AMERICA BEWITCHED

Owen Davies is Professor of Social History at the University of Hertfordshire. He has written extensively on the history of magic, witchcraft, ghosts, and popular medicine, including *The Haunted: A Social History of Ghosts* (2007), *Grimoires: A History of Magic Books* (2009), *Paganism: A Very Short Introduction* (2011), and *Magic: A Very Short Introduction* (2012). He is also the editor of *The Oxford Illustrated History of Witchcraft and Magic*, which is forthcoming from Oxford University Press.

T0096830

'Owen Davies tells a fascinating tale that has never been told before with all the skills of a true craftsman. Its sheer breadth of coverage amazes from the start.'

Ronald Hutton, author of *The Triumph of the Moon: A History of Pagan Witchcraft*

'An extraordinary achievement . . . I was frankly staggered at the range of Davies's research.'

Professor H. C. Erik Midelfort, University of Virginia

'Davies tells a highly original story, yet one that makes instant sense . . . This is a vivid, arresting, insightful book, written with sympathy and human understanding. It extends Davies's reputation as an original thinker in the field, when so much work is derivative or merely illustrative of well-established ideas.'

Malcolm Gaskill, *Fortean Times*

'Davies's catholic approach has produced a volume densely packed with fascinating material. Along with detailed excurses into folklore—there are sustained discussions of hairballs, hag-riding, and skin shedding—the author presents a trove of historical anecdotes and case studies drawn from his wide research into local histories, obscure newspapers, and other neglected byways.'

Nova Religio

'Historians of American witchcraft—and indeed of America generally—need to read this book.'

Adam Jortner, *Magic, Ritual, and Witchcraft*

'. . . a compelling and meticulously researched account . . . Davies's book is an encyclopaedic, insightful and very readable contribution to American and world history . . .'

Marion Gibson, *Social History*

AMERICA BEWITCHED

The story of witchcraft
after Salem

OWEN DAVIES

OXFORD
UNIVERSITY PRESS

OXFORD
UNIVERSITY PRESS

Great Clarendon Street, Oxford, OX2 6DP,
United Kingdom

Oxford University Press is a department of the University of Oxford.
It furthers the University's objective of excellence in research, scholarship,
and education by publishing worldwide. Oxford is a registered trade mark of
Oxford University Press in the UK and in certain other countries

© Owen Davies 2013

The moral rights of the author have been asserted

First published 2013
First published in paperback 2016
Impression: 1

Published in the United States of America by Oxford University Press
198 Madison Avenue, New York, NY 10016, United States of America

British Library Cataloguing in Publication Data
Data available

Library of Congress Cataloging in Publication Data
Data available

ISBN 978-0-19-957871-9 (Hbk.)
ISBN 978-0-19-874538-9 (Pbk.)

Printed in Great Britain by
Clays Ltd, St Ives plc

ACKNOWLEDGEMENTS

Thanks once again to the usual suspects, my family and Céline Chantier, for their ongoing support. I have benefited from discussions regarding various aspects of the book with Willem de Blécourt, Francesca Matteoni, and Rowland Hughes. Thanks also to Luciana O'Flaherty, H. C. Erik Midelfort, and Ronald Hutton who read through the manuscript and made useful comments and corrections. Matthew Cotton of Oxford University Press provided just the right balance of prodding and patience to get the book finished.

TABLE OF CONTENTS

LIST OF PLATES

AFTERMATH

Nineteen people executed, one man pressed to death during interrogation, and four others perished in gaol. This was the human toll of the Salem witch trials of 1692. Many more were bereaved and traumatized, and a community was left counting the economic, social, spiritual, and moral costs. It all began with the antics of two young girls, the daughter and niece of Samuel Parris, the minister of Salem Village. Within months over 150 people from twenty-four different towns were being investigated for witchcraft. As historians have shown, though, the development of the Salem witch trials was as much a story of the multiple tensions of a developing colonial community as the result of the terrible lies of adolescent girls and prejudices of the male Puritan authorities.

The Salem trials resulted in the last of the estimated thirty-eight to forty executions for witchcraft recorded in the British colony.[1] Without the Salem toll the record of official persecution of witches in America would have been mild compared with much of Europe. To say Salem was an aberration, though, would be to misrepresent the popular fear and hatred of witches at the time. This did not diminish despite the changing legal response to witchcraft following Salem. After years of petitioning by those who had suffered, on 17 October 1711 the Massachusetts legislature reversed the guilty verdicts of twenty-two of those convicted and paid hundreds of pounds in compensation to their families. The days of the witch trials seemed to be over: its victims now the righteous, and their persecutors the shamed.

Salem: never again?

Through schooling and the media the events of 1692 are etched into the consciousness of modern America. The date, like 1776 and 1865, brings to a close a chapter in the annals of the country's development. The end of the Salem trials, and the immediate soul searching in its aftermath, mark the beginning of the American enlightenment. Over the ensuing centuries Salem served as a metaphor for bigotry, intolerance, religious fanaticism, persecution, popular credulity, personal ambition, and the dangers of mob rule. As the decades passed, it was also used as a milepost to measure the distance America had progressed from a benighted colonial past. During the nineteenth century, 'Remember Salem!' became a term of antiquarian abuse, a playground game of name calling—'Our colonial founders were more level-headed and enlightened than yours!' State historians rummaged through the archives and were satisfied to find themselves well down the witch-trial league table. The near absence of witch trials in Connecticut turned its early historians into enthusiastic finger-waggers gesturing in the direction of their northern neighbours.[2]

The cry of 'Salem!' was frequently heard in the rivalry between North and South, a rhetorical weapon used by the latter to attack New Englanders and their perceived sense of superiority over the southern states and their defence of the barbarity of slavery. 'When a Virginian is in his most unwholesome frame of mind against the "Yankees," he is apt to refer, in terms either derisive or denunciatory, to the New England trials and executions for witchcraft', sighed one commentator in 1869. Another, complaining of the censorship laws in Virginia, warned, 'let her never talk of the hanging of witches by Massachusetts'.[3] In 1919, the South Carolina state historian Alexander Samuel Salley Jr made a barbed comment during a spat over what was the last witch trial in America, suggesting that, 'the early settlers of South Carolina were governed by educated and cultivated officials, and witchcraft and other forms of fanaticism were frowned upon'. The implication was obvious.[4]

Then there was the desire amongst some Massachusetts communities to seek collective forgiveness for a stain on their state's history. In 1852 Jonathan Waite, a 54-year-old woollen manufacturer of North Brookfield, presented a petition to the Massachusetts legislature requesting that monuments be erected to those who were executed for witchcraft in Salem. The proposal was not taken up, but the idea was revived in 1875 when the descendants of one of the victims, Rebecca Nourse, met in the New England Genealogical Rooms, Boston, to plan a fundraising campaign for a monument to commemorate her death. The Nourse Monument Association was founded and raised over $520, enough for a monument to be erected in 1885 at the Nourse ancestral home in Danvers (formerly Salem village). An impressive ceremony was held on the 30 July to mark its completion, at which Danvers' pastor, the

Reverend Fielder Israel, gave an opening address in which he said their witch-hanging forebears had 'an over-wrought belief concerning religious subjects which their ignorance furthered'. He concluded by considering how far Danvers had come since 1692: 'What has caused such wonderful changes? It is the development of a Christian people. The past, with its deeds, is buried: we would not remove the veil of mystery that hides it if we could; we are content with the present and our hopes for the future. Let the dead rest in peace.'[5]

So, much of the discourse on Salem through the eighteenth and nineteenth centuries assumed that the history of witchcraft ended with Salem. The veil was conveniently drawn and tied fast. This book tears open the veil and reveals a very different story. The Salem nineteen were the last to be legally executed for witchcraft in the colony, yet we now know of more people killed as witches in America after 1692 than before it.

For many in late colonial and independent America, witches remained a real and terrible threat. For them, Salem was not a horrific miscarriage of justice. In 1787 the Philadelphia City Sessions of the Mayor's Court heard the case of a woman who died after being brutally treated by a mob who accused her of witchcraft. Five years later a German woman, aged around seventy, was one of four people who were subjected to violent popular justice in Fairfield County, South Carolina, under suspicion of witchcraft. They launched suits against their assaulters in the county court and won nominal damages.[6] Then in 1796 the Court of Common Pleas and General Sessions of the Peace for the County of York, Maine, dealt with a vicious case of assault and battery against a suspected witch.[7] Historians have known for a long time about these cases that emerge from the 'shadow of the Enlightenment', but they have usually been treated as the last gasp of an old world mentality, exceptional events resulting from lingering superstition.[8] As this book will show, though, if anything, witchcraft disputes multiplied as hundreds of thousands of immigrants poured into North America from Europe. These were people who knew nothing of the history of Salem, and for whom witchcraft was still a heinous crime. Witch trials and executions continued into the 1770s in some German states, and the last legal executions for witchcraft took place in Glarus, Switzerland, in 1782, and in Posen, Poland, in 1793.[9] With the influx of new immigrants and the ongoing challenges faced by the settled population, the history of witchcraft in America was entering a new and not a final phase.

The witchcraft of others

One way of distancing newly 'enlightened' America from the dark days of Salem was to reposition witchcraft belief as the affliction of non-Europeans. At first this meant pointing the finger at Native Americans. This was nothing new of course. Seventeenth-century British, French, and Spanish missionaries, explorers, and settlers saw Native Americans, with their strange religions and medicine men, as the Devil's agents, potent workers of malign magic. They were pagan idolaters worshipping the Devil in the guise of their gods. According to Cotton Mather their medicine men or 'powaws' were 'horrid sorcerers, and hellish conjurers, and such as Conversed with Daemons'.[10] A century later the view remained pervasive. 'The Devil's kingdom now is spread, Where'er an *Indian* shews his head', ran a deeply racist broadside entitled *The Indian's Pedigree*, published in 1794. Yet Native Americans were rarely caught up in the legal prosecution of witches in English colonial America. By contrast, the Spanish authorities at the other end of the country were directly involved with prosecuting indigenous peoples. In the early twentieth century the Pueblo population of Taos, New Mexico, had a motto that it was best to avoid contact with Spanish-Mexicans because if they fell ill they accused you of witchcraft.[11] Such caution has a well-founded history.

Spanish chroniclers presented a very broad conception of witchcraft—more broad than was applied back in Spain—that included indigenous medicine as well as religion, so that all medicine men or healers were routinely denounced as sorcerers and witches. A few years after Sante Fe was created as the capital of the province of New Mexico in 1610, in what was Pueblo territory, the missionary Fray Alonso de Benavides, described how the male Pueblo population was divided into warriors and sorcerers, the latter holding the people under their thrall with their power to control the weather, heal, and cause death. Coupled with this was the association of Native American witchery with rebellion. In 1675 accusations of witchcraft and Devil worship were mixed up with a supposed plot involving Pueblos and Apaches conspiring to rise up against Spanish authority. Four Native Americans were sentenced to hang, forty-seven whipped and enslaved, and others jailed.[12] One of those punished was a medicine man named Popé, who would confirm Spanish suspicions by leading a major Pueblo revolt five years later.

Both the Inquisition and civil authorities continued to pursue cases of witchcraft throughout the eighteenth century, mostly instigated by Spaniards accusing Native Americans or those of mixed race known as *mestizos*. In 1708, for example, a twenty-year-old Spanish woman accused two older Pueblo women with witchcraft. One of the defendants complained, in turn, that 'Spanish women say that whatever sickness they have it is bewitchment.'[13] A case from 1733 illustrates the point in more detail. Bicente García and his wife, Spanish residents of Isleta on the Rio Grande, charged a Pueblo named Melchor Trujillo with bewitching them. Under questioning by the *alcalde* or magistrate (a position of both military and civilian authority), the governor of Isleta, El Casique, explained that Trujillo was a medicine man and not a sorcerer, and had been engaged with curing not killing the Garcías. Investigation revealed that he had given them a drink containing peyote, a cactus that had long been used in the region for healing and ritual and is the source of the psychoactive drug mescaline. El Casique then went on to confess that he was, in fact, the head of a group of sorcerers, including an Apache woman, who had bewitched several local leading Spaniards.[14]

Catholic missionaries also instigated witch trials. Following the possession in the late 1750s of several women in the northern New Mexican settlement of Abiquiu, some fifty miles from Santa Fe, Brother Juan José Toledo made formal accusations that led to the most extensive and complex witch trials in New Mexico, involving the Inquisition and secular authorities.[15] At their heart was a clash between Christian conceptions of possession and native healing and religious practices. There was also a heightened level of insecurity as the Commanche harried the Spanish territory. Toledo attempted to exorcize the women, who exhibited the usual symptoms of diabolic possession—paroxysms of shrieking, fulminations, and convulsions. One of the possessed said two Indian women 'controlled her', forcing her to renounce her Christian devotions. Several decades later, in 1799, Father Antonio Barreras of the San Ildefonso mission accused two Pueblo men and a woman of being '*maleficiadores*' or practitioners of harmful magic. He blamed his sickness upon them, and the *alcalde* took the unusual step of handing over the two accused men to the priest along with a pillory, which was rather like the stocks but held the head and hands rather than the feet. So Barreras whipped the men while they were in the pillory to force a confession. One of them, Juan Domingo Caracho, died from this torture.

The Spanish in New Mexico lived more intimately with the Native Americans than did Europeans in the rest of North America at the time. Large numbers of Pueblos, and to a lesser extent Navajos and Apaches, integrated into Hispanic society, mostly as *genízaros*—servants and labourers. Even in Pueblo communities Hispanic influences in terms of dress, Christianity, and modes of living, were adopted without necessarily undermining Pueblo customary life. The accusations of witchcraft were, in a sense, symptomatic of this close relationship.[16] This helps explain why most eighteenth-century New Mexico trials seem to have collapsed or were deliberately truncated, exposing tensions between the prerogatives of the local clergy and secular authorities. The latter may have been obliged to pursue such cases but they were cautious about the evidence presented, and also aware of the potential for unrest if Native Americans were severely punished. Extralegal action against witches was equally frowned upon. When the Spanish Command-ant General in Chihuahua heard of the Barreras case, he acted swiftly to punish the *alcalde* and banished Barreras from New Mexico.

Elsewhere in North America relations between Native Americans and Euro-peans were mediated principally through traders and Protestant missionaries. The

German-Czech Moravians are a case in point. They too equated the practices of the medicine men with European conceptions of diabolic witchcraft; they were expressions of heathenism, and therefore a major hindrance to the spread of the gospel, in their view. The Moravian missionary David Zeisberger (1721–1808), who worked amongst the Delaware, wrote, 'I believed the Indians were too stupid for such satanic practices, but I have been persuaded otherwise. I know for a certainty that witchcraft is common among them.'[17] When, in 1772, Zeisberger and his colleagues founded the village of Schoenbrunn, the first township in Ohio, for his Native American converts, they created a set of rules and regulations that included the stipulation:

> Whosoever tells stories about others' preparing poison, hunting people at night, and practising witchcraft, must prove this before the committee, and he of whom such things are proved shall not live with us. If, however, the accuser has been found lying, we will regard him as a tool of the Devil.[18]

The town was abandoned a few years later during the Revolutionary War.

Missionaries capable of reasonable reflection on Native-American cultural ways often tied themselves in knots when it came to witchcraft, sometimes denouncing the godlessness of the pagans, their lack of religious awareness, and yet labelling obvious expressions of spirituality as superstition and witchcraft.[19] The same Bible that had underpinned the Salem trials was now seen as the ultimate weapon for vanquishing the witchcraft of benighted others. The hypocrisy was all too apparent to some. In 1821 newspapers reported a speech made by the Iroquois chief and Seneca orator Red Jacket at the trial instigated by New York State of a Seneca man, Tommy Jemmy, for killing a supposed witch:

> What! Do you denounce us as fools and bigots, because we still continue to believe that which you, yourselves, sedulously inculcated two centuries ago? Your divines have thundered this doctrine from the pulpit; your judges have pronounced it from the bench; your courts of justice have sanctioned it with the formalities of law; and you would now punish our unfortunate brother for adhering to the superstitions of his fathers! Go to Salem! Look at the records of your government, and you will find hundreds executed for the very crime which has called forth the sentence of condemnation upon this woman, and drawn down the arm of vengeance upon her. What have our brothers done more than the rulers of your people have done? And what crime has this man committed by executing in a summary way the laws of his country and the injunctions of his God?[20]

For some Native Americans, witchcraft was viewed as a problem brought upon them by contact with Europeans, and not as the missionaries would have it, an expression of antique heathenism. The contagious diseases brought by the Europeans caused devastation that was, for some, incomprehensible other than in terms of witchcraft. So in the seventeenth century the Iroquois accused Jesuit missionaries of being plague-spreading witches.[21] Then the cultural and social disruption caused by encroachment, alcohol, Christianity, and war, led to movements that attempted to pull back from the world of the European settlers, and sought to redefine native identity. This required eradicating destabilizing influences such as alcohol abuse and witchcraft. Witches were at the same time a manifestation of external forces and also internal enemies undermining kinships and the wider community. Prophets emerged that sought to purge their communities of these evildoers. A couple of such messianic figures active amongst the Delawares in the 1760s preached that their fellow men and women should renounce rum, guns, and other imports, revive old religious ceremonies and rites, and so return to the cultural purity of a time before the Europeans arrived. One of them, a Munsee named Wangomen, launched a campaign against witches as part of this agenda but apparently gave up due to the scale of the problem and disputes with other chiefs over the methods involved.[22]

The most serious anti-witch campaigns emerged after the Revolutionary War (1775–1783).[23] Most Native-American chiefs east of the Mississippi sided with the British during the conflict and subsequently faced increased prejudice; they were forced to accept humiliating treaties and further loss of land and rights. The Senecas felt the wrath of the new Americans more than most, and it is no surprise that a Prophet arose in the guise of the heavy-drinking chief Handsome Lake (1735–1815). In 1799, following a series of terrible visions that revealed the depths to which his people had sunk, he began a campaign to revitalize the Nation. During his trances he claimed the spirits of the dead and angelic messengers had been sent to him by the Great Spirit who was angered by the terrible influence over his people of whiskey, witchcraft, charms, and abortion magic. So, as part of his reform movement, Handsome Lake launched a campaign against witches, who the spirits in his visions had described as 'people without their right minds. They make disease and spread sickness to make the living die'. But many of his followers came to reject the policy, and he was criticized by his political rivals such as Red Jacket, who was himself apparently accused of witchcraft by Handsome Lake. He watered down his rhetoric, and the 'Code of Handsome Lake' included the prohibition of harming witches, instructing that they should be left for God to punish as he saw fit.

A more systematic and brutal campaign was launched in 1805 by Tenskwatawa, the Shawnee Prophet, amongst the Native Americans of the Ohio River Valley.[24]

Another reformed alcoholic, Tenskwatawa, received visions that most of his fellow Shawnees were destined to burn in the afterlife. He had been tasked by the Great Spirit to lead his fellow men and women away from sin and towards salvation. This would be achieved by rejecting European ways, abandoning metal implements, European clothing, and food. The spirits also warned him against the witches operating within. He claimed he had been given the power to identify witches, and so travelled from settlement to settlement among the Delawares and Wyandots like some latter-day Witchfinder General pointing out the evil ones. His accusations were frequently politically inspired, accusing chiefs who sought compromise with European society and converts to Christianity.

Much of what we know of the witch hunting activities of Handsome Lake, the Shawnee Prophet and others, derives from the writings of missionaries. It is no surprise, then, if the extent of their campaigns came to be wildly inflated. Claims that hundreds perished say much about white perceptions of Native Americans credulity, superstition, and brutality, but little about the reality. The movements fizzled out due to resistance and objection by Native-American society, not because of European religious, moral, or martial authority. There was no great panic, no appetite for the destabilizing effect of systematic persecution at an already precarious time. The movements certainly fed from the widespread fear of witch-craft generally, but were alien in their pursuance. Repugnance at Handsome Lake's involvement in the killing of an accused witch in 1809 chipped away at his support. No more than sixteen witch executions can be found in the sources regarding Tenskwatawa's campaign. Most of his accusations against other chiefs did not stick.

In these episodes, rebellion and witchcraft were once again entwined but this time the accusations were not made by Europeans against subjugated and restless indigenous peoples, but by Native Americans against their own kin: the rebellion was not martial but cultural. While the paucity of the evidence needs to be recognized, the suggestion is that due to European influence the conception of the witch changed. Before the mid-eighteenth century the witch in Native-American belief was usually an outsider from another clan or another race. So the Iroquois often cast accusations at the Delaware for instance. But through extensive exposure to Europeans the witch figure became the enemy within, an internalized expression of the external threat to their existence. Despite arguing for the disengagement with European ways that were thought to be corroding the culture of their ancestors, the prophets and their messages were clearly influenced by the religious and moral ideas they had assimilated through contact with Protestant missionaries. Algonquian and Iroquois witchcraft beliefs, for instance, came to incorporate Christian conceptions of the Devil as the source of evil and witchery.[25] The prophets' political denunciations of their medicine men probably chimed more with the missionaries than with popular sentiment. This is not to say that Native Americans were reluctant witch killers. Further periods of witch fear gripped Native-American communities later in the century too, as will be discussed in subsequent chapters.

It is estimated that between the early seventeenth century and the prohibition of the slave trade in 1807, nearly half a million Africans were taken by force to North America. Here was another subjugated people on whom to pin the label of the 'superstitious other'. As with Native Americans, skin colour reinforced prejudice, with Europeans associating blackness with devils and demons, sooty from the depths of Hell. As former New York slave John Jea wrote of his masters, 'Frequently did they tell us we were made by, and like the devil, and commonly called us black devils.'[26] The African slaves also challenged Americans with new religions and forms of worship that deeply disturbed the Christian senses. Once again religious practices, most notably the Voodoo of New Orleans, would be portrayed as an addiction to devil worship and witchcraft. Only the white man wielding his Bible could tame such wild, pagan impulses. Thaddeus Norris, writing on 'Negro Superstitions' in 1870, stated that association with the white man 'humanized' their 'superstitions'. But too much contact could also be detrimental to the white man; African 'superstition' could be contagious. There was concern about the 'nonsense' that black nursemaids might instil in the minds of their masters' children, but it was the cultural intimacy between poor whites and African Americans that disturbed racist sensibilities most.[27] In 1879 the *Indianapolis Sentinel* reported the case of William Padgett of Meade County, Kentucky, who murdered his wife under the delusion that she had bewitched him. The paper described Padgett as 'an ignorant, unsophisticated Kentuckian, who was raised among the Negroes in the old slave times, and partook of their superstitions and wild vagaries. There are many white men of this class now living in Kentucky.'[28] Indeed, for some, these 'crackers' or poor 'white trash' of the southern states were 'worse than the colored man'. While 'the Negro race is naturally superstitious', opined the *Philadelphia Times* in 1890, the cracker 'fondly imagines that he is so much shrewder, and so he does not use what brains he has, nor does he try to learn anything. He has thousands of signs, omens, cures, and beliefs that are a continual source of annoyance to him, and perpetually keep him in a state of dread'. Another editorial making the some observation, decided that the superstition of the 'Kentucky darkies' ultimately trumped that of their 'whiter brethren' thanks to the 'grotesqueness and sometimes the horror that is associated with the former's "hoodoo" worship'.[29]

The nineteenth-century American sense of superiority that consigned witchcraft to dark-skinned 'heathens' also extended to the 'old world' people of Europe. Dripping with condescension, the *St Louis Republic* opined in 1896 that 'Most people believe that witchcraft among civilized people ended when the "Salem witch mania" ran its course and died out in the year 1692. It did, as far as America is concerned, except among savages, but in other countries the belief in the superstition did not die until a much later date.'[30] There followed mention of nineteenth-century trials resulting from the drowning, torturing, and burning of witches in England, France, Spain, Prussia, Russia, Poland, Austria, and Mexico. There was no reflection, of course, on where the hundreds of thousands of recent immigrants in America originated.

Reporting witchcraft

The few contemporary historians who have looked beyond Salem have relied heavily on the raft of antiquarian county and town histories that appeared from the 1840s onwards.[31] By the mid-nineteenth century some thirty local groups and societies had formed, albeit sometimes fleetingly, to record the history of America's communities.[32] The antiquarian purpose in writing these histories was not only to provide an archive, but to foster local pride. To record one's history was a mark of social progress, the stamp of civilization for a community. Celebrating the founding of the Antiquarian Historical Society of Illinois in 1827, a leading Mississippi Valley literary figure hoped the work of the Society would 'remove the film from the eyes of those of our Atlantic readers, who still think, that there is neither taste, oratory, nor fine writing in the backwoods country'. Unfortunately it ceased to exist two years later.[33]

Some local historians ignored the topic of witchcraft altogether as unbefitting, but others included legends of witches to provide a bit of local colour. While there was sometimes a brief recognition that, in the words of the historian of Norton, Massachusetts, there were 'some yet living who hug these ideas to their bosoms', nearly all the legends printed conveniently concerned people and events some forty to a hundred years before. They helped demonstrate how far the community had come. 'The silly doctrine of witchcraft has fled the Schoharie valley, never more to enter it', reported the historian of Schoharie County, New York State, in 1845, after relating a couple of stories of witchcraft from 'many years ago'. The Rev. A. P. Marvin, author of the *History of the Town of Winchendon*, Worcester County, Massachusetts, expressed his satisfaction in 1868 that his section on superstition and witchcraft was 'very meagre'. While noting that there were still those who believed in witches, 'the town traditions are not rich in cases of witchcraft'. Likewise the chronicler of the town of Union, Maine, reported in 1851 that the community was 'now too enlightened' for the absurdity of witchcraft, and that, anyway, superstition 'never gained much credence among the adults in this town'.[34] Still, the authors were clearly picking up stories from oral testimony. As the constitution of the Antiquarian Historical Society of Illinois recognized, 'many important facts respecting its settlement by the present race of inhabitants are preserved only in tradition'. As such they contain useful accounts of beliefs and counter-witchcraft practices, and provide a flavour of the cultural importance of witches, transformed into legendary figures, in what is otherwise a relative blank period in the annals of American witchcraft.

A few perspicacious nineteenth-century observers saw beyond the smeared lens of local pride and stepped above the condescension of racial prejudice to recognize the pervasive belief in witchcraft. One was James Monroe Buckley (1836–1920), a Methodist minister, editor of the Methodist periodical *The Christian Advocate*, travel writer, and self-educated psychologist of religion. On his numerous pedestrian tours across different parts of the States he had many times stayed with farmers, trappers, fishermen, and labourers, and heard tales of witches and their exploits. But his personal experience was supported by his perusal of the American press. In the late 1880s he made note of more than fifty lawsuits that had been instituted in recent years by persons making accusations of witchcraft. Writing in 1892 he concluded that 'Witchcraft is at the present time believed in by a majority of the citizens of the United States.' There was some relief for American sensibilities, as, with the exception of the hotbeds of Pennsylvania and the South, he thought that witchcraft beliefs were even stronger in Canada.[35]

In 1800 there were over 200 newspapers, by 1833 there were at least 1,200 titles, 3,000 by 1860, and over 7,000 by 1880. Many of these were short-lived, or of a political or religious nature and little concerned with local news and events.[36] Urbanization, cheaper production methods, growing literacy, and an expanding population enabled the growth of daily newspapers from mid-century. Their proliferation, the insatiable desire for news to fill their pages, and the growing role of local newspapers as semi-official records of local events and crime, led to greater interest in everyday witchcraft disputes. Instances of the abuse, assault, and murder of suspected witches sometimes ended up in local courts and were occasionally heard at state level. In many such cases, though, only the journalistic reports of the trials survive. Furthermore, the nature of record keeping at the time meant that the legal archives—the few that survive—rarely report the dialogues that took place *during* a trial. It was in the drama of the courtroom that the motives behind accusations were often laid bare in detail. It is the newspapers that provide us with such accounts.

In 1847 the *New-Bedford Mercury* printed a brief thought-piece inspired by the continued belief of witchcraft in Yorkshire, England, as reported in English newspapers. The American journalist observed that he had 'supposed the United States to be too intelligent for such things'.[37] But he was forced to change his mind after reading about a case of witchcraft from Maine in one of the state's papers, the *Northern Tribune*. The journalist came to realize that,

> in this enlightened day, and even in this State, there are many persons who as firmly believe in the existence of witches, as they do in the truth of the Christian religion – men, too, of good common sense in every other respect. We know of neighborhoods where the good women cannot meet with trouble in 'making the butter come,' but some poor, withered old woman has to bear the blame . . . A gate cannot be torn off its hinges, or the cattle get loose in the stable, but the witches have a hand in the matter.[38]

As this suggests, the accumulating weight of press reports regarding witchcraft from the mid-nineteenth century onwards generated a growing realization that the antiquarians had got it wrong. Witchcraft was an ongoing problem and not a matter of legend.

From around the 1870s onwards newspapers, instead of just repeating hearsay, second-hand accounts, or regurgitated titbits from other newspapers, began to quiz the strange news that came their way. In 1899, for example, the Minnesota newspaper the *Winona Daily Republican* reprinted a story from the *Trempealeau Gazette* concerning a court case arising from witchcraft in a German community near Richmond. 'With a view to getting at the facts', the *Republican* newspaper wrote to Justice ʻC. F. Dykeman, who presided over the case, to ask for further particulars. Dykeman duly obliged in order 'to correct a wrong impression that has got abroad and to prevent injustice to the several parties concerned'.[39] The increasing influence of investigative journalism and the growing popularity of human interest stories meant that in the cities journalists could often be found hanging around the police courts waiting for newsworthy cases. Their ears would prick up when some poor souls entered to complain about witches, and instead of just reporting an overheard story they would get talking to the parties involved. Some journalists even visited them at home, accused and accuser alike.

On occasion, journalistic involvement meant the papers also became part of the story. In 1881 a poor Irish couple, Mr and Mrs Richard May, living in Port Richmond, Staten Island, placed the following advertisement in one of New York's numerous daily newspapers:

> If there is any person in New York that can cure witchcraft, man or woman, white or black, let them come and cure if they can, and no cure no pay. Richard May, Port Richmond, S. I.

The *New York Times*, a daily founded in 1851, which had made its name in the 1870s by exposing political corruption, sent out a reporter to investigate. The result was a fascinating insight into both popular feeling about witches and the development of journalistic style.[40]

After asking around in Port Richmond, the journalist was eventually pointed in the direction of a small white-painted cottage in a side street where the old Irish carpenter and his wife lived. The journalist began his report by describing his first impressions of the cottage interior and its two elderly inhabitants. Then the interview began:

> 'Yes,' said he, in answer to a question. 'I had the advertisement put in: at least, my wife did. She has to attend to everything, now. Can you drive out witches?'

> The reporter was inclined to think that he might drive one out, if it was a small witch and he had a big club; but he replied, with some caution, that he proposed to publish an account of this witchcraft in THE TIMES, and such publicity would certainly have a good effect upon the witch, and perhaps drive it out altogether.

> 'Yes,' said the old man, 'yes. I don't know but it might. I'm sure I wish it would. It's very hard to be bewitched this way, and kept away from work and left to starve. But I can't talk much; the witch won't let me talk much. My wife can talk.' . . .

> 'He hasn't done a stroke of work,' said she, 'for four years. There he sits all day, just as you see him now. And me too. I'm all wrong. I am bewitched too, but not a bad as him. I'll tell you all about it, and you can write it down, so as not to forget it. Think you can remember it? Well, some people have great heads. If we were only wise enough we could get over this, and there are plenty of people could cure us – people with great learning – if we could only find them. It was all along of that woman. She did it all.'

> 'What woman?'

> 'The woman that lived in this house with us.'

She went on to tell of a Scots woman that boarded with them who they believed was the witch responsible. 'Did you ever see a witch?' asked Mrs May. The reporter confided to his readers that his experience had been 'confined principally to witches of the ham sand kind'. The discussion then took a darker tone when Mrs May asked him:

> I think a witch is worse than a murderer that kills a person: don't you? For a murderer only just kills you all at once, and it's over, but a witch kills you by inches. I think witches ought to be killed. They used to kill them in this country, and they kill them now in Scotland. This woman is a Scotch woman and I think she ought to be put out of the way, and not let go about bewitching folks.

In 1903 a *Los Angeles Times* reporter made a similar visit to a bewitched German couple living in East Washington Street, Carson. Louis Pfau's wife suffered from rheumatism and they had paid a local quack doctor to massage her for $1.50 a session. They were poor and had to cancel the treatment, with the quack making his disgruntlement very clear. When the Pfaus started to experience a series of misfortunes with their animals and Mrs Pfau got worse they suspected the quack had bewitched them in revenge. Pfau prepared a statement translated from German that he had intended to request be published in the newspaper, which it duly was under the heading 'Victims of the Black Art':

> All people of Los Angeles take warning: There is a certain man in this city who claims to be a great healer, and after making people well he can make them sick again. As a controller of spirits he can do great harm to people for if he has taken a dislike to his neighbor he can bring it about that this neighbor must seek other quarters.
>
> He has brought devil's books, wherein he has learned the art of his evil practices to both man and animal. He has even gone so far that even the hens will cease to lay at his command. He pretends to be a good carpenter, but he is nothing but a practitioner of the black art, and everyone beware of him.[41]

For some, though, press interest was most unwelcome. Minor incidents became national news, and, when named, those abused as witches found their unwarranted reputations amplified across the communities in which they lived. This was what concerned Dykeman when he wrote to the press, and his fears were certainly borne out in 1893 when a nurse named Irena Oles of Washington, Pennsylvania, was accused of bewitching a fourteen-year-old boy. The matter was reported in detail in a local newspaper. Following its publication she was pointed at and stoned in the street, and people refused to employ her as a nurse. She eventually resorted to the courts to sue the family concerned.[42] A few years later it was the press that was similarly threatened with legal action. In 1899, John Dalke, one of numerous Mecklenburg Germans who settled and farmed in Center, Outagamie County, Wisconsin, hired an attorney to institute slander suits against those accusing him of having bewitched his sister-in-law, three of her children, and his neighbours' livestock. He then threatened libel suits against newspapers printing further accounts of the allegations being made against him by his neighbours. The reports do seem to have stopped after this threat was reported.[43]

In the late nineteenth century the refinement of techniques allowing photographic images to be reproduced on newsprint quality paper would have a major impact on how people consumed newspapers. Photojournalism instigated the rise of modern celebrity culture, but also captured momentous historic moments with lasting profound consequences. For us, the photographs of accused witches, the bewitched, and witch killers, some of which are reproduced in this book, bring home both the ordinariness of witchcraft accusations and provoke a more emotional response to the personal tragedies that sometimes resulted. They banish any stereotypical images of the witch that the written word might evoke. In this respect they serve a valuable historical purpose, and yet they raise moral issues. It is not always clear that those concerned wished to be photographed. While some posed for the cameras, enjoying the limelight of notoriety, others were no doubt snapped without consent or regretted their appearance in visual media. When, in 1907, a journalist visited Margaret Gilmore, an accused witch who unfairly found herself in jail (we will return to her in Chapter 3), and asked to take her photograph, she declined saying she did not want her relatives knowing of her predicament. A few years earlier, the witch killer Solomon Hotema expressed reluctance when the press asked to photograph him in prison, but agreed when assured by the journalist that 'it would be done without the least desire to injure him or to exploit him in any other but a truthful attitude'.[44]

The founding of the American Folklore Society in 1888 marked the beginning of a new phase in the recording of witchcraft beliefs across American society. Its journal would provide a valuable vehicle for the publication of material gained from oral sources and culled from the literary archive, but there is no avoiding the fact that in the early years the American folklore movement, as elsewhere, shared and reinforced the same cultural biases and prejudices displayed by the newspapers, antiquarians, and missionaries. Some of those who collected and analysed folktales from the mouths of African Americans and Native Americans concluded that they must have European origins because they recognized many of the motifs from the compendious collections of European folktales by the likes of the Grimm brothers. So, it was argued, they must have spread amongst these cultures through early contact with the white population, the Spanish and Portuguese in particular. These assumptions were also based on the idea that African- and Native-American languages were too primitive to have developed and transmitted such creative and culturally rich stories.[45]

The broad category of 'superstition', under which witchcraft was usually included, was also used as a means of defining racial distance and superiority. This is clear from the work of the Louisiana branch of the American Folklore Association during the 1890s. Its membership was all white and linked to the social web of plantation owners and related businessmen in the state, with a strong showing of women and educators. Their work consciously reinforced racial boundaries, with the belief in witchcraft and the practice of Voodoo providing a useful marker. So, as one of the leading Louisiana members, Alcée Fortier, wrote, 'negroes are still very much afraid of their witchcraft', while Voodoo was 'the best proof of the credulity and superstition of the Blacks'.[46] One of the messages that came through in this early phase of American folklore studies is that 'we' the Europeans gave them sophisticated forms of folklore and 'they' gave 'us' the grosser forms of superstition.

By no means were all early folklore studies so influenced by racial or class prejudice. African Americans were not passive objects of folklore. In the 1890s an African-American folklore society was formed in Virginia, and one of its voices, the monthly journal the *Southern Workman*, published regular folklore columns to preserve and record traditions.[47] Three decades later, the groundbreaking anthropologist and novelist Zora Neale Hurston began presenting her research on the folklore and life of African Americans in the southern states through academic explorations and fiction. It was the folklorists, furthermore, who, through extensive interviewing, confirmed in a more systematic way than the newspapers that witchcraft beliefs were widespread amongst European-American populations and not just those with dark skins. An excellent example is an article published in the *Journal of American Folklore* in 1894 on the 'Folk-Lore of the Mountain Whites of the Alleghanies', in which there is no attempt to argue that the continued belief in witchcraft belief was due to African-American influence. Instead, the author sought to contextualize the beliefs he collected, exploring the European migration history in the area and the geographical and environmental conditions in which settlers scraped a living.[48] Still, one of the great failings of the early American folklorists was their avoidance of urban America. Like their European counterparts, most folklorists were tied to the notion that 'traditional superstitions' lingered longest in the mountains, backwoods, and remote settlements of the country.

While the racial prejudices evident in the early collection of Native-American and African-American folklore must be recognized, the voluminous material the folklorists collected provided a profound resource for understanding the oral and literary cultures of all of America's inhabitants. Later generations of folklorists would take a more sophisticated and objective approach to both collecting and analysis, focusing more on the complex interchange of beliefs and practices between Native Americans, African Americans, and Europeans. For those studying witchcraft, though, the folklore archive presents three major weaknesses. First, folklorists rarely interviewed those who were accused and abused for being witches. The legends and stories are nearly always from those who knew of witches or were bewitched by them. Furthermore, as with the local histories, many of the accounts concerned events that occurred several generations before, and about people long dead. This was often a result of the decision making of interviewees who, concerned about being judged credulous or foolish by their 'betters', deflected questions about the currency of witchcraft by locating it in the past, resulting in the familiar refrain, 'there used to be a lot of witches around here in the old days . . .'.

Thirdly, due to interviewee confidentiality, folklorists did not usually provide full names of people or their place of residence. Fortunately, newspapers often did. This allows the historian to pursue record linkage research, identifying, and then piecing together the individual histories of those involved in witchcraft cases, providing fresh clues to the origins and nature of the disputes recorded in the newspapers. Such work also confirms the general reliability of reportage, though journalists tended to be poor judges of people's ages, sometimes adding a decade or more on the basis of careworn faces and bowed backs. Most of the people mentioned in the disputes in this book have been searched for in the censuses, trade directories, ship passenger lists, and other such sources. In the majority of cases I have been able to trace them. Richard May and his wife mentioned above, for example, can be found in the census, living alone in Northfield, Port Richmond. Just as the journalist had reported, the census tells us they were both Irish-born, and Richard was a carpenter. From the census we find that his wife's name was Ann, and that she was born in 1815 and her husband three years later. The journalist had suggested Richard was nearly seventy, but he was actually sixty-two. There are a number of obstacles to such research, however, one being the destruction of most of the 1890 census in a fire in 1921. Many Americans, particularly recent immigrants, moved around searching for work or a better life, making it difficult to track them down and confirm identities, especially if their name was, say, John Smith. Journalists often misspelt or garbled people's surnames as they busily scribbled notes during court cases. Likewise those conducting the censuses sometimes wrote names differently each time. Through a process of Chinese whispers transmitted via telegraph messages, multiple variants of a person's name sometimes appeared in different newspapers re-reporting the same case. Names also became anglicized over time. Put together the newspaper research and the folklore sources, though, and we have an archive on American witchcraft every bit as rich and important as that of the seventeenth century.

Where to find witchcraft

The history of witchcraft after Salem has primarily focused upon Native Americans and African Americans. But race is not the only influence on the way in which the geography of witchcraft has been imprinted on the American mind. You do not see witches in Westerns, for example, but the belief in them travelled with those pioneers who trekked west in the mid-nineteenth century and settled there. The long history of European witchcraft accusations in the former Spanish territories of

New Mexico and Texas has already been touched upon, but belief in witchcraft was present amongst Europeans elsewhere in the Wild West. Witchcraft crops up in the macabre story of the serial-killing 'Hell Benders' of Cherryvale, Kansas. The Bender family consisted of German immigrants John Bender and his supposed wife, their daughter Kate (not by John), and a young man who posed as her brother. In 1870 they built a cabin and set up a small grocery store and rest stop along a well-worn trail. Kate, in her early twenties made a modest name for herself as a spiritualist medium touring the surrounding settlements. She also had a reputation for darker powers, her 'brother' informing one visitor that 'she could control the devil, and that the devil did her bidding'. Kate apparently accused another female visitor, who escaped their clutches, of bewitching her coffee. In a region notorious for gunfighters and bandits the Benders quietly went about their business murdering weary travellers, taking their possessions and burying the corpses in the garden. The family fled the area in 1873 after a visit by a fifty-strong posse led by Colonel York, who was looking for his missing brother, a physician who was one of the Benders' victims. Despite rumours to the contrary, the Benders were never brought to justice.[49]

Yet many people would find it surreal to see a witch turn up in a Western movie. Pulp literature and films about the Wild West have shaped our perceptions of what life was like, and witches are not part of it. By contrast it would not seem out of place for witchcraft to be central to a late nineteenth-century drama set amongst hillbillies in the Appalachians and Ozarks, or amongst the Pennsylvania Dutch. The hex reputation of the latter will be discussed later in the book, but as a perceptive *New York Times* journalist cautioned in 1911, 'A man named Smith is just as likely to believe in charms and incantations as a man named Schmidt.'[50]

Urbanizing America represents an equally glaring blank in the geography of witchcraft. As already noted, early folklorists tended to avoid the cities as barren ground for the garnering of old traditions and beliefs.[51] Urbanization may have generated terrible squalor and chaotic slums, but they were also characterized as beacons of industry, rationality, and cynicism. Cities represented progress, and although it was recognized that fortune-tellers, astrologers, prophets, and quacks flourished in the search for prosperity and the American dream, despite a few shady spots, the social and physical urban environment was thought to leave little space for 'traditional superstitions' to flourish. But again, the reality was clearly otherwise. Many of the witchcraft dramas studied in this book were acted out in urban America, which, on reflection, is not surprising. It was to the cities that millions of immigrants flocked, and where they found themselves thrown together in a chaotic multicultural whirlwind. Some of the northern industrial towns of the early twentieth century were made up mostly of recent arrivals from diverse cultures. They became American on paper but for at least a generation spoke their old tongue in the home, sent their children to church schools where no English was spoken, and clung to the culture, food, and customs of their homelands. People sought to recreate their old family and community structures in the new world. Italian Americans are an obvious example. In 1870, the Italian-born population of Philadelphia, for instance, was only 300, but by 1930 there were more than 155,000 Italians in the city forming their own close-knit neighbourhoods sometimes based around 'old country' local and regional links. A Chicago social worker in the 1920s reported several instances amongst the city's Calabrian Italian population where sickness was attributed to witchcraft and was cured traditionally within the community.[52]

In the short term, witchcraft accusations were generated through the psychological disorientation and social disruption of rapid urbanization. This was sometimes expressed in terms of mental illness, often played out within intimate, claustrophobic domestic settings. At other times it arose from the suspicion or misunderstanding of other cultures' rituals and beliefs in melting-pot communities.

In the longer term, settled and stable neighbourhoods with broadly shared local identities formed in which certain individuals develop reputations for witchcraft over decades through gossip and the collective accumulation of strange coincidences and misfortunes. As an initial example of such urban witches, let us see how witchcraft disputes played out in the streets of early nineteenth-century New York.

A Five Points witch

In 1838 a magazine correspondent recalled how around seventeen years before he had been told by a schoolmistress of a case of three children having been bewitched in Batavia Street, New York. The teacher earnestly believed it was a genuine case.[53] A few years later witchcraft accusations swirled around the streets of downtown Manhattan.

On 20 January 1829 a New York police court heard a complaint of assault and battery brought by Mary Boman against Martha Ann Sloan and Catharine Lane.[54] The events took place in Water Street, Manhattan, near the docks. It was a crowded bustling place of boarding houses and stores. Brothels and drinking holes catered for the sailors and dockworkers. With its proximity to the marshy waters, the inhabitants were prone to bouts of cholera and malaria. Tenements were built there in the early 1830s, leading to overcrowding, and the street would soon become notorious as a den of moral iniquity. Its population was poor with a considerable proportion being recent immigrants from Europe, the Irish—like Martha Sloan—in particular. But in 1829 it had not yet slid all the way down.

Appearing before the magistrate, Sloan and Lane denied assaulting Boman and instead claimed they were fearful of the threats made by Boman who they suspected was a witch. When questioned as to Boman's being a witch, Catharine Lane replied:

> Why, I do believe some part of it, because she has made her brags that Mrs Dexter should never get off her bed again; and it was so, for she is bed-ridden now; and I have heard that woman say, that Mrs Dexter had sent for her to come in and see her, and she had refused to do it, because in that case all the evil which she had caused to fall upon Mrs Dexter, would recoil upon herself.

Martha Sloan added:

> Yes – and more than that: there is a girl that she has boasted to have given a disease of which she can never be cured. Her face is twisted and deformed by convulsions, so that she is terrible to look upon. They have had a great many physicians to see her, but they have declared her incurable, and one of them said that if he had a hundred dollars down, he could not remove the disease.

Lane described how she had seen Boman making human figures out of rags into which she placed salt and pepper. She stuck pins and needles into them, and then placed them in the fire, muttering some spell as they burned. A sailor named Williams who was present in the police office confirmed he knew of Boman's reputation for witchcraft, noting that her landlady believed she had injured several other people in her boarding house. Williams made it clear, however, that he personally did not believe in witchcraft.

The magistrate also questioned a sailor named Bright who had accompanied the two defendants to the police office and had offered to provide bail for their appearance. Referring to Boman, Bright told the magistrate, 'she is what I call a "Five Point Ranger".... I believe she can do a great many uncommon things. I have heard her say, that she could raise the Forties any time she liked'. The Five Points was an area not far from Water Street named after a large five-pointed junction of roads. During the 1820s the population swelled, predominantly by Irish immigrants but also by a sizeable minority of African Americans. By 1830 it had a reputation as the poorest, most violent and vice ridden spot in the city. Waterborne diseases thrived in the swampy polluted waters that frequently flooded the area. The squalor and violence of the place worsened over the next few years as more and more immigrants poured in and were dragged into the gutter where crime and prostitution flourished. In 1842 the inquisitive Charles Dickens visited the Five Points accompanied by a police escort, and like other

British visitors familiar with the London slums, was nevertheless shocked: 'Ruined houses open to the street, whence, through wide gaps in the walls, other ruins loom upon the eye, as though the world of vice and misery had nothing else to show: hideous tenements which take their name from robbery and murder; all that is loathsome, drooping, and decayed is here.' The powerful 'Forties' that Bright believed Boman could raise through her witchery referred to the criminal gang from the Five Points known as the Forty Thieves. This was the first recorded organized criminal fraternity in America. It was founded in the mid-1820s by immigrant Irishmen and was initially led by one Edward Coleman. The Forty Thieves pretty much controlled the area and to be able to call them up through magic would have been a pretty impressive boast.

'The charge of witchcraft is a somewhat curious one', said the magistrate after hearing all the testimony. 'It is not so serious now, as it would have been some centuries back, although it may have considerable effect upon the minds of the ignorant part of the community.' One of the women was bound over to face criminal prosecution for assault and battery, and when she and her bail were asked to sign the bond they had to mark with a cross because they were illiterate. The magistrate, sharing the widespread assumption that education was an antidote to such beliefs, commented that it was no wonder that they believed in witchcraft.

★★★

Witchcraft after Salem was clearly not just a story of fireside tales, legends, and superstitions. It continued to be a matter of life and death, souring the American dream for many immigrants, and spoiling the lives of those who had been settled for generations. Witches were integral to the cultural fabric of America. They were part of the story of the decimation of the Native Americans, the experience of slavery and emancipation, and the immigrant experience; they were embedded in the religious and social history of the country. Yet the history of American witchcraft also tells a less traumatic story, one that shows how different cultures interacted, and shaped each others' languages and beliefs. It reveals shared cultural traits, fears, thought patterns, and weaknesses. The history presented in the ensuing pages will, I hope, spark greater scholarly and public interest in a subject that plumbs the depths of what it meant to be American.

Magic of A New Land

Post-colonial America was the backdrop for one of the most extraordinary cultural confrontations. The story of human migration and environmental challenges is as old as human existence, but never before in the history of the human race had so many different peoples, their myriad languages, cultures, customs, and beliefs been thrown together so quickly and so chaotically in a new land, facing an environment strange and yet familiar in equal measure. This applies not just to the pioneers who pushed westwards in the mid-nineteenth century, for it is often overlooked that much of the Eastern seaboard was also virgin country to Europeans at the time. Swathes of woodland in New York State, for instance, were turned into farmland through the blood, sweat, and tears of immigrant families during the 1800s. Poverty, starvation, and disease were the lot of many, yet within a generation towns were founded, industries created, roads built, and a myriad churches and prayer houses constructed. In many respects, eighteenth- and nineteenth-century settlers faced the same environmental difficulties, cultural encounters, and social tensions as the seventeenth-century colonists. It is no surprise, then, that the magical beliefs that both comforted and concerned the early settlers were as relevant to the lives of Americans two and three centuries later. In other ways the experience was very different. In the push westwards Europeans were confronted with unfamiliar landscapes and new peoples. With the growth of the slavery system during the eighteenth century, African influences became deeply engrained in the magical and medical cultures of Europeans, while relationships with Native Americans deepened as trade, encroachment, settlement, and state building accelerated. The rapidly expanding cities of the nineteenth century were the destination for millions of new arrivals.

Faced with survival in these challenging environments it is not surprising that those recently settled in the countryside, often forming isolated communities with none of the familiar medical services, magical experts, and communal structures to cope with misfortune, initially resorted to their homelands for succour. So when, in 1885, Mrs John Solomon, of the Swedish community of Belgrade, Minnesota, suspected her lingering illness was due to witchcraft she wrote to friends in Sweden for advice about an appropriate witch doctor. One being suggested, she then wrote to him in Sweden enclosing a lock of her hair and a fragment of her clothing. The witch doctor wrote back that she had been bewitched by an old woman who frequently went to the Solomon's house. This fitted the description of Mrs Solomon's aunt, who was then publicly accused of witchcraft. New life in an urban environment could be equally isolating and disorientating. Who to turn to for magical help? When, in 1901, the sister of Peter Calebrese, of 138 Ewing Street, Chicago, fell ill due to supposed witchcraft, she did not seek relief locally but returned to her family home in Italy to see if the spell could be negated.[1]

Cultural misunderstandings about healing rituals and magic charms occurred in the multi-ethnic environments and dense housing of rapidly expanding towns. In the summer of 1871 a Dutch family moved from Grand Rapids to Watson Street, Detroit. It was not an area with a significant Dutch population and the family spoke no English. The name of the family seems to have been Stupemeyer—or that was at least how a local policeman pronounced it. After a few days Mr Stupemeyer was struck down with a fever and his wife tried a variety of home cures that struck neighbours as quite bizarre and worrying. One woman saw him holding a bag of ash in one hand and a cup of cold water in the other. The idea it seems was that the ash would absorb the fever, which would then be quenched by mixing with the cold water. Concerned neighbours who were unable to communicate with the couple called in the local doctor, but his help was also declined. Others offered to stay up and tend the gravely ill man but Mrs Stupermeyer just shook her head to say no. Finally, after several days, a man who could speak Dutch was brought in and threatened her with arrest if she did not let the doctor tend to her husband.

Margaret Carr of Pittsburgh found herself in a tricky situation in the autumn of 1867 due to similar neighbourhood incomprehension. Carr's grandchild was sick with a respiratory infection know as croup. To cure it she purchased a black cat from which she took three drops of blood to rub into the child's inflamed and swollen throat. This was a fairly well-known cure for various afflictions. The author of a history of Virginia recalled in the early nineteenth century that it was a common sight to see black cats with cropped ears and tails due to the practice of obtaining blood from them to cure the skin infection known as erysipelas. The practice was widespread in Britain and Ireland too. It was noted in 1825, for example, that three drops of blood from a black cat's tail was a very common cure for epilepsy amongst the 'lower orders' of London and Essex. So in some American communities the procedure would have attracted no suspicion at all. But evidently some people in Carr's Pittsburgh neighbourhood were unfamiliar with the cure; for them the desire for cat's blood was proof of witchery. Fearful of retribution, Carr requested the intervention of the authorities. Her lawyer William Owens brought twenty witnesses to court to testify as to the benign nature and efficacy of the cure, and so dispel the suspicions of witchcraft.[2] In the 1920s the New York Board of Health were baffled by the sudden demand for dog fat. An investigation was launched which found that it was being used in a folk remedy to cure tuberculosis.[3] A search through ethnomedical sources shows that the ingestion of dog fat was a widespread practice in Poland, Russia, and other parts of Eastern Europe. It would have been a peculiar practice to those of British or Irish origin, though.

The terminology of magic and witchcraft provides a fascinating indication of the often imperceptible cultural exchanges that took place. Every immigrant brought and used the language of his or her homeland, so no doubt Poles, Croatians, and Swedes in America continued to complain of the *czarownice, vještice,* and *häxor* in their midst. But English, German, Native-American, and African-American terms would come to diffuse widely across the population. The Native-American 'pow-wow' is thought to be of Algonquin origin, and seventeenth-century English colonists used it to refer to Native-American medicine men, although it also had a meaning as a communal, ritual meeting. By the twentieth century its usage was widespread amongst the Pennsylvania Dutch to describe a distinctive type of folk healer or 'doctor' who used magic charms, herbs, and the Bible, with the act of healing being described as 'pow-wowing'. But while the word derived from Native Americans, the practices concerned did not.[4] It is likely that the term became pervasive thanks to its inclusion in the title of a popular printed collection of charms of German origin, the *Long Lost Friend.* The term 'power doctor' recorded in the Ozarks for a similar category of magical healer probably derives from 'pow-wow'.[5]

While the German term '*braucherei*' to describe the same faith-based healing as pow-wow medicine did not permeate beyond the German speaking community, the term for a witch, 'hex' (*hexerei,* witchcraft), became engrained in American popular idiom. As was observed in a study of American speech in 1935, 'the word hex seems as well established in the English of the region as the word pretzel or sauerkraut'.[6] The spread of its usage beyond the German community was in no small part due to the newspapers' adoption of the term as a noun and verb in the regular reports of Pennsylvania Dutch witchcraft that were broadcast across the country during the late nineteenth and early twentieth century. They described people as being 'hexed' or bewitched, while 'hex slayer' was used to label those who murdered suspected witches.

The English terms 'witch' and 'witchcraft' are, of course, the most dominant terms in American popular usage to describe these malign magic workers, though we need to be aware that they do not necessarily equate exactly with Native-American or African-American conceptions. The Navajos, for instance, have distinctly different categories of harmful magic that, it has been argued, cannot be appropriately described by the umbrella term of 'witchcraft'. The titles of 'cunning-man' and 'cunning-woman' to describe those who combated witches, while widespread in England, do not seem to have retained their common usage across the Atlantic by the nineteenth century. 'Wise woman' and 'wise man' were more widely used, but no more so than terms such as 'witch master' and 'witch doctor' that were uncommon in colloquial English speech. 'Witch master' probably derives from the German 'Hexenmeister'. The term 'repeller' crops up in one source from twentieth-century Kentucky. This is intriguing, for the only analogous term in a British context is the west Cornish term 'peller', which was first recorded in print in 1849. Although a Cornish language origin for it has been proposed, it is most likely a contraction of the English words 'repeller' or 'expeller'.[7] Many Cornish miners made their way to America in search of work during the mid-nineteenth century, and played a major role in the industry's development. The widely respected skills of the Cousin Jacks, as the Cornish were known, meant they filled positions as foremen, bosses, and engineers as well as labourers.[8] Some undoubtedly found themselves employed in the rich coal mines of Kentucky, and so it is possible that the state's repeller was of Cornish heritage. The Cousin Jacks interviewed by the folklorist Richard Dorson in the old copper and iron mining communities of the Upper Peninsula of Michigan in 1946, still used the West Country term 'ill wish' to mean 'bewitch', though the couple of instances of witchcraft he collected concerned people back in Cornwall.[9]

In contrast, 'conjure' and 'conjurer'—the latter title used particularly in Wales and southern England, became the most widely employed terms in nineteenth-century African-American magic. The 'conjure doctor' fulfilled a similar role to the cunning-folk of Europe, in that they healed, detected stolen property, provided charms and spells to provoke love, cured bewitchment, and counteracted witches. More so than British cunning-folk, however, they were also thought to bewitch people when angered or for a fee.[10] The eclectic range of magic they practised borrowed from European and Native-American beliefs, with a strong emphasis on the Bible.

Voodoo or Voudou is, strictly speaking, a form of religious worship of West African origin that continued in New Orleans into the late nineteenth century, but it came to be widely used by the media to describe any form of African-American and sometimes European magic.[11] The term 'hoodoo' may be a variant spelling of 'voodoo', although it has also been suggested that it derives from the West African word *juju* for magic. Hoodoo came to represent the same range of magical activities as practised by the conjure doctors, including the malevolent overtones. It was quite widely adopted as a noun, adjective and verb, with white miners referring to divining rods as 'hoodoo sticks' during the late nineteenth century for example. A range of other terms were also known in regional contexts across the South. 'Goomer doctor' was used in parts of the Ozarks and beyond. The adjective 'goomered' to mean bewitched was also in use in the early nineteenth century. Possibly of African origin, it was also uttered by whites in the Carolinas. In the early nineteenth century the South Carolina plantation owner, Mason Lee, who was originally from North Carolina, used it. As we will see later, Lee's will was contested, and when the term 'goomered' was used by his acquaintances in court it left one reporter completely baffled as to its meaning.[12] The word 'tricked' was also used in African-American communities to describe the casting of spells both benign and malign, though most often as a synonym for bewitched. The term crops up in a report dated 1822 on the murder of an African American for witchcraft. His assailant believed the man 'had *tricked*' him and his wife.[13]

In Louisiana the West African word *gri-gri* for charms was well established in African-American language, as was *wanga* for the practice of both good and bad magic.[14] Under French influence, *wangateur* and *wangateuse* developed as names for male and female practitioners. One final term of note is 'goopher' or 'goofer', used quite widely in Georgia and the Carolinas to describe the magical use of the dead. It probably derives from the Kongo word *kufwa* meaning 'to die', but in America it had a broader sense. Graveyard dirt used in magic was known as goopher dust, and 'goofering' was to walk over a goofer or trick-bag containing graveyard dirt, hair, broken needles, and the like that activated a curse. The goopher doctor, like a conjure doctor, was someone who could both create goopher bags but also remove the curses.[15]

Snakes and roots

Europeans and Africans had accrued a huge store of knowledge about the healing and magical properties of animals and plants over the millennia. This was transmitted orally, via manuscripts, and then, in sixteenth-century Europe, by printed herbals, healing manuals, and books of secrets.[16] Some, but by no means all, of this knowledge was irrelevant in the American environment. Thomas Short's *Medicina Britannica*, published in England in the 1740s, noted that amongst the many healing properties of the plant herb Paris was its action against witchcraft, but the Philadelphia edition of 1751 reminded readers that the plant did not grow in the American provinces.[17]

Still, much was also familiar to the new arrivals. The alligators in the swamps of the eastern and southern states may have been strange beasts to many Europeans, but for West African slaves they were pretty much the same as the crocodiles in their homelands. So they knew how to exploit them as a source of food and medicine, including the use of the gall bladder as a poison. Then there were animal equivalents, so that German Americans transferred the healing properties of badger grease to that of the skunk.[18] The European rowan and service tree, the berries of which Thomas Short noted were 'formerly the dernier Resort against Witchcraft', had close relatives in parts of America.[19] European settlers also found hazel trees (*Corylus americana*) in north-eastern America similar to those in Europe, and so continued to exploit its anti-witchcraft properties. In the Ozarks crosses made from hazel twigs were a frequent sight nailed in barns and stables.[20]

New arrivals to America also brought plants that enabled them to continue traditional practices. Angelica, for example, was widely used in Europe for its anti-witchcraft properties, and became a staple of the colonial herb garden. In the mid-eighteenth century, the Pennsylvania apothecary and printer Christopher Sauer wrote in his German-language *Compendious Herbal* that 'it has been discovered through everyday use that angelica provides a particularly good remedy for injuries brought about by witchcraft'.[21] Sauer was clear about using European angelica rather than Native-American varieties, which also had curative properties and were used by the indigenous population. In some cases imports had a major impact on the country's agricultural development. The Goober or goober pea, otherwise known as the peanut, is a good example. Now a staple American snacking food, in African and early African-American belief it was associated in some contexts with witchcraft and bad luck.[22]

But American fauna and flora presented fantastic new medical and magical possibilities. Tobacco was one of the earliest examples, of course, but there were many more. One we shall encounter later is the puccoon or blood root (*Sanguinaria canedensis*), found along the eastern seaboard. This produces a red sap which was used by Native Americans as a dye and in herbal medicine. In African-American folk magic it was considered to bring good luck if rubbed on the body.[23] This is not the place to engage in an extensive discussion of herbal medicine, so let us instead concentrate on two aspects of America's fauna and flora, snakes and roots, which illustrate the exchange of knowledge between

Native Americans, African Americans, and Europeans, and how it generated new expressions of magic.

North Europeans were no stranger to poisonous snakes in the form of the zigzag-patterned adder, but the range and deadliness of venomous snakes in America presented a new challenge for rural settlers. There was the swamp-loving cottonmouth in the south-eastern states that made the task of drainage a risky business, and the pretty but deadly coral snake. But it was the rattlesnake that understandably caused the most concern. In 1683 a French immigrant named Louis Thibou wrote that there had been much talk in England about the dangers of the rattlesnake, but in an effort to reassure his fellow Frenchman he stated that, 'a few people have been bitten by accident, but there is a good remedy for that here and no one has ever died of their bite'.[24] The early Carolina authorities and businessmen feared, nevertheless, that the rumours of the rattler's power would put off potential settlers. Interest in them was enduring, though. In 1729 an English newspaper advertised that two live rattlesnakes, supposedly caught by American 'Indians', were on display in a wire cage for six pence a peek at a coffee house in Covent Garden, London. Visitors could also handle the rattle of a dead compatriot.[25] It was not just the deadliness of the rattlesnake's poison that attracted interest but its power to fascinate with its stare. While early colonial literature reported the rattlesnake as a matter-of-fact danger, from the late seventeenth century onwards there emerged a growing literature discussing the power of the rattlesnake to entrance animals and humans before it struck.[26] The matter was a fitting subject for that esteemed scientific body the Royal Society. Around the same time its members were pondering the reports of second sight in the Scottish Highlands. Both were discussed in terms of the power of charming or 'fascination'.

The occult world was still a matter of intellectual curiosity and imagination. In 1723 one colonial fellow of the Royal Society, Paul Dudley, wrote that he was 'abundantly satisfied' that the rattlesnake 'charmed' its prey into its mouth. 'The Eye of this Creature has something so singular and terrible, that there is no looking stedfastly on him' he asserted. Others reported how they felt sick and feeble once caught in a rattlesnake's hypnotic glare. Christopher Witt, writing in 1735, took the argument into the realms of witchcraft discourse—'Seeing that this fascinating Power of the Snake cannot be denied, why may it not be also allow'd in some malicious wicked old women.' Witt was an unusual individual, an English-born botanist and occultist of Germantown, Pennsylvania, but his view was probably widely shared.

Snakes played a significant role in Native-American myth, but there was confusion at the time as to whether the notion of the rattlesnake's powers of ocular fascination derived from Native-American belief. Rattlesnakes were certainly used in some cursing rituals. Amongst the Shoshoni, during the late nineteenth century, people who wished to cause harm cooked the heads of rattlesnakes on hot coals, along with other ingredients, and placed the mixture in a buckskin bag. Whoever wore the bag could kill people by looking intently at them while muttering a charm. A Zuni witch was accused of making a missile from rattlesnake hearts, which she directed at children.[27] It is clear, though, that settlers borrowed much from Native-American treatments for rattlesnake bites. A British herbal published in 1790 noted in its entry on rattlesnake root (*Polygala senega*), 'we are indebted for our knowledge of this plant, and its virtues, to the Indians'.[28] As its name suggested, the twisted yellow root of this perennial plant was considered a cure for rattlesnake bite by the Seneca, but was also used more widely for inflammation, fever, and as an expectorant. Commerce was created with one South Carolina physician advertising in 1750 that he would give five shillings for a pound of snakeroot.[29] By the nineteenth century, *Polygala senega* was being exported to Europe for sale in druggists and chemists shops. Yet, there was reluctance on behalf of some to give credence to Native-American cures. This was alluded to by a correspondent to the *Virginia Gazette* in 1738, who found 'many Persons railing against the Rattlesnake-Root . . . some through Disrespect to the Discoverer'. The correspondent, however, was convinced that it had saved the lives of himself and many of his slaves from pleurisy and the ague.[30]

By the 1800s Native-American herbal knowledge formed the basis of much of the published manuals of American pharmacy.[31] This is evident in medical guides such as Abel Tennant's 1837 *Vegetable Materia Medica*. Tennant recalled that his knowledge of one plant was 'obtained from a man who was taken prisoner by the Indians when small, and to whom the Indian doctor gave a full account of the plants used by them in curing diseases'.[32] One important contribution to the medicine chest was the use of pinkroot or Indian pink, which the Cherokee called *Unsteetla*, to cure the widespread problem of intestinal worms.[33] There are numerous others, such as the Louisiana Houma Nation's use of an infusion of magnolia leaves for cramps, which was adopted by the Cajun population.[34] 'Indian doctor' became a title to describe any purveyor of medicines purportedly or actually obtained from Native Americans. There were numerous, often itinerant practitioners who claimed in newspaper adverts, handbills, and on the stump, to have learned their knowledge during captivity by or long association with the Nations. One Peter Carlton advertised in a German-language Philadelphia newspaper in 1775: 'Peter Carlton, doctor according to the Indian method, lives on Christopher Mussel's plantation . . . While held captive by the Indians for fourteen years, he learned their medical methods, and he now gives treatment and also instruction.' Another Indian doctor named Cook, who settled near the town of Union, Maine, around 1805, claimed he obtained his herbal medicines from a medicinal garden cultivated and then abandoned by the Indians.[35]

Tennant recorded six species of plant under the heading of 'snakeroots', all of which possessed curative properties beyond snakebite, including the cure of gangrene, fevers, stomach upsets, and measles.[36] Snakeroot could also be used in unorthodox ways. In 1901 a quack doctor named Thomas Everhart joined an Atlanta chain gang for a month after defrauding an African-American woman of $3 for professing to cure her of deafness by rubbing snakeroot powder on her ears.[37] Most of the plants were so named because of the serpentine form of their roots. Their association with snake bites was, therefore, an example of the doctrine of signatures, a global concept understood by cultures that shared no common religious or intellectual origin. It encapsulated the idea that the shape and colour of plants that were similar to parts of the animal kingdom or symptoms of bodily illness had an associated curative value.

Europeans learned not only from Native Americans but also the African-American peoples they had enslaved. West African medical traditions, like those of Native Americans, placed considerable emphasis on the use of roots in both healing and spiritual matters. The two groups interacted closely with each other. After all, significant numbers of Native Americans were enslaved during the early eighteenth century and intermarriage was not uncommon. Some Native-American tribes also practised slavery. Economically and culturally both peoples were more reliant on the natural resources around them, while the European Americans of the late eighteenth and nineteenth centuries were increasingly locked into the commercialized medical world of patent medicines and under the influence of the expanding medical profession. Necessity and confidence, furthermore, made them more willing to experiment. Indeed, empirical knowledge of herbal medicine was one route to freedom. One of the most popular herbal cures for snakebites was created by an African-American slave named Caesar, who was freed and paid an annuity by the South Carolina General Assembly in the mid-eighteenth century. The cure was based on the juice from the roots of plantain and horehound, both of which were recorded as being used by the Seneca as snakebite remedies. Dr Caesar gained legendary status over the ensuing decades, and his remedies for snakebite and poison were printed in Carolina newspapers and in almanacs produced in Virginia, Maryland, and Pennsylvania.[38]

Across the slaving colonies during the mid-eighteenth-century fears grew about the occult use of poisons. In 1756 the Charleston physician Alexander Garden wrote to Charles Alston, Professor of Botany at Edinburgh University, requesting 'what information you could about the African Poisons, as I greatly and do still suspect that the Negroes bring their knowledge of the poisonous plants, which they use here'.[39] Ordinances and edicts were instituted prohibiting slaves from practising herb medicine to stem the perceived epidemic of poisoning of plantation owners and their staff. Conjure was now viewed as an act of rebellion. South

Carolina instituted a law in 1751 ordering 'That in case any slave shall teach or instruct another slave in the knowledge of any poisonous root, plant, herb, or other poison whatever, he or she, so offending, shall upon conviction thereof, suffer death.' Similar legislation was introduced in Georgia and some French colonies.[40]

A series of trials during the late eighteenth and early nineteenth centuries confirm that poisoning was employed as a weapon against both white plantation owners and also against fellow slaves. Those charged with poisoning were often also accused of conjuring, such as a Virginia domestic slave and reputed conjurer named Delphy who was executed in 1816. She was said to have slipped a decoction of pokeroot, a plant with toxic compounds that was commonly used as an ingredient in cancer cures, into her mistress's coffee every morning. The poisons used were usually herbal in nature; laws prevented druggists and chemists selling to slaves such notable European poisons as strychnine and arsenic. But snakeheads, in which poisons was thought to reside, were also mentioned in cases. A North Carolina bondman and conjurer, tried in 1800 for the murder of a white slave holder, was overheard expressing a 'wish for a Rattle snake's head' to make a powerful poison. Poisons need not be ingested to be deemed effective. A slave in Mecklenberg County was transported after attempting to poison his master by beating some leaves with a rattlesnake's head and leaving them on the master's doorstep.[41]

While poisoning had long been considered an adjunct of witchcraft in Europe from antiquity to the courtly intrigues of the medieval and early modern aristocracy, accusations of the use of natural poisons were far from ubiquitous in those witch trials concerning the common people. The fear of accepting food stuffs or being touched by suspected witches was widespread, but the way such contamination was thought to operate was rarely described in the language of 'poison' as distinct from bewitchment. Cunning-folk and other magical healers were occasionally prosecuted for prescribing potions to deliberately poison clients for one reason or another, but in the West African sorcery tradition the relationship between witchcraft and the use of poison was inseparable. Witches were commonly thought to enact their malicious work through the direct and ritual use of poisons. One early nineteenth-century missionary working among the Bassa tribe of Liberia, observed that 'they live in much dread of being poisoned, and, as they seem generally to connect this poisoning with witchcraft, they wear on their bodies something furnished by their grigri men'.[42] The judicial use of poison to try African witches was also much reported during the nineteenth and early twentieth century. The suspects were made to swallow poison either voluntarily or forcibly; if they died they were guilty, if they vomited it up and survived they were innocent. So Europeans came to equate poisoning with Africanness. Writing in 1803, Thomas Winterbottom, a physician posted to Sierra Leone in the 1790s, noted that the English lower classes believed that poison naturally accumulated under the fingernails of black people, which they used to destroy their enemies.[43]

White fears of conjure poisoning seem to have calmed down by the mid-nineteenth century as the slavery system crumbled, but it remained prominent in African-American tradition. An African American from Wilmington, North Carolina, interviewed in the twentieth century illustrates this nicely. 'I've been hurt by a woman', he said. 'Well, I wus poisoned in good fashion. I liked to died.' The regular doctor did not help, so he cured himself with a drink of silk root, blacksnake root, and devil-shoestring root, and bathed in a concoction of cherry bark, red oak bark, and dogwood root after which he threw the water in the direction of the sunrise. Poisoning in a conjure context did not necessarily mean the victim had ingested or touched a poison. The act of poisoning could be achieved at a distance by burying substances in the ground, throwing them in the river, or hanging them up.[44]

The American term 'root doctor' was born out of this eighteenth-century medical exchange in the southern states, and became a common term used by African-American healers along with the more generic title of 'yarb' or 'erb' doctor. It subsequently became culturally and geographically diffuse. Sixteen people described themselves as 'root doctors' in the 1880 census, all were male, ten were white, and six black. Root doctor William Baker, of Raleigh, North Carolina, was born in Prussia and Ulf Nydrum, of Ludington, Michigan, was a Norwegian.[45] There were, of course, many more root doctors operating than these, and many women amongst them. Very few of those who ended up in court or were reported in the newspapers turn up in the census, which is not surprising considering their itinerant status and sometimes shady practices. Some stuck strictly to natural herbal cures, but other root doctors were involved in magical activities known as 'root working', in which sense they were no different to conjure and hoodoo doctors. We will return to all these characters in a later chapter.

Witch balls

The notion that witches harmed livestock by shooting or throwing hair balls that passed through the animals' hides without leaving any visible trace was a widespread and prominent belief in America.[46] Yet I have found no such tradition in Europe. It was obviously well established by the early nineteenth century as the clergyman and historian of West Virginia and Pennsylvania, Joseph Doddridge (1769–1826), referred to witches shooting cattle with hair balls.[47] Methodist minister Rev. James Jenkins (b. 1764), whose preaching style was epitomized by his nickname 'Bawling Jenkins', recalled attending a class meeting in South Carolina at which a reputed witch was present. He asked one of the members why they 'suffered her to stay in class', and was told, '"Suffer her! Why we are afraid of her"...and he went on to tell of the poor woman's cows she had shot with hair-balls, or a great many of them fired at once, she had killed in a moment every fowl in the yard of some poor woman whom she had a grudge against.'[48] Later in the century newspapers mentioned the notion. In 1875, for instance, the press reported that Nancy Lewis of Hazel Dell Township, Iowa, made public complaints that her 83-year-old mother-in-law Clarinda Lewis was a witch, and accused her of manufacturing witch balls and tormenting her and her daughters at night. A newspaper account of a witch drama unfolding in Newton County, Georgia, in the same year, explained that an elderly widow stood accused, amongst other crimes, of making 'witch balls' of hair gathered from the tail of a cow.[49] As to how these balls were thought to be produced, an old Ozark witch was said to have made hers by rolling a small bunch of black hair with beeswax into hard pellets. These she threw at her victims and they would enter their bodies. A more sophisticated method of firing them was reported from Rowan County, North Carolina. Witches there were supposed to make bullets of twisted and knotted hair that they shot from a glass phial open at both ends.[50]

The popular conception of hair balls as the product of witchcraft was supported by physical evidence, for as one nineteenth-century American folklorist noted, butchers frequently found them in the stomachs of oxen and cows. Reports and correspondence on the subject cropped up periodically in the American agricultural press.[51] The Boston veterinary surgeon, and author of popular veterinary guides, George Dadd, considered the topic in his book on *The Diseases of Cattle* (1859). Let us read his description:

> In consequence of the propensity which some animals have of licking their own bodies, or those of their associates, they manage to swallow large quantities of hair, which being indigestible, accumulates in a compartment of the stomach in the form of a dense ball, which is occasionally regurgitated.... These balls sometimes accumulate material until they are bigger than ordinary sized goose eggs. It is not surprising that death ensues from the irritation of such an indigestible mass in the stomach of an ox or cow, and it is also not surprising that many deaths of cattle cannot be accounted for by their owners.[52]

Dadd was well aware that 'not a few' people believed that they were the work of witchcraft. Likewise, in 1853, an Indiana doctor, the author of what was probably the first chemical analysis of an ox concretion in America, noted that the superstitious called them witch balls but their origin was obvious to the 'intelligent observer' as he set about explaining.[53]

The belief in witch balls was clearly widely held in African-American farming communities as well. The editors of the *Western Farmer & Gardener*, one of whom was the Presbyterian pastor Henry Ward Beecher, noted that African Americans in Kentucky were 'exceedingly superstitious' with respect to hair balls, and refused to touch or be near them when found. In 1846 an Iowa correspondent sent to the editors an example of one of thirteen hair balls taken from the stomachs of a calf on his farm. The calf had belonged to an African American who, after its death, told the correspondent that it was killed by witches and cited the balls as proof. Further investigation revealed the true cause. The original owner of the calf was a barber and the calf had evidently eaten considerable quantities of hair clippings from the barbershop, and these had coalesced into the hairballs. In the 1890s it was also reported that African-American conjurer doctors in the southern states laid curses by throwing hair balls at their target, and in Georgia and South Carolina by burying them under doorsteps.[54]

Humans are also susceptible to gastric hairballs, although identifiable medical examples were rare in the period concerned. A medical paper on the subject in 1902 reported that only twenty-four cases, twenty-two recorded from inquests, had been formally noted in European and American medical literature. Twenty-three of them concerned women between eighteen and thirty-four years of age.[55] The reason for this striking gender bias was the habit amongst girls of chewing locks of their long loose hair or the ends of their braids. One case was reported of a male victim who was in the habit of chewing his beard. Those working with cotton, wool, or coconut fibres were also prone. Twentieth-century autopsies confirm that new items such as chewing gum and popcorn have been known to cause similar gastric concretions. Considering that very few people were ever dissected, the notion that witches shot humans with hair balls must have been an extrapolation from the many examples found in livestock. Still, claims of finding witch shots associated with human casualties were made in folklore. So we have accounts of examples being discovered in the mouths of those shot by witches or close by their bodies, having rolled out of their mouths as they were suddenly and inexplicably struck down dead (from a heart attack, for example). No doubt some witch doctors also played tricks, revealing to clients the witchery behind their loved ones' mysterious deaths.[56]

But hair balls could also have beneficial properties. Examples were apparently much sought after as protective amulets amongst African Americans in Georgia and South Carolina. In southern Illinois 'witch masters' moved hair balls over the heads of those plagued with witchcraft or evil spirits.[57] Mark Twain introduced such a hair ball to the readers of the *Adventures of Huckleberry Finn*. Huck's companion Jim, an escaped slave who is a repository of African-American occult lore, and claims to have seen the Devil, possessed a 'hair-ball as big as your fist, which had been took out of the fourth stomach of an ox, and he used to do magic with it. He said there was a spirit inside of it, and it knowed everything.'[58] A manufacturing tradition developed. The roving adventurer Griffin Tipsoward (d. 1840), who was born in Pennsylvania, lived with the Kickapoo Indians, and was an early settler in Illinois, made part of his living as a healer. He employed 'witch balls' consisting of deer and cow hair held together by string. These he would move about the person bewitched while muttering some charm.[59]

In fact the desirable properties of certain hair balls known as bezoars, a word that has recently generated interest thanks to its inclusion as a potion ingredient in the *Harry Potter* novels, has a very long history.[60] The word bezoar derives from the Persian meaning 'expelling poison'. Information about its medical properties seems to have been introduced to Europe by Arab physicians in the medieval period, and bezoars became hugely desirable items in the medicine cabinets of rich Europeans into the eighteenth century. These were not the hair balls of common livestock, though, but those from the stomachs of wild animals from exotic lands, such as Persian goats and South American llamas.[61] An early nineteenth-century encyclopaedia listed six types of bezoar, including *Bezoar simiæ* from certain Brazilian monkeys, and *Bezoar porcinum* or *pedro del porco*, which derived from the porcupine.[62]

Although most prized as a means of extracting poison, they were also thought to cure the plague, epilepsy, witchcraft, and other ailments. What with the concerns over poisoning amongst plantation owners, and snakebites, it is no surprise that eighteenth-century American settlers were keen to source bezoars. At the beginning of the eighteenth century the Englishman settler John Lawson (1674–1711) recorded in his journal *Native Americans of the Carolinas*:

> Enquiry of them, if they never got any of the Bezoar Stone, and giving them a Description how it was found, the Indians told me, they had great plenty of it; and ask'd me, what use I could make of it? I answer'd them, That the white Men us'd it in Physick, and that I would buy some off them ... Thereupon, one of them pull'd out a Leather- Pouch, wherein was some of it in Powder; he was a notable Hunter, and affirm'd to me, That the Powder blown into the Eyes, strengthen'd the Sight and Brain exceedingly, that being the most common Use made of it.[63]

In the early 1740s broadsides were distributed along the Eastern seaboard advertising that a Frenchman named Francis Torres had for sale a number of 'Chinese snake-stones', which were almost certainly bezoars. They cured the 'Bites of all venomous or poisonous Creatures, as Rattle (and other) Snakes, Scorpions, mad

Dogs, etc'. When applied to the wound the stone drew out the poison, and when placed in a glass of water purged itself ready for reuse. The broadside bore testimonials from several South Carolina slave owners. That the advertising campaign proved successful is suggested by a letter to a medical journal from a Virginian man in 1807 who praised the healing power of a Chinese snake stone in the possession of the Rev. Lewis Chaustien of Frederick County. It was accompanied by a certificate that stated it came from Bombay in 1740. Chaustien generally did not charge the numerous applicants bitten by mad dogs or snakes who came to him.[64] In 1840 a North Carolina man offered a similar snake stone for sale for the princely sum of $20.[65]

During the early nineteenth century the idea of the foreign 'snake stone' gave way to the distinctly American 'madstone' in folk medical tradition.[66] The most efficacious madstones were the bezoars from deer, and they became much prized for curing rabies (hydrophobia) in particular, the disease having spread considerably since the 1770s.[67] One Alabama quack doctor who possessed two madstones explained in an advertising puff: 'What is a Mad-stone? It is a compact of Vegetable and Mucus Matters, and formed by a freak of nature in the small or second stomach of a Hermaphrodite Deer, and so constructed with its innumerable cells that when applied to lacerated flesh, it adheres at once and every cell exercises a suction power, but does not absorb any substance except Virus.' Those who possessed them became important figures in rural communities. The 'Stoll Stone' of Cass County, Missouri, which 'had saved a good many lives' according to its mid-twentieth-century custodian, was handed down through the Stoll family after the first emigrant member of the family arrived from Alsace-Loraine around 1850 and found the madstone in the stomach of a deer he shot during a sojourn in California. In 1879 a madstone derived from the stomach of a deer was bought by a Texas druggist for $250.[68]

I have strayed somewhat from the topic of witch balls but the comparison with madstones reveals a significant distinction. Hair balls found in *wild* animals, principally deer in America, accrued natural beneficial properties but hair balls found in *domesticated* livestock were symptomatic of supernatural assault and generally but always considered harmful. But why did hair balls in livestock develop into the witch ball tradition? The fact that American veterinarians and agriculturalists seemed to be more concerned about hair balls than their European counterparts might be a clue. Can answers be found by exploring environmental and agricultural developments in America? Perhaps hair balls were more prevalent in American livestock in the nineteenth century. Huge numbers of European dairy cows were exported to the states. The Guernsey cow, for instance, was first brought to America in the 1830s and nearly 35,000 were exported live over the next century. The last two decades of the nineteenth century saw a substantial increase in imports, not only from Britain but also breeds such as the Holstein-Friesian from the Netherlands and the Brown Swiss from Switzerland.[69] Just like their human owners, imported livestock breeds had to adapt to the indigenous flora and new grazing regimes. New fodder plants were also imported from Europe. In 1896 the United States Department of Agriculture received reports of numerous horse deaths from Delaware, Virginia, and North Carolina. The cause—hair balls from eating the dry prickly stems of deflowered crimson clover.[70] This form of clover is indigenous to southern Europe and was first introduced to America as a fodder crop in the mid-nineteenth century, although it only began to be grown widely in the 1940s.[71] It is pure speculation, of course, but maybe the exposure of northern and central European livestock to new fibrous plants with which they were unfamiliar led to a greater incidence of stomach concretions. While this might help explain the prominence of hair balls in American rural tradition, it does not get us any further in understanding where the witch ball concept came from. Perhaps the fairies had something to do with it.

What happened to the fairies?

'There are no fairies in our meadows, and no elves to spirit away our children'. So wrote the Massachusetts Unitarian minister and novelist Sylvester Judd (1813–1853). Reflecting on the fading influence of superstition in New England he went on to observe that 'witches have quite vanished'.[72] So what did he know? Then again, it is true that fairies are very rarely mentioned in the ethnographic sources of the nineteenth and early twentieth century. When the great American folklorist Wayland D. Hand wrote an article on 'European Fairy Lore in the New World' some thirty years ago, a lot of his references concerned Canada and Newfoundland rather than the United States, and he recognized that in America the influence of print on recorded fairy lore was 'considerable, if not decisive'.[73] From surveying a wider array of sources than Hand it is patently clear that European oral traditions and beliefs concerning fairies did not migrate as well as ghosts and witches. This failure of fairy tradition to survive the Atlantic crossing has been remarked upon but little studied.[74] One obvious reason for the weakness of fairy lore is that in Western Europe the fairies were rooted in local geographies and popular interpretations of the ancient landscape. They inhabited liminal places, physical and metaphysical boundaries between the past and present, this world and other realms, natural features that represented portals between different states of being. So we find fairy legends and sightings focused around prehistoric earth-works and burial mounds, and landscape features such as venerable trees, streams and bridges. Now, all these features could also be found in the North American landscape of course. The difference is that in the old world landscape associations with fairies had their roots in centuries of accumulated tradition and experience. The fairies lost their relevance once divorced from these long-held associations.[75] This is not to say, though, that American immigrants ceased believing in fairies. Fairy beliefs have been collected in both Canada and America, usually from Irish or Highland Scots families, but they invariably pertain to events and people back in the old homelands.[76] Ghosts on the other hand, while sharing motifs, characteristics, and landscape associations with fairies, were attached not only to places but self-evidently to people. So ghosts repopulated America because they multiplied as people died, allowing new legends to form in new locations.

The curious thing is, though, that fairy belief seems to have been maintained in greater strength in some French Canadian settlements and amongst Newfoundlandlers. Twentieth-century folklorists have collected numerous stories of the French *lutins* and British fairies in these communities.[77] It is no surprise that one of the stronger records of fairy faith collected in mid-twentieth-century America was amongst the French Canadian inhabitants of the Upper Peninsula, Michigan, who settled in the area during the logging boom of the late nineteenth century. In 1946 some still expressed a belief in the *lutins* that rode the farmers' horses at night leaving their manes knotted. No one interviewed had caught them in the act though.[78] One suggestion for the strength of belief in Newfoundland at least, is that the settlement pattern and economy, which were based primarily on fishing, created small close-knit communities connected to those in the homeland, with life existing in familiar environmental conditions.[79] A significant proportion of the population of Newfoundland, furthermore, was drawn from Ireland and the English West Country. Fairy beliefs remained stronger in western England than most other parts of the country in the nineteenth century. In this context it is worth noting that witchcraft beliefs recorded in Newfoundland in the second half of the twentieth century were also strongest amongst communities with a West Country heritage, mirroring the fact that the counties of Somerset, Devon, and Dorset are richer in court cases and recorded witchcraft disputes than most other parts of England.[80] Isolation is often considered the key factor in the preservation of traditions, but with regard to fairies this does not necessarily hold true. The Newfoundland evidence suggests a more complex condition whereby geographical remoteness was in play but where the fishing economy reduced cultural and social isolation, providing an environment conducive to limited fairy migration.

I have raised the matter of fairies here because the American witch ball tradition is clearly related to the European fairy or elf shot tradition—or that of Scotland and Ireland, to be more precise. Fairy shooting consisted of two main elements. The first was diagnostic. Unexpected deaths amongst humans and livestock, probably often from heart attacks and strokes, whose bodies displayed no external signs of harm were sometimes thought to have been shot with invisible missiles by elves or fairies, a condition known as *elfschuss* in German and *alfskot* in Norwegian.[81] The terms 'elfshot' or 'elfshotten' were still used in eighteenth-century America to describe a specific medical condition in horned cattle. As Samuel Deane, one-time Vice President of Bowdoin College, Brunswick, Maine, explained in his book *The New-England Farmer* (1790), the symptoms were sluggishness and loss of appetite:

> The original of the name seems to have been a superstitious opinion, that cattle were shotten and wounded by elves, or fairies. The disease, how-ever, is not imaginary. It is believed to be an opening in the peritonæum, or film of the belly, caused by relaxation. It resembles a hole made by a bullet, and may be felt through the skin which remains unhurt.[82]

This corresponds to information collected in Ireland and Scotland in the same period. It was reported in early nineteenth-century Ireland that the inhabitants of County Antrim, 'will show you the spot where you may feel a hole in the flesh, but not in the skin, where the cow has been struck'. In Sutherland, Scotland, the symptoms of elf shot were described as the animal feeling uneasy, breathing hard, and refusing food. Samuel Deane advised that elfshot could be cured by rubbing the part with salt and water, and we find similar advice from Highland Scotland, where an agricultural survey of 1812 noted that the country people rubbed salt over the holes, and a draft of salted water in which silver had been dipped was dabbed on the ears of the sick animals and poured down their throat.[83]

The second element of the fairy shooting tradition was evidential. While the entry points of their missiles left no visible wound, the reality of such assaults was confirmed by the existence of the prehistoric stone arrowheads that were brought to the surface by ploughing, particularly the distinctive barbed and tanged arrow-heads of the late Neolithic and Bronze Age. In societies where the use of such stone tools was far beyond distant memory but it was recognized that they were fabricated, it is not surprising that they were attributed to a race of supernatural beings. Across much of nineteenth-century Europe, Stone Age arrowheads and axes were believed in popular culture to be produced by thunder storms and were kept to ward off lightening.[84] But during the nineteenth century at least, it would seem that only in Scotland and Ireland did a direct connection continued to be made between these flint arrowheads and the *condition* of being fairy shot. The fairies did not use bows to fire their arrows though, just as American witches did not fire their balls from guns. In late seventeenth-century Scotland Robert Kirk wrote that these flints were 'shaped like a barbed arrow head, but flung as a dart with great force'. Likewise those witches who learned the technique from the fairies. Isobel Gowdie, who was tried for witchcraft in 1662, explained that she flicked them off her thumbnail.[85] One fairy doctor in north-west Ireland kept four flint arrowheads that he showed to clients to show the cause of their cows' ailment. His grandfather had found them near a rath or fort on a farm plagued by elf shot. The fairies, or 'gentry' as they were euphemistically known in Ireland, fired them to keep inquisitive cows from their sacred areas.[86]

Wherever Europeans settled in America they also found familiar-looking arrowheads.[87] In 1699 the antiquarian Edward Lhwyd (1660–1708) after visiting the highlands of Scotland and seeing arrowhead amulets, wrote: 'I doubt not but you have often seen of these Arrowheads they ascribe to elfs or fairies: they are just the same chip'd flints the natives of New England head their arrows with at this day.'[88] Many of the examples collected in America over the centuries are prehistoric or date to the early colonial years, but amongst some Native Americans stone technology and the production of stone arrowheads continued into the nineteenth century. That is not to say it was widespread, but the well-worn narrative of Native Americans swiftly ditching their ancient technologies for metal hatchets, knives, arrow tips, and guns is not entirely accurate. There were cultural, economic, and practical reasons for continuing to use stone tools.[89] Probably the last of the traditional arrowhead makers was a man who came to be known to the public as Ishi, the last surviving member of the Yahi hunter-gatherer group of north-central California. In 1908 he had fired his arrows at a party of engineers surveying a pipeline to frighten them off his ancestral lands. In 1911 starving and close to death, he made his way to a European settlement. He was taken to the county jail in Oroville but following widespread newspaper coverage of his plight, he was brought to the Museum of Anthropology at the University of California. Here he lived for a further five years demonstrating his tool-making skills, and helping academics record his people's language and culture, before succumbing to tuberculosis.[90]

Some Native-American peoples ascribed magical powers to stone arrowheads, but in contexts somewhat different to the Europeans. Amongst the Cheyenne, arrowheads that had killed enemies or those of enemies that had failed to kill their intended victims, were kept on necklaces. The Pueblos wore arrowheads as protection against witches, and they and the Apache used quartz found at the base of trees blasted by lightening to fashion 'medicine arrows' used by women in healing rituals. The colour of arrowheads also had spiritual associations.[91]

There is little evidence, though, of European settlers ascribing supernatural powers or causation to the Native-American stone arrows and axes they found. A rare example of the old elf shot tradition being associated with Native-American stone arrows was recorded by a folklorist in the Appalachians during the 1930s. An informant told how he had been riding home at dusk and had seen a small red-headed fairy at a distance. He then felt something whiz past him, upon which his horse went lame. On searching the spot the next day he found a flint point typical of the sort used by some Native Americans for shooting birds and small game. Elsewhere there are a couple of examples from southern Illinois, an area settled primarily by English and Scots-Irish, of worked flints being used against childbirth pains and to protect chickens from hawks. It was noted that in the area it was by no means rare to find Native-American flint arrows in cultivated fields or old abandoned middens.[92] Likewise, African-American use of Indian arrowheads was known but not widespread. A Mississippi conjure doctor told the folklorist Newbell Niles Puckett that the Indian arrowheads found in the area were not made by human hands but forged from thunder and lightning. The ashes remaining from a piece of punk burnt by a spark from an arrowhead gave good luck. Excavations from several nineteenth-century African-American occupation sites have turned up examples of Native-American stone tools, suggesting that their ritual employment might have been in more common use than the literary sources suggest.[93]

As the reference to Isobel Gowdie shows, the notion of witches shooting like the fairies was not unknown in parts of Europe. In Germany, for instance, 'hexenschuss' or 'witch shot' was used to describe lumbago or sudden back pain, and the term was certainly in use in early twentieth-century German communities in America.[94] But hairballs were not elements in these European projectile traditions. They were, however, in Native-American belief. The late eighteenth-century Moravian missionary David Zeisberger, writing of the Delaware Indians, amongst whom he lived and worked, provides us with a crucial bit of evidence. He described a common form of causing harm amongst the Delaware that involved 'a little piece of an old blanket or something else. This they rub in their hands until formed into a little ball. Naming the one who is marked for death, they throw this ball at him, saying that he shall die. They call this shooting the witchball.'[95] The same notion was reported amongst the Choctaws of Mississippi, with one account describing how a woman was killed by a 'witch ball' or *Isht-ul-bih* shot from an invisible rifle.[96] A 1923 report on the shooting of a supposed witch, the ninety-year-old Choctaw David Houston, in the mountains of Push-mataha County, Oklahoma, related that his alleged victim and possible murderer, Choctaw Johnnie Hobson, was told by a medicine man that the red blotches on his feet were caused by him having been shot by a witch ball.[97]

So in some Native-American cultures witches shot not arrowheads but balls with invisible rifles. We shall see in a later chapter how the concept of witchcraft-inspired object intrusion was an important aspect of their medical beliefs. For the moment it is enough to suggest that the American witch ball tradition that developed amongst European settlers and African Americans was a Native-American influence. The concept of supernatural shooting was common to all, but the notion that witches fired balls or bullets seems to have developed from

Native-American conceptualization of European technology within a supernatural framework of disease, which then was passed back to the European colonizers. The hair balls found in animal stomachs, such as buffalo, which we know from John Lawson's early eighteenth-century account that some tribes collected, provided the physical evidence for this new formulation of witch shooting.

They shoot witches don't they?

If witches shot their victims, then people shot witches. The history of gun culture in America is controversial and emotive, attracting considerable published debate. In contrast much less attention has been given to popular gun ownership in the European countries from which people emigrated. We do know that in nineteenth-century Switzerland private ownership of firearms was unrestricted and widespread. In parts of France, Corsica in particular, gun ownership was commonplace at all social levels.[98] In Britain, though, restrictions were placed on gun ownership in the early nineteenth century in response to concerns over poaching and vagrant demobbed soldiers after the Napoleonic war. Hunting with guns became the preserve of land-owning society and the gamekeepers in its employ, with the middle classes taking up the sporting pastime of pigeon shooting. The situation in the many German states and principalities before unification is less clear. Suffice it to say, though, that emigrant German gunsmiths were influential in late eighteenth- and nineteenth-century America.

Without getting entangled in the thicket of the US debate, it is clear that although before the American Civil War gun ownership was not as widespread as has sometimes been assumed, possession and use of guns by the general populace was certainly far more widespread than in Britain and other parts of Europe at the time.[99] One reason for this was the importance of the militia to the defence of communities, states and country against the attacks of Native Americans, slave uprisings, and wars with the French, Spanish, and British. The militia could not function as a fighting force without the private ownership of firearms, although in the late eighteenth and early nineteenth centuries there were frequent complaints that militiamen attended muster unarmed. Whether this was because substantial numbers of men did not possess guns or because they were reluctant to use their private property is one of the many debates raised by the archival sources. There was a shortage of firearms generally, though, and America was reliant upon imports of firearms and their components from Europe to distribute public guns to the militia. There were a variety of other influences on the pattern of ownership. The pacifist heritage of Pennsylvania and Delaware, for example, meant there was probably a considerably reduced level of armament. But from the Civil War onwards, American gun production began to match that of Europe, prices dropped, and the love affair with the firearm really began. Guns were not kept solely for military purposes, of course; they were used for personal protection and hunting. But the use of simple snares and traps was undoubtedly more widespread because they were far cheaper in comparison to the maintenance and repair of guns, and the cost of shot and gunpowder. Yet if the quarry were witches then you were better off reaching for your gun.

In 1901 a thirty-seven-year-old resident of Burt, Iowa, a German farm servant named Matt Hammerly was recommitted to a hospital for the insane after applying to the County Clerk for a permit to carry a gun to protect himself against the witches that had plagued him for a long time.[100] This was no doubt a good decision on behalf of the authorities. Various cases of suspected witches being shot dead are described in this book. While such instances were exceptional they were, nevertheless, more frequent than people might think. There was more than one way to shoot a witch though. A widespread tradition existed in nineteenth-century America of firing at the images of suspected witches with bullets containing silver, usually obtained from melting down dimes. This was a classic bit of sympathetic magic whereby the real witch would suffer the agonies of the bullet piercing his or her image.

Writing in 1824 the historian Joseph Doddridge remembered how 'For the cure of the diseases inflicted by witchcraft, the picture of the supposed witch was drawn on a stump or piece of board and shot at with a bullet containing a little bit of silver.'[101] In 1828 it was reported that in North Carolina 'Many a plank and tree, will bear the marks of silver bullets, some of which have been discharged within a short time past, at certain figures made of chalk and charcoal, and said to represent sundry old ladies, in the form of witches.' A Virginia man used the bloody sap of the puccoon root to draw the outline of the witch he suspected. The practice left a lasting mark in the woodlands of America. In 1899 timber cutters in Sampson County, North Carolina, found the image of a woman carved into a cypress tree and embedded within were several pieces of silver shot and a silver dime minted in 1850. The tradition kept pace with the spread of new technologies. In 1901 a folklorist was advised by a resident of Frederick County, Maryland, whose population had a strong Germanic background, to shoot a silver bullet at a photograph of a witch: 'If you can't get hold of her photograph, just draw her profile on the end of the barn, and shoot at that.'[102] No wonder that witches were commonly thought to work their spells over guns to make them misfire or malfunction. An eighteenth-century cure book in German kept by the Dahmer family of Pendleton County, West Virginia, includes one such charm:

> To stay a shot: Shot stand still in the name of God. Give neither fire nor
> flames. As sure as the beloved mother of God has remained a pure virgin
> (rock of Gibralta) + + +

A range of counter-magic remedies existed. Placing a dime in the barrel was an obvious solution, seeing as witches hated silver. Another 'de-witchifying' ritual consisted of placing the barrel in a stream of water, first upstream and then downstream.[103]

It was not only Americans who turned guns on witches—the French were pretty handy too.[104] In Britain, by contrast, there are no recorded shootings of witches. There are certainly references to the use of silver bullets made from a sixpenny piece in the nineteenth- and twentieth-century British folklore record. Most are legends, however, and I have come across no verifiable cases of the practice having been carried out. In 1957 an old Somerset gardener pondered on this, remarking, 'perhaps we can't melt down a silver bullet out of our present-day coining, and no one wears silver buttons nowadays.' The legends, furthermore, only concern shooting witches in animal form, usually a hare, with the witches exhibiting wounds once back in human form, although they were rarely said to have died as a result. Similar stories of shooting witch hares with silver bullets were also widespread in Germany and Scandinavia, and so it is no surprise that the motif was prevalent in American folk belief, with deer taking the place of hares in many accounts.[105] In the late nineteenth century a man of Logan, Mifflin County, Pennsylvania, was said to have shot a deer on the advice of a witch doctor believing it to be his aunt who he thought had bewitched him.[106]

The ritual shooting of witch images with silver bullets seems to be distinctively American then, a product of the country's love affair with the gun and the freedom unavailable to many Europeans to just go out into the woods and fire.

But if symbolic killing did not work, then the next step taken by the bewitched might be fatal. In September 1838 newspapers reported the shooting of a 'peaceable free', mixed-race man called Yates as he rode home on horseback near Abingdon, Virginia. At the subsequent murder trial the defendant, an elderly white man named Marsh, said in his defence that Yates had bewitched him, causing him to be afflicted with scrofula, and his 'dumb critters' to fall ill.[107] Marsh testified that he had initially tried to combat Yates's influence by drawing his likeness in chicken blood, taking this image into the woods and shooting at it with bullets that contained a small quantity of silver. One of the bullets used to kill Yates was produced in court, where it was observed there were cross marks on the surface that were thought to provide further anti-witch potency.

THE LAW

During the early eighteenth century, a few years after the last witch trials had taken place in America, several states adopted a raft of English statutes: amongst them was the 1604 Act against Witchcraft and Conjuration. This was the law under which hundreds of suspected witches were arrested in seventeenth-century England. So at a time when prosecutions for witchcraft were ceasing on both sides of the pond, the 1604 Act, with its death penalty for invoking evil spirits, became law in South Carolina in 1712 and Pennsylvania in 1718. In 1728 the Rhode Island legislators enacted 'That Witchcraft is, and shall be Felony; and whosoever shall be lawfully convicted thereof, shall suffer the Pains of Death.'[1] While these may seem reactionary impulses, we must bear in mind that witch trials continued in parts of central Europe into the mid-eighteenth century.

The adoption of the 1604 Act cannot simply be dismissed as an oversight by otherwise enlightened American legislatures. After all, the South Carolina Chief Justice Nicholas Trott (1663–1740), who was born and educated in England, believed in witchcraft and considered it a crime. 'We live in an Age of Atheism and Infidelity,' he complained in March 1706, 'and some Persons that are no great Friends to Religion, have made it their Business to decry all Stories of Apparitions and of Witches.' His opinions failed to convince a grand jury, however, to proceed with the prosecution of a suspected witch whom Trott considered guilty.[2] Trott was a staunch Anglican and his linking of atheism with scepticism regarding witchcraft was a common refrain in Anglican polemic at a time when the Church felt threatened by the growing influence of religious nonconformity and rationalist tendencies within the Church itself. Yet he was not uncritical about the standard of evidence required to try accused witches, questioning the legal basis of the Salem trials and rejecting the spectral evidence that played such a part in the prosecutions.

Back in Britain, the 1604 law against witchcraft was finally repealed in 1736 and a new statute was enacted that enshrined the prevailing legal view that witchcraft was a fraudulent practice rather than a real satanic activity.[3] So, from then on, if any person

> pretend to exercise or use any kind of Witchcraft, Sorcery, Inchantment, or Conjuration, or undertake to tell Fortunes, or pretend, from his or her Skill or Knowledge in any occult or crafty Science, to discover where or in what manner any Goods or Chattels, supposed to have been stolen or lost, may be found, every Person, so offending, being thereof lawfully convicted.

The punishment was one year's imprisonment, quarterly stints in the pillory for one hour, and the payment of sureties for good behaviour. The passing of the Act was by no means universally supported in Britain, and a considerable portion of educated society continued to believe in the power of witchcraft. The 1736 Act remained on the British statute books until 1951, and was occasionally dusted off and used against fortune-tellers, cunning-folk, and spiritualist mediums.[4]

Although English common law held sway in colonial America, the complex political situations in the various states meant that the enlightened 1736 Act was not adopted automatically. Witchcraft apparently remained a capital crime in Rhode Island into the 1740s. It was only in the 1770s, following independence, that Thomas Jefferson proposed Virginia enact an Americanized version of the 1736 statute, recommending that: 'All attempts to delude the people, or to abuse their understanding by exercise of the pretended arts of witchcraft, conjuration, enchantment or sorcery or by pretended prophecies, shall be punished by ducking and whipping at the discretion of a jury, not exceeding 15 stripes.' New Jersey followed suit in 1796.[5]

Pennsylvania provides a particularly interesting case. In February 1754, the Pennsylvania House of Representatives considered a proposal by Benjamin Franklin and others to repeal the 1718 adoption of the 1604 act, as it was deemed 'unnecessary here'. They further proposed that the 1736 Witchcraft Act be introduced to replace it.[6] But the legislature did not listen. It was not until September 1794 that the 1604 act was finally repealed in Pennsylvania. Why was Franklin's proposal not adopted at the time? Maybe the minor issue of witchcraft was lost in a bigger debate about the rejection of British common law. Maybe it was simply because of legislative timetabling and oversight. After all, by a statute of 1587, witchcraft remained a criminal offence in Ireland until it was belatedly repealed by the British parliament in 1821.[7] Still, we should not dismiss the possibility that it was obstructed by the continued educated belief in witchcraft. We need only consider the views of Thomas Cooper (1759–1839), an English-born, Oxford-educated lawyer, philosopher, and president of South Carolina College. A political radical who supported the French Revolution, Cooper left for America after being accused of trying to undermine British constitutional institutions.[8] Yet he was a believer in the literal truth of the Bible. In his *Statutes at Large of South Carolina*, Cooper inferred that the 1604 Act was still active in the state because its repeal in England and Scotland by the British parliament in 1736 did not extend explicitly to the colonies, and South Carolina and other states had not devised their own equivalent. Cooper then devoted several pages of notes to the history of the laws against witchcraft and their interpretation based on the volumes on the subject he possessed in his extensive library.

Without in any way expressing the view that the 1604 statute should remain active, Cooper defended the scriptural reality of witchcraft and so believed it could not be dismissed as mere pretence and imposture. He called upon the authority of Nicholas Trott, and the similar opinion of the eminent English jurist William Blackstone. 'Whatever therefore may be the opinions of the educated and enlightened part of the community in the present day', Cooper concluded, 'very many persons of good sense, as well as Christian piety, have been, and many still remain, firm believers in the reality and occasional existence of this presumed crime.'[9]

The squire

In nineteenth-century America the title of 'squire', short for 'Esquire', became a synonym for a justice of the peace. A century earlier it had simply denoted a gentleman landowner—the sort of man that often filled the role of the justice. It was an unpaid but coveted post, bringing with it political influence and the prestige of being a royal officer. The holders were all well educated, but despite wielding considerable legal power and authority in their localities, the position did not require any formal legal training. Nevertheless, they ruled on a range of petty civil and criminal offences. During the America Republic, however, the squire-archy changed. The royal association was severed, but the influence and power of the post remained attractive to ambitious social climbers. The new breed of justice was no longer a squire in old world terms. While the role attracted many law graduates it also opened up to tradesmen and small farmers. One of the allures was that, once in post, the respected title of 'squire' stuck to them for life in popular custom. If Massachusetts is indicative of a broader trend, then in the early decades of the new republic the number of justices expanded considerably.[10]

Judging from contemporary opinion, the new breed of squire-justice was not well regarded. The provocative English journalist William Cobbett (1763–1835) spent several years in Pennsylvania in the 1790s and gained a very poor impression of them: 'The moment these illiterate and unprincipled wretches receive the commission of the peace, they assume the title of Esquire, which their shoeless wives and children bestow on them on all occasions. It is not at all uncommon to see a Squire as ragged as a colt.' He went on to recall one justice of the peace in the neighbourhood of Philadelphia who sold greens and potatoes in the city's market. He described such squires as a greater curse upon Pennsylvania than dysentery and yellow fever.[11] A pen portrait of a New Hampshire justice of the peace by another author was no less flattering. Squire Jock was 'an arrant *pettifogger*' whose 'mind was on a very small scale, and his studies had been but few and limited'.[12]

The squires have been rather peripheral figures in the history of America, but they were clearly an important part of the social fabric of American society in the eighteenth and nineteenth centuries. More to the point, they were the arbiters in many witchcraft disputes, and it was their role to try and resolve the personal and social conflicts that generated accusations. To carry out their duties eighteenth-century squires relied heavily on the numerous manuals that explained the role of the justice of the peace and provided the basics regarding the statutory misdemeanours over which they held jurisdiction. The reliance on such manuals further cemented the practices of British common law in the everyday application of justice in America.[13] William Nelson's *Office and Authority of the Justice of Peace*, which was first published in England in 1704 and went through numerous subsequent editions, was one of the most popular manuals on both sides of the Atlantic. The first and most popular American guide was the *Conductor Generalis or a Guide for Justices of the Peace*. It appeared in 1711 and went through eleven editions published in six cities in three colonies. While indispensible tools of the trade, these well-thumbed guides did not necessarily reflect current legal thought, and despite the production of numerous editions, they could quickly go out of date. The legal status of witchcraft highlights this all too well. Several justices' manuals published in England and America in the year 1736 continued to reiterate the 1604 laws against witchcraft without any caveats or reflection, even though the last convictions for the crime had been several decades before. As the 1729 edition of Nelson's *Office of a Justice of Peace* stated: 'It seems plain, that there are Witches, because Laws have been made to punish such Offenders, tho' few have been convicted of Witchcraft.'[14] Hardly a sophisticated or nuanced argument: the letter of the law was the law.

After the passing of the 1736 Witchcraft Act, the next editions of the popular British manuals were updated, but American ones reflected the confused legal situation in the colony. Editions of the *Conductor Generalis* for 1749 and 1750, published in New York and Philadelphia respectively, continued to instruct justices on the content of the 1604 Act without any mention of its repeal. By the 1780s the crime of witchcraft had been expunged from its pages, but there was no mention of the 1736 Act. Not much help to the squire. Those reading a poorly edited North Carolina handbook for justices of the peace published in 1774 would have been further confused by reading details of the 1604 Act, being informed of its repeal in England, and then being told that witchcraft was still an offence in common law![15]

It is not surprising then that some squires without legal training and relying on such manuals, were unclear about the status of witchcraft and the means of proceeding when confronted with cases brought before them. We need to bear in mind, furthermore, the considerable weight of popular pressure they were subject to in isolated communities. Some justices of the peace believed in witchcraft and were willing to bend to the will of those that did. In 1820, for instance, a Baltimore newspaper reported that a newly appointed justice of the peace in Frederick County, Maryland, had recently burned one of his pigs alive as a counter against an old woman who he believed had bewitched his pig sty.[16] Now we can better understand the sensational actions of Squire French of Fentress County.

Fiasco in Fentress

The Methodist preacher and local historian Rev. A. B. Wright knew the area of Fentress County, Tennessee, and the surrounding area intimately. Recalling his time preaching in the neighbourhood in the 1880s, he wrote: 'Superstition has a strong grasp on many. It is a popular opinion among some, that witches are prevalent and doing a great deal of harm; and some even profess to know how to kill them.'[17] Little had evidently changed in half a century. For in 1831 a complicated case of suit and counter suit arising from accusations of witchcraft against a man in Fentress County revealed both the depth of feeling about witches and the ambiguous operation of local justice at the time.[18]

In the summer of 1830 several young women in Fentress County, which had been created only seven years before, suffered from fits and other symptoms attributable to witchcraft. They all recovered after several months except for Rebecca French, aged in her thirties, daughter of Joseph French.[19] Originally from Virginia, French had brought his family to Fentress County sometime around 1807. His was a prosperous and respected family in the area. Joseph was a justice of the peace, and at the time of these events Rebecca and her parents lived on a 600-acre spread a few miles west of Clarkrange in the south-western corner of the county.

Before going any further, though, it is best to clear up some problems with the sources in this case. Brief details have been reprinted several times based on those in a biography of the Tennessee judge Jefferson Dillard Goodpasture published in 1897. Its author was his son Albert Virgil, a lawyer and clerk of the State Supreme Court. Goodpasture Sr knew those involved in the Fentress case well. Yet in the account of events provided by his son no mention is made of the French family. Furthermore, in recent references the date of the case is put as 1835. It is a newspaper report from the *Nashville Herald*, reprinted in several other newspapers, that confirms the date as 1831 and puts the French family centre stage. Genealogical research confirms the details of the French family as recorded in the *Nashville Herald*, so it would seem that either the Goodpastures did not know the full story or deliberately erased the French family from the case, perhaps out of sensitivities towards relatives. There was good reason to do so, as we shall see. The court records would have clarified these details but they no longer survive, having probably perished in the fire that destroyed Fentress County Courthouse in 1905.[20]

Back to events then: during the winter of 1830 Rebecca was treated for bewitchment by Isaac Taylor and Pleasant Taylor, who the *Nashville Herald* described as 'celebrated for their skill in putting witches to flight'. Both men were recorded in the County Tax List of 1833. Genealogies indicate that Pleasant was a young blacksmith who lived in Jamestown, the county seat, while Isaac Taylor was a well-established surveyor in the area.[21] In January an old man named Stout who lived along the Obeds River that flows through the county, paid a visit to Squire French's house. As soon as he appeared Rebecca was seized with the tell-tale signs of violent jerks and trembling. She demanded that Stout give her a rope that he had brought with him. He initially declined to do so, but, concerned for his personal safety, he reluctantly handed it over. When the rope was tied around her waist her symptoms stopped. In the minds of some of those present, this was a sure sign that Stout was the witch responsible for Rebecca's condition. Stout understandably made a quick exit. Rebecca's torments returned.

One Charles Staunton now requested a warrant for the arrest of Stout, which was granted by Esquire French. A constable and five men armed with guns and silver bullets apprehended the suspected witch and brought him before French and a crowd of locals. Further proof was now sought of Stout's guilt. Those present were ordered to take Rebecca by the hand and pronounce the words: 'May the Great God of heaven, in the name of the Father, Son, and Holy Ghost, bless you.' Several people went through this process but without any effect. When Stout was forced to go through the same ritual at gunpoint her tortures immediately ceased. Rebecca now procured a warrant, presumably from her father, for the arrest of Stout on the charge of witchcraft. Stout, in turn, took out a warrant against Isaac

Taylor, Pleasant Taylor, Charles Staunton, and others for assault and battery and false arrest. In the midst of winter, with snow deep on the ground, the parties made there way to Jamestown, some twenty miles or so away, to have the merits of their cases assessed by the county magistrate Joshua Owens, who was a good friend of Judge Goodpasture. The charge against Stout was considered first. Owens decided to hold him to bail in the considerable sum of $2,000 to appear before the next county court in February.

On the due date Rebecca failed to turn up at the courthouse, which had been completed only four years earlier from plans drawn up by John M. Clemens, who was the father of Mark Twain and one of the town's lawyers. Rebecca French was ordered to pay costs. She appealed and the case was brought before a jury at the next Tennessee Circuit Court. Evidence was given that Stout had been seen exiting through the keyholes of houses, and that as well as afflicting the local women he had harmed horses and livestock through his witchery. The prosecuting attorney General John B. McCormick decided, however, that the prosecution could not be sustained and refused to proceed with the indictment. The decision apparently caused uproar amongst the Fentress hill folk who believed justice had not been done.

At the May session of the county court it was the turn of Stout's persecutors to stand trial. Squire Joseph French was called for the defence and deposed that he had never believed in witchcraft until confronted with his daughter's suffering, and that no attempt to harm Stout took place at his house—other than the unpleasant business of knocking him down with a chair. Pleasant Taylor also affirmed his belief in witchcraft. Isaac Taylor pleaded not guilty but was found guilty. He appealed, and once again the Circuit Court was confronted with the issue of witchcraft. Judge Abraham Caruthers, founder of the Cumberland School of Law, presided over the appeal. The prosecution rested its case on the fact that the handling of Stout for his supposed crime was permissible under the English Conjuration and Witchcraft Act of 1604, which, it was stated, had never been repealed in the state of Tennessee. Judge Caruthers gave this argument short shrift, stating that the Act had never been in force in the state. He informed the jury that the prosecution's case was 'destructive of, repugnant to, or inconsistent with the freedom and independence of this state, and form of government'. The decision of the county court was upheld.

Delaware witches beware

It would seem that reference to 'witchcraft', even as a fraudulent activity, was expunged from the statute books of most of the old states of the Eastern seaboard by the early nineteenth century. New laws were instituted against fortune-tellers and magical practitioners that took elements of the 1736 Witchcraft Act, namely the prohibition of magic as a false pretence, and married them with the essence of the British vagrancy laws that targeted simple fortune-telling and 'immoral' street activities. So in the 1840s the revised statutes of Maine included a section that bundled together nightwalkers, brawlers, railers, pilferers, common pipers, fiddlers, and those 'feigning themselves to have knowledge in physiognomy, palmistry, or, for the like purpose, pretending that they can tell destinies or fortunes, or discover where lost or stolen goods may be found'. In Pennsylvania an act against fortune-telling covered those who pretended 'to effect any purpose by spells, charms, necromancy or incantation'.[22] No mention of 'witchcraft' though. Yet a few east coast states adhered closely to the old English witchcraft laws. In 1847 the statutes of New Jersey continued to reiterate the main contents of the 1736 Witchcraft Act, with pretenders to 'witchcraft' punished by fines of up to $50 and up to three months' imprisonment.[23] Neighbouring Delaware adopted a tougher approach.

The 2010 mid-term elections cast a spotlight on Delaware, where the campaign of the high profile, Tea Party Republican candidate Christine O'Donnell faltered during its latter stages after she took to the airwaves to publicly deny ever having been a witch. But this was by no means the first time that witchcraft had caused embarrassment in the state. In December 1892 newspapers reported that two fortune tellers, Mrs Purrle of New York City and Madame Merill of Elmira, were arrested for fortune-telling in Wilmington, Delaware, and charged by the authorities with 'witchcraft'. The penalty for the crime was one year's imprisonment, one hour in the pillory (only for men), and a $100 fine. The two women were understandably frightened at being charged with witchcraft, and as the press noted, 'The law is very old, and this is the first time the present authorities remember that it has even been enforced.'[24] Did the crime of witchcraft really continue to exist in late nineteenth-century Delaware?

Move forward to 1950 and the Wilmington authorities once again found themselves in the same awkward position.[25] A 23-year-old 'character reader' named Helen Evans was arrested on the 13 March after receiving a complaint from one of her female clients who suffered from a nervous disposition. After analysing her handwriting, Evans had told the woman that she was under a curse. She gave the woman some bread and sugar wrapped in a handkerchief, saying that might help, and told her to return in several days and for $10 she would remove the curse. The complainant then informed the police, accusing Evans of putting the curse upon her. She was arrested, and charged by Detective Lt. George Keinburger with practising the 'art of witchcraft'. The press scented a good story. Evans was interviewed and was reported as saying, 'Do they mean I'm one of those things that fly around on broomsticks? If that's what they mean, then I should have a big black cauldron and be stirring things up in it shouldn't I? Why, I should even have black cats crawling around.' When asked if she had any black cats, she replied, 'No, only a Great Dane puppy named Baron.' The next journalistic port of call was Delaware's chief archivist Leon De Valinger who traced the witchcraft portion of the state's law back to the English Witchcraft and Conjuration Act of 1604. The state's attorney general, Albert W. James, was reported as saying that he was unfamiliar with the statute and was at a loss to explain what the 'art' of witchcraft entailed.

Judge Thomas Herlihy Jr presided over the case. He had taken up the position of judge four years earlier with a remit to clean up and modernize the municipal court. One of his first acts was to end racial segregation in the courtroom, and he also formalized the practice of informing defendants of their rights.[26] Dealing with the offence of witchcraft was clearly not something he was going to tolerate. On accepting a request to postpone the trial due to Evans's ill health, he remarked, 'It is unbelievable that a charge of practising the art of witchcraft could be brought in the enlightened state of Delaware.' With the glare of the American press on them, the postponement meant there was time to find a solution that dampened media interest in the story. But, first, let us now turn to the actual rather than reported legal status of witchcraft in Delaware.

In 1719 an 'Act for the advancement of Justice, and more certain administration thereof' instituted a raft of English common law statutes. Amongst them was the 1604 Act referred to by Leon De Valinger. So section 9 of this Delaware Act, stated:

> And be it further enacted by the authority aforesaid, That another statute, made in the first year of the reign of King James the first, chapter the twelfth, intituled, 'An act against conjuration, witchcraft, and dealing with evil and wicked spirits,' shall be duly put in execution in this government, and of like force and effect, as if the same were here repeated and enacted.[27]

On 7 February 1777 the Assembly of the Lower Counties on the Delaware recommended that this Act against Conjuration be repealed.[28] This was duly instituted two years later to conform to the English Witchcraft Act of 1736, thereby allow for the prosecution of the 'pretence' of witchcraft. So, by the early nineteenth century the Delaware law concerning witchcraft ran as follows:

> If any person or persons shall pretend to exercise the art of witchcraft, conjuration, fortune telling or dealing with spirits; every person or persons so offending, upon conviction thereof, shall be publicly whipped with

twenty-one lashes on the bare back well laid on, and shall forfeit and pay to the state a fine not exceeding one hundred dollars.[29]

By 1852 the punishment of whipping had been removed and in a nod to the prevailing western shift in penal policy, those convicted were to 'be imprisoned not exceeding one year'. Yet counter to the general trend, the Delaware legislature decided that some form of public punishment was still necessary, and so it was decreed that culprits should also 'stand one hour in the pillory'.[30]

So this was the state of the law at the time of the trial of Mrs Purrle and Madame Merill in 1892. When the journalist and novelist Theodore Dreiser (1871–1945) cast his keen eye on Delaware's laws during a visit in 1901 he did not fail to remark on the witchcraft statute, noting that 'such statements must certainly sound antiquated to the residents of every other state; but Delaware is peculiar in its old fashioned attitude'.[31] This peculiarity extended to Delaware's fondness for the pillory. The pillory had been abolished in England in 1837 and was last used in 1821. It was phased out in nearly all the American states during the mid-nineteenth century. Delaware's reluctance to pay for a state prison and adopt a penal policy based on incarceration and hard labour meant that at the dawn of the twentieth century it was still pillorying and whipping convicted criminals.[32] Dreiser attended one session where several men where pilloried and whipped as a crowd of some two hundred winced, smiled, and laughed.[33]

The journal of the Delaware House of Representatives for 1905 records that in the previous year a man in Sussex County had been convicted of 'pretending to practice the art of witchcraft' and was ordered to stand in the pillory on Saturday, 5 November 1904.[34] It is unlikely this was carried out though, for the authorities were, at the time, debating the future of the pillory. In 1905 it was abolished by a near unanimous vote. The witchcraft law received further discussion in the House in 1927 when Representative William E. Virden introduced a bill to add the word 'phrenology' to the list of other supernatural frauds—'witchcraft, conjuration, fortune telling or dealing with spirits'. The amendment was passed, Senate Attorney Lynch explaining that it was added to prevent gypsies from divining the bumps on people's head. The law needed sharper teeth.[35] So, by the time of the trial of Helen Evans, one legal anachronism had been expunged from the state statute books, but another remained. Although the Delaware code was quite clear that witchcraft was not an offence but rather the *pretence* of witchcraft—a fundamental distinction—it was easily confused in the public consciousness and prone to journalistic manipulation and misunderstanding. This was what troubled Judge Herlihy and also Evans's lawyer, James Gallo, who told a reporter that he thought the charge would be changed prior to her trial.

The press had a field day mocking the small east coast state. An editorial in the Alabama newspaper *The Dothan Eagle* opined: 'Maybe Delaware doesn't have any laws to cover curse-removing except this one. If so, this is certainly a case of "there oughta be a law". Charging somebody with witchcraft these days is ridiculous, even if it is resorting to a technicality. It doesn't speak much of the modernity of the State of Delaware.' A Californian paper similarly noted with humorous understatement, 'Delaware is well on the road to becoming one of the most civilized localities.'[36] In early May, Judge Herlihy ruled that Evans would stand trial on charges of fortune-telling only and she was granted $300 bail. So a much anticipated 'witchcraft trial' was avoided and press interest duly evaporated. Delaware was hardly the most talked about state in America, and the authorities' discomfort over the national attention given to the case was clear: the jibes hurt.

Action was taken. In 1951 the New Castle attorney and member of the House, Stephen E. Hamilton, introduced a Bill to the Delaware House of Representatives calling for an amendment to the law 'relating to skill in witchcraft'.[37] It was one of a number of 'obsolete statutes' identified by the state's revised code commission. It could not be struck from the law books without the approval of the Delaware Assembly, though, and this duly happened in February 1953. It was widely reported in the national press, and headlines such as that in the *Tucson Daily Citizen* no doubt caused further teeth-grinding. 'Witchcraft Now Legal in Delaware' it exclaimed.[38] The Speaker of the House, Frank Albert Jones, welcomed the move but said he would ensure that a new provision was instituted prohibiting fortune-telling, and dealing with spirits. This was duly done so that in 1955 a clause was returned that was the same as the old statute only with 'witchcraft' removed.[39] Spirits and conjuration seemingly remained troublesome to the state.

What's in a name?

For some the American dream crumbled when rumours of witchcraft began to fly. Just as in the period of the witch trials, they ripped families apart, led to communal ostracism, destroyed livelihoods, and were potentially life threatening. Take the tragic case of Annie Weber, for example. She and her husband Carl, a wood turner by trade, had emigrated from Germany and settled in New York where they produced five children. They were part of a great wave of German immigrants. In 1880 there were around 500,000 German Americans in the city, and nearly a third of its population was either German born or the children of German immigrants.[40] In February 1889 the family were living at 316 Rivington Street, now a fashionable destination for restaurant goers, then described as a desolate place of cheap tenements. One morning Annie went to Madison Square Park and swallowed some arsenic. A policeman found her writhing in agony and took her to hospital where she died. Poverty had driven her to despair. Carl could not get full-time work, the young children were going hungry, and their fifteen-year-old daughter hung around the streets late into the night and had to be sent to a reformatory. The accusations of witchcraft that had been repeatedly flung at her over the previous two months tipped her over the edge. The source of the slander was a woman named Soine who lived across the hall from the Webers. A journalist for the *New York Herald* paid her a visit. Soine freely admitted that she had called Annie a witch on a number of occasions during frequent domestic quarrels. She said, however, that she always withdrew the charge when her anger subsided, and did not think that Annie would take her words to heart.[41] That is the danger of harmful words.

Some of those accused of witchcraft moved away to physically distance themselves from their tormentors, others decide to fight back through the courts. This is what Mrs William Geiser, of Paterson, New Jersey, did in 1893 after accusations of witchcraft against her led to two families moving out of her house.[42] In 1914, in Lower Towamensing township, Pennsylvania, a young married woman named Lizzie Silliman made public accusations of witchcraft against Emma Hollenbach. On 25 April, for instance, she was alleged to have said: 'Old Mrs Hollenbach is a witch. She can practise witchcraft. She was also after my baby, and your twins. She has bewitched them.'[43] As a result, Hollenbach, who made a living selling eggs, butter, and poultry, had lost much of her trade. She too decided to take legal action.

Slander unlike witchcraft was not a crime against society, and, therefore, it was prosecutable as a civil rather than a criminal offence; that is to say, cases were brought by private suit between individuals. If successful, the defendant paid damages to the plaintiff commensurate with the harm done. The damages awarded reflected the seriousness of the imputed crime and the reputation of the plaintiff. So the cost of a slanderous witchcraft accusation was likely to go down as the threat of prosecution for the capital offence receded. In 1724 Sarah Spence sued Elizabeth and James Ackley at the county court in Colchester, Connecticut. She had moved to there from East Haddam, but her repute as a witch followed her despite having a certificate for 'good religion and virtue' from her minister John Buckley. On returning to Haddam the Ackleys accused her of being a witch. She sued for the considerable sum of £500 and received £5. This was then reduced to one shilling on appeal.[44] Move on a couple of decades, and in 1742 Elizabeth Gould, a New Haven widow, was awarded a mere sixpence in damages from Benjamin Chittenden, despite Gould's claim that the charge of witchcraft made against her had brought her into 'Abhorrence' and led to her being 'vexed, grieved and molested' by her neighbours.[45]

As the legal system and jurisprudence became more sophisticated during the eighteenth century, defamation became more problematic for the authorities. This was compounded by the decline of the formal role of the churches in dealing with moral offences, and the growing pressure on justices and the courts by an expanding population. In America there was an explosion of litigation during the first half of the eighteenth century, mostly concerning debtors and business dealings, but there was a substantial decrease in slander suits, particularly those brought by women, over the course of the century.[46] Some of this decline may have come from the bottom up, but it is also clear that the judiciary were tightening access to the courts for non-criminal offences.

Defamation concerning witchcraft became particularly knotty. In his *Treatise of the Law of Slander* (1813) Thomas Starkie simply gave up trying to come to a firm legal principle on the issue. The case law was so inconsistent 'as to appear incapable of affording any illustration of the subject of this treatise'.[47] The numerous cases compiled by Charles Viner (1678–1756) in his much-thumbed 23-volume *General Abridgment of Law and Equity* undoubtedly furnished the sources that led Starkie to reach his weary conclusion. A perusal of Viner's lengthy section on witchcraft slander certainly reveals a history of legal contradiction and contestation. So in one instance it was decided that to say to another 'he is a witch' was not actionable, that is giving cause for legal action, because it was a 'common word of passion'. Yet to say 'he is a witch, and deserves to be hanged' was actionable slander because 'deserves to be hanged' confirmed that the slanderer used 'witch' in terms of the capital offence of witchcraft. Another ruling decided that to call someone a witch was not an actionable slander unless some act of witchcraft was also alleged.[48]

All of Viner's cases dated to the period in England when the 1604 Witchcraft and Conjuration Act was still in force and being implemented. The interpretation of slander changed once the Act was repealed in 1736. From then on, as reported in a volume of case law argued in the New Jersey supreme court, witchcraft was no longer slanderous as the crime did not exist.[49] As the British lawyer Lord Chief Justice de Grey concluded in 1771, slanderous words 'must contain an express imputation of some crime liable to punishment, some capital offence, or other infamous crime or misdemeanour'.[50] This was why Viner ended his section by concluding that because of the 1736 Act 'it may be impertinent to add anything more as to witches or witchcraft, &c'.

But the matter was not clear-cut, as the much more frequent incidence of sexual defamation in the late eighteenth century revealed. On both sides of the Atlantic judges struggled to find a common position on what was another decidedly female concern. Some sexual improprieties that may have offended common sensibilities were not criminal or at least not serious crimes, so imputing them to someone was not necessarily actionable. In England the ecclesiastical courts continued to deal with sexual defamation up until 1855, but could only deal with cases not actionable under common law, such as the imputation of adultery and fornication. So a woman could go to the Church courts if she was called a 'lazy stinking strumpet', but not if she was called 'a thief and a whore'. Most of the women who resorted to the Church courts in this late period were from the upper-working class.[51] In America there was no such alternative, and during the first half of the nineteenth century state legislatures came to different decisions about how to accommodate sexual slander against women. North Carolina and Kentucky, for instance, enacted laws that facilitated female access to litigation over sexual slander. Other states stuck closely to English common law for much of the century. There was a general awareness, though, that common law was inadequate when it came to the protection of female honour. The evidence suggests, however, that popular resort to the courts for sexual slander was far from the familiar path it had been a century and a half before. New York's appellate courts heard only twenty-four sexual slander cases between 1807 and 1880.[52]

During the late eighteenth century uncertainty as to whether the 1604 Conjuration Act had been repealed or not, caused further head scratching as to how to proceed with witchcraft slander, as a rare detailed case from Massachusetts illustrates. In October 1787 John Estes and his wife Eleanor sought an action of slander against Alcut Stover, before the Court of Common Pleas, Cumberland County, Maine (then part of Massachusetts).[53] The setting for the events that led to the suit was Harpswell Township, where both the Estes family and the Stovers were well established.[54] This coastal community comprised a promontory and several islands and was populated mostly by farmers and fishermen. It was described a few decades later as a delightful place in summer that attracted pleasure seekers and convalescing invalids. But reminiscing of life in the area around 1780, James Curtis wrote in his journal: 'Every sorry old woman was deputed a witch, and spirits were frequently seen, and much feared.'[55] Eleanor Estes was one such sorry woman.

Stovers had been uttering accusations against Eleanor for several years. One witness deposed that in 1784, while he and Stovers were out on Goose Island, they had observed a number of young cattle behaving unusually wildly, running around very quickly. The witness remarked to Stovers that perhaps the cattle were bewitched and suggested that Eleanor Estes might be the witch responsible. Stovers replied that he did, indeed, think as much, and went on to say, 'I can prove it, and if she don't mind, I'll have her hanged.' The following spring, according to another witness, Stovers repeated his opinion that she was a witch, but said he was unsure as to whether he could prove enough to have her hanged. The next year, Stover told an acquaintance that he believed John Estes and his wife had been 'wishing bad wishes upon his creatures; and her wishes generally came to pass'. Stover's said Eleanor was a witch, but as the acquaintance deposed, he 'said that he did not think she was so bad a one as they were in former times'. Another resident, Andrew Webber, deposed that he heard Alcut Stover say that he believed Eleanor Estes 'was a witch'. Webber continued: 'I have heard that Eleanor Estes, the wife of John Estes, was a tattling woman, and made mischief among her neighbours; but as to my own knowledge, I don't know any harm of Eleanor Estes, except the common report about town.'

As to the legal situation, it would seem that the 1604 Act had not yet been formerly expunged from the statute books of Massachusetts. According to the early nineteenth-century Cumberland County lawyer James D. Hopkins, around the same time as the Estes case Judge Wells had informed a jury that, regrettably, the old statute against witchcraft remained unrepealed and was therefore still in force.[56] No wonder then that Stover repeatedly stated that he hoped to see Eleanor hang. Because the 1604 statute was deemed still law the slander was actionable and so the Court decided in Estes's favour. This was not the end of the matter though. Stover appealed against the decision and in July 1789 the Superior Court reversed the judgement. Despite the rule of common law, the declaration of the Court of Common Pleas was deemed insufficient, perhaps because it was considered absurd that a prosecution for witchcraft was a serious possibility. Stovers recovered a large sum in damages, and the poor Estes were left counting the costs of trying to solve their terrible predicament in a peaceful and measured way.

During the early nineteenth century growing concerns were expressed that the defamation laws were counter-productive in terms of their social value. In the opinion of Judge Jasper Yeates (1745–1817), who sat on the bench of the Pennsylvania Supreme Court, the reiteration of slanderous accusations in such a public forum as the courtroom should be discouraged. Encouraging legal 'actions for general expressions of censure by individuals in their daily intercourse with their fellow citizens, would not conduce to the peace of society', he said.[57] From the 1830s onwards the judiciary tried to restrict further the flow of petty slander, with the squires playing a significant role in ensuring that potential cases were nipped in the bud. By the latter stages of the century the flow of slander cases, most concerning sexual defamation, had been reduced. But new cultural pressures exerted themselves with regard to witchcraft.

Dealing with slander German-style

Witchcraft defamation cases still found their way to court during the late nineteenth and early twentieth century; if anything they probably increased. Nearly all of them were brought by German immigrants or members of

Pennsylvania's well-established German community. This reflected developments back in the homeland where insult laws introduced by the legislature of the recently united Germany were bolstered during the 1870s. These Imperial German defamation laws focused on the preservation of personal honour at all levels of society, and encouraged the working classes to resort to the courts for petty slander in their thousands. Malicious slander intended to sully a person's reputation, even amongst a small circle of people, was punishable with imprisonment. It was a criminal offence to defame the memory of a dead person.[58] This was different from British and American common law where slander was treated as a civil not a criminal offence and usually required evidence of material injury to the plaintiff. The insult laws introduced in the 1870s led to a huge increase in defamation proceedings in Germany, much to the chagrin and annoyance of judges and magistrates. They wrote of their exasperation as the courts clogged up with defamation cases deriving from gossip, idle tongues, and petty squabbles. One Berlin newspaper complained in 1913 that defamation suits 'poison the social climate of small towns more than all other lawsuits'.[59]

The American slander laws gave Germans the opportunity to pursue this new litigious custom. German was sometimes also the language in which the cases were conducted, such as the suit brought by Mary Ann Swartz of Lancaster County, Pennsylvania in 1915, against Alice Honshour, who had declared publicly in German, 'Mary Ann Swartz is a witch. She has bewitched me and I cannot get well.'[60]

As to the sums involved, Swartz demanded $5,000. Annie Lukach, who brought a slander suit against Susie Malarik before the Hammond superior court, Chicago, in 1918, asked for $2,000 in damages. Malarik had said, 'That woman is a witch and possessed of supernatural powers by compact with evil spirits and the devil and is a dangerous woman.' She also accused Lukach of bewitching her son to death. A year earlier, Mrs John Dissinger of Auburn, Pennsylvania, demanded $20,000 from her neighbour Augustus Sigfried, for accusing her of bewitching one of his sons.[61] Emma Hollenbach, who we heard about earlier, requested $10,000 to compensate for her loss of business. These are huge sums and may seem like crazy opportunism. As we have seen, though, the financial and social consequences of witchcraft accusations were serious. In this light, the sums involved seem reasonable.

The workings of common law and its Americanized versions meant that the outcome of such suits was usually less than satisfactory. The old legal issues continued to be raised, as we can see from a slander trial heard before a Cincinnati court in 1877. Judge William Ledyard Avery presided over the case. The defendant J. C. Bruckman was accused of saying of the plaintiff John Ziegler: 'He is a damn son of——; I am going to kill him, the accursed wizard. Look up! There walks the wizard who bewitched my sister in law.' Avery deliberated on whether the words were actionable, and evidently resorted to Viner's *General Abridgment of Law and Equity* in search of precedents. He concluded that the only actionable words were those that concerned accusations of offences punishable by law or the attribution of a disease that would lead to a plaintiff's exclusion from society. 'There walks the wizard who bewitched my sister in law' constituted neither of these. It was mere abuse, not slander. Avery ruled in Bruckman's favour leaving Ziegler to pay costs.[62]

The slander suit brought before a Jersey City civil court in February 1885 by Frederick Weissing and his wife Theresa, of Union Hill, New Jersey, went the same way. They sought damages for slander after a neighbour named Louisa Schrick told neighbours that Theresa was a witch and had put a fatal spell on one of her daughters who had died of convulsions. Theresa was ostracized and children ran away from her as she walked down the street. The District Court was packed to hear Judge Randolph give his judgement. After Theresa Weissing and her witnesses had given their testimony, the Judge opened a musty old volume of the *Laws of the State of New Jersey* and read out a relevant passage from the act of 1796, namely that: 'no prosecution, suit or proceeding, shall be commenced or carried on in any court of this State, against any person for conjuration, witchcraft, sorcery or inchantment, or for charging another with any such offence'. Randolph did not trouble himself with the niceties of the slander laws as Ledyard Avery had done. In his opinion the 1796 New Jersey legislation meant that witchcraft could not be recognized by the courts no matter the context. He dismissed the suit.[63]

Making a civil claim for slander was not the only legal avenue for pursuing defamation, though. Various state and city ordinances provided opportunities. In 1883 a Mrs Snyder of Scranton, Pennsylvania, was accused by Mrs Sarah Kochert of bewitching her daughter to death. Instead of suing for slander, Snyder, perhaps following legal advice, instituted a suit under a Scranton city ordinance prohibiting insulting language. This brought a fine of between one and twenty-five dollars for anyone found guilty of 'loud, boisterous, or insulting language, tending to excite a breach of the peace'.[64] Another victim of accusations from Detroit adopted a similar strategy. In 1917 John Burcicki was fined $50 for accusing Mary Biskupa of being a witch and having bewitched his sauerkraut. The lawyer acting on Biskupa's behalf, Charles Turic, said he had taken on the case to prevent future outbreaks of 'superstitious fears' amongst Detroit's Polish community.[65] It is likely that Burcicki was prosecuted under a Michigan statute of 1897 that prohibited using 'indecent, immoral, obscene, or insulting language in the presence of any woman or child . . . within the limits of any township, village, or city in the state of Michigan'. The penalty was a fine of up to $100.[66] A similar outcome happened in 1899 to resolve a dispute concerned two German farming families living in

Pleasant Hill Township, Minnesota. The accused witch was Carl Kinstler (1839–1906) and his accuser was his son-in-law Albert Pappenfuss (1865–1951) who had married Matilda Kinstler in 1889. The two families had emigrated from Pomerania, on the Baltic Germany coast, in the 1880s. Kinstler apparently enjoyed a reputation for magical skill, but when he decided to divide his property amongst his children, discord was sown and his reputation soured. After Carl had visited the Pappenfuss farm on several occasions their turkeys began to die, their pigs fell sick, their horse collapsed, and one of their young sons was taken ill. Albert publicly accused his father-in-law of witchcraft. Kinstler went to Justice C. F. Dykeman at Richmond and asked for a warrant for the arrest of Albert and Matilda for having circulated slanderous reports of his witchery. Dykeman informed him that 'the Minnesota penal code did not cover cases of that kind'. Frustrated, Kinstler returned later and charged them with 'abusive language tending to cause a breach of the peace'. Dykeman duly proceeded with the case, and the Pappenfusses were brought to court, where the proceedings were conducted in German as Carl spoke no English. One of them was found guilty, but because it was a family matter Dykeman imposed only a nominal penalty and sent them away with some strong advice as to their future conduct.[67]

Pursuing this path did not bring any payments for damages, but the aim, as in most slander cases, was to silence the harmful accusations rather than receive financial compensation. If the resort to the courts was too expensive, frightening, or frustrating then magic was always a private alternative. The popular nineteenth-century American book of German charms, the *Long Lost Friend*, fittingly provided a 'good remedy against calumniation or slander':

> If you are calumniated or slandered to your very skin, to your very flesh, to your very bones, cast it back upon the false tongues. † † † Take off your shirt, and turn it wrong side out, and then run your two thumbs along your body, close under the ribs, starting at the pit of the heart down to the thighs.[68]

Popular understanding

In July 1891 a reporter from the New York paper *The World* interviewed a thirty-year-old woman named Mary Ruth of Greshville, Pennsylvania, who suffered from depression and anxiety due to the accusations of witchcraft made against her by neighbours. The tormented and confused Mary told how she had visited a Reading witch doctor to ask whether she had really bewitched a neighbour named Mrs Boyer. The witch doctor said Mrs Boyer was indeed bewitched, but declined to confirm that Mary was responsible. Nevertheless, her possible guilt weighed heavily on Mary, and she explained to the journalist that: 'Someone told me that the penalty was $1,000 fine for witchcraft, and that we would be sued and all our property taken from us. This worried me and I've had no rest and peace of mind since.'[69] Ruth was not alone in her concern. An Irish St Louis woman, Rose Downey, who was accused of bewitching her infant grandson, visited the deputy coroner in 1898 to know if she could be charged for bewitching the child. She left much relieved.[70] The confusion was, no doubt, due to popular misunderstanding of the legal status of witchcraft. Remember that in Pennsylvania the law punished the *pretence* 'to effect any purpose by spells, charms, necromancy or incantation'. But as we have seen, the newspapers misrepresented the crucial distinction between witchcraft and the pretence of witchcraft. No wonder the likes of Ruth and Rose were confused.

There were not a few who firmly believed that witchcraft was still a prosecut-able offence. A Mississippi man known to the psychiatrist James Kiernan was one such person. He had, it has to be said, spent spells in prison and asylums, but he was an intelligent man. He had pestered justices on several occasions to have people prosecuted for bewitching him, and during one stay in the state prison studied law so that he could push through a legal case against a witch. When some fellow inmates convinced him that General Grant had repealed the witchcraft laws, his mental state deteriorated.[71] Periodic cases occurred where those who considered themselves bewitched applied to the local justice fully convinced that witchcraft was a crime that the authorities would punish. In the summer of 1850 one such case occurred in Philadelphia and another in the neighbouring town of Camden. In the first an elderly gentleman lodged a complaint before Alderman McKinley that a female neighbour had cast a spell upon him over the last eighteen months. McKinley dismissed the case. Across the Delaware River in Camden, a few days later, Mrs Eliza Toy charged Sara A. Pearson with witchcraft before a local justice. Toy accused Pearson of bewitching her child. Both women and Mr Toy were bound over to keep the peace in the sum of $100 each.[72] In November 1901 Peter Calebrese, lodging at 138 Ewing Street, Chicago, went to the Maxwell Street police station and requested the presiding magistrate, Captain Wheeler, to arrest one Mary Devito of 138 West Polk Street, for having cast a spell over him and his sister. Wheeler, who was described as a modest man prone to good deeds, said, rather generously, he would have to look up the law on witchcraft before taking any action. The impatient Calebrese instead went to consult the well-known neighbourhood priest, Father Dunne.[73]

While in most instances the squire swiftly dismissed such cases or resolved them by converting them into breaches of the peace, a perplexed and overly accommo-dating local judiciary occasionally followed up on demands to restrain suspected witches. This was the unfortunate fate of Margaret Gilmore of Vincennes, Indiana, in 1907.[74] The son of a neighbour, John Paris, accidentally injured one of her chickens. Paris subsequently heard from neighbours that Gilmore had declared, 'If that chicken dies one of his children dies too.' The chicken died, and not long after so did Paris's two-year-old son. He suffered from whooping cough, but for the Paris family the cause of death was witchcraft. John Paris sought official help against Gilmore's spells, visited a local justice of the peace, and paid for a peace warrant against her as a disturber of the peace. Once sworn and paid for, Gilmore was arrested. The next stage in the process of swearing a peace warrant was for the arrested person to be brought before a magistrate at the nearest convenience to answer the charge. In Gilmore's case that meant a stint in Knox county jail. Considering the origin of the complaint, there was no chance of the case going any further though. As one local newspaper observed, 'the peace bond under which he seeks to place the "witch" would be about as binding as the rich widow's appeal "now you stop!" to the robbers who were murdering her for her wealth'.[75] But by now Gilmore had already suffered. Innocent of any crime, she had spent time in jail and the newspapers had broadcast the accusations against her far and wide. It was not uncommon for those arrested under such a peace warrant to sue for malicious prosecution, but there is no evidence that Gilmore did so. Not surprisingly, three years later, she was no longer living in Vincennes.

In a peculiar case from 1924, the Princess Anne county court, Virginia, banished an elderly root doctor, Annie Taylor, wife of a longshoreman, from the county, with her husband having to pay a bond of $2,000 to ensure that she stayed away. Her crime was being a nuisance to her neighbours. The decision was a triumph of popular pressure over legal probity. Banishment from town, county, or state, had been used in colonial days, and later as a strategy for dealing with vagrants and other miscreants, but by the twentieth century it was deeply problematic and rarely invoked. It broke the *national* right to freedom of movement, and generated inter-county and inter-state friction, as one state dumped vagrants on another. Some state constitutions, such as West Virginia's, explicitly forbade banishment as a punishment. During the first half of the century a series of rulings by a number of supreme courts confirmed that county courts did not have the judicial powers to banish citizens.[76] This did not stop Princess Anne county magistrate Frank Bell from issuing the banishment order against Taylor. He did so after hearing the complaints of several African American and white residents of Kempsville, who testified as to Taylor's healing and bewitching activities. Farmer Walter Johnson swore that she had killed his mule by waving her stick over its head. Lucy Brown accused Taylor of cursing her by place some roots and horsehair in a bottle and burying it under her front door. A wealthy Kempsville farmer, Columbus C. Hudgins, had a rather different complaint. Some of his chickens and pigs had been stolen and he believed the thieves had given them to Taylor as payment for her charms and medicine. Bell concluded that he could find no law that provided punishment for her alleged crimes, but that something must be done. Lawyer and former Jamestown councilman John G. Tilton defended Taylor, and his presence apparently calmed the hostile crowd in the courtroom, even if he was unable to get the charges dropped. Taylor had her supporters too, and they gathered at the railway station to see her off when she was dumped across the state border to become North Carolina's 'problem'.[77]

Popular understanding of the legal position of witchcraft was shaped to a considerable degree by the adherence of many to the literal truth of the Bible. For centuries the persecution and execution of witches had been justified by reference to the Old Testament. Did it not state in Exodus chapter 22, verse 18, as printed in the King James Bible, that 'thou shalt not suffer a witch to live'? As far back as the sixteenth century, sceptics had argued that the vernacular Bibles of Protestant Europe had mistranslated this and other passages referring to witches and sorcerers. They argued that the original Hebrew and Greek texts condemned poisoners and not witches—as they were understood at the time of the witch trials. While this was increasingly accepted by the clergy and intellectual society during the eighteenth and early nineteenth century, nothing was done to correct the King James Bible in this respect despite the various revisions that were undertaken by the American Bible Society and others.[78] So there it remained in the millions of well-thumbed Bibles in American homes: witches had to be killed.

In 1875 the family of John Berry, well known and respected in Clinton County, Kentucky, ended up in court before they could enact Mosaic Law. One of Berry's married daughters, who lived with her husband on the edge of Ballard County, suffered a lingering illness and believed she had received a visitation from the spirit of a man named McDonald. The spirit told her that certain female neighbours were witches and that in the form of cats they would do great harm to her family. Being devout believers, the family turned to their Bible for help and found the passage from Exodus. The accused women were made aware of the Berry family's views and feared for their safety. One day, one of John Berry's teenage sons espied a cat, and believing it to be a witch he took his gun to shoot it. The cat seemed to vanish though, so he made threats against the suspected women believing they had just resumed their human form. Fortunately, other neighbours in the community did not share the Berry's suspicions, and after this episode, they instigated the arrest of John, his wife, and two sons. Under oath they testified that they believed that according to the Scriptures the witches should be killed. Then after conceding their views might be erroneous, they were released on giving a bond of $300 for their good behaviour.[79]

When, in June 1912, farm labourer Clinton Baugher of Walkersville, Maryland, was brought before Justice Aaron R. Anders for assaulting his brother, Joseph Baugher, whose wife he accused of witchcraft, a brief exchange took place on the content of the Bible. Anders instructed those present in court that witches did not exist, to which Baugher replied, 'The Bible says there are witches, but you mustn't believe in 'em', by which it was presumed he meant 'could not trust them'. A member of Baugher's family then piped up to explain that the Bible directed that 'she that hath bewitched me be slain'. Anders told them firmly that there was no such statement in the Bible.[80] He was right, but the Baughers oral version of Exodus 22:18 indicates how its message was ingrained in folk conceptions of witchcraft. Biblical support for the existence of witches rested on more than just Exodus though. Both Old and New Testaments referred to malign magical practices and practitioners. The account in 1 Samuel Chapter 28 of the 'Witch of Endor' who raised up the prophet Samuel was often referred to as proof, even though in the King James Bible and others she is not actually referred to as a 'witch'. When, in July 1871, a newspaper reporter interviewed a bewitched woman of New Albany, Indiana, and stated he did not believe in witchcraft, she 'wondered if we had ever read the Bible, especially that part relating to the witch of Endor, whom she declared had never died, and she had ample opportunity to teach her vile arts to others'.[81]

To explain away all these references as mistranslation was a tall order, as was proven by the determined campaign of a Swedish witch believer named Leopold Weedstrand. In 1875, Weedstrand, who had arrived in the US six years before, and believed he was persecuted by witches based in Meadville, Pennsylvania, wrote letters of complaint to the United States District Attorney Reed at Pittsburgh. Receiving no reply, he turned up at his office and was duly kicked out. When a journalist told him, 'You know you can't bring an action at law against the witches', Weedstrand replied, 'I can bring an action against whoever keeps them. There is no law for people keeping devils or witches. The devil can't hurt anybody unless he is kept by somebody. Haven't you read in the Bible about people keeping a devil?' 'Where do you find it in the Bible?' Inquired the journalist. 'I read it in the writings of Moses, and the Acts of the Apostles, and I tell you I'm going to law to find out about this thing at Meadville.'[82] Weedstrand was a litigious fellow, and sued the editor of the Scranton paper the *Morning Republican*, John E. Barrett, for libel regarding an article ridiculing Weedstrand's claims.

WITCHES

Native Americans, Africans, and Europeans shared the same fundamental conception of witches. Motivated by the disruptive forces of spite and envy, they were troublemakers, the spreaders of sickness, sowers of discord. Their malicious activities explained otherwise inexplicable misfortunes, the reason why bad things happened at certain times to certain people in certain places. In short, witches made sense of a chaotic world. That said, this chapter will also highlight some of the significant differences too, mostly with regard to how witches were thought to go about their work, the sources of their power, and conceptions of their spiritual essence. We also need to recognize that many different regional beliefs and legends about witches existed in Europe, amongst the different Native-American tribes, and the various ethnic groups of West Africa. How these influenced each other is a fascinating part of the story of witchcraft in America, but one that is obviously difficult to map. The pathways of influence and exchange of beliefs are usually imperceptible, but the clues are there if not always the answers.[1]

The witch of legend and folklore is at times a somewhat different creature from the witch of the everyday disputes that make up the bulk of this book. Folk beliefs tell of witch status being an accident of birth, such as the Italian American notion that any woman born at midnight on Christmas Eve became a witch or *strega*. Legends relate how people sought and achieved witch-hood through ritual and rite. In the Ozarks it was thought that this could be done by shooting at the moon with a silver bullet.[2] The idea that people became witches by making a pact with the Devil was at the core of the Christian theological conception of the diabolic witch. But look closely at the witch trial records, at the complaints that the common people lodged against accused witches, and the Devil is usually absent. The victims of witchcraft saw their misfortune primarily in terms of the witch and not the actions of the satanic puppet master who so concerned the authorities. Likewise the 'reverse witch trial' material of the American post-colonial era rarely contains references to the Devil.

The notion of the diabolic pact was stronger in folklore and legend. One of the more common stories about achieving witch-hood through satanic patronage describes how the want-to-be witch went up a nearby mountain before sunrise. As the sun began to appear he or she uttered insults and curses at God, praised the Devil, held up a white handkerchief, fired a silver bullet through it and watched the blood drip.[3] The notion that witchcraft could be learned from evil 'Black Art' books was also fairly widespread in legends. But the witch was not alone in seeking out the Evil One. The male desire to obtain power and wealth—or musical genius, as in the famous legend regarding the bluesman Robert Johnson—from the Devil was equally represented in folklore.

Christianity was the major European influence on Native-and African-American notions and legends of witchcraft, with its concept of the Devil, biblical support for the existence of witches, the intercessionary power of the saints, and the magical potency of the Bible. A more subtle European Christian influence has also been traced with regard to the gender of the witch figure. Around 78 per cent of those accused of witchcraft in colonial New England were women, a figure that mirrors the general statistics for Europe at the time. A sample of 142 cases of assault, slander, murder, and abuse concerning European Americans from the 1780s to the 1950s reveals that 85 per cent of those accused of witchcraft were women, with little variation over time.[4] There were theological reasons for this gender bias. Women were thought to be made in the image of Eve and inherited her vulnerability to temptation. The Devil knew this well and sought to recruit them to his army, seducing them with his physical charms, flattering their vanity, enticing them with the prospect of power over the stronger in society. Christian conceptions of feminine weakness alone, though, do not explain the preponderance of women amongst those accused of witchcraft. As we shall see shortly, women's social and economic position in society made them vulnerable to accusations. Considering that much witchcraft was associated with the home, children, and dairying, all areas of female responsibility, it is no surprise that many accusations were made by women against other women.

The notion of female weakness and women's moral corruptibility was amplified in European views regarding Native-American women. The eighteenth-century Moravian minister David Zeisberger commented, for instance, how Delaware Indian women were 'much given to lying and gossiping. They carry evil report from house to house.'[5] It has been argued that witchcraft amongst the Seneca became more feminized during the late eighteenth century, in part due to the influence of Quaker and Moravian teachings on women's subservient domestic role in the godly household. This found expression in the preaching of Handsome Lake who attempted to instate a more strict patriarchal division of responsibilities and domestic behaviour, and presented a more demonized view of female sin. No wonder, perhaps, that the Seneca in the period persecuted females as witches much more than men. Otherwise medicine men were frequently the target of accusations when they were thought to be suspiciously helpless in the face of epidemics, crop failure, and drought.[6]

The gender bias in African-American accusations is less obvious. A sample of cases arising from harmful magic amongst African Americans shows that just under half of those accused were men. It is clear that this is largely due to witchcraft's location *within* the conjure tradition rather than as a separate category of malicious magic. While it was certainly not unknown for cunning-folk and fortune-tellers to be accused of witchcraft in European-American communities, the conjure doctors and their ilk, many of whom were women, were deemed as likely to inflict harm upon you as cure you.[7] They were as much the source of misfortune as good fortune, not necessarily because they were inherently evil, but because they serviced the enmities and malign impulses of the general public, providing the magical means for others to commit vengeance and manifest spite. That is not to say that the female witch figure as understood in European culture was absent from African-American belief. The supernatural witch figure, who we shall encounter later, was inherently feminine, and stereotyping in terms of age and gender were in play in all cultures.

Three sorts of witch

Folk belief and legend shaped fantasies and hallucinations about the marvellous things that witches were capable of doing, which in turn nourished the development of gossip and accusations. But the origin of most reputations for witchcraft can be found in emotional, social, and cultural relationships. Legends presented a world where witches created themselves, whereas the reality was generally that people bestowed witch-hood on others. Through looking at the many accusations and assaults made against identifiable people over the last two centuries and more, three main types of witch emerge.

First up there was the *outsider witch*, someone who accrued a reputation because of their social position, where they lived, how they lived, and what they looked like. The archetypal example, and one which we find over and over again in the era of the witch trials, is the elderly widow or spinster who called upon the charity of neighbours to survive. Age, gender, and marginality marked her out. Writing in 1824 the clergymen and historian Joseph Doddridge, who lived at various times in Pennsylvania, Virginia, and Ohio, recalled, 'I have known several poor old women much surprised at being refused requests which had usually been granted without hesitation, and almost heart broken when informed of the cause of the refusal'.[8] The cause was witchcraft. The scenario of the begging witch was a familiar old narrative in reportage and storytelling, and the psychological origin of witchcraft accusations born of charity denied was discussed as far back as four centuries ago.[9] The beggar woman muttered words of anger at being refused, and when misfortune next struck the suspicions of the unforthcoming household focused on the unwelcome visitor. Even if the woman went off without a murmur, the guilt of the uncharitable was projected on to her and manifested in hostility and suspicion. The role of ostension is significant here. This is when people carry out activities that have been learned from legends, or they respond to situations influenced by folkloric stereotypes. In other words, narratives become facts or 'maps for action'.[10] So if it was known from stories and legends that witches went begging and cursed you if they were refused, then when the begging scenario played out in reality, the associated set of beliefs, suspicions, and responses kicked in. .

The turning of Margaret 'Mag' Gilmore, of Vincennes, Indiana, into a feared witch followed a similar trajectory. While begging was not behind the build-up of tension that led to open accusations, the uttering of threats by an elderly woman in a marginal social position was interpreted as witchcraft by her neighbours. Mag had been married three times, and had family in Monroe and Owen counties. She had arrived in Vincennes around 1906, a single, independent middle-aged woman. She moved into a one-room shack in the suburb of Oklahoma, named as such in 1893 because land lots had been offered in the manner of the Oklahoma land run of 1889.[11] Mag made a living from her chickens and selling home-grown vegetables at the city market. At some point she adopted a little girl named Bertha Lee Anderson. Mag was apparently more educated and of a higher social level than her neighbours. All in all, she did not fit in well with the poor families around her. Rumours began to circulate that she had not slept in fourteen years, that she spent night after night hammering mysteriously on the floor of her home. Then there were the accounts of her coming to the front door and calling in a ghostly voice. When she came out to sweep her porch with a broom the local children fled in terror. All that was required was for an unfortunate coincidence to generate outright accusations, which, as was related in the previous chapter, duly happened in July 1907 when John Paris's son died after she allegedly threatened his death.[12]

As Gilmore's case suggests, children played a significant role in the development of the outsider witch. Many readers of this book can probably remember as children fixing upon one or two elderly or eccentric people in their communities who they believed were at least uncanny and witch-like if not considered as witches. They became the focus of childhood pestering, which sometimes descended to more malign levels of harassment. An elderly German woman named Christina Meyer, who lived at a boarding house at 45 Peete Street, Cincinnati, was one such victim of childish persecution in 1878. The area was a heartland of the German immigrant community in the city, so she certainly did not stand out because of her background. She did arouse curiosity, however, for regularly sitting on the floor of her room at night with a candle between her feet reading an old book. Her window gave on to the street so she was something of a public spectacle. One suspects she was browsing her Bible or some German religious text, but the local children imagined the solitary old woman was reading up on her charms and spells. Meyer was pestered by children peering at her through the window and by the protective crosses they drew on her door and the threshold. Two girls named Clara and Lena Roher were particularly troublesome. The Roher parents were also German immigrants, and the family lived in the same house as Meyer. A newspaper report on the case suggested the girls were nineteen and seventeen respectively, which would, perhaps, give a different complexion to the situation, but the census shows they were only sixteen and thirteen at the time. Meyer was so disturbed by the accusations and activities that she prosecuted the two girls. Brought before the local court, Squire Schwab lectured the girls on their foolish beliefs and persecution of Meyer and ordered bonds of $100 to ensure their good behaviour. This no doubt caused some disruption to relations in the street and we find that two years later Meyer was no longer living in Peete Street and the Rohers had moved around the corner to Mulberry Street.[13]

On occasion the outsider witch was a religious intruder. Obvious examples are the cases where Native-American communities accused missionaries of witchcraft. In 1839 the Reverend Edmund Franklin Ely, who was stationed at the Ojibwa village of Fond du Lac, Minnesota, found himself accused of being a witch after one of his cows charged at and wounded a young native named Makwawaian, with whom relations were already strained. Ely was not considered to be a witch because he was foreign as such—the Ojibwa had dealt with traders for years—but because he denounced their religion, and refused to engage in customary communal behaviour as a result. He lived outside their social conventions, and yet his own religion was seen as giving him spiritual powers to cause harm.[14]

Strange medical practices could also attract suspicion when practised by an incomer, as a poor New York seamstress named Meta Immerman found to her cost. Meta suffered from failing eyesight and in 1911 decided to visit Allentown,

Pennsylvania, to take the Kneipp cure, finding lodgings with the family of George Kipp, a butcher living at 207 South Thirteenth Street. Kneipp treatment was named after the Bavarian priest Sebastian Kneipp who advocated a system of healing combining herbalism, a diet of grains, vegetables and fruit, exercise, cold water treatment or hydrotherapy, and spiritual purity. It came into vogue in America during the 1890s and the movement still has a significant following in Germany today. As part of her treatment Meta engaged in activities that her new neighbours found most peculiar. She walked barefoot in the dewy grass early in the morning and late at night, and followed a diet consisting solely of nuts and raw eggs. When one of the other lodgers, a young man named John Sobers, fell ill with stomach pains, witchcraft was suspected. The Kipps and the Sobers began to interpret Meta's every actions as confirmation of her witchery. George said he passed her door one night and her eyes burned like a cat's. The small electric flashlight she used to help her see at night was re-imagined as fire flashes emanating from her fingers. Rumours spread beyond No. 207. When Kipp's young daughter Winnie also fell ill they decided to take action. While Meta was out they put her bags on the porch and locked the door. When she banged on the door to get her key, the Kipps called the police on the basis that she had not paid rent. As she was led through the streets a crowd gathered shouting 'Witch!', and boys pelted her with stones. Meta spent forty-eight hours in jail before being released, and she returned in haste to New York.[15]

Ethnicity could also play its part, particularly with regard to gypsies who had always been considered outsiders and who often settled on the physical outskirts of communities. European states had transported Romani gypsies to the American colonies as undesirable vagrants back in the seventeenth century, and they began to arrive of their own accord in significant numbers from Britain and central and south-eastern Europe during the second half of the nineteenth century, although it is impossible to fix on an exact figure. They operated as they had done in Europe, working in the horse trade, copper-smithing, and fortune-telling.[16] It was an elderly German gypsy named Elizabeth Fullerman who became the focus of witchcraft stories in New Orleans in 1855. She lived in a hut on the outskirts of the city, near the Union Race Course which had begun operating three years earlier. The horse races were a natural meeting point for the Romani, and Fullerman made a meagre living as a fortune-teller amongst the crowds that attended the races. Rumours of her malign powers circulated around the Gentilly Road, and a kerfuffle ensued when a young Swiss woman, Elizabeth Hinney, who lived nearby, began to suffer from convulsions and shaking. Some suspected she suffered from the symptoms of malaria or St Vitus's Dance—a condition more recently equated with the rheumatic fever or autoimmune response known as Sydenham's chorea—but which others considered witchcraft.[17] Crowds gathered daily at the

Hinney home, and rumours about Fullerman abounded. The police decided to arrest Fullerman for disturbing the peace, which seems grossly unfair, but perhaps they had her safety in mind. A mixed-race crowd, apparently numbering up to five hundred, gathered around the police office to see the witch.[18]

Racial suspicion as well as gender and lifestyle led to the perfect storm of witchcraft accusations that whirled around sixty-year-old Irene Ray of Rochester, Indiana. Around 1932, Irene, who was part Miami Indian, her second husband Charles, their daughter Iloe, and her husband Stanley Carter, and the family cat Fuzzy, moved into an abandoned shack just outside Rochester. They had previously been living in Plymouth, a town some twenty miles to the north, where Charles had worked as a foreman on the Nickle Plate railroad. The family applied for state relief and received a large but shabby house to live in on Audubon Avenue. Charles got employment from the Works Progress Administration, which had been created as part of Roosevelt's New Deal. As they were strangers and therefore not strictly a charge on local taxpayers, the generosity of the Rochester authorities seemed rather curious as well as unfair to some locals. Irene's boast of being descended from an Indian witch doctor, along with her powerful beady eyes, evident from photographs of her, further fuelled the stories that started to develop. The local children teased her, adults made unflattering comments, and rumours of her witchery began to circulate. As Stanley Carter told a journalist, 'It's a lot of hooey. They didn't like the way we lived and just trumped up all those yarns. But I'd better not say much because Iloe and I are trying to live here.'

There is no doubt that some of those who accrued outsider witch status decided to turn it to their advantage as a means of leveraging charity, or deflecting petty conflicts with neighbours: witchcraft was power, but those who exploited it had to be very careful not to actually state that, yes, they were witches. Their powers had to be insinuated and implied, not explicitly confirmed. So it was that Irene played upon the reputation that had been bestowed upon her, in the process confirming the initial unfounded rumours. Mr Friday Castle, a plumber's assistant, related that Irene used to make a shortcut across his garden, in which he had planted potatoes. This understandably annoyed him and so he confronted her one day. 'That old witch ran her eyes back and forth over the patch until they had covered every inch of it', recalled Castle. 'Then she looked at me, and said: "It won't make a bit of difference now whether anybody walks on it or not".' When, in 1937, Chief of Police Lewis Clay Sheets supervised the removal of Irene's grandchild after complaints of the moral state of the Ray-Carter household, she screamed at him, 'You are just a tool of that Knight woman and you will be sorry, too!' He died a few days later of a heart attack.[19] It was Mrs Knight who voiced the accusations of witchcraft against Irene, and requested the authorities take action against her for being a witch. The new Police Chief Paul Whitcomb attracted considerable criticism when he chose to arrest Irene on vagrancy charges while investigating the accusations. She said later, 'I am not a witch, never said I was and never did any of the things they say I did', but she added, 'just the same anything that happened to anybody serves 'em right.'[20]

The possessors of the evil eye sometimes fit the outsider witch category. The term 'evil eye' was and is much bandied about in discussions of witchcraft, and in the nineteenth and twentieth century the American press used it liberally in reports of witchcraft disputes. But while the idea that witches could cast a spell through sight was widespread in different cultures, and was encapsulated in such English terms as 'forelooked' or 'overlooked', the evil eye as a concept is best understood as a distinct tradition found in Mediterranean cultures. Known as the *mal ojo* in Spanish and *malocchio* in Italian, the young and the old were considered most vulnerable to its power, with most accusations concerning the illness of infants. A folklore survey of belief in the evil eye conducted in New York in the 1940s found it alive and well, mostly among the Italian and Jewish populations. Other sources show it was also widespread in Mexican-American communities in the south, and amongst the scattered Syrian-Lebanese communities that settled across America in the late nineteenth and early twentieth century.[21]

All witches were thought able to bewitch by sight, but not all possessors of the evil eye were bad people: some were involuntary witches born with eyes or eyebrows that marked them out. For some Italians, a particularly heavy 'mono-brow' was a sign, for instance. Unusually coloured or particularly piercing eyes were other indicators. Having an 'electric' gaze was a common description in twentieth-century cases. Most obvious of all was the possession of a squint. This was revealed in a 1929 divorce case. Giuseppina Porcello, who had a squint or cast in one eye, appealed to the New York Supreme Court for a separation against her husband. Justice Philip J. McCook presided. Giuseppina's husband Giuseppe Porcello had emigrated from Sicily nine years earlier, and the couple were married in December 1928. Conjugal bliss did not ensue. Only four days after the wedding he accused her of having cast an evil eye over him, thereby coercing him into marriage. Giuseppina told Justice McCook, 'My husband was continually pointing his finger at me as a person who had an evil eye that cast a spell over him. He said that unless he was freed from the evil influence he would die and I would be to blame.' Her 'evil eye penetrated to his very bones', he said. He made her go to several cunning-women in Brooklyn, including a woman named Hipolito whose reputation had been considerable back in Palermo, in order to counteract her malign eye. It was best for all concerned that Giuseppina was granted her separation.[22]

In 1901 a German named Carrie Merklem or Merckle lodged a complaint at the southern police station, Baltimore, against Greek neighbours. Carrie was a washerwoman in a tenement block. One day she picked up the four-month-old child of the Greek family. Several hours later it fell ill and the Greeks believed Carrie had cast an evil eye on it. They demanded that she spit in the child's face, a common act of counter magic in evil eye cases, which she duly did to avoid further confrontation. Carrie told the police that she would have to leave her job because the Greeks had convinced her neighbours she had an evil eye.[23] As this case suggests, while different racial and linguistic communities shared the same belief in the malign influence of a witch's eye, there was a degree of ethnic bias in terms of who was thought to possess it. There is a sense that the holder of the evil eye was a malign tool of outsider influence. As the following case indicates, this could work both ways in that the evil eye could be seen as a speciality *of* those of Mediterranean stock.

Johanna McKinley and her family lived in Florham Park, Morris County, New Jersey, where her husband was a teamster. As the census shows, all her neighbours were of Irish descent apart from an Italian couple, Francesco Sena and his wife. They all worked on the Florham Estate and stud, built up in the 1890s by the heiress Florence Vanderbilt and her financier husband, Hamilton McKown Twombly. In 1907 McKinley complained to the Morris County Society for the Prevention of Cruelty to Animals that an Italian neighbour was 'exercising an evil eye' over her cow and pig. McKinley had written down an itemized list of grievances against 'No. 3', as she called the Italian. She accused him of stealing celery and poisoning her dogs and chickens, but most serious of all he had cast an evil eye on her pig so that it became a skeleton, and on her cow so that it dried up. Agent Van Dyke was sent to investigate but said he could do nothing unless the Italian was caught in the act, which McKinley said was impossible.[24]

The *conflict witch* was the product of long-term personal feuds and unresolved tensions, usually within families or between neighbours. This meant that men figure more frequently as conflict witches, although the old stereotypical attributes of the female outsider came into play as well. Relationship disputes built up from envy, jealousy, incompatible personalities, inheritance disputes, sexual passions, and financial frustrations. The accusation of witchcraft acted as a pressure valve, but the results could be devastating for individuals, families, and communities. So it was that in 1796 pent-up suspicions and accusations within three related families exploded in terrible violence in the coastal town of Arundel, York County, Maine (then part of Massachusetts). Arundel was not some rural backwater recently settled by European emigrants. It was a prosperous town, its nineteen-hundred or so inhabitants benefiting from the shipbuilding and fishing industries of Kennebunkport. In the 1730s and 1740s three families, the Smiths, Cleaves, and Hiltons, had firmly rooted themselves in the community and were prominent enough to have brief biographies in a history of Arundel published in 1837.[25]

The events of 1796 centred on Elizabeth Hilton, daughter of Abraham Hilton and his wife Dorothy Lindsey. Elizabeth married Daniel Smith, son of Captain Daniel Smith and Hannah Harding. By 1796 Elizabeth had become a widow. It is likely she is the 'Widow Smith' recorded in the 1790 census. It would seem though, that she could not count on any support from her relatives in her solitary old age, for she was thought to have bewitched a neighbour and relative named John Hilton.

In October 1796 John was returning home one evening, just before dark, when Elizabeth Smith appeared before him, walking some six yards distant. He held an ox goad in his hand and it now began to move of its own accord, as if it was trying to slip free. Quickly putting two-and-two together he thought such trickery must be the work of Elizabeth's witchcraft. This was confirmed when he went to strike her with the goad, only for the goad, controlled by some supernatural force, to turn upon himself, beating him violently on his own back. John now declared publicly that Smith was a witch, and sought to find a cure for the spell she had cast upon him. In this he was aided by two of his nieces, Sarah and Molly Hilton, and also Dolly and Elizabeth Smith—the latter was the late Daniel Smith's sister, and so Widow Smith's sister-in-law. They had boiled some of John's urine, a widely used method of dealing with witches. Widow Smith had even consented to be scratched by Hilton to draw blood and so break her supposed power over him. But nothing seemed to end John's mental torment. The Smith and Hilton women began to make death threats against the widow, saying she should have been in Hell with the damned a long time ago. They apparently urged on John to carry out the task, and on 15 October he ran to Widow Smith's house, beat her, drove her out of her house, and began to throttle her. The Smith and Hilton women joined in, crying out 'kill her uncle John'. Fortunately for all involved she did not die.

The following month, Sarah and Molly Hilton, and Dolly and Elizabeth Smith, were tried for assault and battery at the General Sessions of the Peace for the County of York held at Biddeford, and presided over by Judge Wells. It is unclear why John Hilton was not prosecuted, though it could have been due to presumed insanity. Eaton Cleaves was the key witness for the defence. His father, a black-smith named Robert Cleaves, had come to Arundel around 1740, and the family gave their name to the nearby Cleaves Cove, now a desirable seafront property location. Eaton married Miriam Smith, sister of Daniel Smith, and so was related to Widow Smith by marriage. Eaton testified in court that until the evening with the ox goad, John Hilton had been of sound mind, and that he had been firm and consistent in has accusations against Widow Smith. The four female defendants were fined $100 each, bound over to keep the peace, and ordered to appear at the next session of the court for a ruling on their subsequent behaviour.[26]

The origin of the antagonism against Widow Smith is now lost to us, but a case a century later reveals one possible cause—the tensions between a young mother and her mother-in-law. The notion that post-menopausal women envied the fertility of younger women and vented it by magically harming infants was a significant theme in the early-modern witch trials, and is evident in numerous disputes in the modern era.[27] The much-employed comedy stereotype of the jealous mother-in-law, which reflects a venerable truth, can be interpreted in similar deep-rooted psychological terms. In July 1898 Mrs Rose Downey, a careworn, widowed Irish woman, fifty-three-years old, visited the St Louis coroner's office to report to the deputy coroner that her daughter-in-law accused her of bewitching to death her three-month-old grandson. Her daughter-in-law, Mary E. Downey had arrived from Ireland three years earlier to visit relatives. She claimed to be the sister of William O'Brien, the Irish Nationalist politician, member of parliament and newspaper publisher. She met and married Rose's son Bernard, a foundry worker, in 1897, and their first child was born the following year. The infant in question was their second. Mary would go on to lose nine other children over the years, but the first losses obviously hurt terribly. Someone was to blame, and the person with whom she got on least well was her mother-in-law. As she explained to a journalist:

> My mother-in-law is actuated by spite. She has been prejudiced against me ever since I married her son and has tried to separate us, because he was her main support before our marriage. At the time she tried to throw obstacles in our way and even claimed that we were not legally married. She has caused trouble ever since then. Before my first child was born she wished that it would have a dog's head. The child was perfectly developed, but did not live. Then again, she wished me trouble when my second child was born. An aunt of Mr Downey's died about two weeks ago and I was told by Mrs Dougherty, a woman who attended the funeral, that my mother-in-law wished over the corpse that my baby would follow her to Calvary Cemetery. Now she hopes that I will follow the child in two weeks' time.[28]

In the romantic fantasy film *I Married a Witch* (1942), the time-travelling Salem sorceress played by Veronica Lake murmurs, 'Love is stronger than witchcraft.' But in reality it was usually the other way around. The film is yet to be made, but any studio interested in a film entitled 'I Divorced a Witch' might take a look at the probate court suit filed by a St Louis printer named Hugo Lambey in 1899. The son of Prussian immigrants, the twenty-eight-year-old Hugo petitioned that his wife Anna's belief in witchcraft and preoccupation with charms and magical rituals tended 'to turn plaintiff into ridicule and contempt among his neighbours and friends'. He accused her of putting a witch's love potion in his coffee. It patently failed, causing him a gastric upset instead. Over and above the annoying accusations of witchcraft she made against neighbours, there was also her habit of boiling certain ingredients in a pot at night which she stirred with a feather. Lambey's divorce was evidently granted for we find him newly married the following year.[29] A couple of years later, the boot was on the other foot when Eliza Norris of Worthington, Ohio, brought a divorce suit against her husband Amos before the probate court after thirty-five years of marriage. For two hours in the witness stand Eliza related how her husband, a farmer, practised experimental witchery upon her, aided by a book of witchcraft in his possession. He would seek out and swallow four-leaved clovers to enhance his powers, and to make her fall sick would put seven one dollar bills in his shirt pocket, place his right hand over it, and then touch her with his left elbow.[30]

And so to our final category of witch, the *accidental witch*. Many accusations arose not because the accused fitted stereotypes or were in dispute with their alleged victims; it was because people appeared in the wrong place at the wrong time—including in dreams and nightmares, or did or said something completely innocently but which subsequent misfortune rendered suspicious with hindsight. Admiring glances and words at the sight of a beautiful baby were behind many accusations of *mal ojo*. Elderly women who kissed babies were hostages to fortune. In 1903 a Chicago court heard how Frank Galenski and his wife, who kept a grocery shop, became convinced that an elderly customer, Francesca Krejewski, was a witch when one of her children fell ill after having been kissed by Krejewski while she was in their shop. A doctor diagnosed the child had blood poisoning.[31] Other acts of kindness by strangers could easily be interpreted sinisterly. As a butcher's wife named Mrs Malinda Balthazar, of 82 Elm Street, Reading, PA, explained to a journalist in 1883, 'None of the family are allowed to accept any gifts, and everything that comes into the family must be paid for.' She told of a countrywoman she knew well who called to offer her some luscious looking pears. 'I told her that we could not accept them as a gift. Before she left I bought the pears by paying her a cent.'[32] Close friendship was no immunity to accusations either if coincidence struck. In 1903 a court in Newark, New Jersey, heard Mary Guth accuse her friend Anna Lesnik, of 28 Albert Avenue, of having witched her by the means of a cup of tea. 'Ever since I drank that tea I have felt queer', asserted Guth. 'When I go out in the street everything seems to be turned wrong.' 'Mary Guth talks nonsense', countered Lesnik, 'I gave her just a cup of plain, ordinary tea, such as people drink every day.'[33]

Magical practitioners played a major role in the creation of accidental witches through prescribing rituals that relied in drawing the guilty to the victim's house, but which in actuality often led to visiting neighbours and other passers-by being fingered and left bewildered. In his autobiography, the spiritualist Andrew Jackson Davis (1826–1910) described a typical example of this that shaped his childhood. One time the family cow dried up while their neighbour's ones pastured in the same meadow continued to produce. Family and friends offered up a range of natural explanations for this conundrum. His mother had other ideas: 'Her confidence in the supernatural, as I have heretofore said, had never been impaired or disturbed. Superstition seemed an inevitable concomitant of her genuine spiritual experiences.' Witchcraft was suspected and a 'witch master' was called in who advised boiling some of the cow's urine in an iron pot containing nine needles. This would draw the witch responsible to their door he said. The family duly undertook the ritual, during which an elderly neighbour came calling for a teaspoon of salt. They did not think anything of it, but when the witch master called the next day and asked if anyone had come a-knocking, Davis's mother mentioned the old neighbour: why, he announced, the old woman was the witch! To her credit she did not believe so, and she ended up feeling embarrassed by the whole affair, about which the family kept very quiet.[34]

Doing witchcraft: lizards, bags, and dolls

While witches were commonly thought to enact witchcraft by thought, touch, and sight, they were also believed to practise ritual forms of harmful magic. One of the most pervasive in American cultures concerned bodily intrusion. In other words, the notion that witches invisibly sent objects into their victims. Elf shot and witch balls are examples that have already been discussed. The Zuni Pueblo considered this intrusive magic the commonest way in which witches harmed people. They sent bone splinters, thorns, cactus needles, insects, shreds of funerary cloth, and corpse flesh into their victims' bodies. Amongst Californian Native Americans, nail clippings, blood clots, and individual hairs were also thought to be intruded, and among the Apaches, frogs and stones. Jesuit accounts of the Iroquois relate how medicine men expelled the intrusions using emetics, or magically used a knife but without making an incision.[35] Other records attest that they also claimed to massage the intrusive material to the surface or more spectacularly cut an incision into the body and sucked it out. Both procedures obviously gave ample opportunity for magic of the sleight-of-hand kind. Consider another Jesuit observation regarding the medicine men of the Iroquois: 'In this, some jugglers are so expert in their art that with the point of a knife they seem to extract or rather, they cause to appear whatever pleases them,—a piece of iron, or a pebble which they say they have drawn from the heart, or from inside of the patient's bones, without, however, making an incision'.[36]

Amongst African Americans we find the similar notion that witches sent lizards and snakes into their victims' bodies. The same concept is well recorded from West Africa. In 1867 an African-American woman named Emily McClellan, who had moved from Virginia to Washington, came to believe she was conjured by another woman after a dispute over a skirt. Emily began to bark uncontrollably like a dog, and she felt something gnawing its way from her stomach to her neck. Some who watched over her said they saw the form of a lizard crawling under the skin of her chest, moving up to her neck and back again. At the time McClellan lived in a tenement in Campbell Barracks, upper Seventh Street. The area simmered with racial tensions, with regular assaults on African Americans. Only the year before there had been pitched battles between poor white and black residents.[37] This time the place was raised to a pitch of excitement due to McClellan's bewitchment, with both white and black neighbours confirming the sightings of the lizard in her body.[38]

Mrs Bailey Johnson, of Augusta, Georgia, died in January 1895 after a root doctor told her that she was filled with lizards. Her children believed their father had conjured her. A fight ensued in which the father killed one of her sons.[39] In the same year Mary Rogers, a young African-American woman of 487 Myrtle Avenue, Brooklyn, died. It was believed a spell had been put upon her years before by a mixed-race woman with whom she vied for the affections of a man during her girlhood in Virginia. Rogers's step-sister said that a local white 'voodoo' doctor, Dr Parrett of 851 Fulton Street, had treated Mary and told her that he had extracted snakes and lizards from her. Parrett told the coroner that he merely treated her with rhubarb and bitter aloes. The autopsy revealed that she died from a tumour.[40]

One magical explanation for how witches performed bodily intrusion involved placing the powder of ground, dried snake heads, and scorpions in their victims' water or food: they would come back to life in the stomach and slowly eat up their hosts.[41] As to natural explanations, some of the experiences of lizard and snake intrusion were probable due to tapeworms, cancerous growths, and nervous disorders, and it has been suggested that the symptoms of severe stomach acid were another common cause.[42] Most important though, was that many people claimed to have actually seen lizards removed from a person's body by a conjure or root doctor—or *thought* they had seen them to be more precise, since it is obvious that those practitioners used illusory tricks like their Native-American counterparts. There are instances of lizards being tucked up sleeves and retrieved at the appropriate moment of the ritual, or concealed in a poultice applied to the skin, or likewise hidden in a cabbage leaf for the same purpose.

Witchcraft was not all imaginary though: people really did practise harmful magic in all cultures. The fabrication of conjure bags or balls was a common form of cursing magic in African-American tradition. The following examples illustrate what they consisted of and how they were employed. In 1888 Colonel Dewey Moore Wisdom, Chief Clerk of the Union Indian Agency in Muskogee, in what would later be the state of Oklahoma, presided over the trial of an African-American gospel minister named Willis Loren and his two sons who were charged with witchcraft by one of their neighbours named Island Renty, who lived in Cane Creek Bottom. Many African Americans in the neighbourhood were descended from people enslaved by the Creek Nation. Island claimed that Loren's two sons visited his home at midnight and buried in his yard a quantity of dirt, broken bottles, and horse hair tied up in a cloth. These items were duly produced in court and the Lorens did not deny that they had placed them in Renty's yard. Although they believed in the power of witchcraft, the Lorens pleaded that they were not trying to injure anyone, but had only been trying to scare folks in the neighbourhood. The locals were not so convinced. A large and threatening crowd gathered as the Lorens were escorted away.[43]

In the summer of 1885 the North Carolina family of Henry McCorckle fell ill after he quarrelled with a hoodoo doctress who had lodged with them. She threatened to conjure them all, which she duly did by collecting some mud from a nearby stream, adding some of her own hair and six crooked pins, and rolling it into a ball. She returned to McCorckle's house, dropped to her knees and threw the conjure ball so that it stuck to the wall. Within hours the family was suffering from griping stomach pains. A few months later, a similar case was reported from Ellijay, Georgia. A black root gatherer had begged for bread from an African-American woman named Clements, who lived alone with her four sons. Clements refused to provide charity whereupon the root digger uttered a curse against her and her cabin. A few hours later Clements died of convulsions. A conjure ball consisting of red rags, hairs from a black dog's tail, and crooked pins were found lodged over the door of the cabin. An autopsy of Clements' body found no evidence of poisoning.[44]

The conjure ball concept had limited penetration into European-American practices, chiming a little with the widespread notion of the witch hair ball. It became a part of the folk beliefs of white North Carolinians. One elderly woman named Lucy Britt of Gates County, who was born in 1844, recalled, 'I went to see a herb doctor who told me if I'd find the conjure [bag] and throw it in runnin' water, without touchin' it with my naked hands, I'd never be troubled no more. I never found nary a thing; so I've had to suffer with colic and rheumatism all my life.'[45] We find reference to it much farther afield too, such as in the Wisconsin state board of health's legal action against a 'hex woman' named Anna Jurich in 1934. This forty-nine-year-old single mother with no stated occupation lived with her daughter in what was then 2nd Avenue in Milwaukee, providing magical services to the Yugoslav community. One Mrs Obradovich (there were several in the town) had failed to pay Jurich for a spell to ward of harm during childbirth, and in retaliation a 'witch ball' was thrown through the Obradovich's window. It consisted of a thimble filled with toe and fingernail parings, wrapped in human hair and vari-coloured string. This was covered with a patchwork of cloth cut in triangles, crosses, crescents, squares, and ovals. The family burned it and scattered the ashes in an attempt to avert the curse.[46] It is likely that Jurich, who had emigrated in 1900, picked up the idea from Milwaukee's substantial African-American population. Perhaps she purchased it ready made from a local conjure doctor.

The origin of the conjure ball is linked to the West African *gris gris* bags, also known as *juju* bags, and the *nkisi* or *minkisi* containers of Congo. These consisted of a collection of ritual objects, powders, and oils placed most commonly in a red pouch. They gave their possessors spiritual power that could be used for benign and malign purposes. A case from Spanish Louisiana in 1773 demonstrates the African link. Several slaves were accused of requesting a man from Guinea, who spoke only Mandinga, to create a '*gri gri*' consisting of herbs and the gallbladder and heart of an alligator to murder a plantation overseer.[47] In nineteenth-century America bottles also came to be used as vessels. In 1883, for instance, it was reported that an Atlanta conjurer had bewitched another by placing some water (probably a euphemism for urine) in a bottle along with six hairs from the right hind leg of a cat.[48]

Native-American tribes shared the similar concept of the medicine bundle. This was a sacred collection of objects such as arrowheads, fossils, feathers, pipes, animal bones, tobacco, and other items of personal or tribal significance, kept in a skin bag or pouch. Together with associated rituals they enabled access to the spirit world, and provided protection for the individual, usually a chief, medicine man or woman, and ensured the well-being of the community.[49] What is unclear is whether in pre-contact times the medicine bundle was imbued solely with beneficial powers. Christians demonized the medicine bundles as the tools of the maligned medicine men and they became associated with witchcraft amongst some Native Americans by the late eighteenth century. The Shawnee Prophet Tenskwatawa, for instance, denounced medicine bundles as witch bags. In 1806 an aged Christian chief, Teteboxti, was murdered at a Moravian mission by the Prophet's followers after a catch-22 situation whereby they promised to give him a pardon if he gave up his medicine bag, which was believed to contain tobacco, bones, and other magical elements. He did not have one, but under torture confessed to burying it under a stone. It was not found were he said it was, though, and under further torture he confessed he had hidden it in a fellow Christian's house. He was subsequently executed.

The inheritance of such medicine bundles became problematic. The impulse was to destroy them. A Pueblo legend relates how a man burned a 'witch bag' he had found containing hairs, rags, fingers, and a small rag doll. A local witch went mad searching for it and was soon discovered dead.[50] Yet at the same time they were ancestral objects that one should not destroy. The spirit of the deceased owner might not rest if separated from his or her bag. The Ojibwa of Minnesota ensured that they were buried with their owners, a process that would ensure the tradition was allocated to the past.[51] A Menomini woman interviewed in the mid-twentieth century explained regarding her great-grandmother, 'I inherited her two "medicine bags"—the very powerful one, and another one. I no longer have them. Having them in my possession put me under an obligation to kill one person each year with each bag. This is our old belief. But I do not wish to kill persons. . . . I gave the two bags to two old, distant relatives.'[52]

A distinctively African-American tradition with clear roots in the West African kingdom of Kongo was the use of goopher dust or graveyard dirt. In Africa it was usually employed for protective purposes but in nineteenth-century America it also became a tool of harmful magic.[53] It could be blown at a victim, or added to the ingredients of a conjure ball. The use of poisons, as we have seen, was also considered an aspect of African harmful magic, and was expressed in the use of snakes and lizards heads, often dried and powdered, in conjure practices. Plugging was a technique more widely known across American cultures. Amongst the Kwakiutl a charm to cause fainting fits consisted of a hole made in the end of a stick into which was placed some hair or menstrual blood. This was then covered with a bit of snake or corpse skin and a wooden plug inserted.[54] A variation of the practice was used by African Americans in Georgia and Alabama, whereby some excrement of the intended victim was obtained and plugged in the hole of a tree. This caused the intended victim to be constipated. To counter it the plug had to be taken out and the tree chopped down and burned.[55] European Americans used similar plugging techniques for causing harm and as a medical cure.

The concept of harmful image magic was based on the 'laws of sympathy'—that like affects like or that lasting associations are formed between things that have been in close contact with each other, was common to all cultures in America. The fabrication of dolls in the form of an intended victim that were then mutilated dates back to antiquity and can be found across the globe. Amongst the Menomini of Wisconsin, witches were thought to make dolls of their victims out of grass and wood, or drew their likeness on the ground or on birch bark, and then shot, stabbed or mutilated the images.[56] Amongst the Nambe 'witch dolls' filled with chilli seeds, dirt, and rags were thought to inflict disease, and an old prohibition amongst the Pueblo against making rag dolls for their children derives from the fear over their evil usage. It has been suggested that the Pueblo knowledge of witch dolls derives from Spanish Americans. During the Abiquiu witch trials in mid-eighteenth-century New Mexico, for instance, it was claimed that the suspected witches had made a clay image of Father Toledo in which they stuck pins.[57] But it is likely that it was a practice independent of European influence.

Although in the twentieth century the voodoo doll became an iconic and commercial vehicle for expressing African-American magic, it was not a common element in conjure; at least it was by no means as ubiquitous as conjure balls for the same purpose.[58] As a term, it does not appear in newspapers or other literary sources until the twentieth century, although the concept of such image magic was certainly a part of hoodoo or conjure. In 1906 a Galveston woman who lived near Winnie Street asked the police for protection after what was described as a 'hoodoo doll' was left hanging on her door knob along with a bunch of carrots. The doll's features were those of an elderly woman with grey hair, and attached to it was a placard on which was pencilled a skull and crossbones and the word 'Death'.[59] A children's prank perhaps, but indicative of the fear that such objects inspired.

There is a difference, of course, between the folklore reports of the many ways in which people could try to harm through magic, and proof that such rituals were actually used. I have provided some concrete examples above, but most of the evidence we have for people conducting such rituals, particularly amongst European Americans, concerned actions *against* suspected witches and not *by* accused witches. We shall return to this in the next chapter.

Witchcraft fantasies

Around 1813 or 1814 the residents of Chesterfield and Lancaster in South Carolina were stirred up by sensational rumours. A girl accused one Barbara Powers of Chesterfield of transforming her into a horse and riding her to exhaustion. The supposed witchery began when the girl laid down to rest after a tiring day's labour. While in this state she claimed that Powers appeared and sat upon her chest, violently choking her. Family and friends of the girl forced Powers to come and touch her and say over her 'God bless you', thereby breaking the spell. The girl apparently recovered. But this was not the end of the matter.

Chesterfield County, named after the English statesman Lord Chesterfield (1694–1773), was created in 1785, and was predominantly settled by people of British descent. The village of Chesterfield was founded as the county town, and around 1813 probably numbered less than a hundred people. It was not a complete backwater though; a decade before the events above a stagecoach and post road had been constructed a few miles south and the village's proximity would slowly but surely increase the size of Chesterfield.[60] Chesterfield village had its own courthouse and jail by 1843, but in 1813 the prosecution case brought by Powers had to be heard at Lancaster. Judge David Johnson, later elected governor of South Carolina, oversaw the trial, and one of the lawyers in the case, Stephen D. Miller, would follow in his footsteps, becoming the twenty-fifth Governor of the state.

Seven or eight of those involved in coercing Powers were tried. They stood accused of assault, battery, and false imprisonment. The girl was sworn to give testimony and explained how during her drowsy torment Powers turned her into a horse and rode her to Lancaster village. There Powers passed through the keyhole of several shops and brought out valuable goods, and then rode her back to Chesterfield. She subsequently set out on another similar raid to steal items from shops in Cheraw—the oldest settlement in Chesterfield. The girl said she was left utterly worn out and ill from such supernatural abuse. Judge Thompson stopped further testimony, and apparently said later that he had proceeded with the trial out of curiosity.[61]

A decade later, similar evidence was heard during the trial of a folk healer before the Superior Court of Exeter County, New Hampshire. An Irishman, aged around sixty-years-old, testified how he sank into despondency after the death of his wife and became convinced that he was bewitched by an elderly woman who lodged in the same house, and another woman in the neighbourhood.[62] After he lay down to rest they would enter through the keyhole of his bedroom door and flash strange lights at him, making peculiar signs and gestures. Sometimes the spirits of other women joined them and they would sit down in the chimney corner and smoke pipes. They also appeared to him in the shape of horses: 'once I heard a horse come near the house in the evening, and pass into the field directly under my window. I looked out and saw him feeding. I took a halter in my hand and went to catch him. I went close up to him, put my arm round his neck and was just drawing the halter when—faith, there was no horse!' He consulted one Dr Scoby who offered medicine that was 'good against witches', and who subsequently defrauded him.

Such extraordinary testimonies could be put down to the mental illness of the individuals concerned; the hallucinatory symptoms of the Chesterfield girl's nervous exhaustion, and the Irishman's obvious depression. Medical factors no doubt played their part, but the content of their hallucinations were not an aberration. The notion of being ridden by witches and the nocturnal visits of witches in spirit form were rooted deep in the relationship between legends, tales, dreams, the waking imagination, and physical experience. Witch riding provides the most vivid illustration that witches were more than mere vindictive humans: they were spiritual entities too.

Accounts of witches riding to gatherings on people they had transformed into horses can be found in legends and folk tales from across the USA, so too the belief that they rode horses at night leaving them sweating and with tangled manes when their owners found them in the stable the following morning.[63] The prevalence of these stories is hardly surprising considering they were also integral to witchcraft beliefs in Europe, encountered in the witch trials, depicted in the art of the period, and recorded many times by folklorists. In nineteenth-century Europe witch riding was not just the subject of idle storytelling. Considerable social disruption was caused in the rural Swedish village of Gagnef in 1858, when 130 or so children, mostly girls under nine years of age, claimed they had been abducted by witches and ridden to nocturnal Sabbats. Over 700 people were directly affected by the rumours.[64]

Witch riding was also a strong theme in African-American belief. The folklorist Harry Hyatt collected numerous accounts during the mid-twentieth century, including the experience of a gentleman from New York:

> my mother and father had gone to bed, and mother was making a funny noise like they do when they try to get their breath. And my father saw this old witch leaning over my mother. And my father knew it was her. They called it riding her. So he jumped up and grabbed her. He saw her. She looked like herself but she was not as visible. And my father said she changed just as quick. She turned into a leather strap and slipped through his hand. He stood there holding the strap.[65]

There has been speculation that witch riding was one of those folk notions that derived from Europeans. One argument for this was that riding horseback was little known to West Africans, and although other animals were ridden, the act of saddling and bridling, which are common to most witch-riding legends, was not relevant.[66] Yet the concept of flying witches and the magical significance of riding were a part of African belief systems. Equestrianism was actually an important iconic element in West African art, with ritual sculptures and carvings depicting the act of riding horses and other animals in Kongo and Yoruba cultures.[67] It is well recorded in East Africa that witches were thought to ride on hyenas in a similar fashion and for a similar purpose as the European riding witches.[68] So, again, as with a lot witchcraft belief, not so much wholesale borrowing but adaptation and assimilation of similar concepts and notions between different cultures.

The *experience* of being witch-ridden was more than just a fantasy born of dreams and legends. The clinical condition known as sleep paralysis was clearly responsible for many such manifestations of witchcraft. Sleep paralysis occurs as a result of the interruption of REM sleep episodes when there is intense central nervous system activity but muscles are rested. For a brief moment, but for what can seem like an age, those whose REM sleep is interrupted, usually when sleeping in a supine position, can see and hear but cannot move. In this half-awake half-dream state, sufferers feel a crushing weight on the chest and legs, or the sensation of being choked, and can experience hallucinations of entities either in the room, sitting on them or smothering their paralysed body. These hallucinations are culturally determined. So a number of well-recorded cases of supposed alien abduction from the 1970s and 1980s can be put down to sleep paralysis. When witchcraft belief was widespread and legends of witch riding a staple of fireside stories, people saw old women or 'hags' astride them. Sometimes these were fantastical creatures, sometimes the visions of known individuals. We find examples in the American witch-trial records of the seventeenth century.[69]

There is no better first-hand account of the experience that than of the former slave William Grimes, writing in 1825. He recalled that while in service to a brutal master in Savannah, Georgia, he had

> at different times of the night felt a singular sensation, such as people generally call the night-mare: I would feel her coming towards me, and endeavouring to make a noise, which I could quite plainly at first; but the nearer she approached me the more faintly I would cry out. I called to her, aunt Frankee, aunt Frankee, as plain as I could, until she got upon me and began to exercise her enchantments on me. I was then entirely speechless; making a noise like one apparently choking, or strangling. My master had often heard me make this noise in the night, and had called to me, to know what was the matter; but as long as she remained there I could not answer. She would then leave me and go to her own bed. After my master had called to her a number of times. Frankee, Frankee, when she got to her own bed, she would answer, sair. What ails Theo? (a name I went by there, cutting short the name Theodore) She answered, hag ride him sair. He then called to me, telling me to go and sleep with her. I could then, after she had left me, speak myself, and also have use of my limbs. I got up, and went to her bed, and tried to get under her coverlid; but could not find her. I found her bed clothes wet. I kept feeling for her, but could not find her. Her bed was tumbled from head to foot. I was then convinced she was a witch, and that she rode me. I then lay across the corner of her bed without any covering, because I thought she would not dare to ride me on her own bed, although she was a witch. I have often, at the time she started from her own bed, in some shape or other, felt a shock, and the nigher she advanced towards me, the more severe the shock would be. The next morning my master asked me what was the

matter of me last night. I told him that some old witch rode me, and that old witch, is no other than old Frankee. He cursed me and called me a damned fool, and told me that if he heard any more of it, he would whip me. I then knew he did not believe in witch-craft. He said, why don't she ride me? I will give her a dollar. Ride me you old hag, and I will give you a dollar. I told him she would not dare to ride him.[70]

Being hag-ridden was a traumatic experience causing fear and anxiety that could disrupt sleep patterns further, generating a cycle of sleep paralysis attacks. There was no more physical and disturbing a proof of witches' power over peoples' bodies.

Skin shedding and shape-shifting

One distinctive African-American belief associated with both the notion of witch riding and the experience of being hag-ridden, is that witches physically shed their skins before setting out on their spirit journeys to ride people. If you could find the skin before the witch returned and rubbed pepper and salt into it, you would cause her much discomfort. A great sensation was caused in New Orleans in 1844 when rumours spread that a witch had been arrested, and a large crowd gathered around the high constable's office. It was said that she had been seen slipping out of her skin, washing it in the Mississippi and leaving it to dry by moonlight. Gossip related that at the time of her arrest she had slipped off her skin and someone had managed to fill it with salt, so that 'she was unable to enter it again, and was at that time as raw as a piece of beef'.[71] It has been suggested that the concept was introduced to the Carolinas by Caribbean slaves, and one twentieth-century collection of skin-shedding stories was collected solely from Gullah-speaking areas—the Gullah being African-American communities in South Carolina, the Sea Islands, and Georgia, who have retained a strong African cultural heritage and speak a Creole language similar to that found in Jamaica and Barbados.[72] Indeed, in parts of the Caribbean we find the *soukouyan* or *soucouyant*, a night-flying, blood-sucking female witch that sheds her skin and enters bedrooms through the keyhole. As in African-American belief, the witch intruder could be hindered by sprinkling rice, salt grains, or mustard seeds on the bedroom floor. Witches and other spirits had a great weakness for endlessly counting things: the longer they were so occupied the better for the intended victim.[73]

The concept of skin shedding spread little beyond African-American culture. The story of the Tunica Indian witch in Louisiana who shed her skin before her nocturnal travels, until one day a medicine man found it and filled it with salt, sounds suspiciously like a borrowing from African-American folk belief.[74] But some Native-American tribes held similar beliefs. In Choctaw tradition a witch was not considered entirely human and therefore not a member of society. Witches *inhabited* human bodies, which explains the notion that when performing acts of witchcraft they were thought to throw their entrails over the bough of a tree.[75] There was some limited penetration of skin shedding into European American consciousness. In the case of the New Orleans gypsy Elizabeth Fuller-man, mentioned earlier, it was reported that one of the policeman who dealt with the case had mischievously put it about that she had turned into a cat and escaped from jail leaving her skin behind.[76] In the early twentieth century, a folklorist was told by a white man in North Carolina about a reputed begging witch named Phoebe Ward, also white, who, it was said, possessed a magical grease that she rubbed on herself to slip out of her skin.[77]

Skin shedding leads us on to the widespread notion that witches transformed themselves into animals better to carry out their malicious activities. Such shape-shifting was widely recorded amongst Native Americans. The Ojibwa and Menomini, for instance, believed witches travelled great distances as owls, bears, turkeys, snakes, wolves, foxes, and bats to attack people. They were able to achieve this by slipping on the skins or wearing the feathers of these animals.[78] The folklore archives regarding Europeans in America are likewise full of legends of witches transformed into animals. So in 1894 it was recorded that an Alleghanies witch had 'pressed to death' the sister-in-law of a doctor while in the form of a wild cat that sat on her chest at night.[79] Again, it is useful to turn to concrete examples of how such beliefs were actually acted upon. In 1936 the Hungarian neighbourhood around Franklin Street, Woodbridge, New Jersey, was stirred up by stories of the fantastic doings of a witch. The details were revealed when three women were brought before magistrate Arthur Brown to answer for their abuse of the suspected woman. One told Brown that she had looked through the witch's window and seen how 'her head would shrink to the size of my fist, her body would become large and horns would appear on her head and she would walk on all fours like an animal'. Another related, 'I saw her bend down and her head changed into a dog's head and she had big bumps on her back.' Then, 'one night I saw her at the window. She looked like a frightful animal. She seemed to be dressed in the skin of an animal. There was also a blazing stream of fire above her head.' Brown was having none of it, and threatened the three women that if there were any more complaints he would send them to the workhouse.[80]

The notion that witches had animal spirit helpers in the form of domesticated animals, such as dogs, cats, and mice, has often been represented as a distinctively English witchcraft tradition. While such 'familiars' were certainly an intriguing element in English witch trials, and were transformed by learned conceptions of witchcraft into demonic imps in the seventeenth century, similar notions of domestic animal spirits that enabled witches to perform their work were known in other parts of Europe. And again, it is a concept known in other cultures around the globe in terms of witchcraft, sorcery, and shamanistic beliefs. Still, the familiar was not a major theme in nineteenth- and early twentieth-century American witchcraft belief, though it cropped up from time to time in disputes. In July 1902 the three-year-old son of a tailor named John Eisenhower and his wife Sarah was buried. She and her husband believed he had been bewitched. Neighbours in Douglass and Locust streets, Reading, PA, where the couple lived with their large family, had blamed other recent deaths likewise. Mrs Eisenhower had seen a strange old woman stop in front of their house the moment her son began to suffer. Then around the time he died, a huge black cat appeared on the rear fence of their home. It had an enormous head and glowing eyes. The neighbours instigated a hunt for the evil beast. 'My husband shot a cat', explained Mrs Eisenhower, 'but he did not get the one he was after. It all seems so strange . . . I believe the cat belongs to the woman that cast the spell over my poor child. She perhaps uses her to work her spells.'[81]

In 1904 the Pottsville justice Sidney Shaw heard Cora Hiney accuse her former friend and neighbour Mary Leib of bewitching her child. According to Hiney and other neighbours, Mary's white cat and black dog were possessed of malign powers. They emitted a phosphorescent glow at night, and were heard talking to each other. The cat would cry in distress, but whenever someone approached it would burst into laughter before fading into thin air. The cat had gone into Hiney's house and stolen some meat several days prior to her daughter falling ill. An African-American fortune-teller confirmed that various misfortunes in the neighbourhood had been caused by a witch.[82] An interesting variation on the notion of the familiar was reported from the German community in Memphis during 1866. A Mrs Alvers, whose young daughter had fallen sick, visited a fortune-teller in Elm Street who told her that the suspected witch, a neighbour named Flohr, had a black cat strung up in her garret and that the spirit of the cat had passed into the girl's body causing her sickness. Flohr's husband subsequently sued Alvers for defamation.[83]

The new witches

'Witchcraft Revived!' was a periodic cry in the press. The stories were not always concerned with witchcraft per se, but the actions of mesmerists and spiritualists. During the late eighteenth and early nineteenth centuries two major cultural movements led to a new re-evaluation of the spiritual realm.[84] One was

religious—the Second Great Awakening, which encompassed the revivalist movements led by the Methodists and Baptists and the spawning of a range of new
American evangelical and metaphysical churches and prophets. At its heart was the
appeal to the emotions, a reconnection with the spiritual through divine inspiration, and the expectation of the second coming of Christ. Communication with
angels and the spirits of the dead were central to the faith and worship of groups
like the Shakers. For some this Great Awakening was a glorious era of divine
revelation, a period of divine blessings, confirmation that America was, indeed, the
new Jerusalem ready to receive the imminent return of Christ. For others it was an
embarrassing outbreak of old superstitions, religious frauds, and credulity, unset-
tling the rational foundations of the new Republic. Back in England, Methodist
preaching was accused of inflaming popular 'superstition' and increasing belief in
witchcraft. In America movements such as the Shakers and the Mormons faced
both these accusations *and* that they were practising witchcraft. The Shakers
claimed they were possessed by the spirit of God, but some critics suggested they
were letting in demons.[85]

The other movement was scientific—the development of the theory of animal
magnetism or mesmerism. This was the idea established by the Viennese doctor
Franz Anton Mesmer (1734–1815) that an invisible magnetic fluid existed inside
the human body that could be channelled to influence other bodies. Mesmer and
his followers sought to control the direction of this 'animal magnetism' for medical
purposes, healing the sick by unblocking the channels of flow in patients either
through sheer will power or physical contact. It was not until the 1830s that
mesmerism became a major cultural force in America, and its enthusiastic adoption
was closely linked with the growth of evangelical religion. The seemingly revolutionary science of invisible natural forces opened up new explanations for the
fascinating gaze of the rattle snake, the modus operandi of spiritual communication, and the malign influence of the evil eye. 'With such a lamp to our feet', the
Boston spiritualist Allen Putnam told his readers in 1858, 'let us go back to the dark
day of the most terrific scenes in New England's history.' He was talking about
Salem of course, and in light of mesmerism the old trial records now made clear
sense; all the supposed acts of witchcraft could be explained away as the 'legitimate
operations of natural laws'.[86] Salem needed to be re-evaluated. Those who made
the accusations and pursued the prosecutions were not credulous fools, they just
did not understand the secret *natural* forces at play. 'Salem witchcraft can scarcely
be mentioned without a pitying smile at what we think the absurd folly of our
ancestors; and yet there was a truth in Salem witchcraft', wrote another advocate.[87]

The early mesmeric followers considered themselves Enlightenment figures,
scientifically undermining popular credulity with regard to witchcraft, relocating
witches from the supernatural realm to the natural world. But to others,

mesmerism seemed to be just another recrudescence of the discredited belief of a world governed by spirits.[88] One such critic, David Christy, an Ohio journalist and geologist of an evangelical persuasion, looked to the common people around him rather than the past to seek analogies. Christy was both an apologist for slavery, and an active proponent of the repatriation of African Americans. In various publications published during the mid-nineteenth century he decried the 'superstitious credulity' of witchcraft and *gris-gris*, and what he termed the 'devil worship' of the Africans. He considered it providential that, 'the barbarian was brought to the Christian, instead of awaiting the tardier and more dangerous plan of the Christian going to the barbarian'.[89] In his vision, the emancipated slaves of Ohio would bring Christian civilization back to their African brothers.

In *The Life and Times of Old Billy McConnell,* Christy's attack on witchcraft and modern 'superstition' is far more subtle, satirical, and sarcastic than his crude opinions regarding African beliefs. Set in the area of Cross Creek Township, Ohio, and apparently based on a real character, through the story of the Irish immigrant witch doctor Billy and his battle against witchcraft, Christy sought to demolish the foundations of mesmerism and clairvoyance by equating them with popular witchcraft beliefs. Billy's powers are presented as being mesmerism before it was 'discovered' by the 'imaginative sciences'. Christy explained how olden times' witches usually bewitched the poorer sort amongst the farmers' cattle rather than the well-fed milk cow or labouring ox, because, as experimentation had revealed, animals of nervous temperament were more susceptible to mesmeric impressions. Witches, concluded Christy in mock seriousness, 'were the original mesmerizers, and modern mesmerists are but their pupils and imitators, with this difference. The former operated principally upon quadrupeds—the latter act upon bipeds.' Old Billy's many reported successes at defeating the power of witchcraft was proof, then, that he was a 'profound philosopher . . . far in advance of our most learned professors of the Imaginative Sciences'. As to his methods, Christy reported that he employed his innate understanding of 'sympathetic currents'. To cure a bewitched ox, for instance, He would take a red-hot horseshoe, mumble a Latin charm over it, with 'philosopher-like expressions of countenance', and place it on the animal's neck. This had the effect of reversing the mesmeric sympathetic current so that it reverted to the witch who would feel the burning sensation in her own neck.

Christy next drew upon the recent discovery of 'psychometry', a term coined in 1842 by the Kentucky physician and mesmerist Joseph Rodes Buchanan, to explain how Billy's charms operated so successfully. Psychometry posited that certain gifted individuals with mesmeric sensitivities could unlock the secret properties of objects, or divine the moral or emotional state of their owners, by holding the object. A psychometer could, for instance, detect the character of a murderer by touching the murder weapon. The English-born Boston geology lecturer, William Denton, enthused about its scientific potential for unlocking the origin of species. By handling a fossil, he believed, the psychometer, could get the measure not only of the original forms of the extinct species but also the prehistoric environment in which they lived, 'filling up the great hiatus' in knowledge of geological time.[90] There were also immense medical benefits. By touching someone's skull at points of phrenological significance, for instance, the skilled psychometer could diagnose mental problems and modify a person's character. Buchanan claimed he had even cured those sceptical of mesmerism by placing his hands on the affected parts of their bodies. He described the process of imbuing others and objects in this way as 'sympathetic impressibility'. 'But a short time since in the history of our race', observed Buchanan, the possession of such a gift 'would have entitled them to hanging or drowning as practitioners of witchcraft; and which even now entitles them to be considered eccentric enthusiasts.'[91] It was through sympathetic impressibility that Billy was able to impress his fine moral characteristics upon the material substance of his charms, which repelled the antagonistic, malign influence that the witches had cast upon man and beast.

Subtle and clever, Christy's dual attack on popular witchcraft beliefs and mesmerism, undermining one by associations with the other, received several positive reviews in the medical press. For the medical profession its lively sarcasm made it not only an instructive but an enjoyable journey into the perceived vanities of the pseudo-sciences and the 'absurdities' of popular beliefs. 'We think its circulation will have a decided tendency to "*stop that knocking*"', concluded one reviewer.[92] It had no impact at all, of course, and a few decades later it was described as impossible to find because most of the copies had been bought up and destroyed by the descendents of those mentioned in the book.[93]

Andrew Jackson Davis, an influential product of the enthusiasm for mesmerism and evangelism, was instrumental in starting the 'knocking' that Christy desired to silence. A youthful follower of the millenarian Baptist prophet William Miller (1782–1849), who proclaimed the second coming of Christ on or before 1843, Davis became a mesmeric healer and a leading figure in Universalism—the religious movement that preached the final salvation of all people. Davis believed he could communicate with the world of spirits during mesmeric or somnambulistic trances, but as his recollections show he was no believer in witchcraft. Mesmeric influence 'annihilates this miserable superstition', he wrote with regard to the idea that witches had influence over others thanks to demonic powers.[94] Yet, the spiritualist movement that he helped found attracted numerous accusations of witchcraft.

Spiritualism was born in March 1848 when two teenage daughters of a blacksmith and farmer named John Fox, of Hydesville, New York, claimed they had communicated with the spirit of a murdered peddler. The girls, Kate and Maggie, had heard strange knocks and raps around the house, manifestations of what the Germans called a poltergeist or 'noisy ghost'. Such noisy haunting had been recorded since antiquity, and they were reported in colonial America.[95] Prior to 1848, such phenomena were commonly blamed on witches along with a broader range of possession symptoms. In 1835 hundreds flocked to see a girl in Muskingum County, Ohio, who was afflicted with 'mewing, barking, braying, biting, kicking, jumping, scratching, smelling'. An old lady in the neighbourhood was accused of witchcraft as a consequence. It was popularly thought that witches invisibly tormented people by breaking things and plaguing them with strange sounds, as an 1832 Baltimore court case demonstrates. It concerned a charge of assault by a young woman on a suspected witch who, she believed, was responsible for making crockery fall from her hands and smash on the floor, and who tormented her with a sound like marbles rattling in a tea pot outside her bedroom door at night.[96]

More to the point, in 1831 newspapers reported a case in Albany where a sixteen- or seventeen-year-old girl, daughter of a widow, had been afflicted with fits and repeatedly heard knocks upon the headboard of her bed. They were loud enough to be heard in adjoining houses with the window open, and occurred day and night. There were those who claimed they had caught the girl making the noises, but many considered her bewitched. She was taken to relatives in a village a few miles from Albany, where admittance to her room was refused to those who did not believe in witchcraft, and a 'witch doctor' was called in to cure her. She returned to Albany in restored health, but once back in town the rappings began again, even when she slept in a hammock. Public interest was aroused once more, and the house attracted many visitors, some suggesting how the offending witch should be countered. The newspapers recalled a similar case in Manhattan in 1805, again centred on a teenage girl, as most such cases were, and in Hackensack, New Jersey, around the same time.[97]

Spiritualism reinterpreted these supernatural knockings as the language of the dead. It was not the first time that this had been claimed, though. The famous Cock Lane ghost fraud of 1762 was based on the same premise. But in the religious and mesmeric climate of 1840s America, there was a large receptive audience for the profundity of its significance—for it confirmed the existence of the afterlife and the nature of the celestial realm. While evangelical religions such as the Shakers believed they received divine communications, spiritualism offered a proper spiritual telegraph: the mediums were not one-way receivers but could go knocking on Heaven's door. Spiritualism, furthermore, offered better scope for generating scientific proof of the existence of the spirit world. But just as in the days of the witch trials, the attempt to communicate with spirits for benign purposes was interpreted by some as necromancy and witchery. The rappings and knockings were the work of demons fooling people into sinful practices and assumptions.

In the 1860s the New England Methodist Episcopal pastor and religious magazine editor William McDonald, a well-known New England evangelical, was appointed by the Providence District Ministers' Association to investigate the spiritualist movement. In the resulting essay endorsed by the Association and another association of clergyman at Bridgewater, Massachusetts, McDonald was 'frank to confess that we believe Spiritualism to be, in part at least, the work of demons'. He identified the same diabolically phenomena in the Bible and the European and American witch trials. This was no historic coincidence. 'Stripped of all the foolish notions peculiar to that age', he wrote regarding Salem, 'New England witchcraft stands before us the younger brother of ancient demonology, and the elder brother of modern Spiritualism.'[98] Spiritualism was problematic for the clergy. While the sceptical wing dismissed it as another 'popular delusion' akin to the Salem episode, there was a middle path of neither dismissing nor embracing its basis. The *Church Review* expressed this position in reviewing McDonald's book: 'we have always supposed that the nastiness of the system was, of itself, a sufficient reason for giving the whole thing a wide berth, without asking whether the Devil was the instigator of it.'[99]

Profoundly influenced by both mesmerism and spiritualism in her early adult life, the founder of Christian Science, Mary Baker Eddy (1821–1910), later exerted considerable energy in distancing herself from both movements. Like other faith healers at the time, however, she struggled to disassociate her practice from public notions of mesmeric healing.[100] She denounced mesmerism as the re-emergence of the old errors of witchcraft and necromancy. They were self-deceiving projections of human thought, not the channelling of spiritual essences. The practice of mesmerism, like witchcraft, was essentially a malignant application of psychology, a 'mind crime'.[101] The bulk of Eddy's theology is not relevant to this study, but aspects of Christian Science healing practice, such as the power of the healer to operate at a distance through the capabilities or 'science' of the Christian mind, were equally dismissed as superstitious witchcraft by some. In rejecting mesmerism Eddy defined it as a source of spiritual harm that came to be known as 'malicious animal magnetism' or 'MAM'. This was the malign use of willpower, the projection of harmful thoughts to cause physical damage. The Victorian paranormal investigator Frank Podmore dubbed it the 'New Witchcraft' in his study of faith healing, and the early twentieth-century psychologist Joseph Jastrow saw it as 'a modern variety of witchcraft ... its central doctrine, reflects the hold of a world-wide superstition natural to primitive religions, with interesting survivals among less enlightened communities of modern times'.[102] MAM become something of a preoccupation amongst early members of the movement. Early editions of Eddy's founding text *Science and Health with Key to the Scriptures*, first published in 1875, included a discussion of the matter entitled 'Animal Magnetism Unmasked', and accounts of its influence appeared regularly in the Christian Science *Journal*, frequently described as manifesting itself in the form of having unwanted bad thoughts about Eddy. Such MAM symptoms were relieved through the healing of fellow Christian Scientists.

Malign animal magnetism became a matter of public debate thanks to what was described in the press as the 'Ipswich witchcraft case'. It centred on one of Eddy's earliest disciples 'Dr' Daniel Spofford, who she subsequently accused of 'immorality', which in Eddy's language simply meant disloyalty to Christian Science. In 1870 Spofford and his wife had entered into an agreement with Eddy that she would teach them the healing art for the sum of $100 cash and 10 per cent of the commercial income from their future Christian Science healing practice. The Spoffords fell out with Eddy over other matters and declined to pay the tithe. So in 1878 Eddy launched a lawsuit against them. It was one of several legal actions that the litigious Eddy instigated against former followers at the time.

Things got worse for Spofford when, as this case was pending, Lucretia Brown, a forty-eight-year-old spinster who lived with her mother and sister in one of the oldest houses in Ipswich, lodged a suit against Spofford that was heard in the Supreme Judicial Court at Salem, Massachusetts, in May 1878. The bill of complaint stated:

> That the said Daniel H. Spofford of Newburyport is a mesmerist, and practices the art of mesmerism, and that by his power and influence he is capable of injuring the persons and property and social relations of others, and does by said means so injure them. That the said Daniel H. Spofford has at divers times and places since the year 1875 wrongfully, maliciously and with the intent to injure the plaintiff, caused the plaintiff by means of his said power and art great suffering of body, severe spinal pains and neuralgia, and temporary suspension of mind.

The charge reads remarkably like the indictments for witchcraft two centuries earlier, and the trial's location further underscored the association in the minds of commentators.

Lucretia had suffered a spinal injury as a child, but while an invalid she was able to run a crocheting agency, employing local women working for pin money. An erstwhile Congregationalist, she was converted to Christian Science in 1876 after successful treatment by a female Christian Science healer from the town of Lynn named Dr Dorcas Rawson, herself a former Methodist. Lucretia was rejuvenated and was able to walk for miles for the first time since childhood, but she had a relapse following several visits by Spofford. She consulted Dorcas again who diagnosed that Spofford had been using mesmerism against her. And so Lucretia decided to take legal action, with some subsequently suggesting that Eddy put her up to it. The case was dismissed.[103]

When, in 1882, the cause of the death of her husband Asa Gilbert Eddy was attributed to heart disease, Mary thought otherwise. She told a *Boston Post* reporter that she feared that he had been poisoned by arsenic delivered at a distance through malicious mesmerism. Over the next few years she became constantly alert to her enemies using MAM against her, blaming her illnesses on its malign influence.[104] The notion of MAM came to overshadow the movement, sowing discord and suspicion amongst her followers, and attracting mockery and scorn from critics. One of Eddy's close advisors convinced her to remove much of her discussions of demonology and MAM from future editions of *Science and Health*, and in 1890 Eddy herself wrote in the *Journal* that the discussion of MAM had 'better be dropped'.[105] The issue seems to have been successfully parked for a few years, but the suspicions festered. When, in 1907, Judge Robert N. Chamberlin was slated to preside over a suit concerning the Trustees of Eddy's property, he was taken ill before the proceedings were due to begin. The *New York Times* reported that members of the Christian Science Church gathered at the courthouse to use their concentrated mind power to counter the MAM inflicted upon the judge by those wishing to work against Eddy and her true followers.[106] Accusations resurfaced in spectacular fashion two years later during another big bust up amongst Christian Scientists when Mrs Maude Kissam Babcock accused another Christian Scientist, Mrs Augusta Stetson, of 'mental assassination'.

Stetson, a former confidant of Eddy, was the leader of the First Church of Christ Scientist in New York, a branch of the Christian Science 'Mother Church' in Boston. There were concerns that Stetson was getting too powerful, and rumours began to swirl that she used MAM to increase her power base and destroy her enemies. Stetson, in turn, organized her followers to make 'mental defenses' against the MAM she believed was directed at her from the Boston Mother Church. Giving evidence before the directors of the Mother Church, Babcock, a former student of Stetson, explained how, 'at midnight I was awakened by an icy blast sweeping through the open window from the direction of New York. My teeth chattered. My heart fluttered. Luminous waves rolled toward me covered with the faces of the dead. It seemed, indeed, that my soul went out from my body. And in this hour of agony I saw Mrs Stetson's blue eyes all around the room.' As we have seen, similar experiences had long been blamed on witchcraft. Babcock and others also lodged complaints that Stetson, through her 'death thoughts', had caused several members to commit suicide or go insane.[107] Stetson was subsequently excommunicated from the Church.

While the mesmerist and spiritualist establishment were ever conscious of distancing themselves from the world of witchcraft and popular supernatural beliefs, the myriad huckstering mesmerists, magnetizers, hypnotists, and mediums who plied their science from town to town across America were clearly not always conscientious about explaining the humanitarian purpose of their powers. The magnetic forces they claimed for themselves were readily understood in terms of traditional conceptions of magic, and although the Christian Science concept of MAM had limited social reach, it is no surprise that mesmeric powers accrued an ambiguous reputation in popular cultures.

In the 1870s a Mississippi African American, who clearly suffered from some form of mental illness but was otherwise clear-minded and intelligent, worked for a time for a doctor named Mansfield, and witnessed him experiment with mesmerism. Shortly after, he began to experience hallucinations and strange sensations. The man thought hoodoo and voodoo was all nonsense, but that mesmerism was a real power which he defined in terms of witchcraft. He told a psychiatrist that the first evidence he had of the malign mesmeric influence upon him was when 'he could not think his own thoughts', and then crazy ideas would enter his head that he could not stop thinking about. At one point he attempted to contact President Cleveland to request that his mesmeric persecutor, Mansfield, be prosecuted under the common law against conspiracy.[108] Accusations of witchcraft through mesmerism also emerged from a violent attack on a religious cult that tried to establish itself near the hamlet of Pemberwick, Greenwich, Connecticut, in 1907. The followers of the Apostolic Faith were led by a man claiming to be a Portuguese missionary named Brother Adolph De Rosa, but who also went by the more prosaic name of Henry Spilkins, and his sidekick 'Sister' Lucy M. Leatherman. The cult had set up their tents in Pemberwick and gone about evangelizing in the locality, advocating hypnotism and the casting out of devils. One night a lynch mob headed by Marie Birdsall, the twenty-two-year-old daughter of German immigrants and the wife of house painter Walter Birdsall, set out to destroy the camp. She accused Spilkins of using black arts and mesmerism on her husband and young local girls who had come under his influence. A turpentine petrol bomb was thrown into the main tent of the camp causing a blaze. No one died, fortunately.[109]

No case reveals better the confrontation between 'mental science' and popular magic than the trial in 1901 of Mrs Helen Roth of 1911 Cortez Street, Chicago. She appeared before Justice James Dooley to defend charges of assault and witchcraft brought by Mrs Mary Donovan of 1929 Cortez Street. It transpired that Roth practised healing through hypnotism, but some of her neighbours on whom she tried her benign practice subsequently believed it was the witch's art. Mrs M. Anderson, a grocer's wife, testified that Roth tried to cure her sore throat.

'She looked into my eyes and made peculiar signs', she said, 'but she failed to put me to sleep.' Roth broke down in tears in the court room and explained her predicament:

> I am not a crazy woman. Neither am I insane nor a witch, as these women would have the court believe. I was born in Germany and my father was a colonel in the German army. I was nurse in several hospitals in Holland for years, and a successful one. I am familiar with hypnotism and know how to use it. It is the mysteries of this science which puzzle my neighbours and make them believe I am a witch. In their ignorance they misconstrued my efforts to benefit them and have brought disgrace upon myself and family.[110]

DEALING WITH WITCHES

D ue to the many cultures that make up the population of America, numerous rituals have been recorded for identifying whether witches had been about their business. They could take the form of a customary trial, the most notorious of which was swimming. This was based on the notion that a river or pond, symbolic of baptismal waters, would reject the bodies of such evil people as witches and, therefore, they would float like corks even when pushed under. If the suspected witches were innocent, then they would sink—and hopefully be pulled out before they drowned. Although never a formal legal means of ordeal in early-modern Europe, the swimming of witches was fairly widespread. Communities basically took the law into their own hands, although local officials often tacitly sanctioned proceedings. We have examples from England, Germany, France, the Netherlands, Poland, Hungary, and the Ukraine, and the practice continued long after the laws against witchcraft were repealed.[1]

In America the puritan minister Increase Mather condemned the practice of swimming in 1684 and William Jones, Governor of Connecticut, denounced it as superstitious and unwarrantable. Nevertheless it was instituted a few times, and quite late on. In 1692 Elizabeth Clawson and Mercy Disborough of Stamford, Connecticut, were swum at Fairfield. Mercy requested to undergo the ordeal as a means of proving her innocence. Neither sank, unfortunately. Then, in 1706, Grace Sherwood, of Princess Anne County, Virginia, was swum 'by her own Consent'. The authorities were most considerate, the swimming being postponed initially as inclement weather 'might endanger her health'.[2] But that seems to have been the last recorded instance. A couple of late eighteenth-century almanacs provided an account of a Virginia community's attempts to try a suspected witch in 1727. This relates how, with the help of churchwardens, the witch was about to be placed in a sack and thrown in a river to see if she floated when an Irish colonel arrived on the scene and saved the woman by telling those gathered that in Ireland they had a better test. This Irish method was to weigh the witch against the church Bible and if she proved the heaviest she was no witch. The ritual of weighing against the church Bible was occasionally practised in England during the eighteenth century, but this almanac story was clearly a tall tale along the lines of the much-repeated satire of a witch swimming written by Benjamin Franklin for the *Pennsylvania Gazette* in 1730. This bogus event purportedly took place at Burlington, New Jersey, where a mob first weighed the suspected witches and then swum them in a mill pond. Such subtle critiques of popular credulity may have had the adverse consequence of spreading knowledge about both trial procedures, but there is no convincing record of a swimming beyond the early eighteenth century. The legend of a Bible-weighing and a proposed but not consummated swimming in mid-eighteenth-century Pennsylvania, as related in a *History of Chester County* (1881), sounds suspiciously like a variation on these earlier, dubious published accounts.[3] The early demise of swimming in America is curious considering that the practice occurred periodically in England right through until the mid-nineteenth century, while a swimming took place at Deldenerbruck in the Netherlands in 1823, and at Hela, near Danzig, in 1836. So it would have been far from a distant memory for many immigrants to America in the late eighteenth and early nineteenth centuries.

The notion that witches had insensitive spots on their bodies where the Devil had marked them led to the rise of the witch-pricking trade in seventeenth-century Europe, Scotland in particular. Self-styled prickers travelled the land charging the authorities for their services with Scottish practitioners being hired south of the border. The profession withered as the trials declined, but the practice left traces in European and American folklore. In the Ozarks it was thought that if an awl was secreted in the seat of a chair so that just a small bit of the point came through, then if a person sat on it without feeling it he or she was surely a witch.[4] On to other methods, and in the Ozarks it was also believed that a freshly cut onion would sour instantly and become poisonous in the presence of a witch, and that a witch would become sick if he or she inadvertently smoked tobacco into which had been slipped a bit of pawpaw bark. The most common method of detecting evil eye amongst Mexican Americans concerned the use of eggs. A raw egg was cracked and poured into a plate, saucer, or cup and placed under the head of the bed of the sick child, or under the pillow. If after a while an eye or a pair of eyes appeared in the egg then that was confirmation. If the white appeared cooked then that was also a sign, and could also signify that the evil eye had been negated.

Eggs were also used in cures, with the yoke being rubbed over the victim's body usually by healers known as *curanderos*.[5] Then there was the technique of boiling the urine of a victim, or the milk of a bewitched cow, which would draw the guilty parties to reveal themselves. This was recorded in seventeenth-century colonial trials as well.[6] Dutch immigrants brought the practice of boiling a black chicken alive in a room where every entrance, gap, or crack in the house was sealed to draw the witch to the house. It was carried out in the Dutch village of Graafschap, Michigan, during a witch panic in 1889.[7] The seemingly limited use of the practice in America may be due to the fact that in the nineteenth-century Netherlands it was largely restricted to mid and western areas of the country.[8] One of the most distinctive and best-recorded detection practices also derived from Dutch and German areas and had avian connections.

Pillow talk

In 1883 excitement was generated in a Pittsburgh neighbourhood when it was reported that Mrs John Smith of McLane Avenue, wife of an employee of Oliver's Wire Company, found a bundle of tightly woven feathers in the shape of an alligator, about fifteen inches long and two inches wide, in her husband's pillow. She had cut open the pillow to investigate the cause of his lingering illness after a sick neighbour, Mr Caffrey, had recovered after having found similar strange feather formations in the shape of flowers and crosses in his pillow. 'I did not know what to make of it', said Smith. So she asked some of the neighbours. 'They said it was the work of a witch.' She kept the feather alligator for a couple of days until she became fed up with the number of curious inquirers coming to her door—some even wanted to purchase the wreath, and so she burned it along with her husband's bedding.[9]

If Smith and Caffrey, as their surnames suggest, were of British and Irish extraction, it is not surprising that the meaning of the feather patterns puzzled them, and that Mrs Smith sought advice from neighbours. It is quite likely that those who interpreted it as witchcraft were of Dutch or German origin, as numerous newspaper reports confirm that wherever Dutch and Germans settled in America, they brought the belief with them. In the late eighteenth-century trial of a witch doctor from the province of Drenthe, in the Netherlands, we find several of his clients cutting open their pillows and finding feather wreaths.[10] The notion was also known in Belgium, Westphalia (western Germany), and north-eastern Italy, where feather bundles in the shape of a crown or coffin were burned at crossroads.[11] During the early twentieth century, numerous accounts of feather dogs, birds, roosters, and flowers were collected from the German inhabitants of

Adams County, Illinois. The general interpretation was that these feather formations were created over time by the witch and it was only when the image was complete that the sick person who used the pillow would die.[12]

In 1896, several members of the German community of Carondelet, Missouri, discussed the tell-tale signs of pillow wreaths. A Miss Neubauer had fallen ill while staying with her sister at 261 Schirmer Street. One day several female neighbours gathered there to discuss the girl's strange sickness. Mrs Hoffmeister, a sister of the girl, was asked whether she had opened the bedding to see if anything was suspicious. A friend of hers who believed in witchcraft, she related, had cut open her pillows and had been horrified to find several feather roses. Later, Hoffmeister and Neubauer cut open the pillow she had been using, and found seven roses and a wreath made of feathers. A woman named Spinning, who knew a thing or two about such matters, was called in and she ordered that they be burned.[13]

During a witchcraft dispute in a suburb of Paterson, New Jersey, known as Little Holland, Peter Sandford told a journalist how he knew his son had been bewitched by a local woman named Mrs Geiser (Geeser):

> Little Hendrick tore open the pillow on his bed. While my wife was
> mending the pillow she felt something hard inside of it. She immediately
> cut it open and searched through the feathers. In our country feather ropes
> of three plaits like that one are said to belong to the devil, and witches are
> the only ones who possess them. I took the rope to a Belgian priest who
> lives a distance down the road, and when he saw it he shook his head and
> said: 'Some one is working you harm, Peter. Look out for yourself!'[14]

There was a contagious aspect to the practice, with communal pillow-slashing sessions taking place, as occurred in Graafschap, Michigan. This small village was founded in 1847 by Dutch-speaking settlers from Drenthe and Hanover, Germany. They were part of a wave of close-knit Dutch Reformed Church communities who, led by their pastors, emigrated to western Michigan during the 1840s. A newspaper in 1889 described them as 'contented, but superstitious Dutch people'. This was a conclusion drawn from reports that the Graafschap villagers were in a state of excitement following several cases of supposed witchcraft. People had been cutting open their pillows to look for the 'feather devils', which were described as looking like crowns or chickens. They had been found in several households and a communal burning of them had apparently taken place. In October, the Graafschap pastor delivered a sermon on the subject to try and extinguish the excitement.[15] Seven years later, similar disruption was reported from the Dutch community of East Overisel in the same county, where several feather designs were found in pillows. It was further claimed that a mouse with a ribbon tied to its tail scampered out of one pillow.[16]

A presentation to the Kansas Academy of Science in 1898 put forward a rational explanation for what were described as 'pillow witches' in a discourse on concretions. The speaker explained how a few human hairs would work their way into the pillow, which would become entangled by the movement of the pillow contents when in use. This tangle of hair would form a nucleus around which feathers would accumulate.[17] I doubt this would have convinced the dedicated Dutch pillow slasher.

Confronting the witch

Once the identity of a suspected witch had been confirmed, one course of action was to carry out ritual actions that required physical confrontation. The most striking of these was the practice of scratching. This was carried out numerous times in eighteenth- and nineteenth-century England, leading to court cases, but there is little evidence of the practice amongst those of English descent in America in the same period. We know that in 1796 Elizabeth Smith of Arundel, Maine, consented to being scratched to stop her relatives from persecuting her, and another case occurred in Pittston, Pennsylvania, in 1877.[18] Maybe instances went unrecorded of course, but it does seem that scratching fell largely out of usage amongst English Americans, perhaps supplanted by the less stressful alternative of shooting the image of the witch.

Still, the notion of drawing blood was not restricted to the English.[19] In November 1914 a Polish woman named Michalana Zamowski and her husband, of Turkey Run, PA, were prosecuted after scratching Katie Short, a German, several times on the face to draw blood. Zamowksi had been ill and lost her voice for a year. She suspected the elderly Short, who earned a meagre living making and selling tallow dips, of having put a spell upon her. The two had shared a drink of whisky shortly before Zamowski fell ill. Very suspicious. Zamowski and her husband consulted others about what to do, and someone, perhaps an English person, recommended scratching.[20] Some African Americans also knew something similar. In June 1893 Willis Wesley Shaw, an African-American farmer who farmed near Buchanan, Georgia, had words with a reputed witch while ploughing one day, and she made as if 'to pick up his tracks'. Shaw got out his knife and slashed a three-inch gash in her neck. He caught her jugular but he pleaded that he was trying to cut her 'witch vein' to counteract her spell, not kill her.[21] A European influence? Or a similar but African notion?

Spitting and spittle were thought to have anti-witch properties in many cultures around the world, and no less so amongst the various peoples of America.[22] One tradition required coercing the witch to spit on his or her victim. In 1876 Julia

Welsh, who had emigrated to New Jersey from Mayo, Ireland, ten years before, was told by a Mrs Collins that her bewitched child could only be cured by getting the suspected witch, another Irish woman named Mary Meehan, to 'come and bless the child three times and cast three spits upon her'. Meehan reluctantly agreed to do this, but then refused at the last minute. Collins then advised that the only alternative was the Irish charm of taking a piece of Meehan's clothing and burning it. Welsh duly acted on this advice, leading to a prosecution for assault.[23] This was, indeed, a common Irish technique. In September 1830 an Irish hod carrier named Jamie was charged with assault before the municipal court of Portland, Maine. He had attacked a female neighbour with a razor, crying 'you old witch, I will be the death of you'. He then began to slash her clothing before other neighbours came to the woman's aid. In court Jamie explained that the woman had bewitched his goat to prevent it from kidding. He had asked her to remove the spell but she denied having done anything to it. So he then seized her with the purpose of getting a piece of her gown, which he intended to burn under the goat's nose in order to break the witchery. He told the magistrate that he had heard of many instances of this remedy working successfully when he was in Ireland, though he had not encountered its use in his new homeland.[24] He was ordered to provide sureties to keep the peace, but being unable to pay he was committed to jail. Jamie was telling the truth, for, indeed, we find references to this ritual in Irish folklore sources. In County Leitrim, for instance, a bewitched animal could be cured by either burning the alphabet on a shovel under its nose or, likewise, a piece of the dress of the witch responsible.[25]

A similar practice was known in the Polish community, too. In August 1903 a Chicago court case resulted when a grocer's wife, Mrs Frank Galenski, attempted to cure her sick child by taking a pair of scissors and cutting off some of the hair and a piece of the shawl from the suspected witch, Francesca Krejewski. These she burned over her sick child, following the advice of a local fortune-teller. Twelve years later another Pole, Veronica Bukowski, of South Bend, Indiana, was advised that her bewitched child would only recover if she invited the suspected witch to her home, burned a bit of her shawl, slapped her until the blood ran, and gave it to the child.[26]

In one instance in Goodhue County, Minnesota, in 1872, the forced confrontation between witch and bewitched occurred over a pan of urine. A farmer's wife and young child were ill and the family believed their servant girl had cast a spell over them. Some of his wife's urine was boiled in a pan and the servant girl was forced to inhale the fumes, thereby taking the spell upon herself. Her head was forced so low over the boiling liquid that her lips were scalded, and so she understandably lodged a complaint with the county attorney.[27]

Some assaults had no ritual function; they were base, brutal attempts to bludgeon or torture the witch in to retracting his or her spells. In 1860 Marias Samierez, a wealthy American rancher of Roma, Texas, kidnapped a woman named Antonia Alanis believing she had bewitched his son who lived near Camargo. A witch doctor said that the witch had shot pigeon bones into his head. Alanis was beaten and her body lashed with prickly pear needles. This ordeal was repeated over a period of two weeks but the son did not recover. She was then tied up and a fire set under her feet. Under such torture the witch doctor said she would be forced to retract the pigeon bones and she would pull them out of the sick man's skull. When, in June 1901, a 24-year-old man named Frank Olding of Jasper, Indiana, believed that his neighbour Mrs Catherine Ferry, a German woman in her sixties, was responsible for bewitching his horse, he grabbed his blacksnake whip and badly whipped, kicked, and punched her.[28]

The witch must die

'I would do the like again', said a labourer named Joseph Lewis who lived near Deep Creek, Norfolk County, Virginia, after shooting dead a free African American named Jack Bass in May 1822. He fired his gun after a female fortune-teller named Evans of Portsmouth had confirmed Lewis's suspicion that Bass was responsible for 'tricking' or bewitching him and his wife. At the consequent trial, held at the Norfolk Superior Court, Judge Parker sentenced Lewis to eighteen years imprisonment.[29] 'I had to kill her. I had to', explained Louis De Paoli, a San Francisco florist who specialized in cultivating violets, after beating his sister-in-law Catherine to death with a chair in the autumn of 1905. He and his wife believed she had bewitched them and their three children. They had bought some pills to combat the spell, and Mrs De Paoli had tried whipping the evil out of the children, praying to St Anthony as she did so. In anguish Louis resolved to make the ultimate sacrifice. He said later, 'I was sorry to do it, but she had a spell on the children and they were about to die. It was either I kill her or five of us die from the spell.' His wife agreed. In broken English she told the authorities, 'Better one die than five, that what he say to me. Then he kill. He right. Katy had spell on us.' Louis spent the rest of his life in an insane asylum.[30]

Numerous other witch murders perpetrated by European and African Americans are detailed in this book, proof that all cultures in America had their rationales for executing witches. As we have seen, some referred to the Bible for justification. Insanity explains the actions of others. Like the two cases above, such murders were usually matters of interpersonal relations between a few people. In nineteenth-century Native-American society, however, the execution of witches was very much a community concern led by chiefs. The Nations had their own traditions and laws that justified the ultimate punishment. The Cherokee considered witchcraft a greater crime than homicide, and a Seneca Council at Buffalo Creek decreed in 1801 that 'those persons accused of Witchcraft should be threatened with Death, in case they persisted in bewitching the People'. Amongst the Choctaw, witches were not thought to be human; they were spirits inhabiting human bodies, so they were not recognized in clan laws that otherwise restrained retributive murder. Witches deserved death: it was a communal obligation to punish them. According to an 1819 missionary report, a source that always need to be treated with circumspection, the Choctaws in what is now Yalobusha County, Mississippi, had killed a dozen suspected witches, male and female, in the previous three years alone.[31]

In 1829 the Mississippi Choctaw Nation instituted a law that addressed white concerns regarding the execution of witches. While produced as a result of shrewd political negotiations with missionaries and white authorities, the law did not deny the reality of witchcraft and enshrined Choctaw beliefs. The result was a fascinating fusion of European and indigenous legal custom, a European conception of justice married to a Choctaw sense of customary right.

> Whereas it has been an old custom of the Choctaws to punish persons said to be witches or wizzards with death, without giving them a fair trial by any disinterested persons; and many have fallen victim under the influence of this habit,
>
> We do hereby resolve, in general council of the North, East and Southern Districts, that in future all persons, who shall be accused of being a wizzard or witch, shall be tried before the Chiefs and committees, or by any four Captains, and if they be found guilty, they shall be punished at the discretion of the courts.
>
> Be it further resolved, that if any person or persons shall find at any place the entrails of a wizzard of witch, the said entrails going from or returning to the body, the said body shall be put to death at the place where it may be discovered, and the said body shall be cut open by a proper person, and an examination be made to see whether it has in it any entrails and a report be made of said body'.[32]

In 1834 Major Francis Armstrong, Choctaw reservation agent, reported that the natives had recently executed a man and a woman for witchcraft. He demanded that the killers be handed over and called a council of chiefs to try and stamp out the practice. He persuaded them to institute a new decree on the 6 November stating

That any person or persons who shall kill another for a witch or wizard shall suffer death. And any person who shall publicly state that he himself or she herself is a witch or wizard, or shall say that such a person or persons are witches or wizards, and he or she knows it to be so, shall receive sixty lashes on the bare back.[33]

Armstrong received official praise for his endeavours. 'To his decision and firmness may be ascribed the termination of a superstitious custom, that triumphs in the weakness of human nature, gives a sort of legalized sanction to the most barbarous acts', declared a Senate report.[34] Still, four years later, considerable excitement surged through the Nation when the natives of the Six Towns executed a woman believed to be a witch despite the new law.[35]

Through a process of negotiation and their own decision-making, the Choctaws suppressed the sort of widespread witch purges that had erupted earlier under Handsome Lake and the Shawnee Prophet, but with the multiple pressures of war, European oppression, and epidemics, systematic witch hunts broke out in several other Native-American tribal areas over the century. One evening in 1854 four Pueblo men reported to the governor of Nambé, New Mexico, that they had murdered two male witches. 'They were killed by order of the pueblo and the head men of the pueblo', testified the governor of Nambé. 'It was the duty of the *fiscal* [constable] to execute the order of the pueblo. They commanded him to kill these two men.' He went on to state, 'we have not exercised this custom of killing witches since the Americans came here, because there had not been such doings before'. The federal agent for the area reported in frustration that the killers were acquitted because of the difficulty of proving in what county the crime was committed.[36] Further executions took place over the next decade or so. When, in 1883, the archaeologist and historian Adolph Bandelier investigated the practice of magic in Nambé he was told by locals that the killing of witches had greatly contributed to the depopulation of the community.[37]

An Indian Reservation was established along the Fresno River, California, in 1854, and four years later it was reported that seven or eight medicine men had been executed for having stopped the rains from coming and failing to cure the sick.[38] In 1878 Navajo fears regarding the harmful magic practised by their medicine men came to a head with several executions and the torture of suspects. The central accusation was that the medicine men were shooting stones into the bodies of people on the reservation. It would seem an epidemic had struck the community. Chief Ganado Mucho explained to the American authorities that some medicine men had also killed some of his relatives by putting grass, hair, horse and sheep dung in his brother's grave. The assumed guilty confessed and Mucho killed two of them. When Lt Mitchell questioned three Navajo medicine men he found tied up for shooting stones into people's bodies, he told them, 'The Americans no longer disbelieve in this shooting stones business and it must be stopped... I am here to make Indian doctors promise to stop.' Contemporary reports and later oral histories of the purge indicate that while the American authorities saw the persecution as a manifestation of tribal politics played out through 'superstition', the episode, like that at Nambé, had its roots in a deeper response to communal anxiety and instability arising from epidemics and relations with the encroaching European Americans.[39]

Such destabilizing purges centred on the failure of medicine men were exceptional, and it is likely that most witch executions were not part of larger hunts but the result of disputes between individuals where the punishment was ultimately sanctioned by tribal law. Those punished in this context were more often women, it would seem. In 1873 a middle-aged woman was executed for witchcraft amongst the Native Americans of Pine Nut Valley, Nevada. A grand council ordered her death by stoning. Her outraged husband initially threatened to 'clean out the whole tribe', but was later pacified. When, in 1888, typhoid fever struck the community of Mojave Indians in San Bernardino County, California, the medicine men instituted a ritual for detecting the witch responsible. The eighteen-year-old daughter of a sub-chief named Creso was identified and then burned to death.[40]

Attacking from a distance

Murder apart, many of those who attempted to draw blood or otherwise manhandle accused witches left themselves open to prosecution for assault, so it is not surprising that most people chose to harm witches at a distance through acts of sympathetic magic. As well as the common practice of shooting the images of witches, there were numerous alternatives, some of them the same procedures as witches were thought to use. Driving a nail in to a witch's footprint was quite widespread in African-American and European tradition.[41] Symbolically beating out the witch from the substance or person bewitched was another technique. Sarah Kochert, of Scranton, Pennsylvania, told a court in 1883 that to unbewitch her infant daughter she had been advised to beat the cradle with a briar stick. This she did until she was so tired she could no longer carry on.[42] Milk churns, or the milk, were beaten with a hawthorn, hickory, or hazel switch to drive out witchery. Sometimes it was reported that the witch would appear with whip marks on her body afterwards. Putting a red-hot poker or horseshoe in the churn had a similar effect on the witch.[43] Burning bewitched objects, or items associated with the bewitched, was practised in seventeenth-century America and continued throughout our period. Again it was based on the sympathetic principle with the witch experiencing burning pains. Another variant practised by a German family in Michigan involved placing a chip of wood in the chimney to dry out, with the witch dying slowly in pain as the moisture left the chip.[44]

Witch bottles, which came into vogue in seventeenth-century England, were used either to draw witches to the victims' houses or to force them to remove their spells by causing them great bodily torment. The general recipe was as follows: take a bottle, put some of the bewitched person's urine in it, add some sharp objects such as bent pins, nails, or thorns, some toenail clippings or hair perhaps, and maybe an item such as a felt heart for good measure. Seal the bottle and either bury it under the hearth, put it up a chimney, or boil it in a fire. The bottle represented the witch's bladder, and the sharp objects, particularly when boiled, would cause him or her excruciating pain. Cotton Mather noted the use of such 'Urinary Experiments' in late seventeenth-century New England, and writing in 1824, Joseph Doddridge explained that a common cure for bewitched children involved 'getting some of the child's water, which was closely corked up in a vial and hung up in a chimney'.[45] A handful of examples have been found by American archaeologists. Excavation of a long-demolished house of nineteenth-century date in Kentucky turned up an obvious case. Buried under the hearth was a bottle containing four pins, the cork was still firmly in place when found. Similarly the fragments of a wine bottle of mid-eighteenth-century date, excavated from the hearth of a house at a coastal Maryland site, contained straight and bent pins stuck in either side of the stopper. A wine bottle of around the same date containing brass pins was found near the base of a chimney in Delaware County, Pennsylvania.[46]

Plugging was another technique used to kill and cure. This involved drilling a hole in a beam or tree, placing items within it and then fitting a wooden plug to drive home the sympathetic magic. In America it was used in folk medicine to cure a range of diseases, asthma in particular. Some hair or nail clippings of the afflicted were plugged, usually into a tree but sometimes into a door jamb or post.[47] Its anti-witch potential is well described in a leather-bound manuscript of remedies and charms written down in 1784 by a South Carolina man named Joshua Gordon:

> If you are suspicious of the person that does you Hurt write their name and Sirname on a pice of paper then bore a hole in your horse trough make a pin that will Just fit the hole then put in the pice of paper into the hole and drive in the pin a little way next day drive it a little more and So on Every day till it be driven Home. All this must be dun Without any persons knowledge but yourself.[48]

There were numerous variations on this practice. When, in 1886, a carpenter named Jefferson Grimley was tearing down the cornice of a farmhouse near Schwenksville, Pennsylvania, a town with a strong ethnic German population, he came across a piece of pinewood six-and-a-half inches long whittled into the form of a cylinder. Six holes of varying diameters had been bored into the wood, three of which went all the way through. In the largest hole was a wooden pin. It transpired that the sizes of the hole corresponded to the degree of torment that the suspected witch would suffer, with the placement of the pin in the largest hole causing death. On the same farm a wooden pin was found driven into the door jamb of the plough-horses' stable. When the pin was withdrawn, some horsehair and a piece of paper with magical marks on it were found stuffed into the hole.[49] Farms and buildings changed hands over generations and the original intent of such magic could be misinterpreted. A new tenant coming across such a plug might naturally assume that the charm was *against* the farm rather than having been done to protect it. This seems to have been the false interpretation of a Pennsylvania farmer early in the twentieth century, whose stock ailed mysteriously. In one of the uprights in his barn he found a hole bored out with an auger and fitted with a wooden plug. On taking it out he found a wad of hair. After removing it, he said his fortunes improved.[50]

While plugging was a widespread practice in Europe, its use as an anti-witch remedy is absent from the British archives. So its source in America was probably German settlers considering its widespread usage amongst the Pennsylvania Dutch. It was adopted by African Americans, who developed the distinctive conjure practice of 'locking the bowels' to cause death by placing the excrement of the intended victim in the plugged hole.[51]

Warding off witchery

Attack was a good form of defence, but better to prevent the witches from working their magic in the first place. Salt was the most culturally diffuse antidote against witchcraft, in part due to its whiteness and associated symbolic purity, and in part because of its universal value as a vital substance in preserving foodstuffs and cleansing wounds. During a Pennsylvania Dutch slander suit in 1915, the plaintiff, Mary Ann Swartz, complained that the couple who accused her of witchcraft had annoyed her by employing someone to scatter salt on the chair and bench she used in the hat factory where she worked. In May 1897, a Russian storekeeper named Isaac Simon complained to the mayor of Hagerstown, Maryland, that a fellow compatriot, Solomon Saltzman, laid salt on his doorstep and pavement every morning presumably to limit his supposed malign influence. Simon feared the charm would prevent him from conducting his business.[52] Native Americans also believed in the power of salt as an antidote. A missionary writing of the Nanticoke Indians of Delaware and the Iroquois in the 1790s, observed that they believed that their poisons and witchcraft were ineffective against the Europeans because they ate so much salt in their food. The same was reported of the Choctaws. Pueblos made bundles consisting of salt from the lakes of Estancia Valley, the dried root of a plant that grew in the Jémez Mountains, and a grain of corn, which were buried under the doorsteps of houses to prevent witches and evil spirits.[53]

Salt held the same properties for African Americans, with red pepper serving a similar purpose. In 1828 an elderly African-American woman was brought before a Baltimore magistrate charged with a breach of the peace for throwing salt around the local market and conducting other spells. It was alleged she intended to bewitch the vendors and their goods, but it is more likely she was actually trying to protect the marketplace. In any case, the prosecution was dismissed as the magistrate said he knew of no law against the throwing of salt on the town's pavement.[54] Salt is now regularly thrown over urban pavements in the winter— the impact on the incidence of witchcraft is not known. For the African diaspora in the Americas salt had an added significance in that the placing of salt on the tongue was used in the conversion of slaves in the Congo. An eighteenth-century Catholic catechism used in converting slaves included the questions:

> Do you want to wash your soul with holy water?
> Do you want to eat the salt of God?
> Will you cast all the sins out of your soul?

Legends in the Caribbean relate how those who abstained from eating salt gained the ability to fly back to their African homeland. They were not tainted by a product explicitly associated with Europeans and Christianity, and so were liberated to develop ancestral spiritual powers that enabled them to reconnect with their African roots—roots that had been demonized by Christians.[55]

The power of the silver bullet has been discussed in an earlier chapter, but the metal had general anti-witch properties. African Americans wore silver dimes around their neck or more distinctively around their ankles to ward of conjure. In Illinois 'silver tea', made by boiling a silver coin in water for a long time, was given to bewitched livestock. The practice of depositing or nailing silver dimes to the bottoms of milk churns and buckets was widespread.[56] The following amusing story demonstrates how the practice could have spin-off benefits.

In 1885 the editor of the *Port Jervis Gazette*, James Juniper Shier, encountered an old woman churning milk outside her log cabin whilst he was on a walking tour in the mountains of Sullivan County, New York. He was perplexed to see the woman start beating the churn with a bundle of hazel switches. On enquiring, she confided that she was attempting to beat out the witchery: 'This h'yer churn's bewitched, an' has been fur better'n a month an' I can't make butter enough come to grease a three-inch corn cake'. This method was not proving as effective as the silver quarter (worth 25 cents) she used to put in the churn for the same purpose. Someone had stolen it about a month before though. 'I only wish I could git my quarter back', she sighed. Shier obligingly produced a quarter that the woman dropped in the churn. She then walked backward around it three times before proceeding to churn once more. 'Thar, sir. They've gone! They couldn't stand the silver', she exclaimed in satisfaction. Talking to an acquaintance later, Shier was told that he had fallen victim to a con trick. The old woman's cabin was a regular stop off for hunters and walkers, and she had pulled the same routine many times, thereby half-filling a coffee pot full of quarters. For once the tables were turned with educated credulity regarding popular superstition being exploited by a cunning rustic.[57]

Although recorded from some parts of England, the use of silver coins in churns seems to have been stronger in Ireland and Scotland. On the Isle of Skye, cows could be cured of any ailment by giving them water that had been poured over silver money or a silver ornament.[58] In Ireland, which I suspect was the main influence on the American tradition, we find cunning-folk who healed livestock using silver coins in a similar manner. An account from 1840 describes how a County Mayo cow doctor cured fairy-struck cows by making them drink a decoction of herbs in which silver three-half-pence coins had been boiled.[59] The anti-witch properties of silver were known elsewhere in European folklore, further helping cement the practice amongst non-Irish European immigrant communities.[60] It is intriguing, though, that prior to the nineteenth century there are few reference to silver as having anti-witchcraft properties. Beliefs regarding the power of iron were more widespread and of older tradition.[61]

All the peoples of America wore charms and amulets to protect against witches, evil, and misfortune more generally. Conjure bags and Native-American medicine bundles served this purpose as well as being fabricated to cause harm. As Nathaniel John Lewis, mayor of Tin City, Savannah, told an interviewer, 'cunjuh must be fought with cunjuh'.[62] One ingredient of conjure bags that had a much broader role in protection was the rabbit's foot. In sixteenth-century England it was carried as a remedy against rheumatism or cramps, and seems to have accrued anti-witch properties by the nineteenth century, although it was hardly a common charm for this purpose. It was in America that the rabbit's foot came into its own due in large part to its incorporation into the hoodoo and conjure traditions. In 1884 the Georgia politician Charles Henry Smith, who wrote newspaper articles under the name Bill Arp, reported that the wearing of rabbit's feet was widespread amongst African Americans of his acquaintance, but that it was only considered efficacious against witches if it was the hind foot of a rabbit shot in a graveyard during a full moon.[63] Around the same time it was observed that the rabbit's foot was as popular amongst poor whites in the South. It was prevalent elsewhere. When a Chicago civil engineer, E. G. Nourse, lost his rabbit's foot he advertised in the newspapers for its return. It apparently came from the left hind leg of a rabbit shot by a cross-eyed African American as it hopped over the grave of a murderer at night. They did not come much more potent than that.[64] During the early twentieth century the rabbit's foot became a popular purchase from the commercial charm manufacturers that sprung up with the booming mail order industry, with American-produced lucky rabbit's feet even being exported to England.[65]

As Charles Wisdom, an African American, sat in Missouri penitentiary awaiting his hanging for the murder in 1892 of a St Louis cigar maker named Edward Drexler, he made one last extraordinary appeal. He sent his rabbit's foot and conjure bag to the state Governor William J. Stone (1848–1918), who would later gain notoriety for voting against the USA's declaration of war against Germany in 1917. It was accompanied by the following letter:

> Dear Governor – I would like for you to do me a favour, and it will be highly appreciated – that is, providing you keep this whole matter secret and not tell any one. I inclose a rabbit foot in this letter. I want you to take it and blow on it three times and then rub it on your face, and you will have good luck the rest of your days. You will be successful in all your undertakings.
>
> You must not interfere with the little bag which you will see tied on the foot, for if you let any of it waste out you won't live 24 hours afterward, because there is conjure in this little bag. Now, I want you to do like a tell you. I know my business because I was born in Possum Bottom, near Clarksville, Tenn., and not far from Bear creek. I want you to take a hatchet and go over to the supreme courtyard and dig a little hole and put the rabbit foot in it and sprinkle in a little salt over the foot, and while sprinkling it you must say: 'Silas and Peter, Silas and Paul; the good Lord, he made us all; from ashes to ashes; from dust to dust; in the Lord I will put my trust.'
>
> And then you must cover the foot up with dirt and press it down, and after you have done so you will have to say this short prayer in my behalf: 'O merciful Lord, give the sweetness of thy comfort to thy afflicted servant, and according to thy accustomed mercy remove the heavy burden of his afflictions. Give him, I humbly beseech thee, patience in suffering, resignation to thy adorable will and perseverance in thy service.

Then everything will be all right, and I will make everything all right
with you. And you must let the rabbit foot remain buried three days and
then dig it up and send it back to me. You must be sure and do so, for if
you don't I will never have any more good luck, or you either.

It looks as though Wisdom's intention was to gain power over Stone through
conjure and thereby influence him to obtain a pardon. It was a futile plan. Wisdom
was hanged a few days later in April 1894. The last words in his letter were a dark
threat to the police: 'I will say, depart from me; I know you not. You jobbed me in
the Drexler case. Prepare for the devil and his angels. And I will cast them into hell
and give them the dirty horse laugh.'[66]

Little silver charms in the shape of an open hand, known in Arabic countries as
the Hand of Fatima, were used by immigrants from Jewish, Christian, and Muslims
communities to ward off the evil eye. A variant, the *figa*, which represents a closed
fist with the thumb placed between the first two fingers, was employed by Italian
and Portuguese Americans. It was a symbol of female sexuality and was effective
when made by the human hand to ward off the evil eye, but amulet representations were produced across the Mediterranean. They first came to America with
Spanish colonization, and archaeologists have found examples in South Carolina
and Florida. Jet and coral bracelets and necklaces, sometimes with phallic symbolism, were also employed against the evil eye in Mediterranean diaspora communities and were of equally venerable usage.[67]

The Bible was a powerful protective amulet; sleeping with it under the pillow
prevented witch-riding for instance. In 1922 a court case arising from a witch
accusation in the Slovakian community of West Pottsgrove, Montgomery Pennsylvania, brought to light another example of Bible power. Susan Gofus, aged
fifty-five, whose husband worked in the blast furnaces like many of their Hungarian, Italian, Polish, Russian, and Slovak neighbours, obtained a warrant for the
arrest of another Slovakian named Michael Warge, aged fifty-three. He accused
Gofus of causing his debilitating illness, despite the local doctor diagnosing that he
was suffering from rheumatism with complications. A neighbour named Kryder
Schwenk, a second- or third-generation Pennsylvanian, described as a huckster in
the census, but apparently a hex doctor of sorts, testified that on seeing Warge he
knew at once that he was bewitched. So he went home, took his large family
Bible, returned to Warge and placed it on his chest. Schwenk prayed loud and
long over Warge, and three days later claimed that the witchcraft had been
expelled. Rheumatism does not just go away, of course, so Warge continued to
suffer. The court ordered Warge to pay $10 in fines, and before leaving court
Warge's wife Annie was so violent in her verbal tirade against Gofus that a
constable had to intervene.[68]

The house can be understand as an expression of the human body with its entrances open to spiritual and physical pollution, assault, and intrusion. These thresholds, both physical and symbolic, were weak points and so protective devices were placed near or around them to keep out unwanted spiritual intruders, including witches.[69] Accounts from colonial and modern eras illustrate how the witch was thought to enter down the chimney, window gaps, or through key holes. So it has been suggested that the carved winged cherubs found on gateposts and above entrances in several colonial New England and South Carolina houses served a protective function.[70] Eighteenth-century German immigrants brought with them the tradition in Alpine Germany and Switzerland of carving or painting protective words and images above front doors. Examples recorded in nineteenth-century Europe include the following from the village of Ober-Schönberg, near Innsbruck: 'All persons entering this house are recommended to Divine protection. God and the Virgin Mary guard all such, even though powerful enemies threaten, and lightning and thunder rage without!' Another above a door in the village of Welschnofen, near Bozen, ran: 'Pray for us, holy Florian, that Fire may nor harm our building.' An eye was painted above the inscription, and below a depiction of St Florian pouring water on a burning roof.[71]

Around the mid-nineteenth century this discrete tradition of decorative symbolism gave rise to the various brightly coloured 'hex signs' that the Pennsylvania Dutch and other rural German communities, such as those in Ohio, painted on their barns and outbuildings. The signs include five, six, and eight-pointed stars, rosettes, representations of hearts, birds, tulips, and geometric designs familiar in other forms of German folk art, that draw heavily on spiritual symbolism. We must be historically sensitive to the purpose of this tradition though. While during the second half of the twentieth century, the 'hex signs' came to be widely interpreted by scholars and the general public as having a magical protective function, it would seem that the designs were primarily decorative in origin. A magazine reporter investigating hex signs on Ohio barns in 1950 tellingly observed, 'present owners seldom know anything about the old lore of their barn trimming. I stop at a particularly nice hexy barn and ask about the hex patterns, and the farmer—or his wife—looks at me in astonishment. They haven't the least idea what I'm talking about.'[72] The investment in paint, artistry, and time was a statement of prosperity, cultural identity, and spirituality—not of anxiety about witches.[73] The Pennsylvania Dutch had other more simple, personal, and secretive ways of protecting their homes. They did not need to plaster large charms all over their barns for all the world to see. The occult interpretation of the hex signs was a product of some folklorists peddling fanciful notions of the survival of ancient pagan sun worship, the public fascination with Pennsylvania hex matters, and the burgeoning tourist industry in Pennsylvania Dutch country.

Simple crosses were placed above doors and beds. In 1866 a Memphis resident named Mrs Alvers believed her child was bewitched, and was instructed by a witch doctor to repeat a formula while making three crosses in chalk on every door of the house. A report from Reading, PA, in 1883, stated that the offices of witch doctors in the town were marked out by protective chalk marks in the shape of crosses over the doors and windows. In the Ozarks people would hammer three nails in the form of a triangle on the outside of the door.[74] Printed or copied versions of the *Himmelsbrief* or Heaven's letter, which purported to be a message from God or Jesus that fluttered from the skies in the distant past, were kept in houses as protection against witches and misfortune. Such protective celestial letters were also popular in England and France and soldiers on both sides in the First World War kept copies in their pockets.

The belief in the anti-witch properties of the horseshoe was widespread across Europe and America.[75] One reason for its potency was because it was made of iron, and worn out horseshoes were a source of the metal that could be taken out circulation. Crescent forms also had significance. In 1828 a correspondent said that he had seen horseshoes nailed to the thresholds of houses to ward off witches during his walking tours through the woods of North Carolina. James Monroe Buckley reported in 1892 that he had seen them nailed on or above doors 'in nearly every county, and often in every township' in New England.[76] Examples can be found in the folklore records of numerous other states, and African Americans adopted the practice as well. As one Florida interviewee told the folklorist Harry Hyatt, 'Mah grandmother she used to do dat—she'd take a horseshoe. When dey put shoes on a horse—yo' know, take dose shoes off an' put new ones on, why she'd take dose shoes an' put one ovah her front door an' one over her back door; every do' she had yo' know, an' 'nother one right at de doorstep dere at de right corner.'[77] A broom placed on the floor behind the front door served the same purpose in European and African-American communities. Witches were unable to step over a broom, and the widespread European tradition that married couples complete their vows by jumping over a broom probably relates to the same apotropaic tradition.[78]

We should not consider all such magical practices as timeless and static. There was always room for adaptation and invention when it came to dealing with witches. The most striking example of this was reported from La Plaisance Creek, Michigan, in 1879. A German family who believed that their livestock and dairy produce was bewitched spent $200 on different witch doctors to no avail. They tried other anti-witchcraft measures in vain. Then a neighbour suggested frightening the suspected witch away with a 'witch killer'. This consisted of a bull's head stripped of skin and stuck on a ten-foot-high pole. A horseshoe was attached to the tip of each horn and an ear of wheat placed crossways in its jaws.

Fastened below this macabre object was a board bearing the words 'This is a witch-killer'. It worked, apparently.[79]

Cumulative research in England has confirmed that the secretion of mundane objects such as shoes, dead cats, implements, and items of clothing in walls and around thresholds clearly had an apotropaic or protective function, warding off evil and misfortune. Recent work in Australia shows that these building rituals were brought there by migrants, and excavations are beginning to confirm the same in European-American contexts. There is some meagre evidence from the colonial period, with, for example, the horseshoe and iron eel-spear trident found underneath original weatherboarding of the Danvers house of the late seventeenth-century Massachusetts gentleman, Zerubabbel Endicott. They were secreted in tell-tale locations associated with the chimney and front door.[80] Substantial evidence is beginning to be recorded from modern-era sites. During recent renovation work on the Indiana Statehouse, a late nineteenth-century shoe was found buried under the floorboards in front of a window, and during the 1904 construction of a barracks at Fort Rosecrans, San Diego, a boot was deliberately deposited behind a brick chimney. Iron hoe-blades have been found located in floor joists near a chimney stack of a house in Sussex County, New Jersey, and in a pit outside the door of a cabin in Calvert County, Maryland, occupied during the late nineteenth and early twentieth centuries.[81] Quartz stones have also been found deposited in similar locations in African-American buildings. Two Virginia excavations revealed quartz crystals near the footings of chimneys in nineteenth-century slave quarters. A large crystal was found near the doorway of a building in Maryland that probably housed slaves or servants. Some deposits could be interpreted as being harmful rather than protective. Consider, for example, a cache of nineteenth-century objects found under a door sill at Slayton House, Annapolis, Maryland, that consisted of nine pins (a number of great magical significance), a crab claw, and a blue bead. Compare this find with the examples of cursing conjure balls placed on or in buildings as related in the previous chapter, and the purpose of the deposit becomes ambiguous. What is important is that archaeologists have become more sensitive to the possible ritual meaning of what, in the past, they might have considered mere household detritus, and hopefully new discoveries will help us decode these domestic rituals of the past.[82]

Written charms

Witch doctors drove a thriving trade in producing written apotropaic charms for concealment around farmyards and homes. John Keckler, a Waynesboro hex doctor, laid 'seals' around his clients and their property. These consisted of small muslin bags containing, as he told a court in 1918, the first verse of the thirty-fifth psalm—'... any cause, O Lord with them that strive with me'. 'If you write a Psalm and put it in the barn', he explained, 'it is good for all the stock in the building.'[83] In 1892 a newspaper reported that Swedish and German farmers near Riegelsville, Pennsylvania, warded off witches by writing these characters '†xJxNxRxYx†' on small strips of paper with red ink, which they then placed above every gate and door on their premises.[84] This was a variant or misspelling of the formula INRI or JNRJ, an acronym of 'Jesus of Nazareth, King [Rex] of the Jews', found widely in Christian iconography, and used in protective magic.

The three main sources of inspiration for the signs and texts in these written charms were the Bible and the print and manuscript copies of two magic books of German origin.[85] One was the *Sixth and Seventh Books of Moses*, which claimed to reveal the secret wisdom God transmitted to Moses but that had been deliberately withheld by Jewish and Christian authorities when formalizing the Torah and Old Testament. Various manuscripts with this title circulated in eighteenth-century Germany and several were printed by a Stuttgart antiquarian in the 1840s. One of these was reprinted in German by a Pennsylvania publisher in the 1860s and an English translation followed a decade or so later. New legends formed regarding the *Sixth and Seventh Books of Moses*. In Pennsylvania in the 1890s it was reported that the original was buried somewhere in the Blue Mountains.[86] The published edition included a series of psalms and seals containing spurious Hebraic characters. So Psalm 10 was for those 'plagued with an unclean, restless, and evil spirit', while Psalm 48 was recommended for those who 'have many enemies without cause, who hate you out of pure envy'.

John George Hohman's *Der lang verborgene Freund* was the other key source of protective charms in America. First published in Reading, Pennsylvania, in 1820, further editions were produced over the next few decades, and English versions began to appear entitled *The Long Lost Friend* or *Long Hidden Friend*. It dealt more explicitly with the problem of witchcraft, and contained several helpful charms. The ancient word square

SATOR
AREPO
TENET
OPERA
ROTAS

was recommended for bewitched cattle, and was administered by writing it on paper and putting it in their feed. This might explain the actions of a hex doctor who treated Sarah Kochert's infant daughter in 1883 by giving her a strip of paper to put around the child's breast, and bits of paper in molasses which she was to feed the child.[87] A long blessing through the power of God was given 'to relieve persons or animals after being bewitched'. The formula JRNRJ (Jesus King of Nazareth King of the Jews) was provided to protect houses against sickness, while the following formula written on a piece of white paper was 'against evil spirits and all manner of witchcraft':

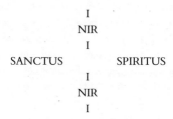

I

NIR

I

SANCTUS   SPIRITUS

I

NIR

I

The *Long Lost Friend* was also the source of the charm below, which was found in an antique sofa purchased by a second-hand dealer in Berks County. One copy was slipped under the top layer of the upholstery of each of the arms. It was written backwards in German, the inversion being integral to its magic:

> Trottenkopf, I, [name of possessor], forbid thee my house and my court-
> yard; I forbid thee my bedstead so that thou wilt not 'trot' over me, [name],
> into another house; and climb over all mountains and fenceposts and over
> all waters. Then the good day will come back into my house. In the name
> of God the Father, God the Son, and God the Holy Ghost. Amen.[88]

The charm was 'to prevent Witches from bewitching Cattle, to be written and placed in the stable; and against Bad Men and Evil Spirits, which nightly torment old and young people, to be written and placed on the bedstead.' Back in Germany the original purpose of the charm was specifically for preventing the nightmare. *Trotten Kopf* derives from the southern German dialect word *Drudenkopf* to describe a 'pressing' elf or spirit. Another German book of charms published in nineteenth-century America, *Albertus Magnus's Egyptian Secrets*, from which derived some of the formulae in the *Long Lost Friend*, included a similar but longer version of the charm, though this time adjuring the *Bettzaierle*, a south-western German term for a nightmare.[89] The English version of *Long Lost Friend* was clearly done without knowledge of the original purpose of the charm, with 'Trotter Kopf' being translated meaninglessly as 'Trotter Head, I forbid thee my house and premises...'.

The Berks County furniture dealer who found the above example, said he frequently came across similar charms in couches, beds, and sofas, and it is highly likely that the one above was written by one of the most successful hex doctors in the region, Dr Hageman of Reading. As will be related in a later chapter, Hage-man's trade was exposed during a libel trial in 1903, during which one of his charms was produced in evidence. It was a version of the Trottenkopf verse written backwards, and in court a translator used a mirror to invert the writing so he could read it to the court.

During the early twentieth century both the *Sixth and Seventh Books of Moses* and the *Long Lost Friend* were published in cheap, pulp paperback formats in their tens of thousands. Their influence spread far beyond the Pennsylvania Dutch, with the *Sixth and Seventh Books of Moses* becoming a key source in hoodoo and conjure. Editions of the latter, along with other compilations of magic and mysticism sold by enterprising American mail-order occult companies, most notably the Delaurence Company of Chicago, would have a major influence on the magical and religious cultures of the Caribbean and parts of West Africa.[90]

Catholic armoury

The religious census of 1890 revealed that there were just over seven million Catholics in America, compared to a total of 15 million Baptists, Methodists, and Presbyterians. Then the substantial Hispanic, Irish, and German Catholic population was joined by the surge of Polish and Italian immigrants over the next few decades. So by 1916 there were nearly sixteen million Catholics, some sixteen per cent of the population. The 1890 statistic came as a shock to the Catholic Church, as it had been assumed that there were millions more. This was because the statistics bandied about in the nineteenth century were wildly inaccurate as they were usually based on the false assumption that all Irish, Italians, Poles, French, and Belgians were practising Catholics.[91]

The reciting of the Catholic Creed, Ave Marias, Hail Mary's, and Our Fathers were all common components of healing charms. In Mexican-American belief, exclaiming 'Madre de Dios!' (Mother of God) had the power to break spells. The sick could also invoke and worship the many saints in Catholic popular religion for both cure and protection from witches. Making the sign of the cross was a potent anti-witchcraft charm. Amongst Texan Mexicans, a cure for the evil eye involved forcing the person who cast it to spit on his or her thumbs and make the sign of the cross on the victim's forehead, and then on either side of the head behind the eyes.[92] Holy water was a venerable weapon. A French priest travelling in the United States during the 1870s observed that it was particularly important in Irish devotional life, and reported a case where it miraculously cured an Irishman of cholera.[93] In 1872 Mr and Mrs Joseph Gutzweiler, a Swiss-German couple from Buffalo in their fifties, told police through an interpreter about their suffering from witchcraft. The witches tormented them at night calling them vile and filthy names. When police visited their apartment at 426 Hickory Street, Mrs Gutzweiler held in her hands a well-worn book of Catholic devotions in large Gothic type. She showed the police a bottle of holy water and a small Catholic medal obtained from a missionary at St Michael's church, Washington Street, that they hoped would see off their tormentors, but they did not. Catholics in the Rio Grande similarly wore medals dedicated to San Benito to ward of witchcraft.[94]

A wealthy Belgian, Father Suitbert Mollinger (1828–1892), was the most successful purveyor of Catholic cure and protection in late nineteenth-century America. He settled in Pittsburgh in the 1860s to work amongst the large German-speaking population in the city, and in 1868 became the first pastor of the Most Holy Name of Jesus Roman Catholic church in Troy Hill.[95] He was an avid collector of relics, employing agents in Europe to seek out and purchase any that came on the market. He paid for the building of a new chapel dedicated to St Anthony of Padua across the street from the church. It opened in 1882, one of eleven pilgrimage shrines created in the United States by that time, and housed the thousands of relics he had collected. It is said that the chapel contains the largest collection of relics outside the Vatican. Amongst its amazing treasures are fabric from the Virgin Mary's veil, a thorn from the Crown of Thorns, splinters from the True Cross, and the skeleton of Saint Demetrius. No wonder people flocked to Troy Hill to visit the chapel in search of spiritual succour.

Father Mollinger accrued a reputation for miraculous cures, attracting considerable attention in the American medical press. He had studied medicine at university, and his name was given to a popular patent medicine that brought in revenue long after his death.[96] But people went on pilgrimage to his church for the potency of his blessings and spiritual healing power. St Anthony's day, 13 June, was the peak in the calendar with thousands flocking to the chapel from hundreds of miles around, and even from abroad. On such days the streetcars were so packed with invalids that they were known locally as ambulances. In June 1891 it was reported in the press that Mollinger's blessing had even cured a disabled fifteen-year-old boy named Martin Lavin, of Somerset, Niagara County, who had been unable to walk since childhood.[97] Mollinger made no charge for his healing work but thousands of dollars in donations were placed in a basket at the side of the altar. We shall see in a later chapter how a bewitched German made his way to Pittsburgh to be blessed by Mollinger.

The Catholic clergy were reluctant to get involved in dealing with witches or witchcraft, and some actively tried to disabuse their flock of the existence of witches in their communities. But the priesthood was comfortable with employing their most potent weapons—blessings and exorcisms—in cases of bodily possession and hauntings; in other words, supernatural assaults that could be attributed directly to the Devil or his minions rather than human intermediaries. In 1904 Monsignor Michael J. Lavelle, Rector of St Patrick's cathedral, New

York, expressed the opinion that people had been and still could be possessed by evil spirits: 'Whether there are any instances at present I do not know. None has ever come to my personal notice. But that the Church recognizes the possibility is evidenced by the rules prepared for exorcising.'[98] While Lavelle had never been approached to deal with evil spirits, in 1901 Father Westharp of St Alphonso's German Catholic church, Lemont, Illinois, paid visits to a German farmer named Seraphim Wilming to rest the troublesome spirits that plagued his farm by making loud noises and moving objects. Three times Westharp returned to bless the house and its grounds, all to no effect. The phenomena were finally revealed to be a hoax perpetrated on Wilming by a man who held a grudge against him.[99]

Not a few of the many thousands who flocked to Mollinger and his fellow priests were Protestants desperate for help. So it was that in 1886 Father Peter Becker, of Holy Trinity church, Woodland Avenue, Cleveland, was called to attend to a middle-aged, Protestant, German woman who believed she was possessed. The church, and Becker's clerical position, had been established only a few years before to serve the swelling German population in the city.[100] The widow lived with her son-in-law and daughter in a cul-de-sac off Madison Avenue. Her husband had died some years earlier, a victim of possession, they believed. The evil spirit of a witch who many years before had bewitched the couple's pigs, transferred itself to the man on the witch's death. On his demise it moved to his wife. She suffered from palpitations, her brain seemed as though it was on fire, while the blood in her veins felt freezing. Father Becker was called in and brought with him a Jesuit priest and a Dominican monk. They held a crucifix before her eyes and went through a rite of exorcism. The woman writhed in agony but felt no relief after. Becker concluded that she was not possessed but suffering from 'religious mania'. He requested that the woman's family not discuss religious matters with her and called in two physicians instead.

When the woman's family came to hear of the amazing cures of Father Mollinger they resolved to take her to him. In July she went to stay with a Troy Hill resident named John Hock. Mollinger paid a visit the next day and placed a medallion containing the bust of St Anthony around her neck. She tried to tear it off and suffered terrible agonies that night. Mollinger returned with some nuns and exorcised her, but found it impossible to feed her holy water, so they secretly put some in her coffee. Still she struggled violently, until she was taken to the Most Holy Name of Jesus church, where a special service was held for her in the presence of the holy relics. The accumulative power of Catholic armaments finally had the desired effect and the woman returned to Cleveland apparently cured.[101] The Catholic Church's role in healing in urban America was further reinforced with the large-scale immigration of Italians during the late nineteenth and early twentieth centuries. The sanctuary of Our Lady of Mount Carmel in 115th Street,

Harlem, New York, became an important focus, for example, with thousands resorting to its statue of the Madonna to heal them of mundane and supernatural ailments such as the *malocchio*.[102]

Bringing in the experts

The reader has already encountered a range of characters who offered to heal the bewitched: medicine men and women, cunning-folk, hex doctors, conjure and hoodoo doctors, wise women, fortune-tellers, root doctors, trick doctors, pow-wows, quacks, mesmeric healers and others, who drove a thriving trade in every part of the country. It is time to explore their world in more detail, for they were usually involved at some point in the many witchcraft disputes discussed in this book.

Nineteenth-century America teamed with people who called themselves 'Doctor' but had no formal medical training. The rewards were meagre for some, but others accrued wealth far beyond the modest lot of the trained medical man. Joseph Doddridge, who like many clergymen of the time also practised medicine for his flock, observed in 1824 that during his sojourns in Pennsylvania, Virginia, and Ohio he had 'known several of those witch masters, as they were called, who made a public profession of curing the diseases inflicted by the influence of witches, and I have known respectable physicians who had no greater portion of business in the line of their profession than many of those witch masters had in theirs'.[103] In general, they were usually literate, and the men often artisans, craftsmen, and tradesmen. If we take a look at Pennsylvania hex doctors we find bricklayers, masons, and farmers amongst them. The Allentown hex doctor Nathan Flickinger, who died in 1916 aged sixty-eight, had been a photographer and insurance salesman.[104] A substantial minority of witch doctors were female, with the magic and healing trade providing good opportunities for single, independent women. The ethnic make-up of practitioners was diverse. An analysis of eighty magical healers and fortune-tellers in New England in the period 1644–1850 revealed that nearly half were African American, Native American, or of mixed ancestry.[105] There seems to have been a considerable degree of interethnic consultation with African Americans consulting European hex doctors, and whites seeking out black root and conjure doctors. Irish and British visited German practitioners and vice versa. In fact, the witch doctors played a crucial role in the transmission of magical ideas and practices from one cultural group to another. People often consulted several different practitioners when bewitched, and based their choice on reputation and proximity. That said, hoodoo and conjure doctors were often sought out by whites because they were thought to possess outsider knowledge unavailable to Europeans, likewise the numerous Chinese fortune-tellers who plied their trade along the Western seaboard, and the small number of itinerant gypsy practitioners.

As to the sources of their power, some practitioners claimed a God-given birth-right, such as being a seventh son of a seventh son or seventh daughter of a seventh daughter. In 1769 one Dr Isaac Calcott landed in Providence claiming to be a German recently arrived from London. He advertised that he possessed the 'art' of curing a wide range of conditions thanks to being a seventh son of a seventh son. He achieved considerable notoriety over the next few years.[106] This European tradition also spread to African-American conjure. A black healer named T. Edwards took to advertising in 1860 in the same way as Calcott a century before. His flyer explained that he was 'naturally a Doctor—having a gift from the Lord. My mother was her mother's seventh daughter, and, I am her seventh son; my father was a seventh son, and I am his seventh son.' He further claimed to have been born with seven cauls—the caul or amniotic sac being known in European and West African belief as conferring healing, divinatory, or spiritual powers on its possessor.[107] In the conjure tradition the possession of some potent artefact such as a ritually obtained black cat bone, root, magnetic lodestone, or the accumulated objects in a conjure bag, were viewed as key means of obtaining magical powers over others.

Access to literary sources of magic was another valuable asset, more so for European-American practitioners at first, but by the late nineteenth century, books, including the Bible, had also become important items in conjure. We have already heard of the *Long Lost Friend* and *Sixth and Seventh Books of Moses*, but other titles circulated in much more limited numbers. Knowledge of the French arsenal of cheap grimoires that were printed in their tens of thousands during the eighteenth and nineteenth centuries found their way to America via French Canadians who emigrated south. The ritual of the *Poule noir* or Black Hen to obtain riches, which was included in several French grimoires, was recounted to the folklorist Richard Dorson by members of the French-Canadian logging community in the Upper Peninsula, Michigan. One man remembered how fifty-four years earlier he knew a hotel proprietor in Escanaba, one of the largest towns in the Upper Peninsula, who possessed a copy of the notorious *Dragon rouge*, or *Red Dragon*: 'One day I went up into his room, I saw this book there. It was written in red, as if with blood . . . . It gave me a fright. I started to read the book; I could not make it out!'[108]

The 'new' powers of mesmerism and hypnotism opened novel avenues for combating witches, and generated a breed of often itinerant mesmerists who were willing to apply their magnetic powers to identify and deal with witchcraft as well as mundane conditions. In 1843 the thirteen-year-old daughter of Absolom

Lawrence, of Pepperell, Massachusetts, was afflicted with terrible fits. Her knees were drawn to her chest, her head was thrown backward, her jaws locked, and she could not swallow anything but a little liquid sucked from a cloth. There were other tell-tale problems. Groaning noises were heard, and the pots and pans in the house banged inexplicably. The family's butter would not come. Witchcraft was suspected. A wandering magnetizer named Dr J. M. Nevens, who advertised in the press that through his magnetized lady companion he could cure 'all complaints that the human frame is subject to', was hired to investigate. Nevens magnetized his companion, who in her trance state saw the spirit of a woman approach the house on an un-shod white horse, then dismount, and enter through a crack under the door. Because of the presence of Nevens magnetic power, said the somnambu-list, the supposed witch did not stay long, leaving via the cellar, groaning and stamping on the stairs in frustration. As a 'doctor', a practitioner of a science, Nevens professed his scepticism about witchcraft, but one suspects that he profited from involvement in such cases, spinning one story to the press and another to his bewitched clients. The girl improved once Lawrence removed his family to another property.[109]

Creating an aura of mystique was important for building a clientele. In the 1880s a distinguished Cincinnati medicine man, an African American who claimed descent from a Native-American tribe, had a distinctive coiffure with a twisted goatee, and wore a scarf baring magical medals. His consultation room at Broad-way and New Street was decked to impress, with two-headed chickens in alcohol jars, and preserved snakes he boasted he had cast out of patients' bodies. But many practitioners relied less on looks and decor and concentrated more on impressing through their arcane rituals in the field. In 1824 one Dr Scoby made a considerable impression on a melancholic Irishman of Exeter County, New Hampshire, who believed he was a victim of witchcraft. The doors and windows of the man's apartment were closed, and then Scoby drew about a quart of blood from him which was then burned over a fire. This proved successful and Scoby was paid nine dollars.[110] In 1883, a peddler and witchdoctor named Armstrong McClain, who operated in the remote Pennsylvania region of Stony Creek Valley, was called in to cure the bewitched daughter of William Kildey. She exhibited symptoms of possession, babbling incoherently in the German tongue, a language she did not speak. This led to an old German woman being accused. McClain began by burning a black, a white, and a brown hair on a shovel. He inspected the ashes and then 'pow-wowed' them. 'If you don't meet a brindle cow on your way home', he told Kildey, who was a river pilot on the Susquehanna, 'sprinkle that ash on the door sill. At sundown the witch's power over your daughter will be broken.' Kildey did not meet a brindle cow, and so sprinkled the ashes as instructed, but to no effect. McClain returned and proceeded to Plan B. He brought some 'snaky looking roots' with him and ordered one of Kildey's daughters to take the first bottle she could from a cupboard while holding her breath. He put the roots in the bottle along with some water, and sprinkled in some white powder while murmuring a charm. He then asked for a hammer, took it, and went outside with the bottle for fifteen minutes. He returned with the hammer and sat at the sick girl's bedside. 'Now I'll kill the witch, old Mrs Boyer!' he exclaimed, before gentle tapping the girl's temple three times with the hammer and then throwing it outside. The witch would die in seven months he said confidently. In the meantime Mrs Boyer's husband and son dealt with McLain the German way and had him arrested for defamation.[111]

Compare McClain's showy series of treatments with the limp, lacklustre rituals of Jacob Shuck, another Pennsylvania hex doctor whose schtick was insufficiently impressive to garner either respect or fear. Nicholas S. Adams of Shamokin, Northumberland County, paid Shuck $1.50 to cure his sick daughter of witchcraft. Shuck merely waved his hand in the air, drew them over the girl's face, and stroked her hair with what he said was the magic palm of his right hand. No improvement was detected and Shuck refused to reimburse Adams. Another dissatisfied client, William Dietrich, related in court that Shuck treated two bewitched cows by stroking their hind legs and tickling their ears, presumably with his magic palm. The cows grew frisky for a bit but when they settled down they were no better. No wonder Dietrich wanted his $4 back.[112]

Proficiency in sleight-of-hand trickery was a useful skill. We have seen this with regard to the cure of witch intrusions. Similar craftiness was almost certainly involved in extracting pillow witches, as in an instance from New Albany, Indiana, in 1871. A woman, who would appear to have suffered from dropsy or oedema in the legs, but who believed she was bewitched, called in a witch doctor named Anderson. He visited and slashed her pillows open. 'Why, he got some beautiful little fans, some of the feathers were sewed up in knots, several cloth cats, just as perfect as live animals, and bunches of hair sewed together in different forms', she said. As the journalist who recorded this conversation suggested, it seems that the good Doctor had introduced the cloth cats and other items during his bedroom investigations.[113]

While witch doctors were instrumental in the process of identifying witches, for the sake of their communal reputations and with possible legal consequences in mind, they were generally very careful not to name people explicitly. Armstrong McClain's downfall is a case in point. Part of their art was to use insinuations or divinatory rituals that led clients to confirm their own suspicions. When in 1883 a witch doctor came to see the sick child of Scranton resident Sarah Kochert, she told him that the neighbour she suspected, Mrs Snyder, had asked her, 'What is the witch doctor doing here?' He sagely told Kockert,

'When you tread on a dog's tail he howls.'[114] The implication was clear. In the same year a butcher's wife named Mrs Malinda Balthazar, of 82 Elm Street, Reading, PA, told a journalist about her consultation with a local witch doctor regarding her bewitched son:

> 'I sent for a witch doctor, who as soon as he saw the child said he knew what was the matter with it – "bad people"'. 'I was not surprised', she said, 'as I had suspected this to be the cause. The doctor said that several persons were concerned in it, but that this one woman was the leader of them, and she would bring something to present me, but under no circumstances should I accept it, as that would give her a fresh hold on the child ... He described the woman who would call, and I immediately recognized her as the same woman who had come and admired and kissed the child when it was only a few days old'.[115]

And so another innocent woman ended up ostracized.

Newspapers considered themselves beacons of enlightened thought, regularly reporting instances of superstition and popular credulity to remind educators, clergy, and the authorities that more needed to be done to combat such beliefs. Yet in a cut-throat business they were willing to accept the advertising revenue generated from astrologers, quacks, and magical healers seeking to drum up new clients. Press advertising was of particular importance to itinerant practitioners who moved from town to town, staying for weeks and months, moving on before the authorities took an interest or the number of unsatisfied clients achieved critical mass. The following three adverts from just one 1861 edition of the *Sun*, a Maryland newspaper, demonstrate the wide range of practitioner styles and practices.[116] First there was the Germanic Dr Samuel Funterbaugh:

> The most wonderful Astrologist and phrenologist in the world, can now be found at his residence, No 7 FOUNTAIN ST., between Alexander and Fleet sts. He uses all kind of Witchcraft and Conjuring; cures all diseases and spells; does anything wished for by the Ladies and Gentlemen; and anything that is stolen or lost returned by witchcraft or conjuring, or describe the person that does anything, and give any person love that wants it.

Then there was the African-sounding R. Deeyou:

> *Herb Doctor and Scientific and Reliable Egyptian Astrologer*, 9 SOUTH GREEN ST. The suffering in body and mind will do well to call. Lowest fee 50 cts. No trickery, cards or humbuggery resorted to. Drunkenness positively cured.

Finally, Hispanic Madame Marientes:

> NO HUMBUG. – Those who wish to know all affairs of late correctly should not fail to call on MADAME MARIENTES. She can bring together those separated, and cause love to be mutual where it does not exist. Consultation hours from 10 A.M. to 5 P.M. No 290 N. GAY ST.

During the mid-nineteenth century the press's hypocritical role in condemning and yet promoting the occult arts was subjected to repeated attack. Writing under the nom de plume Q. K. Philander Doesticks, the gifted humorist and journalist Mortimer Thomson, a former actor and jewellery salesman, campaigned against slavery and humbuggery. In 1859 he wrote a book investigating and demolishing the 'Witches of New York'. By witches he meant the multitude of fortune-tellers, clairvoyants, and astrologers who advertised in the newspapers, and who, with some justification, he linked to the city's underworld of abortionists and brothels. 'It is to be desired that the day may come when they will be no longer classed with harmless mountebanks, but with dangerous criminals', he wrote.[117]

The American medical profession was also understandably sensitive about this plague of competing doctors. While there was an obvious and clear boundary between a licensed physician and an unlicensed healer in official terms, from a popular perspective there was often little difference with regard to the efficacy of their respective treatments. As well as charms and rituals, many witch doctors employed the same drugs and herbs as their official competitors. From a popular perspective, then, the distinction between orthodox general practitioners and unofficial healers was far from obvious, particularly as many of the latter were listed in trade directories as physicians, and operated like licensed doctors with nameplates on their doors, fixed consultation hours, and regular surgeries in different settlements. Dr Andrew Hoff of 818 North Park Avenue Alliance, Ohio, is a good example. Listed in the 1900 census as a 'physician', who would know from this that he was not a licensed doctor and was, in fact, as described in 1893, 'the best witchfinder in Eastern Ohio'? We know all about his trade from his exposure in the press in the 1890s as a result of his involvement in a witchcraft dispute. Hoff (b. 1815), whose parents and wife were Swiss, was open in his belief in the power of witchcraft, and bold enough to name suspected witches. Yet he was a regular customer at an Alliance apothecary shop, whose proprietor had no problem with servicing his requirements and noted approvingly that Hoff seemed to have a thriving business.[118] The history of another German 'Doctor' listed in the trade directories as a physician shows how such people operated openly and with a considerable degree of impunity despite laws against both unlicensed medical practice and the pretence to magic.

Franz Bacher was born in Forst, a town in Karlsruhe district, western Germany, in 1828. He arrived in America as a young man, claiming to have a medical diploma from Heidelberg University. He began practising medicine in New Orleans, and then moved to St Louis until the outbreak of the Civil War. After a spell in the Home Guards he spent the next few years as a travelling medicine man before finally settling at 327 Maine Street, Quincy, Illinois. Here he developed a reputation as a cancer curer, using a special herb plaster. In 1888 he became entangled in a public legal dispute with a dissatisfied cancer patient. The press stirred things up and Bacher wrote to the *Quincy Daily Journal* defending his medical probity, claiming he had successfully cured fifty cases of cancer in the last twelve years. So far in this history there is no hint of any magical practices, and no suspicion was cast on his medical training—at least in the press. His presence clearly irritated licensed physicians in the area however, and in 1901 the State Medical Society brought a charge against him for practising medicine without a licence. Someone did not do their homework though, because the law only applied to people practising after the 1 July 1899, and Bacher had been plying his trade in Quincy for a quarter of a century. The jury found him not guilty. Various appeals were launched and the case rumbled on for another year, eventually concluding in Bacher's favour.

Then, in 1904, Bacher's witch-doctoring business was exposed after a nineteen-year-old client, Bessie Bement, committed suicide. Bement had visited his house in Broadway, Quincy, a small one-storey building with a large sign outside bearing the words 'Dr Franz Bacher'. He confirmed that she was bewitched and provided her with a steel belt one inch in width on which she was to sprinkle some powder he gave her. He also advised her to check her pillow. As he related in a public statement written by his nephew and student William Knopfmeier, and printed in the press:

> In the case of Bessie Bement it now is stated that she was not entirely personally responsible for her deed of self-destruction. It is stated by Dr. F. Bacher that Miss Bement applied to him for advice as she thought she was bewitched. Dr Bacher told her to examine her pillow. She did so and found a reeth in it, a combination of string with feathers attached to it. Dr. Bacher told her to burn it, which she did, as far as known. It is stated that she was mostly downcast, and acted as though she was not entirely responsible for such a deed as to commit suicide. Miss Bement received some medicine from Dr. Bacher after which he heard nothing from Miss Bement until he seen the notice in the Whig that Miss Bement had committed Suicide.

The authorities investigated to see whether any charge could be laid against the now elderly Bacher. He, meanwhile, decided to give an interview at his home to a local journalist in which he spoke openly about his dealings with witchcraft. 'Are you both an M. D. and a hoodoo doctor?' the journalist asked. Bacher replied,

> Don't call me a hoodoo doctor please. I have been practising medicine since 1873, and I know when a person is suffering from a visitation of a hoodoo or bewitchery. But don't say anything about that in your paper, for people are skeptical and many only laugh when we claim what we can do. I know it is for real though. Why it is bewitchery that fills our insane asylums – poor people there suffering and pining away because their physicians doctor them for something else, when they are under the spell of some hoodoo. I believe in medicine, but only a very little of it.

Despite the State Medical Board's campaign against Bacher, he was never black-listed and the *Illinois Medical Journal* noted his death stating that he was an 'M. D., Heidelberg, Germany'. The death of his wife in 1913 was considered newsworthy. Their nephew Knopfmeier does not seem to have stuck with the business, though. He was drafted during the First World War and then settled into a number of mundane desk jobs. This is no indication that the hex doctoring business was in decline: early twentieth-century America was still full of witch believers.[119]

DEALING WITH WITCH BELIEVERS

Writing in 1883, the Illinois historian William Henry Perrin blamed the widespread belief in witchcraft on the fireside stories that made children's hair stand on end 'like quills upon the fretted porcupine'. He believed the notion was a major retardant to the development of the United States. It had 'done far more to beat back the cause of civilization among the common people than could all the swarms of greenhead flies, the murderous Indians, the poisonous snakes and wild beasts, the deadly malaria, disease and poverty.'[1] How could it be combatted? As in Europe, confidence was placed in the expansion of public schooling, much of it provided by religious denominations. The oft-repeated British refrain 'the schoolmaster is abroad' was no less uttered across the Atlantic. Literacy rates in America were certainly impressive compared with much of Europe. The 1850 census indicates that 90 per cent of white Americans were literate, compared to 50–60 per cent in England, for example. Such figures mask a great deal of regional, ethnic, class. and gender variations of course, which in turn fuelled the view that certain social groups such as backwoods folk and African Americans were more superstitious than other because they were less educated.[2] The newspapers reinforced this view, promoting their own influence in shaping a godly but rational America. So in 1831 the editor of the *Baltimore Patriot* explained the enlightening benefits of the press on the nation's youth: 'it habituates their minds to reading and its consequences, in place of talking about ghosts and witches, attending frolics, swearing and lying.'[3]

The medical profession had a vested interest in the fight, for it saw 'superstition' as nourishing the myriad unlicensed healers with whom they competed. In the first volume of the *American Journal of Dental Science* printed in 1839, the secretary of the publishing committee urged: 'Send the school master still more abroad in the land; but more especially, let medical men and their public lecturers expose the folly and the madness of entrusting human life to the secret spells of alchemy and witch-craft.'[4] The presence of witchcraft beliefs became a barometer of the success or otherwise of the education mission. The *Maryland and Virginia Medical Journal* gave poor marks in 1859, complaining that the multitude of quacks and astrologers did not 'say overmuch for the lessons taught by the schoolmaster, who has now for some time had the credit of being abroad'.[5]

The rise of spiritualism provided both a further challenge and a boost to those rationalizers who viewed scientific advancement as inimical to supernatural beliefs. As we have seen, some mesmerists saw their pseudo-scientific discoveries as erasing the 'super' from supernatural. Stage magicians travelled the country debunking mediumship, putting nails in the coffins of the dead through demonstrating the illusions that they believed upheld the belief in the spirit world. A few months after accounts of the Fox Sisters' shenanigans began to circulate, the people of Wash-ington DC were agog at the antics of a young married woman whose convulsions and urge to swallow pins, often plucked from the clothing of visitors, were considered by some neighbours as the work of witchcraft. People flocked to see the wonder, apparently paying a dollar for access to the sick bed. Most of the city's doctors had examined her, but no cure could be found. Step forward Charles Grafton Page (1812–1868), physician and pioneering inventor of electromagnetic motors, who at the time was an examiner at the Washington Patent Office and a Professor of Chemistry. Page caught the woman out simulating the swallowing of pins and denounced her imposture in the local press. He recounted his experience a few years later:

> Knowing that the witches of old had a special fancy for pins, and fully prepared to see nothing more than a dextrous feat of legerdemain, we consented to go, late as it was, and as soon as the pretty little elf, who was lying upon a pallet upon the floor, had become convulsed, and pulled a pin from our person, and swallowed it, we discovered the *quomodò*, and the next day, with a little practice, we were able to go into very fair convulsions, and could draw out pins and swallow them as skilfully as the witch herself.[6]

Page went on to conduct a series of tests upon the Fox sisters and other mediums to expose their fraudulent methods.

Reporting on a case of witchcraft abuse amongst Germans in Hancock County, Illinois, in 1889, the *Daily Inter Ocean* stated its view that the local authorities needed to be proactive. 'The State's Attorney of Hancock County has a novel but plain duty to perform', it advised, 'and there should be no hesitation in doing all that prudence may suggest as necessary to make it understood by all whom it may concern that punishing witches or exorcising devils cannot be practiced with impunity anywhere in the State of Illinois.'[7] Attorneys and magistrates could not do much as they usually dealt with the consequences of such actions. Large fines and prison sentences were not effective deterrents either. At street level it was the police who were often responsible for dealing with disputes before they turned nasty. They were, as the English police of the period have been described, 'domestic missionaries', charged with controlling and suppressing what the authorities viewed as the vice, sloth, and prejudice prevalent on the streets of rapidly expanding cities. So, in December 1920, police had to guard the home of an elderly Italian woman in the Italian quarter of Ellwood City, Pennsylvania, because of the threats she was receiving from neighbours after a peddler of a protective charm, known as the 'paper of the enchanted crosses', spread rumours she was a witch after she had refused to purchase one.[8]

At eleven o'clock one night in March 1883 Michael Schaffler, a labourer from Prussia, entered the Bremen Street Police Station, Cincinnati.[9] With him were his wife Gottliebe, his eighteen-year-old son Frederic, a foundry worker, their teen-age daughter Caroline, and two young boys August and William. All but the six-year-old William had been born in Prussia. In broken English mixed with German, Michael told Lieutenant Westendorf that their lodgings were haunted and requested that they be allowed to spend the night in the police station. Westendorf replied matter-of-factly, 'The police have nothing to do with ghosts.' Michael explained further that witchcraft was behind the supernatural disturbance and they suspected that one Frau Lindecker, a fortune-teller and petty healer, was the witch responsible. Getting into the spirit of things, Sergeant Austin was detailed to investigate the goings on at the Schafflers home. So with a rabble of journalists in tow, who had been hanging around the station kicking their heels waiting for a good story, Austin and Frederic ventured into the night and made their way to 108 Liberty Street. Apart from an initial shock at noises that turned out to derive from a puppy, once inside the spirit manifestations failed to materialize.

The party now moved off down the road to the corner of Race and Liberty Street where Frau Landecker resided. There they found her sitting peacefully in a rocking chair, a shawl over her head. As a disappointed journalist wrote, she did not look like a witch out of Macbeth, but rather 'the usual old German woman in every particular of form and feature and attire'. Austin was unsure as to how to proceed and so decided to take Landecker back to Bremen Street police station, where the rest of the Schaffler family had stayed warming themselves around a stove in the cell room. The police now brought the two parties together and asked

Michael to make his accusations to Landecker's face. So, in broken English, the story unravelled.

It transpired that Landecker had been providing the Schefflers with herbal remedies for a variety of complaints. When the family began to experience various poltergeist-like manifestations, they pretty quickly concluded that the evil spirits that tormented them had been sent by Landecker. Mrs Scheffler burned some consecrated paper flowers, but the family felt no relief. After all had been said, the police allowed the Schefflers to stay the night at the station, and the next day they went in search of new accommodation. We find them a year or so later at a house in the Miami area of the city. Frau Landecker was charged with practising medicine without a diploma and locked up to await trial. A year later, Bremen Street police had their hands full with a full-scale riot, one of the most serious in nineteenth-century America, after the decision of a jury, in what was a very corrupt city, to hand down a manslaughter verdict to a young German and his accomplice who clearly murdered their employer. The courthouse was burned down destroying many records, jurors were terrorized, barricades were set up in the streets, several dozen people died in running battles with National Guard troops.

If the police were domestic missionaries then the clergy were moral police. If witchcraft belief was to be vanquished then they would have to play their part. Up until the eighteenth century Anglican parish vestries dealt with moral offences and malicious defamation, and Baptist churches similarly disciplined the moral behaviour and disputes of its members. Quaker Church courts continued with such business well into the eighteenth century.[10] In 1759 the Pennsylvania Quakers, at their Goshen monthly meeting, heard a complaint against one Robert Jones for participating 'in forcing a poor woman from her habitation (under a pretence of her bewitching a certain child), whereby she has suffered damage'. Jones was subsequently disowned.[11] The Moravian authorities in North Carolina repeatedly expressed concern. Their 1786 Conference noted with frustration that 'superstition regarding hex and other preposterous things has not entirely ceased among us'. A couple of years later it warned that 'any one who believed in such supernatural powers and made use of them could not be permitted to attend the Lord's Supper'. In 1807 Moravian ministers recorded their condemnation of 'congregation members who believe far too much in magic and sorcery and have sought the counsel of the so-called Hexenmeister'.[12]

The huge influx of immigrants during the second half of the nineteenth century generated renewed clerical concerns. In November 1877 the Joint Columbus Conference of Lutheran ministers deliberated on the topic of witchcraft. It became clear from the discussions that the belief in witchcraft was widespread in German and Anglo-American congregations across the country. The debate was based upon a thesis on witchcraft prepared for conference by the Rev. Henry G. Cramer of Zanesville, Ohio, who had emigrated from Hanover, Germany, and preached in German to his flock. From what little we know of its contents it would seem that his definition of witchcraft was largely concerned with hex doctors and pow-wow. Witchcraft, it was agreed, overstepped 'the boundaries prescribed in God's Word to execute that which lies beyond the ordinary effect of nature, and is contrary to the employment of rightful means'.[13] But talking amongst themselves was not going to solve anything. The clergy had to get the message out amongst the people. After three Hungarian women were charged with annoying a woman for being a witch at a police court in Woodbridge, New Jersey, in October 1936, the local Hungarian Catholic priest Vincent Lenyi, who would later play a key role in the care of a new wave of Hungarian immigrants following the Second World War, decided to speak out. At the urging of the magistrate, Lenyi toured the Hungarian community going house to house, disabusing inhabitants of the notion of witchcraft in his native tongue. 'Witchcraft is a rubbish heap of worn out creeds and superstitions', he told them. 'It is all the product of fevered imagination.'[14]

But the clergy were far from speaking with one voice on the matter, just as spiritualism caused fissures between and across different churches. In 1828 it was reported that in North Carolina 'there are hundreds of people in this state, and some preachers too, that have the same belief and dread of witchcraft, as characterized the inhabitants of Salem'.[15] In 1885 the Swedish Lutheran church in Belgrade, Nicollet County, Minnesota, a township first settled in 1854, decided to step in and adjudicate over a public witchcraft accusation amongst its Swedish flock. Mrs John Solomon, who had languished for three years, became convinced that her aunt, a Mrs Johnson, of Hebron, Nicollet County, had bewitched her. The Solomons complained to the preacher A. Anderson, who ordered Mrs Johnson to appear after Sunday service. She did not attend, but a jury of deacons considered various testimonies of her powers. The newspapers reported that Anderson believed in witchcraft.[16] Perhaps he was just very cautious about criticizing those that did for fear of alienating his parishioners. A clergyman in York, Pennsylvania, confided in 1929, 'I don't speak of it in my congregation because my people believe it so thoroughly that they might not come to church at all if I started knocking it.'[17] The following striking case bears out his concerns, and illustrates the challenge the churches faced in converting witch believers.

The other Salem witch trials

The town of Salem, Columbiana County, Ohio, was a thriving settlement founded by the Quakers. Its inhabitants numbered over 6,000 by the end of the nineteenth century, at which time it was described by one observer as displaying 'order, prosperity, thrift, and comfort'. But in 1893 the peace, after which the town was named, as in Jeru*salem* the 'city of peace', was shattered by a virulent witchcraft dispute.

A few miles south of Salem, at a place known as McCracken Corner, lived a farmer named Jacob Culp. Born in Germany around 1839, he and his family emigrated to America when he was a boy. By 1860 the young man had taken up farming and married Hannah Loop, a Pennsylvanian woman fifteen years his senior, becoming stepfather to two children from her previous marriage. Culp worked hard and became one of the most prosperous members of the community. He was a member of Hart Methodist Episcopal Church, which had been founded in the 1820s. He probably contributed to the rebuilding of the old log cabin prayer-house in the 1860s when it was replaced with a smart, white timber-framed church.

Sometime during the 1870s Hannah's mother Mary Loop and her disabled brother Ephraim, described as an 'idiot' and 'dumb' in the censuses, moved in to the Culp's home for a few years before removing to another of Hannah's sisters. When Mary died some neighbours, including a couple of the Loop sisters, cast accusing glances at Jacob. As Jacob told a journalist, when Mary lay dying

> they said I had "spelled" the old woman and was killing her. My wife and I went over and when we went into the room the others got out. They looked at me as if I had smallpox. Mrs Loop died while I was there. I left right off after there had been some hard words passed. On the day of the burying I looked at Mrs Bleam as I met her at the stairs. She set up a scream and ran out of my sight.

When Hannah also died sometime around 1887 and Jacob married Hattie, a woman twenty-five years younger, rumour had it he had bumped Hannah off too.

Stories began to circulate around the area that witchcraft was on the increase. One of those to suffer its depredations was a big-shouldered, long-armed farmer named Norman Bleam, who was related to Culp through his marriage to another of the Loop women. Bleam had heard how a neighbour's cow had been cured by taking its milk, pouring it around an apple tree, and thrashing the ground with a thorn bush. This piece of sympathetic magic tormented the witch responsible who appeared scratched all over. Bleam said he did not believe the story at first but changed his mind when his own cows' milk would not churn. His neighbours said they were bewitched, and he was advised to send for the old cunning-man Dr Andrew Hoff, who lived at Alliance. Hoff was brought over to the farm to inspect the cow. After whispering in its ear he declared it was bewitched by a he-witch, a man with a long, grey beard. He told Bleam that the witch 'talked like a preacher' and went to the local church. 'Who could he mean but Jacob Culp?' wondered Bleam. 'We thought so at home.' A young farmer named Howard Hughes, also married to a Loop, came to a similar conclusion with regard to his agricultural misfortunes. Then there was the sickness of Mrs Sidney Fife, and the bewitchment of the children of the Greenawalts family.

The principal rumour-monger was Culp's sister-in-law, Sadie Loop. A single woman aged thirty-eight in 1890. Sadie was a key member of Hart Methodist Church, having served it as a Sunday School teacher and sexton. In her latter role, she assumed jealous charge of keeping the church building spic and span. In November 1892, following further family misfortunes and illnesses which no doctor could help, Sadie decided to call upon a herb doctress—or 'physician' as she was listed in the census, named Louise Burns. This widow of German birth operated from a house in Maple Street, Salem. She told Sadie that she had a very bad brother-in-law, and when she was asked which one, Burns replied 'the one that came across the ocean'. This could only be Jacob.

On 2 April 1893 Sadie consulted Andrew Hoff. He confirmed that witchcraft was at work, and in Sadie's words, 'described a man living in the neighborhood in such a way that Mr Culp was the only man that fitted the description'. Hoff advised her to cease attending church until he could engineer Culp's death, which would take up to six months to achieve. They must avoid Culp's breath or gaze falling upon them. Sadie and other family members followed his advice, and she informed neighbours of Hoff's words. Culp was understandably riled by the accusations and went to the pastor for help. 'He was afraid he would get into trouble', explained Culp later, 'and didn't want to take sides. He didn't believe in the witches, I think, but he wasn't ready to go with me and face the folks who talked.'

One of those Sadie told, in explanation for her absence at church, was a farmer and Class Leader named Homer B. Shelton. It was only when he subsequently made a formal complaint to the Pastor J. E. Cope that the church finally acted. Shelton's letter runs as follows:

> Dear Brother: - The undersigned a member of the Methodist Episcopal church, complains to you that Sadie Loop, a member of the same church, has been guilty of immoral conduct, and she is hereby charged therewith as follows: Charge, falsehood.

> Specification 1. The said Sadie Loop on or about the 27th day of April, 1893, did utter and publish, contrary to the word of God and the discipline, the following false and evil matter of and concerning Jacob Culp, to wit that he, meaning the said Jacob Culp was a wizard and practiced witchcraft.

> H. B. Shelton

The Columbiana Circuit was obliged to take such a request seriously, and in May 1893 a rare Church court was organized to consider the charge against Sadie Loop. The account we have is exceptional in that the court took the unusual step of allowing representatives of the local press to attend.

The trial was held in the classroom of Salem Methodist Church. Rev. S. Y. Kennedy, of Columbiana, represented the Church in the prosecution, and the Revs J. K. Grimes and J. K. Shaffer, of North Benton, acted for the defence. There were five jurors, Emmett Freed, Robert Hole, William Kelley, J. E. Bonsall, and William Parrish. Before the trial commenced the presiding judge, Rev. G. B. Smith, of Alliance, conducted religious service, and hymn no. 166 was sung by those present. Shelton's charge against Loop was read out and the Rev Kennedy told the court that 'this trial was a prosecution; the church never persecutes', reminding those present that in this particular instance the church and not Shelton was the prosecutor. Sadie Loop was brought in briefly to lodge that she pleaded 'not guilty'. Then Shelton took the stand and the questioning commenced.

Shelton related his conversation with Loop about Culp and his witchcraft. Loop told him how many years before Culp had bought a black art book that he used to become wealthier than his neighbours. She complained that Culp had done nothing to support the church and what little he had given did it no good. When asked whether he had counselled Loop against pursuing her course of action against Culp, Shelton replied, 'No, not personally. I expressed myself as not believing in anything of the kind.' Several of Loops female neighbours were now questioned, relating their conversations regarding Dr Hoff's advice. Shelton returned to give evidence.

What effect did Miss Loop's counsel have on your people at Hart's?

It was a matter of query that anyone should believe such a thing.

Were you impressed that Miss Loop was sincere in her belief about the matter at that time?

I was impressed that she was entirely given up to that belief.

Did Miss Loop come to you confidentially as her leader about this matter?

I do not know, but she requested that this be made known to other members of the church through me, and that it should be kept from Mr Culp, as Dr Hoff claimed he would have much more power over Culp if the matter was kept from him; also that Culp's wife would be in great danger if she should know of this, as he would likely kill her.

After further questions, Shelton was asked:

Have these reports concerning Mr Culp had any serious effect upon the church at Hart's?

Not upon the membership, but they have brought the church into disrepute with those outside.

The defence now had its turn and called John Akin, who had been a class leader for forty years, and had known Sadie for twenty. His testimony was not entirely helpful to the defence. When asked if she had been the source of any trouble in the church, he replied 'not lately', and under further questioning stated that the church had problems with her in the past. Then Sadie took the stand.

Was anything said about witchcraft before you met Dr Hoff?

I did not know there was any such thing and went to the dictionary to find out the definition of the word.

When Dr Hoff explained the condition of affairs did you believe in his theory?

We did not understand anything about it.

She then went on to say she still did not believe the opinions of Dr Hoff:

If you did not believe it, why did you circulate this story?

I did not circulate the story, as I understand it. I went to my class leader and pastor in confidence and told them of the mysterious occurrences which I could not understand, and asked for information and advice.

Shelton was next asked about Loop's reputation, and he replied, 'Personally, at the present time, I would not place much confidence in what she would say.' Jacob Culp was the final witness. He related the various accusations made against him and his relations with the Bleams and Loops. Sadie 'gets into trouble and tries to lie out if it', he said, giving as an instance an episode involving the sending of a valentine.

The questioning closed and the jury consulted for about ten minutes before returning the following verdict:

We, the committee in the case of Miss Sadie Loop, charged with false-hood under the specification that she had on or about the 27th day of April, 1893, published contrary to the word of God and the discipline, the following false and evil matter of and concerning Jacob Culp, to-wit, that he (Jacob Culp) was a wizard and practiced witchcraft, find that said specification is proven and the charge of falsehood sustained.

The Judge, Rev. Smith, informed those present that he had no alternative but to expel Sadie Loop from the membership of the Methodist Episcopal Church.[18]

This was not the end of the matter. Sadie was not one to let things lie, and in June she went to the office of the *Salem Daily News* to request that the paper publish a statement complaining that the church authorities had made no effort to settle the witchcraft trouble, and to clarify that she had never made an assertion that Culp was a witch, but had merely told others what Dr Hoff had said.[19] Rev Cope was removed to another charge at the next Conference, and Rev J. E. Hollister of Alliance became pastor of Hart Church.

The rumours rumbled on around McCracken Corner, and Dr Hoff was never far from them. In November a new accusation of witchery reopened the festering scar in the community's spiritual life. Howard Hughes had been digging a well on his farm and when he got to what he thought was a sufficient depth, no water appeared. He called in Dr Hoff, who burned some herbs and muttered some charm before declaring that the dry well was the fault of witchcraft, and would remain dry until Culp was dead. Rev. Hollister acted decisively, requesting Hughes and others to disavow their belief in witchcraft and treat Culp as a brother. This they refused to do, so another Church court was arranged for 24 January 1894. Rev. Kingsbury of Alliance was the appointed judge, with the Rev. Kennedy appearing for the prosecution and Rev. Shipman for the defence. The Hughes and the Bleams were called to defend themselves but on the appointed morning none of them turned up. The Reverends spent an hour discussing the Church's jurisdiction in such circumstances and in conclusion they decided to expel Howard Hughes, and Norman Bleam and his wife, from Hart Church. An attorney gave notice of their right to appeal at the next quarterly conference of the Methodist church.[20]

Hart Church never recovered from these traumatic events. Numerous members left as a result, the congregation went into terminal decline, and it was finally disbanded in the 1930s. In 1937 the church was pulled down and parts of it used for lumber. Today it is marked only by a small graveyard along Route 45 a few miles south of Salem.[21]

Alaska: of barbers and gunboats

From the moment the United States purchased Alaska from the Russian Empire in 1867 through to the present day, governors of Alaska have had issues with witchcraft. On taking over the vast region the army moved in to impose 'order' on indigenous populations that were liberally described as heathens, pagans, and idolaters. The natives had their own judicial and social mechanisms for maintaining law and order, but as with other Native-American peoples these were often at odds with European conceptions of justice and morality. In fact the real law-and-order problem concerned the thousands of unruly gold prospectors that headed north, while the soldiers who were meant to be keeping the peace were frequent breakers of it. Still, witchcraft clearly posed a serious problem from the 1870s onwards. Missionaries assumed that it had always been thus, but maybe it was the social and cultural stresses generated by the arrival en masse of the Europeans that exacerbated native fears of a witch epidemic. It has been suggested that this is what happened to the Kaska Indians of British Columbia and the Yukon during the early twentieth century. The Kaska way of life was disrupted by miners making their way to the Klondike goldfields, and concern regarding witches increased with greater contact with the Tlingit peoples to the west amongst whom witchcraft had already assumed epidemic proportions.[22]

The old naval flagship the USS Jamestown was one of the hubs of American Alaskan administration in the early years. It had been launched in 1844 and first served off the West African coast to suppress the slave trade. In 1867–8 it served as a guard and store ship at Sitka, the capital of the new American territory.[23] The land here in the panhandle of Alaska, along the Pacific coast, was populated by the Tlingit people. They had already had decades of semi-colonial rule under the Russian-American Company, which had a commercial monopoly in the territory trading principally in furs. The Russian Orthodox Church had also set up a mission, created parishes, and founded schools. An 1850 Church report was confident that the power of the native medicine doctors was weakening due to such missionary activity. The Russian physicians, who the Tlingit initially suspected of being workers of witchcraft, also reported some success at convincing them that their knowledge was better than that of their medicine men, and that witches were not responsible for diseases.[24]

Under the captaincy of Lester Beardslee the Jamestown returned again between 1879 and 1881 to protect American interests and preserve the peace after the withdrawal of the army from Alaska. Ten days after arriving in Sitka, Beardslee, who took a keen interest in native customary law, was informed of an elderly native woman who had fled from her people fearing she would be killed as a witch. She was brought to the customs house along with those who had made the threats. The latter were informed in no uncertain terms that they would be hanged if they carried out their intentions. The accusers promised not to harm the woman but requested the captain banish her to another country. Commander Henry Glass, who took over from Beardslee, performed a similar role as judge and jury in May 1881 when another accused witch escaped certain death and fled to the Jamestown. After investigating the case Glass ordered a party to arrest the local medicine man involved and other leading men in the village. The medicine man fled but two chiefs were brought back, and one of them was fined and imprisoned after questioning.[25] And so the US Navy joined the fight against the witch believers.

A report drawn up by the Alaskan division of the Bureau of Education in 1897 concerning the station in Hoonah territory, thirty miles west of the modern capital

Juneau, noted that in previous years officials had denied the existence of witchcraft fearing that it would put off migrants.[26] It was a pointless attempt since from the late 1870s onwards, American newspapers and journals had relished shocking their readers with tales of human sacrifice, polygamy, female slavery, the sinister influence of the medicine men, and the brutal manner in which they dealt with witches. One news item in 1882 ran, 'It is one of the pleasing customs of our fellow countrymen of Alaska to torture witches.'[27] Witchcraft became the symbol of Alaskan moral, spiritual, and intellectual turpitude. Never mind the white folks killing each other across the 'civilized' United States.

Much of the information fed to the public derived from Presbyterian missionaries who had pretty much free reign in the territory. In 1882, for instance, the Ohio missionary and teacher Maggie J. Dunbar, who was posted at Fort Wrangell, described in a letter read before the Presbyterian Women's Board of Missions in St Louis, and then printed in the press, the torturing to death of several children and old men as witches. She told of an orphaned young girl locked up and whipped for having bewitched her aunt.[28] Dunbar came to Fort Wrangell, an old Tlingit settlement that became a centre for gold-rush prospectors, at the request of the Presbyterian missionary Sheldon Jackson (1834–1909). He became the First General Agent of Education in Alaska, and never lost an opportunity to highlight the witchcraft 'problem' to further his religious, educational, and political aims. The disseminating of lurid tales of tortured and murdered witches both helped bring in donations to the mission, and justified what has been described as the Americanization of Alaska through the schools set up for native children.[29]

Female missionaries were amongst the most active in Alaska, and there were several converted native women amongst them. At Hoonah two widows, Amanda McFarland and Mary Howell, led the fight against witchcraft in the 1890s. Before that, McFarland, sometimes described as the first white woman in Alaska, had dealt with a number of cases at Fort Wrangell, in Tlingit territory. She wrote a letter from there in 1878, which was printed by Sheldon Jackson,

> We have had more witchcraft here, and the effect has been very bad on the minds of the young people. Some of my brightest and best scholars have been led away by it. As we have no kind of law, none of the whites felt that they had any right to interfere. It has frequently been said to me, 'If you will get a minister here, so that the Indians will see that he is permanent, and one who will make them understand he is determined to break up all such things, it will more than anything else tend to prevent the recurrence of such scenes.'[30]

A Reverend came in the shape of Samuel Hall Young (1847–1927), who did, indeed, set about tackling the witch believers head on. He reckoned that in the

summer of 1878 alone the wave of witch fear amongst the Tlingit in the archipelago around Sitka had led to the deaths of over a hundred suspected witches, with
two or three times as many people tortured.[31] Before arriving in his new parish he
had done some reading on witchcraft, shamans, and medicine. They had formerly
been remote topics, he reflected, but now became part of his daily experience. On
one occasion he called together several chiefs and caused uproar when he
announced, 'I am going to put down all persecution for witchcraft and banish
the medicine-men from this town. This is going to be a Christian town, and the
law of love shall take the place of the law of hatred and wrong.' At another
gathering he admitted that the whites used to hold to such beliefs too, but that was
in the past. Now witch persecutors were law breakers, and had to be punished: 'It
is for you to say now which side you are on—whether on the side of the
government and law of the Unites States to which you belong, or on the side of
murder and superstition and error and savagery.'[32]

The missionaries, and later the secular authorities, saw themselves in a Mani-
chean struggle with the medicine men. It was they who were responsible for the
witchcraft problem. Undermine them, suppress them, and the atrocities committed against accused witches would end. In an interview given in 1927, Hall Young
said that the grip of 'superstition' over the Alaskans broke once the 'bushy hair' of
the medicine men had been cropped.[33] By this he meant the belief that the power
of an *ixt* was associated with his long, uncut hair. The barber strategy was adopted
by the navy early on. During his tenure in Alaska, Glass, of whom one Russian
priest observed 'hunting shamans was his favourite pastime and sport', sentenced
one troublesome *ixt* to have his hair cut off in public. A decade later the
commander of the USS *Pinta*, William T. Burwell, ordered a similar punishment
during a stopover in Shakan, a Henya Tlingit tribal village. An officer, Robert
E. Coontz, later US Chief of Naval Operations, recalled:

> We erected a small platform on the quarter deck, brought out the barber's
> chair, and, while two sturdy bluejackets held him fast, his long, black,
> flowing hair was removed with the barber's clippers. The inhabitants
> thronged on the nearby beach and watched the operation. When shorn
> of his locks, the power of the witch doctor vanished![34]

Chilkat chief Skun-doo-ooh (Skundoo) was another of those who suffered this
fate during an eventful career as an *ixt*. He was said to be the only red-headed
native in south-eastern Alaska, and his name meant 'one is enraged at him'. He was
involved in several cases of witch torture, and was considered a major obstacle to
missionary success—more of him shortly.[35]

For decades there was no fully functional judiciary in Alaska.[36] It did not have
the administrative status to institute a system of courts. During the 1870s and early

1880s settlers tried for capital offences had to be sent down to Oregon, where a supreme court had been founded when it became the thirty-third state in 1859, and with the completion of a grand courthouse in 1875. But the expense and distance made it prohibitive. The respective legal rights of whites and natives in Alaska were also an ongoing matter of debate. As in other areas of the frontier West, miners law filled some of the gap, and in the early 1880s an ad hoc uniformed native police force was created under the auspices of missionaries such as John G. Brady. According to an interview with his children, Brady had once, on being tipped-off by the native police, personally rescued a boy-witch pinned to the shoreline, cutting the bonds before the tide took its victim. The Brady family looked after him for a year before he was sent to school and later began a maritime career.[37]

The Alaskan Organic Act of 1884 introduced the laws of the State of Oregon, leading to the creation of a district court, and the appointment of a judge, marshal, and attorney. This effectively brought all native peoples under white jurisdiction. Yet, initially, the new judiciary conflicted with the moral law imposed by the missionaries and actually gave natives a better degree of control over their lives. The activities of the Presbyterian mission in Sitka came under legal scrutiny. The first judge of the new district, Judge Samuel Ward McAllister, ruled that the mission schools had no right to enforce native students' attendance, and that parents could remove their children from the schools as and when they wanted. This had a direct impact on the missionaries' adoption of those children who fled or were banished because they were thought to be witches. Sheldon Jackson immediately started pulling strings to reverse this and other decisions of the new government. He held up the terrible treatment of child witches as an example. McAllister and others were soon removed from their posts.[38]

In 1898, as John Green Brady began a term as Governor of Alaska, he wrote that apart from the drinking of rum, witchcraft was 'the greatest curse of the Alaskan people'.[39] The navy had continued to deal with the witchcraft problem wherever and whenever circumstances arose. When, in 1898, Brady inspected the various settlements along the coast in the USS Wheeling, he lectured on the evils of witchcraft belief wherever they docked, reminding his native Alaskan audience through an interpreter that he would not deal with them leniently in such matters in the future. To reinforce the point, the Wheeling's captain ordered gun practice—the first time in history gun-boat diplomacy had been used against the witchcraft problem.[40] Such tactics were hardly effective. Only three years earlier one Illinois newspaper had scoffed at the official denials of the prevalence of medicine men and witchcraft in Alaska, stating that scores had died recently. It noted that the authorities clearly had inadequate resources to deal with the problem and called for an army post to be established to suppress the belief.[41]

The new Alaskan judiciary had plenty on its plate, including the liquor problem, the practice of slavery amongst the Tlingits, mining disputes, and pervasive violence amongst the white population. It only began to be seriously proactive regarding witch murders during the mid-1890s, under pressure from the American government and missionaries. In 1894 Skun-doo-ooh was sent down to San Quentin prison in California for three years for manslaughter following his involvement in the killing of a woman for witchcraft by binding her to a tree and leaving her to starve to death. His head was shaved in prison, but he returned home to Chilkat with an enhanced reputation. He said he had become a Christian, but appears to have resumed his old activities. In 1902 he was described as 'a constant terror' to the Presbyterian missionary in Chilkat, and had recently been involved in the torture of an eleven-year-old native boy, Willie Jackson. Skun-doo-ooh told the brother of a local chief that Jackson had bewitched his family. As a result Jackson was hung up by the toes for several hours and placed in a cellar while the application of further torture was debated. He was rescued by the local missionary and Canadian mounted police, and sent to a school in Sitka.[42] It is somewhat ironic that around this time the aged Skun-doo-ooh made some money by posing for studio set 'ethnographic' photos of himself in action.[43] A few years after his death another *ixt* began trading on his name. In 1910 this Skun-doo-ooh impersonator was jailed at Skagway for wood stealing and while there he was held down by two white inmates as the jail barber cut off his locks.[44]

Skun-doo-ooh was not the only luminary to be prosecuted. In 1896 a Hoonah chief from Chichagof Island, some hundred miles south-west of Juneau, was arrested and put on trial for torturing and murdering his nephew for bewitching him.[45] Two years later, Judge Johnson, acting under instructions from Washington, addressed the issue of witchcraft before the Alaskan grand jury. Many murders could be traced to witchcraft belief, he said, and 'it is your duty not to ignore, but to make patient inquiry into the alleged offenses growing out of the practice of witchcraft, and return true bills where evidence so warrants'.[46] The authorities now became more proactive, pursuing investigations and not just waiting for victims to turn up on their doorsteps. Shortly after Johnson's address, the jail in Juneau was reported to be full of Native Alaskans brought in on charges relating to witchcraft. In February 1900 district marshal Grant travelled to Kake to investigate reports of two witch murders and four impending ones.[47] Two years later, the United State Commissioner H. H. Folsom, accompanied by the marshal and attorney, chartered a special steamboat to take them to a Hoonah village forty miles from Juneau to hold an inquest on the remains of two Tlingits who had been starved to death. One of them had been bound to a tree to drive out spirits. Federal officers arrested the entire tribe responsible and charged four with murder.[48]

A legislative act passed in 1915 allowed Native-Alaskan settlements with more than forty permanent members over the age of twenty-one to form self-governing organizations overseen by elected councilmen. They were given the power to pass local ordinances as long as they did not conflict with federal or territorial law. One ordinance that these new organizations were expected to enact was against 'the practice of witchcraft', by which the authorities meant the activities of the *ixt*, though the communities probably had a broader definition.[49] So the first ordinance passed by the Tlingit village of Kake was, indeed, against witchcraft under penalty of a fine or imprisonment. The 'problem' had clearly not been resolved. The same year William Gilbert Beattie, a Presbyterian minister and superintendent of native schools for Alaska, told the district court in Juneau:

> The question of witchcraft is one of the most difficult problems we have to handle among the natives. The existence of witches is a certainty with them, and there is absolutely no possibility of convincing them that there are no such things as witches. It isn't stubbornness on their part. It is simply and sincerely their belief that there are among their tribesmen persons who have power to cast a spell over others of their number.[50]

His comments were occasioned by having brought several members of the Killisnoo community to Juneau to be questioned by the district attorney regarding a blind man in Killisnoo who claimed to be responsible for all the deaths in the village by his witchcraft. His fifteen-year-old daughter, Mary Moses, or Klantosh to give her Tlingit name, testified to the district attorney James A. Smiser regarding her father's power, expressing her fear that he might kill her grandmother. Smiser ruminated that the evidence brought to mind the power of hypnotism, but concluded that as there was no tangible evidence there was no law in place by which he could take action against the man.[51]

Further arrests were made over the next few years, but the substance of two of the last instances suggests the tide was turning. In 1917 Judge Jennings fined a native woman, a Mrs Hansen, for carving up another woman who had accused her of being a witch. Her husband was sent to jail for three months. He sent Hansen from court with the injunction to spread the word, 'that there is no witchcraft in Alaska, and when an Indian man or woman stabs another for being called a witch it will mean the penitentiary for 10 years'. This did not prevent the Tlingit Peter Lawrence, from Yakutat, shooting dead Billy James for accusing him of witchcraft in 1919.[52] Those accused of witchcraft were now taking the law into their own hands, and the dynamics of accusations were no longer communal but interpersonal.

While abuses against suspected witches continued in the rest of America, they seem to have died out by the 1920s in Tlingit Alaska. Was this due to the success of the missionaries and educationalists—to the Americanization of the Tlingits? It is true that by 1920 all Tlingit communities had become at least nominally Christian. This 'success' was not just down to the Presbyterians either. A revitalized Russian Orthodox mission during the late nineteenth century proved successful in attracting Native Alaskans, who were drawn, perhaps, to the ritual aspects of the faith and the priests' greater willingness to embrace their language. The Salvation Army also moved in with some success. But as this book demonstrates in graphic detail, becoming a school-educated American was no cure for witch belief. And, as ethnographic studies show, the Christian population did not reject the belief in witchcraft. Everything points to the declining influence of the *ixt* as diminishing the punishment of suspected witches. So in one sense, the missionaries were astute in targeting them as 'preachers of witchcraft', but wrong in assuming that belief would swiftly disappear as a consequence. Their demise, furthermore, was not necessarily a direct result of the application of scissors, naval diplomacy, missionaries, and district marshals. The acculturation process that exacerbated their waning influence was more complex than that—as Skun-doo-ooh's long career in the witch-detection business showed.

Under both the Russians and Americans the *ixt* had to compete with the challenge to their power from new medicines and theologies.[53] There is evidence they attempted to adapt to the latter by adopting or accepting elements of Christian doctrine and practice. One *ixt* claimed to have received his power from a 'big Russian'. Europeans also brought with them devastating new diseases such as smallpox against which the *ixt* demonstrably had no power. Again, some tried to adapt by conjuring up smallpox spirits with whom they could communicate to counter the disease. European doctors brought medicines and vaccine in the case of smallpox that challenged both the *ixt*'s diagnoses and methods. The shamanistic elements of the *ixt*'s practice and their paraphernalia, such as rattles and masks, impressed less and less, so that by 1920 their status had dwindled to that of fortune-tellers and modest spiritual healers. They were no longer the arbiters of life and death.

Finally, there is a missing chapter in the annals of Alaskan witchcraft. What of the no doubt many witch believers amongst the fluctuating white and Chinese labouring population during the late nineteenth and early twentieth century? A few scant references help balance the picture a tiny bit. A Russian diarist writing from Sitka in the 1880s referred to the witchcraft beliefs of his fellow Russian inhabitants as well as the Tlingits.[54] Hall Young recalled a Jewish storekeeper in Wrangell who confided in Tlingit customers that he too believed in witchcraft, and that it was not long ago that Americans had tortured and executed witches just as they did. Young believed the storekeeper only sympathized with them to keep their custom.[55] There is no reason to take Young's side of the story: just look at Pennsylvania.

The Pennsylvania problem

Alaskans were not the only objects of opprobrium regarding witch belief during the late nineteenth and early twentieth century. 'We are given to refer to the superstitious colored people of the South', wrote Baltimore Baptist Pastor Joshua E. Wills in 1911, 'but the genuine Pennsylvania Dutchman has more superstition to the square inch than any other man on the American continent.' 'I believe,' he continued, 'no better field in the wide world offers opportunity for missionary endeavors than among country districts of Eastern Pennsylvania.'[56] The sentiment was not new. The nation-wide reputation of Pennsylvania, its German population in particular, for being a state of staunch witchcraft believers had developed since the 1880s when a drip-feed of stories about hex doctors and witches began to circulate across the United States.

In 1889 a newspaper reporter covering a case of witch abuse in a German community in Tioga, Hancock County, Illinois, commented: 'especially remarkable is it that the witch believers should be Germans, the people of all others who have the least superstition, at least that is the reputation they enjoy'.[57] If that reputation ever existed it was already being trashed by events in Pennsylvania. In 1883 a series of witchcraft disputes in Reading, Pottstown, Scranton, Philadelphia, and Pittsburg led to headlines such as 'The Witch Epidemic'.[58] While cases from elsewhere in the US were usually treated as isolated cases, every Pennsylvania case was an accumulation. Headlines began to appear with titles such as, 'Weird Stories: People in Pennsylvania Said to Believe in Witches'.[59] Some of this was inspired by inter-state niggling—as we have seen elsewhere. But the Pennsylvania press was the source of many of the stories. In January 1891 the *Philadelphia Inquirer* ran with an exclusive headed, 'Witches in Berks County: Reading "Doctors" Minister to the Delusive'. It began: 'A veritable nest or hot-bed of supposed witches and witchcraft exists among the hills of Earl and Douglass townships.'[60] From this and other subsequent reports there was clearly a degree to which the Pennsylvania press engaged in a tacit policy of geographical isolation of the problem—for them it was never the whole state, but certain populations in certain places. Berks County, and its seat Reading, and Lancaster County, were the culprits. In 1902, for instance the *Philadelphia Inquirer* commented, 'Reading would be a rare field for the student in psychology just now. The only reason that she is not burning witches is because the law won't let her.'[61]

The press of the period nearly always referred to the 'superstitious' people of the two counties as Pennsylvania Dutch or Germans, but Lancaster and Berks County were the seats of the Amish, Mennonites, and other 'plain people' communities. The first Amish in America settled in Berks County back in the eighteenth century before other communities took root elsewhere in America and Canada. They were not particularly noticeable to the outside world until the 1930s because until the rise of mass car ownership, mechanization of small-scale farming, and changes in popular fashion, the look and lifestyle of the 'plain people' were not that different from the wider farming population around them.

In 1892 another Pennsylvania report headed 'Queer Witch Stories' circulated around the press: 'What funny stories come out of Berks county, Pa, about witches and witch doctors, and those who enjoy them most are the educated Berks county people, who laugh at the superstitious fears of foolish and ignorant neighbours.'[62] But such stories were increasingly being read with concern and contemplation rather than merriment. Pennsylvania witch belief was becoming seen as a social, moral, and health problem—an embarrassment to the state. There was no sign of it going away either, and the problem could not be pinned on recent credulous immigrants from Europe. Yet there was no religious mission to purge the witch believers: the Alaskans were pagans and the Pennsylvanians staunch Christians after all! It was up to the medical establishment to lead the crusade.

In December 1899 a Reading general practitioner, John M. Bertolet, read a paper to the Berks County Medical Society bearing the title 'Witch Doctors and their Deceptions'. He had on many occasions had to treat people who had first consulted a hex doctor. The following year the world of the hex doctor was sensationally exposed by the tough, crusading journalist Alice Rix. She paid a visit to the Elm Street consulting room of the prosperous Reading hex doctor Joseph H. Hageman posing as a client seeking help for a sick relative. The sixty-seven-year-old Hageman was the offspring of German immigrants and had built up a large clientele over the years. He was listed as a 'physician' in the census and in the Reading *Directory*, but his business was pure pow-wow. Rix's pen portrait was none too flattering, 'He is a gross, grizzled, dirty old man, huge of head and face and jowl and hanging chin, with a monstrous body . . . big, fat, greasy hands, like suet puddings boiled in bags . . . bright, blue, questioning, kindly eyes—two spots of innocent blue upon a field of filth, like forget-me-nots dropped on a dirt heap.' Hageman took affront at the article she wrote about him for the Philadelphia newspaper the *North American*—not at his unflattering physical description, but at Rix's questioning of the good doctor's medical credentials. His reputation for the 'legitimate and scientific practice of medicine' had been traduced.

Hageman mobilized support, with some of his clients writing to the press in his defence. He also brought a libel suit against the newspaper's proprietor and one-time US Postmaster General, John Wanamaker. This was a very unwise move considering Wanamaker was a rich and powerful man. The trial took place in Philadelphia's Common Pleas Court in March 1903 before Judge McCarthy. One of those present to watch the spectacle was Baltimore Pastor Joshua E. Wills, a friend of McCarthy's. Over six days a succession of Hageman's clients, nearly a

Plate 1. Iroquois chief and Seneca orator Sagoyewatha, also known as Red Jacket (d. 1830). He gave a powerful speech at the trial of Tommy Jemmy, who was prosecuted for killing a supposed witch.

Plate 2. Giuseppina Porcello, who had a squint or cast in one eye, appealed to the New York Supreme Court in 1929 for a separation from her husband who accused her of having an evil eye.

STONE WOMAN WHOM THEY CALL A WITCH

Crowd's Treatment of Mrs. Immerman Recalls Days of Salem Witchcraft.

Allentown, Pa.—From occurences here ending with the stoning and jailing of Mrs. Meta Immerman one would think that the days of Salem witchcraft had been revived. Mrs. Immerman, a seamstress, of New York, came here to take barefoot treatment for a nervous trouble. She boarded at the home of George Kipp, a butcher. In the house were John Sobers and his wife.

After the woman had gone there to live Sobers was attacked with indigestion. A fake doctor told him he was the victim of evil spirits. The

Stone Woman as a Witch.

Kipps and Sobers then suspected Mrs. Immerman of working the evil spell. All sorts of witchcraft stories were circulated about the town, and she was told to go. Her trunk was put out of the house, and when she argued about it the police were called. The crowd called her witch and stoned her as she was taken to jail.

She was in a cell forty-eight hours before being released. The Sobers and Kipps now wear charms of broken needles and sawdust and have cabalistic crosses chalked on the home to drive away the evil spirits.

Plate 3. In 1911, New York seamstress, Meta Immerman, visited Allentown, Pennsylvania, to take the Kneipp cure. Her 'strange' health regime led to her being stoned in the streets for being a witch.

Plate 4. The founder of Christian Science, Mary Baker Eddy (1821–1910), promoted the notion of 'malicious animal magnetism' or 'MAM', a force akin to witchcraft.

Plate 5. Louis De Paoli, a San Francisco florist, beat his sister-in-law to death with a chair in the autumn of 1905 believing she had bewitched his family.

Plate 6. A bezoar from a cow's stomach—or a 'witch ball'.

Plate 7. Cartoon of a Pennsylvania pow-wow doctor with a client, drawn by David Heckert, a wealthy and prominent citizen of York, Pa., who was murdered in 1908.

Science Studies Pow-Wowing

Jacob Zellers . . . the big charm and spell man from York . . . administering a cure for erysipelas. . . . Many "patients" attest the success of his methods in curing and helping them.

Killing five people by witchcraft was but one of the startling things scientists heard about from Jacob Zellers, brought down to Washington from his Pennsylvania home to explain his charms, cures and curses

Zellers takes a stone from running water . . . and makes three series of passes with it . . . over the afflicted horse that has the "sweeny." . . . Then he mutters a charm, replaces the stone in the stream from which it came, and goodby "sweeny."

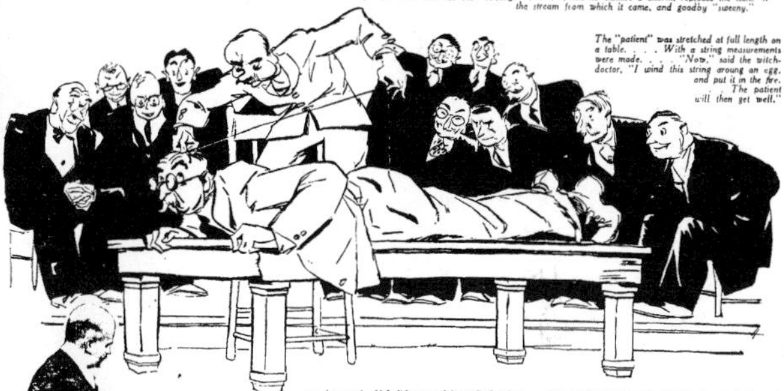

The "patient" was stretched at full length on a table. . . . With a string measurements were made. . . . "Now," said the witch-doctor, "I wind this string around an egg, and put it in the fire. . . . The patient will then get well."

By CLARA LOUISE LESLIE

"I MYSELF have killed five people!"

The witch doctor was quite matter-of-fact as he made the statement. He was a matter-of-fact person, not at all the sort of man you would connect with 20th century witchcraft. Evidently a hard worker, he was a sturdy little Pennsylvanian of German ancestry, and plainly very much in earnest. But he was one of the greatest witch doctors in the country today.

Three deep, a semi-circle of listeners leaned forward eagerly around a big table in the Graduate School of American University at Washington, D. C. A student, Edwin R. Danner, of York, Pa., famous for its recent "hex murder," had brought Jacob Zellers to tell of his first-hand knowledge of how the "black arts" are practiced today.

The audience, all advanced students and educators working under Dr. Walton Colcord John, watched Zellers closely as he stood behind the table and talked on.

His countenance reflected nothing of the mysterious or occult. With flashing eyes, good humor, and in phraseology and accent so unique that it brought a smile to the faces of his learned audience, he regaled his hearers for three hours with pointers on his craft, leaning forward over the table, thoroughly engrossed in telling "how he did it." When questions began coming too fast, however, he warned the class that "beyond a certain point I will not reveal my secrecy."

"I have been powwowing for 27 years," he declared. "The laws of Pennsylvania forbid it, but I turn out for no doctor or church or lawyer." He then emphasized seriously that he has never charged a cent for any of his services to the bewitched people of his country. "Sometimes," he said, "a 'spy' comes to get 'cured,' but since I present him with no bill, what can he do?"

UTTERLY sincere, he went on to explain that powwowing is the good influence with which to oppose witchcraft and hexing, the evil influence. If the case is serious enough to demand it, magic of a kind to kill is inflicted upon the caster of the evil spell. It was in this way that Zellers said he had "already killed five people." A "hex" is a spell cast by an enemy, usually from a jealous motive. It is black magic.

"To place a 'hex,'" it was explained, "all a person has to do is to obtain an object from the subject and chant prayers from the sixth and seventh books of Moses. These books are not now included in the Bible, but you can get them.

"Moses," said the witch doctor, "used the prayers in the books for a good purpose, while his descendants used them for evil. By praying before a personal object once owned by the person to be 'hexed,' an intense hatred is projected from the 'hexer' to the 'hexed.'" Zellers mentioned having once seen a woman with a fork she had borrowed or obtained, chopping it against the rafters in the barn, 'hexing' her rival with it.

"I don't know where I get my power," he replied to a question. "This was taught me by a famous witch doctor on his deathbed. A teacher of the art loses his own power as soon as he has taught it or transferred it to another. When I first realized I had the power, it frightened me and I told my old aunt not to tell anybody that I had it."

THOROUGHLY aware of the intellectual gap between himself and his listeners, he said, "I admit you know more than I do, and you'll laugh at some of the things I tell you." Then, from little folded notes which he took from his pocket and referred to occasionally through big gold-rimmed spectacles, he proceeded to cite instances of some of his cures, giving the names and addresses of his "patients."

"If a patient comes to me who hasn't been to a doctor first, I make him go, so the authorities can't hold anything against me. The kind of patients I like best are the ones who have already been to three or four doctors who have failed to help them. Then I take them."

Hemorrhages of all kinds yield readily to Zeller's magic, the class was told. "Suppose you cut an artery in your arm—accidentally, not on purpose to try me. I could stop the blood. I breathe on the patient and say the Lord's Prayer till I get to the words 'Thy will be done on earth.' There I stop! I do this three different times and then the bleeding will stop!" A number of healings of this type were described in detail.

A boy having 72 warts came and asked to have them removed. Zellers said he removed them without difficulty by his magic. "It is necessary for one to *ask* for what be wants," the witch doctor insisted.

"A woman who came from Fort Wayne, Indiana, for me to cure her had been 'hexed' by another woman and had gotten so fat that she couldn't get through doors.

Children are often brought by their parents . . . for treatment by Zellers and other powwow-doctors . . . and in many instances astonishing results are claimed.

"She weighed 560 pounds," he added. Due to his influence, he said, she reduced to about 150 pounds. "The last I heard she was back in Fort Wayne, a normal woman."

"Don't you think there is a fortune for a man with such remarkable weight-reducing process?"

"I don't sell this for money," was the rather abrupt reply.

ONCE Zellers was called, he related, to the home of a farmer whose house and whose barns, also, had become tenanted to an amazing degree with bedbugs. "Your boy has the sixth and seventh Books of Moses around here," warned the witch doctor, "and this plague is the result. 'Hunt for those books and get them out of your possession.' Sure enough, the farmer found them, he destroyed them and was soon rid of the bugs."

An account was then given of a woman who threw a "hex" on her son's wife, so that the latter was seized with a strange illness which "four or five doctors could not diagnose." Then Zellers was called in.

He found that the mother-in-law was casting the spell. In the case of strongly-projected hatred, the "hexer," according to Zellers, can be "seen" by looking into a crystal, into clear water, or into a fire.

Applying secret remedies, Zellers drove the evil spirit away. Part of his prescription in "unhexing" a person is to forbid the loaning or giving of anything from the patient's house for nine days. According to witchcraft authority, when an evil influence or spell has been broken by a witch doctor, the original witch will seek to borrow something from the afflicted person in order to relieve his or her own agony which has resulted concomitant to the thwarting of his or her own desires by some outside agent or witch practitioner.

In this case, the mother-in-law used trickery and ruined the cure. So Zellers was forced to use stronger magic, knowing, as he said, that it would result in death for the witch. Zellers fixed his deadly magic, the daughter-in-law began to grow strong and the evil "hex" was "driven back to its source." The mother-in-law died of a mysterious malady within nine days.

"Were you ever questioned in regard to the five deaths you claim to have been responsible for?"

"No! If a person gets sick from some strange illness that no doctor can diagnose and dies of it and I'm five miles away, what can they do to me? But the victim dies just the same! If I did wrong I hope God judges me, but if it's a life for a life, what would you do? Anyhow, it's they that kill themselves, because if the 'hex' hadn't belonged to them it wouldn't have come back."

WHEN from among this professional group Zellers chose a "victim" to demonstrate some of his methods for treating disease, the spectators were unable to restrain merriment. The "patient" was to be measured with a string, which was one of the powwow doctor's methods for diagnosing and curing disease. The "patient" was asked to stretch himself full length, face downward, on the large table in front of the class. "I *should* do this on your bare skin," said the "doctor." He began at the crown of the professor's head.

Down the "patient's" neck, down his spine, went the string until it had been pressed to the limit of the heel. The man's length was then noted. "Now stand up," he was ordered. The string was next held to the man's forehead. "Now put your finger on your navel if you can find out where it's at." Measurements from the forehead to the navel completed the operations.

"Now," said the witch doctor, holding up the string quite as earnestly as though he had performed a serious operation, "I take this and wind it around an egg and put the egg in the fire. The egg will burn to a cinder, but the string will not burn—and the patient will get well!"

Pernicious anemia, erysipelas, headache, rash, fits, nervous disorders, fever and gangrene were subjects of some of the other cures described. Most of these cures, just as Zellers related them, had already been witnessed through Mr. Danner, who had personally interviewed 125 people in and around York for the purpose of substantiating the witchcraft stories.

"How many people in Pennsylvania take stock in this?" Zellers was asked.

"Oh, about seven out of eight," confidently.

"Hexing," it was declared, may even be extended to livestock. One of the strangest stories Zellers told was about the bewitched pigs. A farmer who raised hogs for a living refused to sell one to a certain neighbor woman. Immediately he was pursued with bad luck in his hog raising. The pigs acquired freakish habits, drooped and died. Finally there remained a litter of nine so weak that "they couldn't live and they couldn't die."

In the case of strongly-projected hatred . . . the "hexer" may be seen by looking into a fire.

WHEN the farmer came for help, Zellers told him to make a brush pile and with straw to make nine beds in the pile. The brush was saturated with kerosene and the pigs that "couldn't live and couldn't die" were placed in the beds. A fire was lighted. Eight pigs ran out, but one stayed in and was burned to death. A neighbor woman ran out crying, "My God! I am in that fire," and immediately dropped dead. The eight pigs lived, and from then on the farmer had no more trouble with his hog raising. "If the ninth pig had ran out of the fire," Zellers explained, "the woman would not have done that and the spell would not have been broken."

A farmer known as "Ben," with two span of mules hitched to a wagon, could not get his mules to pull on level ground.

"I told him," said Zellers, "that he was bewitched." The mules pulled as hard as they could and were unable to budge the load, he said. Then the farmer took down an ax from his wagon. He was just about to chop a spoke out of a rear wheel of the wagon when an old man behind a tree nearby cried out in a loud voice, "Ben, don't cut!" The spell was removed and then the mules easily pulled the wagon, Zellers said. It is claimed that cutting a spoke in the wheel would more than likely have killed the old man who was casting the spell. That old man, Zellers said, had spellbound the mules, but the threat of the ax broke the spell.

The witch doctor did "reveal his secrecy" to the extent of telling how he cures the "sweeny" (a severe ailment in horses). He takes a stone from running water and makes three series of passes with it over the afflicted flesh, saying German words that mean in effect, "Flesh and blood, bones and marrow, no more than this stone shall you have pain." The stone must then be returned to the running water and the sweeny will disappear.

"What do you think brought about the cures at the priest's grave in Boston a few months ago?" Zellers was asked.

"That was faith. They went there and *believed* that if they prayed at his grave they would get well, and so they did."

ZELLERS quoted the Bible freely and referred to the miracles of Christ and Moses as proof of some of his own claims. "You've got to be conscientious," he emphasized. "It's no use for anyone to do something just on purpose to try me. That is mocking. When a person does that he doesn't believe."

"How can a cow be conscientious?"

"It's the person who owns the cow that makes the difference. He believes or he wouldn't come with the cow."

"Do you think any of your power comes to you through those who have departed from this life?"

"I don't know anything about that. But people who have been bothered by those kind of things have come to me and I've fixed them." (Zellers' expressions for treating a patient were invariably "I did for her," or "I fixed her.")

"Often people who are under 'hexes' see thought forms that represent these 'hexes.' Sometimes they see them in the form of snakes or devils or pigs, or sometimes cats. One woman would see a devil come through the keyhole, with a small devil after that one, and a snake following the two devils. She put salt on them, but that only made them [illegible] at her. But I fixed her," he added.

"Could a person be 'hexed' at a distance?"

"Yes, if you get in contact with them in some way."

"Any person, man or woman, who casts a spell is a 'witch.' It's the women that get mixed up most in this 'hexing.' Men don't have so much time alone to think.

"This power is given to me," he said, modestly. "I have a son 24 years old, but I cannot tell whether I will be able to teach him this."

IN a modest house in the workingman's district of York lives Jacob Zellers, his retiring little wife and a goodly brood of children. One or two healthy tow-heads may be seen peeping around doors at visitors. "We're just common folks," the witch doctor apologizes. You look around and feel that at least he is not exploiting his powers, whatever they are, for personal gain.

On the dining table under a big square, old-fashioned light dome lay a "chain letter," probably waiting to be copied nine times and sent traveling again. In his own home you feel more than ever that in Zellers' personality lies a great deal of his power to influence or affect those who may come to him for help. He has a clear brain, shrewd, concentrated gaze and full solar plexus development which is usually associated with personal magnetism. And above all he is kindly. Zellers, in addition to powwowing, works steadily at his trade of auto painting.

That results do sometimes follow powwowing and witchcraft seems to be an undisputed fact.

The question is, "What is the power underlying witchcraft?" Is it purely suggestion, and if so, how and under what circumstances does it work?

(Copyright, 1931, by EveryWeek Magazine—Printed in U. S. A.)

Plate 8. Jacob Zellers, an automobile painter and pow-wow doctor of York, Pa., in action during the early 1930s.

WHERE WITCHES FLOURISH IN THIS TWENTIETH CENTURY

New York Woman Haled to Court as a Magician in Allentown, Penn.— Big Modern Communities Where Spells and Incantations Are Used Daily for Every Ill That Flesh Is Heir To.

Sir John Klos, to Whom Mrs. Innocent Went For the Kinp-e Cure.

The Kipp House.

Mrs. George Kipp and Her Children.

Mrs. John Baker, the Bride.

John Baker, Who Charged That Mrs. Innocenzo Bewitched Him.

"Dr." Charles Kistler, the Pow-Wow Doctor.

The Klos Hut Near Bethlehem Where the Kninp Cure Was Practiced.

The New York Times
Published September 10, 1911
Copyright © The New York Times

Plate 9. The Allentown, Pa., pow-wow doctor Charles Kistler (*top right*), who, in 1911, told a journalist that he had 1,200 patients in the previous year alone.

Plate 10. Chilkat chief Skun-doo-ooh (Skundoo), the most notorious Alaskan medicine man or *ixt* during the late nineteenth century.

Plate 11. Matilda Waldman. In 1935 Waldman, of Cleveland, Ohio, accused delicatessen owner Ida Cooper of witchcraft and shot her dead.

HAPPY AS BULLET KILLS WOMAN FEARED AS WITCH

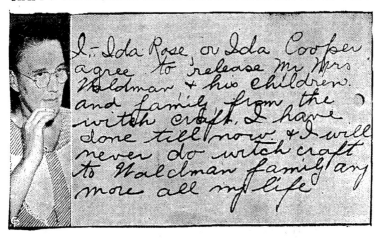

Mrs. Waldman

Note Mrs. Waldman requested "witch" to sign.

Asserting she was glad she "broke the witch's spell" under which she said she and her husband had been "held for years", Mrs. Matilda Waldman was held on a first degree murder charge by Cleveland police after the slaying of Mrs. Ida Cooper. A note that Mrs. Waldman asked Mrs. Cooper, proprietor of a neighborhood grocery, to sign just before the shooting, is pictured, with Mrs. Waldman, above. Mrs. Waldman told police the witchcraft often took the form of fireballs which she and her husband nailed to the walls, keeping a hammer handy for the purpose. Police planned to have mentality of both Mr. and Mrs. Waldman tested. He also was held under a murder charge.

Plate 12. The note Waldman passed to Cooper before shooting her.

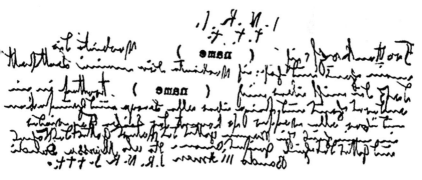

Plate 13. A hexzettel, or anti-witch charm, found in an antique sofa purchased by a secondhand dealer in Berks County, Pa. It was written backwards in German.

ADAM HEIDT.
NOW ON TRIAL AT MONTICELLO.

JOSEPH HEIDT.
JOINTLY INDICTED WITH ADAM.

TRIED FOR MURDER.

THE CRIME OF WHICH ADAM HEIDT AND HIS SON JOSEPH STANDS CHARGED.

A Jury at Monticello Listens to the Evidence Against Them.

The jury to try Adam Heidt at Monticello, was completed yesterday afternoon by the selection of A. Rudolph, as the twelfth juror, and District Attorney Couch opened the case on the part of the people.

The PRESS has already given a full and complete account of the murder for which Adam Heidt and Joseph Heidt, his son, were indicted by the grand jury of Sullivan county. Briefly restated the murder occurred the 19th of January last, shading his eyes. Through the whole day he did not for one moment allow his eyes to be seen but once, and that was when the jurors were being sworn and he was required to stand up. Adam Heidt, the father, wept frequently, but appeared more cheerful than his son.

THE DISTRICT ATTORNEY OPENS THE CASE.

At 3 o'clock a recess was taken for 20 minutes. After the recess, District Attorney Couch detailed to the jury the circumstances of the murder of George Markert on the evening of the 19th of January, 1892. The evidence at the coroner's inquest pointed to Joseph Heidt as being one of the participants in the murder of Markert. They expected to prove that Joseph killed George Markert and that Joseph believed that Markert had the power of witchcraft, which he exercised over his father, and on that belief he proceeded to put Markert out of the way.

Plate 14. Adam and Joseph Heidt. The Heidts, who migrated to New York State from Bavaria in the 1850s, were charged with the murder of George Markert. They believed he was a witch.

Plate 15. Deputy United States Marshal Daniel Cunningham (1850–1942), who investigated the mysterious slaying of Annie Boggs in Booger Hole, West Virginia.

Plate 16. In 1899 the highly educated and respected Oklahoma Choctaw, Solomon Hotema, went on a witch-killing spree, aided by Sam Fry. Tarnatubby was a reputed medicine man.

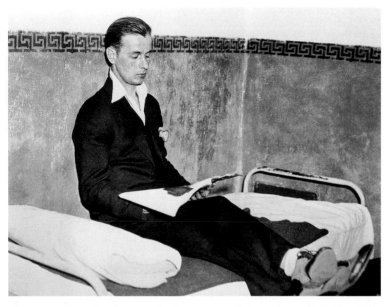

Plate 17. Albert Shinsky in gaol. The 24-year-old from Shenandoah, Shuylkill County, Pa., murdered Susan Mummey believing she was a witch who tormented him at night in the form of a cat.

Plate 18. The interior of the evangelical 'witchmobile', a van containing an anti-occult display of diabolic paraphernalia that toured the US in the early 1970s.

Plate 19. Actress Elizabeth Montgomery played the glamorous suburban witch Samantha Stephens in the hit television comedy series *Bewitched*, which ran between 1964 and 1972.

Plate 20. The house of Nelson Rehmeyer in North Hopewell Township, Pennsylvania. Rehmeyer was the victim in the sensational 1928 'hex murder'.

hundred of them, took the stand to praise his healing powers. His modus operandi was revealed in great detail. Some of his potions underwent chemical analysis, revealing that one of his tonics for bad blood was no more than cherry-flavoured grain alcohol. There was his lucrative trade in *Himmelsbriefs*, and his potent charm against witches—a small canvas cloth bag inscribed with I. N. R. I. containing slips of paper with words in German, Latin, Greek, and Hebrew. Hageman sat nervously, fidgeting in his seat as the hours and days passed. He knew he had made a big mistake. When it came to his own turn to give evidence, he was mauled by the defence lawyer, ex-Judge James Gay Gordon. Hageman, who held no medical licence or evidence of formal training, was made to reveal that he knew nothing of the circulation of blood, was unfamiliar with the word 'pathology', could not define 'hygiene', and was ignorant of the chemical name for common salt. His claim to medical competence was shredded and the case was dismissed.[63]

In 1904 the journal *American Medicine* reported that the Pennsylvania State Medical Board intended to institute a campaign to wipe out hex doctors and *hexerei*. 'The duty has been too long postponed', grumbled the editor, but he hoped that if pursued thoroughly lives would be saved.[64] The increased attention was due in part to the Hageman trial, and in part to the frequent reports from the state's coroners regarding the link between hex doctors and high infant mortality. As he made out the death certificate for eight-month-old Elmer Eckenroth in September 1900, Reading doctor S. Banks Taylor heard how the infant had been unsuccessfully treated by hex doctors.[65] The cause of death was marasmus, or severe malnutrition, a common manifestation of dietary poverty at the time—a lack of protein in particular. A few years later the Reading coroner dealt with the infant of Frederick Carl who had also succumbed to marasmus. A pow-wow doctor had brought a copy of the *Seventh Book of Moses* to Carl's home and written out a passage in red ink on a piece of paper. This he slipped into a muslin bag and hung it at the head of the cradle.[66] When the Pottsville coroner launched an investigation into the death of the child of Michael Cubich, of St Clair, he heard how it had been taken to a hex doctor at Shenandoah. A regular physician was not called in until it died.[67]

By the end of the summer of 1909 Reading coroner Robert E. Strasser had had enough. In one day alone he had investigated six infant deaths all of which involved treatment by hex doctors. He made a public statement saying that the hex doctors were to blame for a large percentage of the infant deaths during the summer months. 'It is time that the authorities investigate the illegal practice that has existed so long in Reading and Berks county, and which is the fundamental reason for the many deaths of our young.' The Allentown coroner expressed similar determination the following summer after yet another such case.[68]

The chorus of complaint was joined by a branch of the Visiting Nurse Association. These Associations had been founded around the country from the 1880s onwards, inspired by the system of charitable district nursing founded by Florence Nightingale in Britain. With regard to Pennsylvania, by 1902 there were Associations in Philadelphia, Harrisburg, and Scranton. A Reading branch was formed in 1918. Charitable donations paid for nurses to go into the homes of the poor to improve sanitary conditions, instruct mothers on childcare, and wash and dress the sick. They were at the frontline of popular healthcare wherever an Association was active.[69] It is not surprising, therefore, that they joined the battle. In 1912 a supervisor of the Visiting Nurse Association, Anna Barlow, put out a statement from Reading denouncing the activities of the local hex doctors. Barlow said that her nurses had saved the lives of numerous children that had been maltreated by hex doctors. She explained the challenge, 'they are an exclusive set of men and women numbering about 20 in this city. Their workings are secret. Ask one of the victims and they will say, "we don't know where their home is. We don't know their names. If we would tell their names the charm would be broken"'.[70]

Did the authorities listen to the chorus of professional criticism? Well, substantive action was finally taken in 1911 with the passing of the Medical Practices Act of Pennsylvania. It reinforced existing legislature, creating a Bureau of Medical Education and Licensure. Henceforth no one in the state could call themselves a doctor or treat diseases by the use of medicines without obtaining a certificate of licensure from the Bureau.[71] If one were polite, one might say that it was an abject failure, an object lesson in how legislature remains an empty gesture if not backed up with the resources and sustained will to implement it.

As the reader will have gathered by now the hex doctors were hardly shy, retiring types skulking in the shadows. The Allentown practitioner Charles Kistler was entered matter-of-factly as 'pow wow doctor' in the 1910 census, and in 1911 he told a journalist that he had 1,200 patients in the previous year alone. An upstanding local citizen confirmed that this was no idle boast.[72] If anything, the negative publicity did them good. The hex doctors thrived. This was revealed all too frustratingly during a probate hearing regarding the will of Martha Adams of Harrisburg in 1915. She had died at the age of fifty-six leaving the bulk of her $12,000 estate to a hex doctor named Harrison Seiferd, a fifty-nine-year-old married man living in South Cameron Street, Harrisburg, whose principal occupation was a bricklayer in a local furnace works. He had been treating both Martha and her deceased husband regularly for some years, and she had complete faith in his ability to communicate to her deceased husband, provide her with magical protection, and put hexes on others. She was, in short, in thrall to the man. His principal treatment consisted of 'force bags' that gave the possessor power over others. These he apparently sold for between $1 and $1,000 depending on the wealth of his clients. One of the bags possessed by Adams was opened and revealed to contain a toenail and a written charm. The will was upheld, justifying Seiferd's demeanour at the probate hearing where he wore a perpetual grin.[73]

Then, in the same year, there was the reprehensible behaviour of Waynesboro hex doctor John Keckler, another bricklayer. His sordid practices were exposed in a long-running legal saga between 1918 and 1921. At the age of fifty-nine Keckler, married with several children, was sentenced to serve five to seven years in the penitentiary for raping the daughters of one of his clients. Like several English cunning-folk I have studied, he abused his magical reputation to coerce clients into having sex with him.[74] Keckler's victims were Ada and Grace Kriner, aged twelve and fifteen respectively at the time of the crime. Keckler had been brought to the Kriner farm at Lemasters, Franklin County, in 1915, to lay a number of his seals around the place to protect it against witchcraft. Keckler told Kriner that a malign influence had been cursing his place for thirty years, and reckoned he could cure its latest manifestation, a sick hog. The seals would be insufficient though, and he would need to involve Ada and Grace in his rituals to remove the hex upon the family. The two young girls were brought to a neighbour's house, the Heckmans, to spend the night. Here, on several occasions between 1915 and May 1917, Keckler had sex with the two girls. He told the Heckmans that as part of his secret magical ritual the girls had 'to touch the hem of his garment'. On one occasion he drew a circle around one of them and uttered an incantation. Grace testified during the trial in 1918 that Keckler would be awaiting them in bed and after performing some ceremonies, including the placement of seals upon them, he would commit the crime. They were sworn to secrecy with the threat that telling anyone would 'do no good'. After Keckler's imprisonment, Kriner launched a $20,000 suit against Keckler and the Heckmans—$10,000 for the debauchment of each of his daughters. The suit rumbled on until April 1921 when Kriner was finally awarded $17,690.50.[75]

For a few years the hex doctor problem slipped into the background, only to explode into the national consciousness in November 1928 when the burned and bound body of a York County farmer and small-time pow-wow doctor named Nelson D. Rehmeyer was found. It transpired that he had been murdered by John Blymyer and two young accomplices. Blymyer believed Rehmeyer had hexed him, and so he and his two companions went to his farmhouse to seize and burn the copy of the *Long Lost Friend* that he was thought to possess, and also to cut a lock of his hair and burn it to break the hex. There is no evidence to suggest the three men had murder on their minds, but a scuffle ensued in which Rehmeyer was knocked dead. They tried to burn down the house to destroy the evidence.[76] The subsequent trial of the three men was a national and international sensation. Years later, one of Rehmeyer's closest neighbours recalled the media fuss and how it intruded on his own life. 'For weeks on end I could hardly get any work done day or night without some male or female reporter interruptin' me askin' to interview me . . . . It got so I could hardly eat my meals without the front doorbell ringin' . . . And in York, man! You shouda been there. Cars with the license tags from twenty different states; more strangers on the streets than durin' the Fair. Every hotel room taken and every restaurant jammed to the doors.'[77]

The case also stoked the creative imagination. The well-connected writer John Lineaweaver wrote a short story in 1931 called 'Hexa buch' concerning a Pennsylvania hex doctor named Dr Hoffmeyer. The title referred to Hoffmeyer's books which included the *Sixth and Seventh Books of Moses*, *Albertus Magnus*, and the *Long Lost Friend*.[78] Then, in 1932, the Potomac Playmakers, a theatre troupe based in Hagerstown, Maryland, which is still going today, staged a comedy by the playwright and inventor Elmer Greenfelder, who was inspired by the Blymyer trial. It was called *Broomsticks, Amen!* and concerned the contemporary beliefs of the Pennsylvania Dutch. The central character was a hex doctor called Emil Hofnagel. Hofnagel hates licensed doctors, and is incensed when his daughter marries a Harrisburg physician. Their child gets sick, and the hex doctor shoots his son-in-law in the shoulder and begins to pow-wow the child himself, but it dies. The three-act play then charts how the wounded doctor sets about combatting the influence of the hex doctors over the community. Despite the serious theme, fun was had with the mangled English of the Pennsylvania Dutch. So when Hofnagel's doorbell ceases to work, he puts out a sign requesting, 'the bell don't make. Please bump!' When, in 1933, it was staged at the Pelham Theater, New York, the lead actor was comedian Lew Fields (born Moses Schoenfeld) who was well known for his 'Dutch Act' portraying German immigrants. It even had a very brief run on Broadway the following year with Jean Adair playing the hex doctor's wife. Adair went on to play one of the aunts in the Cary Grant feature film *Arsenic and Old Lace* (1944).[79] Its Broadway stint was damned by faint praise. The critic Burns Mantle, who was intrigued enough to do some background reading on the topic and referenced the Blymyer trial in his review, thought it well played but concluded it was, 'an earnest folk play, as said, but as foreign to the tastes of this theater center as might be a folk drama of Bavarian peasants'.[80]

The hex doctors also had their public defenders. One hex doctor who stood up and faced the whirlwind of criticism gave a rather remarkable defence of his profession at the Graduate School of the American University, Washington DC, in 1931. Jacob Zellers, an automobile painter living with his wife Daisy and large brood of children in West College Avenue, York, had been pow-wowing for twenty-seven years. He was invited to explain his line of work by a student, Edwin R. Danner, who was also from York and would, a couple of decades later, write a dictionary of the Pennsylvania Dutch dialect. Zellers audience consisted of students and staff under the tutelage of Dr Walton Colcord John, Adjunct Professor of Education. If this was not unusual enough, Zellers was quite open about witches and hexing. He had hexed people himself using the *Sixth and Seventh Books of Moses* he told his audience. He had been responsible for the death of five witches acting in magical self-defence. Much of his business was, however, concerned with pow-wowing simple ailments such as warts. He was most conscious of the authorities' attempts to entrap him, saying that he knew spies came to his surgery masquerading as clients, but as he charged no money, and presented to bill, what could they do? 'If a patient comes to me who hasn't been to a doctor first, I make him go, so the authorities can't hold anything against me. The kind of patients I like best are the ones who have already been to three or four doctors who have failed to help them. Then I take them.'[81]

The most influential defender was no practitioner, though. Meet Ammon Monroe Aurand Jr (1895–1956). The Aurands had been settled in Beaver Springs, Snyder County, for generations. The town was built by German settlers and was originally called Reigertown. The family belonged to the Christ Reformed Church, a Calvinist denomination that originated in the Netherlands.[82] Aurand Sr built up a prosperous publishing company that included the nationwide sale of Bibles, and Aurand Jr was groomed to follow in his father's footsteps from an early age. In 1906 he was described (in a publication by his father) 'as one of the hustling and enterprising young boys of the town and will someday make his mark in the business world'. He was something of a prodigy for having learned typesetting at the age of five, and by the age of eleven he was the librarian of the town's free library. Aurand Jr went on to establish his own more modest publishing house in Harrisburg, and made his reputation by producing a series of idiosyncratic and populist publications explaining and defending Pennsylvania Dutch customs, traditions, and beliefs that pandered to outsider curiosity about them. Indeed, the publishing longevity of Aurand's pamphlets both fuelled and were fuelled by the beginnings of the tourist industry regarding the Lancaster County Amish during the 1930s.[83] Not surprisingly, some of his publications, those regarding the Amish in particular, were not well received within the community. Words such as 'exploitation', 'misrepresentation', and 'disservice' were levelled against him over the years. A case in point was his various publications on the custom of bundling in which courting couples were bundled together in bed fully clothed. Aurand suggested controversially that the custom was particularly prevalent in the Amish community of Mifflin County.[84]

In 1918 the family firm had printed copies of a *Himmelsbrief* for a client who disseminated them amongst the National Guard and draftees in the central counties of Pennsylvania. But his most influential publication on magic was undoubtedly *The Pow Wow Book* (1929), skilfully marketed to tap into the national interest in the

Blymyer case, it was widely reviewed by the American press and frequently praised as an important insight into a 'strange' world. Greenfelder used Aurand's *Pow Wow Book* when researching *Broomsticks, Amen!*, and Aurand sent a copy to Burns Mantle on hearing he was reviewing the play. He became the 'go-to' man for a journalistic quote on *hexerei*. In the preface, Aurand stated he did not believe in the existence of witches but sought to sift the wheat from the chaff in witchcraft—the wheat he identified was pow-wow healing, which if it had no medical benefit certainly did no harm. Aurand said he was 'a disinterested spectator in a war between classes which will not end with the present generation—nor the next'. What ensued was a mish-mash of information. He provided an account of the Blymyer trial, the Medical Practices Act, a useful history of pow-wow books, a collection of charms culled from other texts, and an interview with a pow-wow doctor. Appended was a copy of Hohman's *Long Lost Friend*. It was a publication that appealed to a wide audience, as Aurand well knew.

What genuinely annoyed Aurand was the fingering of Pennsylvanian Germans as being more prone to superstition. In 1933 he gave a newspaper interview in which he pointed out, 'These practices are part of their religion . . . These ideas cannot be taken away from these people as long as constitutional privileges exist.' He was less sympathetic to those hex doctors who commercialized their practices, though.[85] He made a good point. In the farmland of southern Schuylkill County, for instance, ethnic Germans did, indeed, predominate, but to the north of the county, in the coalfields, 85 five per cent of the population in some towns were recent immigrants, mostly from southern and eastern Europe. We have already encountered cases of witchcraft in these communities. The sensational 'poison widows' trials in Philadelphia between 1938 and 1939, which concerned a life insurance racket involving numerous murders, exposed the profound belief in magic and the evil eye amongst the city's Italian community. One of the ringleaders, Paul Petrillo, practised *la fattura* or spell working, and another, a Russian Jew named Morris Bolber, also known as 'Louis the Rabbi', professed to being an adept of the Kabbalah and having learned magic secrets from a Chinese sorceress.[86] Aurand was part of the problem, however, as well as the solution. He helped reinforce the association between persistent witch belief and the Pennsylvania Dutch. Another of his witchcraft pamphlets published in 1942 was entitled *The Realness of Witchcraft in America*, but focused primarily on the Pennsylvania Dutch.

Following the Blymyer case, hex doctors were once again implicated in every evil act and suspicious tragedy. When Mrs Harry MacDonald of Reading burned to death at her home in January 1930 officials sought a hex link. Over a hundred witnesses were summoned by the coroner. One theory was that she had smeared her body with some oily substance provided by a hex doctor, and then set herself alight to purify herself. But no evidence emerged that she had ever visited a hex doctor.[87] Still, the District Attorney threatened to clean up the county once again, and the main weapon against the hex doctors, the 1911 Medical Practices Act, was now brought into action. The following year Charles N. Fry, a State Medical Licensure Bureau investigator instigated prosecutions against Charles W. Dice, a York medicine salesman and pow-wow doctor, who was sentenced to leave the county. Then Dr George E. Murry of Mount Nebo, a farm manager, was arrested and charged with holding an illegal Wednesday night surgery in York.[88]

In September 1933 Robert W. Semenow, law enforcement director of the State Bureau of Medical Licensure, issued a public statement saying, 'this is the beginning of a fight to the finish. We mean to get rid of every last one of these pow-wow people before we are finished'.[89] But for all the tough talk, six months later Semenow admitted to a journalist that they were struggling—and not with the weight of information. Lancaster County was the hotbed of the whole racket he complained, and the greatest barrier to success was the patients and not the hex doctors. 'We would be only too glad to prosecute these so-called hex doctors,' he said, 'but we are handicapped because of the fear of patients.' Only two prosecutions were launched between December and April, with one conviction.[90] The 'baby slasher' case from Salladasburg, Lycoming County, is a good example of the problem Semenow faced. The five-year-old son of John Fritz was diagnosed as a 'mental deficient', and it was recommended that he be taken to the state hospital after he cut his eight-month-old baby brother James Leroy with a butcher's knife. John Fritz resented the involvement of the authorities, claiming his family had been 'hissed up on by neighbors'. The family believed their five-year-old son, who had attacked their baby boy on other occasions, was possessed by an evil spirit and so they had brought in a female pow-wow doctor to drive it out. She went through some ritual and declared that he had been 'cured by faith'. John Fritz rejected criticism of the pow-wow and refused to divulge any information about her, much to the frustration of the authorities.[91] A similar response was met during the trial of Warren Faust, of Fleetwood, Berks County, for shooting dead his father Alvin, in March 1940. Alvin had repeatedly visited hex doctors, and a written charm was found on his corpse. Warren, a twenty-five-year-old showbill artist, crippled in early childhood, said his father raved variously that he was God or that Moses had given him special powers. When questioned in jail as to the name of the hex doctor his father consulted, Warren refused to say.[92]

From the 1940s onwards, hex fatigue set in amongst the Pennsylvania authorities and press. The result, perhaps, of a sullen admittance that pow-wowing and witchcraft beliefs could not be suppressed by laws and interventions. Or perhaps a consequence of a deluded belief that year on year the miraculous power of state education was doing the job without further intervention. There is no doubt that the strength of witchcraft belief diminished, as will be discussed in the final chapter, but hexing was only one part of the pow-wow tradition, which was, as Aurand said, ingrained in the religious and cultural life of many Pennsylvania Dutch. In 1961 the minister Jacob J. Hershberger stirred things up when he wrote in the Amish newspaper *The Budget* that pow-wowing and *braucherei* were the work of the Devil. One respondent, who accepted *brauch* but did not believe in witchcraft, suggested it was false to link the two. She further questioned, 'are you absolutely sure that powwowing and "brauch" are one and the same?'[93]

During the 1960s Pennsylvania Dutch folk culture began to attract serious rather than sensational explorations, particularly in the work of the scholar Don Yoder, co-founder of the Pennsylvania Folklife Society. Health care professionals turned from campaigning against to understanding pow-wow. Mennonite and Amish traditional medicine, and ethnic German pow-wow healing more generally, began to be embraced as an honourable tradition—an aspect of legitimate complementary medicine. This was part of a broader shift in western medicine at the time that sought engagement with folk medicine, holistic, and faith-based healing methods from around the globe, such as meditation, acupuncture, and homeopathy.[94] There was a realization that modern medicine and folk medicine could coexist; an either/or situation was not necessary. This is a view now accepted widely in popular culture and partially by the medical establishment. So the Amish, for instance, have no problem with certain aspects of institutional medicine, going to hospital and consulting physicians, but they retain a strong reliance on aspects of pow-wow, such as herbalism and faith healing, for certain ailments.[95]

INSANITY

One October morning in 1825 Richard Neal, aged thirty-seven, of Eliot, Maine, rose from his bed with the fixed intention of killing the family cat. He searched in vain, even taking up some of the flooring of his barn with an axe. His wife told him to leave the cat alone. In response Neal knocked her down and chopped off her head. He then proceeded to the town of Berwick and gave himself up. Neal was a man of good character, with no private quarrels, and seemingly happily married to his wife of seven years and mother of his four young children. How to make sense of a senseless murder? The noise resulting from Neal hacking off the head of his wife quickly brought neighbours to the scene. He told them that his cat was possessed by witches and that they had transferred themselves to his wife—presumably explaining why he could not find the cat. He said he had no intention of killing his wife when he left the house that morning. The conclusion of the press and others was that such an 'unnatural' murder must have resulted from a delusion induced by insanity. There had to be a medical cause. It was reported that eight or nine years before Neal had contracted hydrophobia after saliva from a rabid pig came into contact with a cut on one of his hands. As a result, he had suffered from a period of mental derangement. It was assumed that the murder must be a recurrence of this malady.[1] Was Neal really insane from a modern medical perspective? We will never know. But the issue of gauging the sanity of witch killers cropped up repeatedly over the next century raising profound and difficult legal and ethical questions.

The psychiatric profession in America, as in Europe, has its origins in the growth of mental hospitals during the early nineteenth century in response to changing welfare and penal policies. It was a period when the medical profession was increasingly turning its focus from the body to the mind, exploring the physiology of hallucinations, emotions, and the impulses behind abnormal social behaviour. Insanity was categorized to improve our understanding of it, and research was conducted on asylum inmates to identify the causes of different types of insanity and whether and how they could be cured.

Some early psychiatrists thought they could detect the predisposition to insanity and superstition by applying the science of phrenology. In his 1841 popular guide to the subject, the eccentric San Francisco phrenologist, showman, and photographer Frederick Coombs identified the organ of 'marvellousness' in the brain as being the seat of the problem. Those with a large one were prone to being credulous and superstitious, while those with a very large marvellousness exhibited a propensity to believe in witchcraft and demonology.[2] According to Coomb's head measurements, the archetype of feminine cranial perfection, which he termed 'New England's Fairest Flower', had a very large marvellousness, as did the Chinook Indians. It should be noted that Coombs believed he was George Washington. Other phrenologists explained that a diseased organ of 'destructiveness' exhibited itself in the propensity to irrational violence and murder, sometimes under the delusion of satanic agency. In the days when witchcraft was widely believed in, opined the Scottish phrenologist George Combe, such people were frequently believed to be possessed by evil spirits.[3]

The understanding of insanity in these early days of the profession was deeply influenced by America's racial history. In the 1840s a note published in the first volume of the *American Journal of Insanity* reported observations by physicians in the field that insanity was unheard of amongst the Cherokees and seldom found amongst Africans. An elderly Chief was reported as saying that 'he had never known a case of insanity among his people, such as he had seen in the Hospital at Philadelphia'.[4] The view was pervasive in nineteenth-century psychiatry that insanity was a product of 'civilized' society because life in a modern, urban-industrial environment generated a higher degree of mental excitement. 'Primitive' or 'barbarous' peoples did not need to think beyond satisfying their immediate needs, and so had undeveloped emotional faculties. Once African Americans and Native Americans became civilized or were given their freedom they too experienced increased levels of insanity, but not necessarily because they become more intellectually sophisticated. The perceived intellectual inferiority of African Americans made them even less able to cope emotionally with the disorientation of urban life, and less equipped to handle the responsibilities of civilized society. In 1896 the asylum superintendent Theophilus Powell concluded from the results of a survey of inmates in Georgia that there had been a substantial rise in insanity and tuberculosis amongst blacks since 1860. This he attributed to their enthusiasm for sexual debauchery and drink once freed from slavery. The obvious racist conclusion to be drawn from such fundamentally flawed studies was that emancipation was more traumatic than enslavement and not in the interests of the general well-being of African Americans.

Some early psychiatrists and physicians, particularly those in the southern states, believed the slave population was more prone to conditions such as hysteria and epilepsy, and that they had mental and physical ailments peculiar to themselves. The racist physician Samuel Cartwright (1793–1863) conjured up the term 'drapetomania' to describe a form of insanity that caused slaves to abscond, while *dysaesthesia aethiopis* was a condition explaining 'Negro rascality', which particularly affected freed slaves who lived amongst themselves. The condition of *Cachexia Africana* or dirt eating was also considered peculiar to the African.[5] Amongst African Americans, forms of insanity such as dementia expressed itself in a regressive way that brought out their primitive, pagan, magical impulses. Furthermore, their profound belief in witchcraft rendered them more prone to insanity. A. P. Merrill, a Memphis physician, wrote in the mid-nineteenth century that the negro was 'easily depressed by his confidence in witchcraft, and much of his unhappiness as well as many of his diseases, proceed from purely imaginary causes'.[6] James Kiernan, Superintendent of Cook County Hospital for the Insane, Illinois, and respected author of numerous psychiatric studies, examined several cases of paranoia concerning witchcraft amongst African-American patients. He observed that 'the talk of witchcraft renders a practical business man suspicious of insanity, and would soon bring the mental condition of an otherwise seemingly intelligent negro under suspicion'.[7]

In exploring the relationship between insanity and witchcraft belief in historic contexts we also need to recognize that our modern conceptions of insanity do not necessarily map directly on to historic notions and experiences, and vice versa. Old terminologies such as 'madness', lunacy', and 'melancholy' were shaped by historic religious, cultural, moral, as well as medical notions; they have to be understood within the context of the time and place they were applied. The condition of 'hysteria', or uncontrolled emotional excess, is a pertinent case in point. Its origins lie in the ancient notion that female maladies resulted from a disturbed uterus (*hystera*), but in the nineteenth century it came to be applied widely in relation to the 'mania' or 'madness' of the witch trials. 'Witch hysteria' and the term 'witch craze', which imply that the trials were an outbreak of gendered and/or pathological behaviour, continue to be widely employed in popular culture, although historians have wisely abandoned the terms in recent years.

Seeking retrospective diagnoses, that is, identifying maladies from the annals of history with the hindsight of modern knowledge, and classifying them according to contemporary categories of illness, was a favourite pastime of the early psychiatric profession and continues to be seductive. It has been argued in recent decades that poisoning by the ingestion of ergot fungus (a source of lysergic acid), outbreaks of Lyme disease, and encephalitis lethargica or 'sleepy sickness' solve the 'puzzle' of early-modern witchcraft persecutions. An attempt has also been made to prove that schizophrenia contributed to the Salem witch hunt.[8] This condition is generally associated with delusions of persecution and aural hallucinations in the form of hostile or critical voices, although again, in popular usage it is incorrectly used to suggest multiple personalities. There has never been full agreement in the medical profession about the origin, diagnosis, and cure of schizophrenia, and today there is debate that it should not be used as a diagnostic category.

The term schizophrenia was coined in the early twentieth century, and its use can be more revealing of the contemporary influence of the pharmaceutical industry, doctor-patient relationships, media, and biological research, than the mental health of people in the more distant past.[9] Still, retrospective diagnoses can be of value. They remind us to take seriously beliefs and experiences that have at times been denounced as the excrescences of racial and cultural backwardness. Consider, for example, the case of the Swedish immigrant Leopold Weedstrand, who in the 1870s, believed he was plagued by witches. He moved from Meadville, Pennsylvania, the centre of the trouble, to Iowa and Minnesota to escape their torment, but their voices followed him. 'For hours at night they whispered strange things to me', he said. 'When I got to Minnesota I found it just the same—witches, witches all the time, and they persecuted me . . . I heard voices and remember what they said . . . I heard them say they'd kill me.'[10] Similarly in 1878 the mental state of a German Iowa farmer, Max Frahm, was assessed after he claimed witches constantly called him foul names, and that whenever people approached him the witches cried to him that he was doomed. He was said to be sane in every other respect.[11]

Labelling these cases as schizophrenia helps us to understand the difficult lives of these otherwise sane people. We can understand their suffering and why they believed themselves bewitched, rather than dismissing them as credulous fools and laughing at them, just as Weedstrand was mocked in the local press at the time. Witchcraft belief was not the cause of his insanity, but his illness was expressed through such notions. His case and others highlight that while witchcraft belief was completely normal, it could easily be interpreted as pathological by others who did not share the same culture of belief. This is no mere academic exercise in definition. As we shall now see, determining normal and abnormal witchcraft belief tested the limits of the law in numerous legal disputes.

Putting it to the test

There was an ever-present tension between bad psychiatry and good law, and bad law and good psychiatry in the courtroom.[12] The source of much of it was the M'Naghten rules as a test of legal insanity. They derived from the trial in 1843 of a Scotsman, Daniel M'Naghten, who, believing he was being persecuted by a conspiracy led by the British Tory government at the time, attempted to assassinate the British Prime Minister Robert Peel, but shot dead his secretary instead. M'Naghten was acquitted on the basis of insanity. This caused public uproar and so Parliament requested a panel of judges to draw up a set of rules that justified the decision. In short, the rules, which became a standard test in many countries including the US, judge that persons be found either 'not guilty by reason of insanity' or 'guilty but insane' if proven that they had a disease of the mind that rendered them unable to understand the 'nature and quality' of the criminal act committed, or if they did not know what they were doing was wrong. Those adjudged so, were to be committed to a secure hospital or asylum, usually for an indefinite period.

An American development born out of dissatisfaction with M'Naghten was the irresistible impulse test. This went beyond cognition of the difference between right and wrong, accepting that some people were unable to prevent themselves from committing a crime—they were not free agents, they were uncontrollably driven. So a defendant might know they were doing wrong but could plead diminished responsibility because of irresistible impulse. This was obviously applicable in cases where people claimed they were driven to commit murder by delusions and hallucinations inspired by evil spirits, witches, and the Devil. The irresistible impulse test was first adopted by an Alabama District Court in the 1880s, and was accepted by a few other state courts, but it received criticism for stretching too far the medico-legal definition of insanity, and raised the difficulty of testing that an impulse was uncontrollable rather than one that was not resisted.[13]

The judicial opinion on witchcraft and insanity was forged in the probate courts, during the fraught and often interminable disputes over the validity of wills. The seminal test case of the nineteenth century was that of a South Carolina plantation owner named Mason Lee, who in July 1820, being 'of perfect mind, memory, and understanding', bequeathed his entire $50,000 dollar estate to the states of Tennessee and South Carolina. Doing so, he disinherited his family and two illegitimate sons known as the Pennywinkle twins. To ensure there was no ambiguity, Lee's will stated that his relations would not inherit anything 'while wood grows or water runs'. Lee died two years later aged fifty-two. Over the next seven years his relatives, the Wiggins', contested the will in various courts on the basis that he was insane at the time of making the will, the principal evidence being his conviction that he was plagued by witches and evil spirits.

Lee was born to a respectable North Carolina family. He settled in Georgia before fleeing the state after killing one of his plantation slaves. He then bought a plantation in South Carolina on the Pee Dee River, near Bennettsville, where he prospered. Yet despite his wealth, towards the end of his life Lee lived in a dirty hovel, eating frugally, sleeping in a hollowed out gum-tree log, and wearing the coarsest of clothing. The spoon he ate with had iron rivets, which Lee said helped keep the witches away. He constantly feared that his relatives had 'goomered' him, and believed that all women were witches. Urinating on the ground made him vulnerable to spells, so he carried with him a tin cup into which he peed. A local blacksmith made several swords for him that he thought would protect him against the Devil and his witches. He accused the Wiggins' of bewitching his penis and his teeth. To counteract the latter he had fourteen healthy teeth removed. Various other proofs were given of his eccentric ideas regarding farming techniques.[14]

Lee was certainly obsessed by his fear of witches, and held some unusual views on farming practice, but in both the original court hearing and the subsequent appeals it was ruled that his 'foolishness' regarding witchcraft was considered explicable in terms of his fondness for whisky, and his suffering from the complaint known as the 'gravel' or kidney stones. Indeed, one witness said that Lee had, during his final moments, denied the existence of witchcraft, stating that the cause of all his problems was the gravel. But the outcome of the suit still hung on the relationship between witchcraft belief and insanity. Presiding over the case, the eminent Judge Thomas Waties, great-grandfather of the outspoken South Carolina anti-segregation Judge Julius Waties Waring (1880–1968), instructed the jury that 'a belief in witchcraft, although sometimes the symptom of a disordered mind, was not of itself any proof of it, as it had often been entertained by persons who were above all suspicions of insanity, and even by men who were distinguished for their wisdom'.[15] Case law was made.

Similar decisions were reached in subsequent probate appeals. In 1854 the will of an Indiana farmer named Francis Stephen was upheld despite the fact that he declared his deceased wife was a witch and that the children he disinherited were also witches and had inherited their mother's 'witch-sticks'.[16] The judgement in favour of the validity of the will consisted of a rambling disquisition on belief in the supernatural from the Bible through to spiritualism, concluding that belief in witchcraft was not, in itself, sufficient evidence of insanity, even though Stephen had *acted* upon this belief by disinheriting his children. A couple of years later a similar story to that of Mason Lee was heard during an appeal regarding the will of the bachelor Obed Woodbury, of Beverly, Massachussetts, which cut out the principal heirs, a nephew and niece of his brother named Zebulon Woodbury and Elizabeth Ludden. Obed had intimated that the two would inherit his estate; that is, until a year before his death, when Obed began to harbour the conviction that

Zebulon had poisoned and bewitched him. He kept an iron nail in his pantry to ward of witchcraft, and accused Zebulon of removing it. He also believed that Zebulon's wife had a bottle with seeds in it, which by swinging over her head she could cause him agonies. Obed's convictions were, he had confided, based on conversations with spirits. He even believed he had seen Jesus Christ in the air. Two physicians who attended Obed testified that in their opinion he was suffering insane delusions regarding his nephew. The appeal was successful this time, on the basis that the executor, who was also a legatee, Josiah Ober, had undue influence on Obed in making his will.[17]

In the three cases above, the deceased had expressed their witchcraft belief in terms of persecution complexes that have similarities to the symptoms and behavioural patterns of illnesses such as dementia, but the next case, brought before the New York Surrogate Court in 1888, shows how what we might describe as 'normal' witchcraft beliefs were now being interpreted by some as symptomatic of enfeebled minds. Eliza Ann Vedder, of Albany County, New York, and of Dutch descent, died on 19 January 1887, aged seventy-seven. Four years earlier she had made out her will leaving nearly all her property to her husband. The couple had no children. Once again nephews and nieces contested the will. The principal evidence consisted of her various beliefs and practices. So it was heard that she made the sign of the cross at the bottom of her churn and put irons in the cream to ensure the butter came. She believed that her horses were ridden at night by witches. She told a neighbour that her child was bewitched, and advised her to search its pillow to see if there was a feather wreath. She once took a nephew on a treasure-hunting expedition on her farm. Aspects of Vedder's beliefs, such as feather wreaths, may indeed have seemed peculiar to those who had no knowledge of Dutch popular magic, but to a distant eye there was nothing monomaniacal or paranoid in her behaviour. Evidence in support of the will was given that demonstrated she was perfectly competent in running her farm and domestic life, was a lifelong member of the local Reformed Dutch Church, and that her belief in visions was an aspect of her faith. The defence lawyer concluded reasonably: 'The Bible was the book of books to the aged testatrix. Its lessons had sunk deep in her heart, its language was often on her lips, it was to her the precious fountain of God's inspiration. It is not passing strange that the ancient belief in witchcraft survived in her.' The court agreed.[18]

In this case, and others, illustrious men of the past were cited as evidence that belief in witchcraft was not incompatible with the highest intellect and moral purity. So the lawyer defending Vedder's will mused that Martin Luther and John Wesley had expressed a belief in the evil of witchcraft. In 1903 Judge John Vestal Hadley of the Indiana Supreme Court drew upon his historical knowledge when he reversed a local court decision invalidating the will of an avid treasure-hunter and farmer named Joseph Watt, observing that the influential English judge Matthew Hale (1609–1676) and William Blackstone believed in witches and in punishing them.[19]

Murder trials provided the other main legal forums for debating the relationship between witchcraft belief and insanity. The stakes were much higher, of course. Psychiatric opinion could determine whether a murderer lived or died. Studies conducted in the 1970s showed that the American public vastly inflated how often the insanity defence has been used and the extent of its success. It has always been thus.[20] The insanity defence was actually uncommon in murder trials in the nineteenth and early twentieth century. High-profile cases, such as those of the assassins of Presidents James A. Garfield and William McKinley, distorted public perception. There were practical reasons against employing it. The introduction of an insanity defence usually prolonged trials and led to burdensome costs. The success rate was also low, so that it was not an automatic option for defence lawyers. Furthermore, a successful insanity plea did not mean the murderer got off scot-free. If cure was considered possible, then by the letter of the law the murderer would have to face trial once again. The judicial and medical problems posed by the insanity plea are well illustrated in the following case.

In 1937 a forty-year-old Serbian immigrant named Ilija Martinovich shot dead his cousin and childhood friend Nicholas Aleksich, a policeman in Butte, Montana. Martinovich had emigrated from Serbia, in what was then the Austro-Hungarian Empire, in 1913. He spent a few years in casual labouring jobs, working in the mines, but returned home in 1924 after experience 'all sorts of bad luck'. The following year, though, he was drawn back to the US by what he later believed were the malign powers of Aleksich. Thanks to the guidance of a female guardian angel that appeared to him in dreams, by 1931 Martinovich became convinced his old friend was a wizard guided by the Devil and was responsible for all his misfortune. He would do himself and the world a favour by killing such a wizard. Reasoning that he was likely to be caught, Martinovich began saving money for his day in court. In 1934 he was incarcerated for a time in Warm Springs state psychiatric hospital for exhibiting insanity 'shown in acts and fear of witchcraft'. One of his visitors was Aleksich who stood by his old friend despite his unstable mind, and helped get him paroled. Being a model inmate Martinovich was released after a few months, bought a gun, and bided his time for the right moment. Then on Sunday 28 February 1937 he was in Starovich's saloon, 82 East Park Street, when he spotted Aleksich, followed him down the street, and shot him in the back of the head from two feet. He had killed a wizard, and was glad he had done so.

The trial commenced in June. Martinovich's defence team based their insanity plea upon his belief in witches and wizards. Several psychiatrists took the stand to confirm that Martinovich was an incurable paranoiac, and was unable to distinguish between right and wrong at the time of the murder, It was clear from his testimony, though, that Martinovich did know right from wrong. When questioned as to his intention to kill another man, 'Long John' Gurgevich, whom he also believed to be a witch, the following exchange ensued:

Q. Did you change your mind about killing Long John?
A. I am.
Q. You don't want to kill him now?
A. I don't care when that day I didn't get him, he don't do as much wrong as Nick.
Q. You don't want to kill John now?
A. No.
Q. What made you change your mind?
A. He do me no wrong.
Q. Do you feel sorry for killing Nick?
A. No.
Q. You are glad you didn't kill John?
A. I believe I kill, I would have kill.
Q. You don't feel sorry about it?
A. No.
Q. You realize that the law of Montana makes it a crime for you to kill another man?
A. Yes. I say to myself the jury do what you want, this witchcraft that hurt the people the way I feel myself, give me free.
Q. [If] Instead of killing Nick you killed some other man who wasn't a wizard, do you think you have a right to do that?
A. No other man. For man no right to kill other man. No man has right to kill. It's against the law.
Q. How about wizards?
A. I have right to kill wizards.

It was also heard in evidence that Martinovich told his attorney it was all right to kill a snake or a wizard, but it was not all right to kill a man. Under further questioning he testified, 'In Old Testament, I read three or four times during the panic, without work, I read New Testament five or six times "the wizard no live", that means they be killed.' Hospital psychiatrist Dr Gold was asked if a delusion regarding wizards and witches would interfere with a person's knowledge of law and what was unlawful. Gold replied that it would not interfere in this way, as the patient is always bright and intelligent on subjects except those connected with his or her hallucinations.

After nearly seventy hours of deliberation the jury was deadlocked eight to four in favour of a verdict of not guilty by reason of insanity. Judge J. J. Lynch discharged the jury, and the trial closed at a cost of $5,500 dollars to Silver Bow County. Martinovich stayed in jail while a retrial was arranged for February 1939, a year after the murder. But before it went ahead at further great cost, the county attorney petitioned for a sanity hearing, partly on the basis of saving the county money. Doctors testified that Martinovitch's mental condition had deteriorated. He was confined indefinitely to Warm Springs until such time as he was found to be sane and therefore could stand trial for his crime. I have found no evidence that he was ever released. As a postscript, Mrs Aleksich sued the state industrial fund for compensation for her husband's death, but in 1944 was told by the Supreme Court that her claim was unreasonable as the job of policeman was not inherently hazardous.[21] Rough justice indeed.

Blame it on the roots

Murderers blamed their insanity on all sorts of influences. In 1884 a one-legged English tramp named Michael Murray was hanged at Ebensburg, Pennsylvania, for shooting dead a young man named John Hancuff after the latter had verbally abused him. Just prior to his execution he dictated a letter to be published after his death claiming that he had committed the crime under the influence of witchcraft. Some said the Devil made them do it.[22] If the murderer was clearly not what was termed a 'congenital idiot', then lawyers usually opted for a plea of temporary insanity caused by alcoholism, bangs on the head, extreme emotional stress, fever, poison, and drugs. In the 1910 case of Cletus 'Nutty' Williamson the reading of books of magic was said to have caused temporary insanity. Williamson killed his father-in-law Warren Koons and his wife at Canton, Ohio, while, as he claimed, 'the evil spirit was in me'. A relative of the Koons recalled, 'at our home on Easter day 1909, he expressed his belief in witches and ghosts and such things. He said at home he had a book called "The Seven Books of Moses" or some name like that which explained such things fully.' The defence succeeded in getting hold of a copy of the *Egyptian Secrets*, which the arresting detective confirmed as belonging to Williamson, and produced it as material evidence in court. The defence failed and Williamson was put in the electric chair on 29 April 1911.[23]

When Baxter Purnell went on trial in 1938 for murdering his nineteen-year-old sister-in-law Martha Jane Fink, he blamed his actions on the effects of some roots he was given by a black root doctor. Baxter was born in 1906, one of the numerous children of William and Sallie Parnell of Cabarrus County, North Carolina.[24] William worked in a cotton mill and Baxter began his working life there too as a 'doffer boy', whose role was to take the full bobbins from the spinning frames and replace them with empty ones. By the age of thirty-two he was married and scratching a living as a tenant farmer near the historic Rocky River Presbyterian Church, Concord, which had been founded back in the mid-eighteenth century.

On the evening of the 3 July 1938, while his wife and Martha Jane knelt in a pig pen and prayed after a family row, Baxter, in a fit of anger, plunged an ice pick into Martha Jane's chest. He then went to the nearby home of the local pastor, John Ricks (1906–2010), and requested that he be escorted to Concord to give himself up. At the subsequent inquest, Parnell, a burly young man dressed in overalls, gave no testimony, but he pleaded not guilty at the ensuing murder trial. He claimed that he had no recollection of his heinous act, except that half an hour before, he had chewed a conjure root that made his mind 'come and go in waves', and had rendered him temporarily insane.

The root had been provided by a reputed African-American root doctor from Mecklenburg County named Jennie Morris. She was ordered to testify and duly appeared in a pink-flowered dress, black hat, and veil. She knew, no doubt, that if the plea of temporary insanity was upheld, the consequences for her were grave. It transpired that Baxter had paid her a visit the Sunday before the murder. As she explained: 'He was takin' my dust treatment for good luck. His luck had been comin' mighty bad and I thought he needed some rattletongue root. So I gave him some and told him to gnaw it and spit it out.' He returned the day of the murder in an excited state. Morris said she was scared of him. 'He was 'actin' and talkin' crazy as a betsy bug', and she feared that 'he might get me hexed.' When questioned about the ingredients of her concoctions she was none too forthcoming. 'I ain't got time to tell you', she said. She was concerned, however, to clarify that she did not dabble in harmful magic. She worked to 'do people good' and to 'cure miseries and to bring people good luck'.

As well as the 'root made me mad' plea, the jury heard from Purnell's mother that a head injury he had received as a child had left him 'addle-brained'. He had also been injured in the head by an explosion. His educational record was cited as evidence of this. He had not gone beyond the first grade when he left school at fifteen, after seven or eight years' attendance. Although not widely reported, he also told the jury that he had emasculated himself a few years before though he did not know why he did it. This would explain a curious report in a local newspaper a decade earlier which detailed how police had failed to trace two unknown men that Baxter said had mutilated him while out hunting near Rocky River Church on Christmas day. He underwent emergency surgery at Concord hospital.[25]

Found guilty and sentenced to death, Parnell appealed to the Supreme Court and Governor Hoey, but no interventions were forthcoming. At 10.31 a.m. on 9 December 1938, Parnell was led to the death chamber in Raleigh State Prison. It had been installed in 1910 when electrocution replaced hanging in the state. Then in 1935 it was refitted as a gas chamber.[26] Before nineteen witnesses, including the chaplain, the warden, and other prison officials, he was strapped into the execution chair. The chamber was sealed and the gas switched on. After a couple of minutes, during which he remained calm, the gas took effect and Parnell suddenly strained violently against the straps holding him down. Only after a full fourteen minutes was he finally pronounced dead. The chaplain later told reporters that Parnell requested him not to release any information for publication other than the following statement:

> He exonerates the old colored woman and takes the full blame on himself. He says that he did it in a fit of anger and was sorry immediately afterwards. He prayed for the girl's recovery. He asks that word be sent to the colored woman that he is sorry that he brought her into it and he asks her to forgive him. In fear he gave the story about the 'roots', and then understood it is best not to change one's story. He says he would have liked to have given the truth at his trial but didn't know what to do.[27]

Parnell never divulged his true motives. Israel Fink, father of Martha Jane, thought that he had been enraged by the visit of Martha Jane's boyfriend that evening. Mrs Fink said, 'I just don't know ... I don't understand it.' Who really knows what went through his mind, but it seems likely that Baxter was suffering some long-term psychosexual problems. As his comments to the chaplain suggest, though, the case for temporary insanity based on the herb doctor fatally undermined a genuine case of underlying psychological problems.

Temporary insanity, which included the category of irresistible impulse, was much contested throughout the nineteenth century and beyond. The psychiatric profession insisted that only they held the knowledge to decide the boundary between a crime committed in 'heat of passion' and one committed while temporarily insane, but the problem is that they did not agree among themselves. The respected American neurologist William Alexander Hammond wrote in 1870 that 'the act which marks the height of the paroxysm is always preceded by symptoms of mental aberration, while acts done in the heat of passion are not thus foreshadowed'. Furthermore, after the act, the murderer acting under the influence of the passions thinks only of his escape, of his personal safety, whereas the temporarily insane 'never thinks of escape, nor even avoids publicity. He may even boast of his conduct, or deliver himself into the hands of the law.' But the *Baltimore Medical Journal* dismissed Hammond's definitions as a 'charming.

. . specimen of sophistical reasoning'.[28] Some argued philosophically that all crime was symptomatic of mental illness. Where was the line to be drawn?

Paranoia in the heat

Nineteenth- and early-twentieth-century asylums have had a very bad press, but while there were many abuses and poor conditions some historical perspective is required. The bleeding of patients went out of vogue in the mid-nineteenth century and surgical cures were uncommon. The application of chemical treatments in the form of insulin and metrazol convulsive shock treatment only began in the 1930s. The therapeutic use of electroshock therapy was rarely used in public state asylums during the nineteenth and early twentieth centuries. The more notorious electroconvulsive shock treatment, considered good for schizophrenia and depression in particular, which is responsible for much of the bad press, was only widely adopted in America during the mid-twentieth century. Many patients' experience was one of a regulated working life, cultural activity, and contemplation, as much as that was possible in the increasingly crowded accommodation.[29] For others, of course, it was a living hell. More to the point, the intent of asylum employees was not to contain murderers for life but to restore their sanity so that they could be returned to the courts. But was cure possible? It was certainly rare, but here is one 'success' story.

On 2 August 1935 a forty-six-year-old resident of Cleveland, Ohio, named Matilda Waldman, gaunt, prim, and bespectacled, walked into the delicatessen run by Ida Cooper, aged fifty-seven.[30] After a brief exchange of words she took out a revolver and shot Cooper dead. As she fled the store two passers-by, Michael and Edward August, seized Waldman until police arrived. She told them, 'A holdup man just killed Mrs Cooper.'

As Waldman pulled the trigger, her husband Samuel was in the office of Cleveland Police Prosecutor William H. Schneider complaining of the hex magic being worked upon him by Cooper. Ida's husband Isadore was also present. Earlier that day, Samuel had gone to Isadore and begged him to get his wife to remove the spell he was convinced she had cast over them. They argued and Samuel went off to the police station and requested a warrant for Ida's arrest. No action was taken and so a few hours later Samuel returned to the station to renew his request. Meantime, Cooper had gone there too to complain about Samuel's behaviour. Schneider managed to soothe the immediate situation and the two men left in a calmer state. But when Cooper arrived back at the delicatessen he found his wife lying dead on the floor and police sergeant Stephen Tozzer in the act of arresting Matilda.

She told him, 'I killed her because for six years she has been bewitching me and my husband.'

The Waldmans were poor, with Samuel scraping a meagre living peddling razor blades. Newspapers reported they had two children, but the prior history of the Waldmans is difficult to pin down.[31] The Coopers were first-generation Jewish immigrants. Isadore was from Poland and his wife emigrated from Kiev in 1892—following in the footsteps of many other Jews from the then Russian city to escape its systematic repression and periodic pogroms. They spoke Yiddish to their clutch of children. In America the Coopers had moved around, settling for a while in Pennsylvania and Maryland, Isadore working as a plumber. They eventually put down firm roots in a poor district of Cleveland where Isadore ran a secondhand store before setting up the delicatessen. Ida supplemented their modest income by telling fortunes using cards and a crystal ball.

In 1912 Samuel Waldman went to have his fortune told by Ida. She gazed into her crystal, and the strong impression this left upon him sowed the seeds of the tragedy that would unfold twenty-three years later. For six years after his consultation, he believed that Ida had bewitched him. He only felt relief when he left Cleveland and settled elsewhere. He met and married Matilda and all was well until he bumped into Ida again. The couple began to be tormented by nocturnal disturbances and plagued by strange illnesses. They could not eat or sleep, and experienced bouts of paralysis and blindness. Worst of all, they were periodically menaced by fireballs that danced through their bedroom. They kept all the windows and doors shut, blocked up the keyholes and papered over the windows. All to no avail.

The summer of 1934 had been the hottest on record in Ohio since state weather records began in 1883. July and early August in 1935 saw a return of the sweltering temperatures. Life in the city's tenements was verging on unbearable. Like many other residents, the Waldmans could have left their windows and doors open to provide some ventilated relief. But the Waldmans could not take this risk because of the fireballs. And so on the 2 August, at their wits' end, they finally decided to force Ida to cease her torments. While Samuel went to get a warrant from the police, Matilda decided to take matters into her own hands. As she explained to police, 'At 2:00 pm, I lay down on the bed and some power told me I was in great danger, so I got my husband's gun and went to the Cooper store. "I'm Waldman's wife," I told Mrs Cooper. "Oh, yes, you're the wife of the fellow who thinks I've put the witch on him".' Matilda then handed her the following letter, which she ordered Ida to sign:

I, Ida Rose or Ida Cooper, agree to release Mr Mrs Waldman & his children and family from the witch craft. I have done till now & I'll never do witch craft to Waldman family any more all my life.

Ida merely laughed, at which Matilda reached for the pistol in her handbag and fired three shots.

Matilda was charged with first-degree murder. Samuel was also arrested. On 3 August she was brought to the police court where she pleaded 'not guilty' and stated she felt no remorse for her actions. 'I feel like a new person . . . I feel so relieved I can't explain it.' 'Would you do it again?' asked the presiding judge. 'Well, judge, I hope I never have to', she replied. Matilda was charged, without bond, to stand before the next Grand Jury. The trial never took place though, because following psychiatric tests she was declared to be a paranoiac suffering from delusions of persecution. On 13 November she was committed to Lima State Hospital for treatment. Samuel was declared temporarily insane and taken to Cleveland City Hospital. He was subsequently released and apparently moved to Detroit.

The fortress-like Lima State Hospital had been built at great expense in the countryside a few kilometres north of the town of Lima, following a decision of the Ohio General Assembly in 1906. It was dedicated to the incarceration and cure of the criminally insane, and could house over 1,200 inmates who were put to work in the kitchens, laundry, gardens and dairy farm. Matilda remained there until December 1938. Her case was overseen by Dr Herman Turk, who was promoted to superintendent at the Hospital in 1938. He was not one of the 'strap 'em down and stick in the needle' psychiatrists of the period, dismissing the padded cell as a relic. We gain some insight regarding his professional views from an article he wrote in 1941 on the therapeutic value of libraries in curing insanity. 'Reading furnishes one of the greatest means of relaxation to the emotional tension . . . Reading subdues angers, fears, and dreads, and the intense delusional ideas that may be present.'[32]

Turk was an expert witness in several murder cases before and after his involvement with the Waldman case. According to Turk, Matilda had ceased to suffer from delusions after about a year at Lima, and in December 1938 he declared she was completely sane. This meant a return to Cleveland to face trial. On 6 January 1939 the judges acquitted her of murder on the basis that she was insane on 2 August 1935. Matilda nearly collapsed, though, when the court ordered that she would have to return to Lima State Hospital due to a legal technicality. This concerned a requirement that Turk and another psychiatrist agree on her sanity, after further observation, and formally notify the judge of Allen County. Her case was heard again at a sanity hearing in March 1939. Turk told the court that Waldman's case was 'the most clear-cut case of induced insanity, I ever saw'.[33] Shortly afterwards Matilde was finally released from Lima Hospital. She made her way to her parents in Detroit and so out of the limelight for good. Had justice truly been done?

Another 1930s' witch killer, Albert Shinsky of Shenandoah, Shuylkill County, Pennsylvania, was less fortunate than Waldman.[34] His case highlights the inconsistencies in the post-trial judicial and medical treatment of those sent to psychiatric hospitals. Waldman was fortunate to be under Turk's care. 'We find the border between insanity and sanity so slight that only one trained in the subject can define it', Turk once said. In Shinksy's case it took decades to detect.

Like the Waldmans, Shinsky, a twenty-four-year-old Lithuanian American, one-time farm labourer, miner, and taxi driver, suffered from nocturnal disturbances. He believed a fifty-nine-year-old widow named Susan Mummey, a former neighbour of his family when they occupied a farm in nearby Ringtown, sent a black cat to torment him at night. 'Often', he said, 'the cat grew so large that I was almost smothered by its fur.' Sometimes he saw Mummey's face in that of the cat. He visited numerous hex doctors, one of whom put him on a special diet of raw milk straight from the udder. Convinced by his Bible reading, on 17 March he went to Mummey's home and shot her dead. While in jail, Shinsky explained, 'I was hexed. There was nothing else for me to do. I had to kill her . . . the electric chair will be better than the suffering of the last seven years.' 'I am a new man', he told journalists, and relished eating his first hearty meals in years.

The district attorney Leroy Enterline was determined that Shinsky be sent to the chair, but the medical profession had other ideas. Dr Walter G. Bowers, the respected superintendent of the Shuylkill County Hospital for the Insane was brought in by the jail's warden to assess Shinsky's mental state. Bowers had considerable experience, having worked as a psychiatrist at hospitals in Philadelphia and Norristown. His experiments in hydrotherapy and massage twenty-five years earlier had attracted interest in the profession. He suggested that therapeutic bathing and massage helped improve the mental condition of those suffering from mania and *dementia praecox*.[35] After a two-hour examination Bowers declared Shinsky to be suffering from the latter condition. *Dementia praecox*, or premature dementia, was defined by German psychiatrists in the late nineteenth century and began to be used widely in American medical literature in the 1910s. While its cause was unknown, it was thought to be incurable. It was used interchangeably with schizophrenia, which became the orthodox term for the same set of symptoms when *dementia praecox* fell out of formal medical usage in the early 1950s. There have been recent calls for the term to be reintroduced to replace schizophrenia.[36]

Shinsky's case was brought to an insanity commission where his condition was confirmed. Instead of frying in the electric chair, a spell at the Fairview state hospital for the insane beckoned. Whether bathing was part of his treatment I do not know. Enterline did not forget, though, and in 1937 he sought an indictment against Shinsky 'as a safeguard' in case he was released from the hospital. Ten years passed before a petition was lodged for Shinsky's release. It was unsuccessful. Thirty-four years after the crime, Shinsky was still in Fairview State Hospital, but a local attorney, William J. Krencewicz, was trying to obtain a psychiatric re-evaluation to have him declared sane. Arthur Lewis interviewed him—'I know if this happens I'll have to stand trial for killing Mrs Mummey, an act I deeply regret', he said. 'But I'm willing to take that gamble. I was a stupid, foolish, superstitious young man when I did it. God knows I've been sorry ever since. But I do think I've been punished enough.'[37] The petition was unsuccessful.

In October 1975, forty-one years after the hex murder, Shinsky was brought back to Schuylkill County where he was put in the Wernersville State Hospital pending a hearing as to whether he was sufficiently recovered from insanity to finally stand trial. As the record of the hearing shows, the decision was based considerably on whether he still believed in witchcraft or not. One medical expert testified that in his opinion Shinsky 'never has really given up this belief in witches'. On the subject of witchcraft 'he tends to become evasive or guarded in his replies'. This was born out when Shinsky was questioned and asked point-blank, 'Do you still have a belief in witchcraft?' 'As I said', he replied, 'if I knew what I know now, it wouldn't have happened in the first place. It was all a bad mistake.' He was asked if he believed in hex signs. On this he was clear. 'I do not', Shinsky said. 'Did you believe in witches back in the early 1930s?' 'Well, it seems so.' 'I was just an ignorant youth at the time that I shot that poor woman', he explained. The hearing found Shinsky to be sufficiently sane, and in 1976 he finally got his wish to be tried for the murder of Susan Mummey. He died back at home in Ringtown in May 1983.[38]

A danger to the public: incarcerating witch believers

As the psychiatric profession developed, so the asylum population increased. In 1840 some 2,500 people diagnosed as insane were living in asylums, prisons, or almshouses. This figure rose to over 40,000 in 1880, and by 1923 there were more than 263,000 asylum inmates. This increase far outstripped the population increase in America, which had risen from 17 million in 1840 to over 106 million in 1920.[39] One of the consequences of the pressure this placed on asylums was an increasing shift from the curative role of the asylum to one of containment.

While the increasing number of insanity pleas in the criminal courts fed this expansion, there was also considerable growth in the resort to civil law to have mentally ill people placed in the custody of asylums and hospitals for the insane, either because they were considered a danger to society or property, or because it was deemed they were unable to manage their own affairs. While in general it was only relatives, guardians, or public officials who could request that someone be certified, in practice the law varied from state to state. In Florida, for example, five reputable citizens could request another to be taken into care. Applications for individuals to be certified were heard by the probate courts in many states, which, following British common law, were decided by a jury after hearing expert medical opinion. But arrangements differed elsewhere. In some states, such as Iowa and North Dakota, County Boards of Commissioners on Insanity assessed requests.[40] In 1878, for instance, an Iowa County Board of Commissioners on Insanity heard the case of Max Frahm after it was petitioned that his family lived in constant fear and that their lives had become unendurable. He was sent to Mount Pleasant Hospital, the state's first public asylum completed in 1861.

It was standard practice for the individual concerned to attend the hearing if their presence was not likely to be deleterious to themselves or those present.[41] In 1903 a twenty-seven-year-old Kentuckian, Ward Boyd, made quite an impression when he spoke before Los Angeles Judge Curtis D. Wilbur. In California, superior court judges presided over examinations before an insanity commission, and as stated in the statutes, the judge 'must inform him [the alleged insane] that he is charged with being insane and of his rights to make a defence'. Standing before the judge and the statutory two physicians, Boyd made full use of his rights, telling his story 'in a cool rational way, using the most excellent language and bringing in the points with the skill of a trained storyteller'. He related how, when as a boy, his family lived in National City, near San Diego, a female boarder, a schoolteacher, had made a disturbing impression on him. 'I have seen her eyes glitter at us like a coyote's', he said. That said, he had no thoughts of her having cast a spell on him until only the previous year when he was working a mining claim in the desert. Alone for long periods he began to see disembodied visions of the woman at night, her face expressing hatred and triumph. In what sounds like a possible case of sleep paralysis, he 'had smothered and oppressed feelings about the head and heart'. As a newspaper reported, 'Although Boyd talked so well and seemed so rational, it seemed best to send him to the asylum as he is so completely upset by his awful experience as to be unable to take care of himself.'[42]

But over the decades some states tinkered with the law respecting such insanity inquests, mainly with regard to the right to a jury and the right of the suspected insane to attend their hearing. In 1903 one Wisconsin probate judge protested that while huge care, attention, and cost was given to assessing the mental state of those tried for brutal murders, legal safeguards were being removed for those affected in civil cases. 'To-day a man be adjudged insane, haled from his home, committed to an insane asylum and placed under guardianship without notice to himself, without notice to his next of kin, without his day in court', he complained.[43] It is not surprising then that during the late nineteenth and early twentieth centuries we find numerous cases of people being sent to the asylum on the basis that their witch beliefs were supposedly a danger to themselves and others if left unregulated. Dr Oscar Altland, head of the York County Almshouse, Pennsylvania, was of the opinion that witchcraft believers were prone to violence, and as a consequence, 'they should be placed in institutions and kept there for life for the safety of society'. Hex-slayer John Blymyer had a spell in the almshouse in 1924 and Altland had treated him again in 1927 when Blymyer told him he was being chased by witches. When he asked Blymyer what treatment he was taking for the delusion, he was told 'Lydia Pinkham', the famous cure-all quack tonic.[44] Here again racist attitudes played a part. The psychiatrist James Kiernan observed, for instance, that 'the fact that Chicago is a commercial city, permitting comparative equality on the part of the negro, leads to the quick incarceration of such persons [displaying paranoia], when brought in contact with Aryans and Shemites [Jews], for the mental phenomena displayed would be such as to lead to a rapid suspicion of insanity by a sceptical, practical Aryan or Shemitic business man.'[45]

So in the early twentieth century we see a number of people carted off to the asylum as a means of dealing with witchcraft disputes. In most such cases there is little evidence in the reports of obvious mental illness that can be retrospectively diagnosed. There is no bias toward the incarceration of aged witch accusers who might have suffered from dementia for instance. What to make of the treatment of a twenty-nine-year-old German woman named Freda Jabens, of Spencer, Nebraska? Described as 'a pretty blonde', in 1907 she and her brother, Peter, aged twenty, were sent to the state insane hospital after they and their family had made repeated accusations of witchcraft against a youthful neighbour named Jennie Swartz, who they believed had put a spell on their brother. They had pestered the local district court to arrest Swartz on suspicion of being a witch.[46] In the same year a young woman named Ellen Peterson, daughter of Swedes Katrina and Lars Peterson of Little Prairie, Nicollet County, Minnesota, was prosecuted for assaulting Martha Norlin having accused her of bewitching the family farm. The Petersons' cows had dried up, their chickens had died, and they experienced various other misfortunes. As Norlin drove past their farm one day, Ellen, with the assistance of her sister, dragged her off and beat her. Ellen was sentenced to a spell in prison, as was her brother Christian who, on hearing the sentence in court, threatened to kill Norlin. Unable to pay bond for keeping the peace he was sentenced to six months' imprisonment. At the time of these events Lars Peterson was into his fourth decade as a patient at the state asylum. One of his son-in-laws had joined him there in 1902. Then in the winter of 1909 Ellen, Christian, and their mother were also committed. All had been quiet between the Petersons and Norlin until November 1909 when Ellen and Katrina gave her another beating for being a witch. Mother, daughter, and son put up resistance when they were subsequently arrested. This time they found themselves not before a criminal court but before the probate court. They refused to answer questions and sat silently as they were committed to the state asylum for treatment.[47]

Mrs Peterson could not read, write, or speak English, and the experience of being judged on their sanity must have been all the more disorientating for people in her situation. We get a sense of this from another contemporary probate court examination from Minnesota. In April 1907 Lena Tornow, of Norton, Minnesota, was taken to Rochester State Hospital for the insane for treatment. Lena and her brother Carl had come to America from Germany in 1867. They owned a small farm but had experienced problems. For years they had believed themselves and their animals bewitched by neighbours—ever since a strange dog with long silky hair had passed by the farm. In March 1907 Carl had been bitten by a suspected rabid dog and had gone to the Pasteur Institute in Chicago for treatment. Lena, who spoke little English, and was in her early fifties, was left to run the farm. She and Carl had assaulted several neighbours for being witches and were considered a nuisance. Now she was alone, some of her neighbours successfully requested she be taken to an asylum. She told the court via a translator about her troubles with witchcraft, while her neighbours testified that she looked after the farm well and was perfectly sane except on the matter of witchcraft. It would seem that she and her brother 'recovered' from their respective illnesses and we find them back on their farm in Norton by 1910. But to what did they return?[48]

A superintendent of the Pennsylvania Society to Protect Children from Cruelty, Margaret Hay, explained the harm that such incarcerations could wreak. In an article on the challenges of social work in Schuylkill County she related how a man came into the office of the Society to complain about a Pennsylvania Dutch farmer whose children were begging. The farmer was able-bodied and his neighbours were sick and tired of supporting his family when he was in possession of fifty acres of prime farmland. A social worker paid a visit and found the farm buildings in disrepair and no stock on the land. Yet the farmer's wife was neatly dressed and kept the house clean and tidy. How had things come to this? It transpired that the farmer had continual arguments with a neighbour who was jealous of his fifty acres. The neighbour hatched a plan to petition for the farmer's commitment for insanity on the basis of his belief in witchcraft. It worked, and the farmer was carted off for a spell in the County Insane Hospital. Meanwhile, without his consent, his stock and implements were sold off to pay some outstanding debts. When he was released he returned to his farm and family to find that he no longer had the wherewithal to farm his fifty acres. Neither would his neighbours give him work, wary of his alleged insanity. As Hay concluded, 'this man and his family presented a most distressing problem from both a social and a legal viewpoint. There was no legal aid to help him, and the social consciousness of his immediate neighbourhood simply took the form of looking upon him as a nuisance to be removed from their midst, rather than as someone to be helped.'[49]

WITCH KILLINGS UP CLOSE

Numerous witch murders have been mentioned in previous chapters. I have found references to at least twenty-two slayings committed by white Americans, and five by African Americans. The annual reports of the commissioner of Indian Affairs mention seventeen witch killings out of 147 murders.[1] Other sources refer to more instances, so we are looking at several dozen executions in Native-American communities at least during the nineteenth and early twentieth century. So no culture was immune from the impulse to kill witches. The purpose of this chapter is to explore in detail what led people to commit such a crime, the interplay of personal psychology, community relations, and cultural influences. What was the impact of the killers' actions on family, friends, and neighbours? How did the authorities react and how did the press go about reporting such an extraordinary crime? Moreover, I explore the aftermath of the trials and prosecutions, the subsequent life stories of those affected. In the process, some pitfalls of historical interpretation and assumption are revealed, illustrating the importance of understanding the consequences of events and not just their origins.

Beard-stroking and friendly words: witchcraft in Sullivan County

In the Empire state of New York, within 110 miles of the great city of New York, in the centre of a prosperous farming community, in a county where thousands of dollars are expended annually for the purpose of education and thousands more for the advance of Christianity, there are persons who believe so thoroughly in the ancient bugaboo called witch-craft, that they could have committed murder to rid the community of a peaceful old man who had lived among them for forty years.[2]

In 1853 the ship Edwiner docked in New York having set sail from the French port of Le Havre. Amongst the many German immigrants on board were a farmer named Pierre Heidt, his wife Maria Catharina, their three sons, Nicholas (aged eighteen), Edward (thirteen), Adam (four), and a daughter Caroline (eleven). They had travelled from Bavaria to start a new life in New York State. They were one of thousands of farming families from south-western Germany that made their way to America via Le Havre during the mid-nineteenth century. Many left due to land pressure, in part because of the tradition of partible inheritance that made the region one of small farms and hampered entrepreneurial opportunity. Repeated crop failures did not help. It was not extreme poverty that motivated many though, but the chance to prosper.[3] A French commentator, writing at the time, described the ordeal of these German migrants as they made their way across France:

> It is a lamentable sight, when you are travelling in the spring and autumn on the Strasburg road, to see the long files of carts that meet you every mile, carrying the whole property of the poor wretches, who are about to cross the Atlantic on the faith of a lying prospectus. There they go slowly along; their miserable tumbrels – drawn by such starved, drooping beasts, that your only wonder is, how they can possibly hope to reach Havre alive.[4]

The Heidts made it alive, and spent their last reserves of money on purchasing land in Sullivan County, New York.

Significant German settlement had begun in the area during the 1840s, and by the time the Heidts arrived there were some 2,600 Germans in the county, mostly living around Callicoon and Cochecton. Many had been drawn there by the German-language prospectus distributed at entry ports by a local surveyor and land agent named Solomon Royce. The first generation had much work to do carving out fields and an agricultural living from the wooded hills. Many endured great hardship. One German settler recalled getting lost in the woods whilst attempting to reach the settlement of Jeffersonville before a road existed from the south. Tired and exhausted, he came upon a settlement of half a dozen German families and begged for food. They were unable to help for they were starving themselves. By the 1870s farming was beginning to pay off though, and the settlers were able to fund the creation of several Catholic, Methodist, Presbyterian, and German Reformed churches.[5]

After the first couple of decades in their new country, the Heidts perhaps congratulated themselves and thanked God that their great trek had paid off. They built a home in what is now Delaware Township, a rural area of small hamlets in the Catskills. Pierre, who anglicized his name to Phillip Peter, began farming with the help of his two eldest sons. One of their neighbours was another German immigrant, George Markert, who was originally from Saxony. He and his father worked a small patch of land nearby. The two families got on well. Around 1860, the twenty-six-year-old George married Phillip's daughter Caroline, and a long-standing friendship developed between him and Adam.

In 1869 Adam Heidt married Barbara Ulrich, the American-born daughter of Bavarian immigrants Anton and Ursula Ulrich, who farmed near Bethel, Sullivan County. The young couple moved to Rockland, where Adam worked as a carpenter. Their first son, Joseph, was born the following year. By 1880 the family had relocated back to Delaware Township, where Adam built up a sizeable farm of 133 acres at a spot called Swiss Hill, just south of Jeffersonville. Joseph attended school in the winter and helped on the farm in the summer, while Barbara looked after three further offspring. Adam became a respected member of the community, acting as an officer of the Callicoon Agricultural Fire Relief Association.[6] His uncle, George Market, had by now also bought a small farm for himself and his second wife in Delaware, some 125 yards from the historic Stone Arch Bridge that crosses Callicoon Creek. It was within hollering distance from the Heidts farm. George had saved up money to buy it after having laboured for years at Gideon Wales' tannery near Kenoza Lake. It was only a fifteen-acre spread and George laboured for neighbouring farmers to make ends meet. In 1888 Adam had to lend $600 dollars to him in a legally binding agreement to help pay off other debts he had accrued.

Yes, the Heidts prospered, but they also went through some dark times. In 1874 Adam's brother Nicholas, who farmed nearby, was hit by a train and died later after sustaining serious injuries. In 1882 Anton Ulrich fell from a load of hay and broke his neck. Around 1884 Adam's sister Caroline, George Market's wife, died in her early forties. Markert soon married again. In 1888 Adam's mother Maria died at the age of seventy-five. Adam administered her will, which stated that her property should be divided up between her children and grandchildren.[7] Her death was hardly a great shock, but it happened not long after his mother-in-law Ursula was murdered at her home in Bethel, a mile or so from Jeffersonville. In October 1887 a drunken ex-sailor named Jack Allen entered her home, where she lived alone, and shot her dead. The motive was robbery. A neighbour, Theodore Kanig, who came calling for a jug of cider, found her lying on the floor in a pool of her own blood. Adam and Barbara gave testimony at her trial.[8] Allen was hanged at Monticello jail in July 1888, after adjusting the rope around his neck and telling the hangman, 'Let 'er go.'[9] It was the last hanging in Sullivan County.

As well as these personal misfortunes, there were also problems on the farm. Two fine horses died inexplicably, and some of Adam's cows dried up. Yet his neighbours' cows seemed to produce richer milk. On top of all this, Adam had been suffering for years from an ailment that no doctors could diagnose or cure. The medicines they gave him only made him worse. He had pains in the teeth and limbs, and his 'stomach beat like his heart'. Then all at once he began to improve—until, that is, Markert came to visit after having spent some time away in Rockville, Connecticut. This was in 1890. After shaking hands with him Adam began to feel pains all over his body. He tried some patent medicine, the first bottle of which seemed to help but the second made him worse. Some pills made no difference.

One day in the spring, Markert visited the Heidt farm and Adam took him down to the cellar for a glass of cider. He began to have strange sensations in his eyes. The two men went back upstairs and sat down, and Adam observed Markert stroking his beard in a strange manner:

> He stroked his whiskers and twisted his hand at the end of each stroke as if he was throwing something from them at me. He saw that I noticed it and he stopped. When I turned my head he did the same thing again. I went and looked in the glass. My face was yellow, with a blue rim around my eyes. He then went home. I told my wife to look at my face, and that Markert was a witch and had cast a spell upon me. She told me she couldn't believe that he would do such a thing because he talked so much religion. I told her I thought he had done it.

Markert repeated the same beard-stroking action the following Sunday.

Now that he had fixed upon the idea that Markert's witchery lay behind all his problems, he wracked his memory for other suspicious words or actions that seemed innocuous at the time but which he now reinterpreted as sinister. He remembered an episode twenty-two years before when Markert had patted him three times on the shoulder and said 'You're good—a right good brother-in-law.' Why the repetition? And *three* times at that? Clearly a spell was worked that moment. Then there was the encounter a couple of years back when Markert had been unusually solicitous regarding Adam's health. 'He said he had met the doctor and had asked him if I was dangerously sick, and the doctor said I was', Heidt recalled. Was he concerned about the progress of his witchery?

The last time that Markert came to Heidt's house was in December 1890. He wanted Adam to file a saw for him. Adam refused. The mere sight of it gave him pains. He went to a local doctor who prescribed vapour baths and a course of medicine. They made him feel even worse. He could not eat or sleep. He was taken to hospital and spent two weeks there. The doctors could not find anything wrong with him. Released from hospital and disillusioned with the medical profession, he took a trip to New York to consult a popular fortune-teller named Mrs Stein who lived on Eighty-fifth Street. She confirmed that he had been bewitched and that from then on he should not shake hands with any man. She wrote down a charm on a piece of paper, instructing him not to look at it, and to carry it at all times. He visited her again in March 1891.

After this last visit Adam confronted Markert, saying he was a witch and demanding that he take back the words 'you are a good, a right good brother-in-law'. Markert only laughed at him. The pains got worse. In November, Adam went to stay with his brother in Bradford, Pennsylvania, for five weeks. During this time he consulted a travelling quack doctor named Clark. Adam did not tell him he was bewitched. The good doctor gave him two glass bulbs connected by a glass tube containing a liquid. He held the two bulbs in his hands and the liquid transferred from one bulb to the other. From this the doctor diagnosed that he had heart disease, liver disease, kidney disease, and a host of other diseases. Fortunately, the quack's medicine could cure them all! Adam declined, for he knew now that his problem was beyond natural help. What he needed was spiritual aid. So he went to Pittsburgh to see the celebrated Father Mollinger. Mollinger gave Adam a blessing and said that there was no need for him now to take any medicine. Adam did not tell Mollinger he was bewitched, but desperately hoped that his blessing would counter Markert's spell. It did not.

Adam talked frequently of Markert's witchery with his son Joseph and recounted other cases of witchcraft to support his conviction. Unlike his mother, Joseph became persuaded that his father was, indeed, under Markert's spell. Adam also expressed his views freely with acquaintances and neighbours. When, in October 1891, he called at the home of Adam Bernhart, a farmer of Kenoza Lake, and a fellow Bavarian, he refused to shake hands, saying that he was under a spell laid upon him by Markert. Another neighbour Conrad Metzger tried to convince him that he was not bewitched when Adam asked to borrow $10 from him to see Mrs Stein in New York. As we see over and over again in witchcraft cases in this and early periods, Adam was cautiously seeking support from the local community in the event that action needed to be taken against Markert.

On the evening of Tuesday 19 January 1892, George Markert left his house and trudged through the falling snow to the Half-way House, a respectable inn run by Philip Hembdt on the road from Jeffersonville to Callicoon depot. Markert often spent the evening there with friends. Around 10 o'clock he left for home, but his wife Catharine and stepson John never saw him alive again. At first they were not concerned, as he often stayed out late, but in the morning Catharine sent John out to ask neighbours if they had seen George. As John got to the farm gate that opened onto the main road he saw blood in the snow.

Two men had also seen the blood that morning. One was a neighbouring farmer and local mailman John Koehler, and the other Casper van Bergen. They found Markert's cap, jack-knife, and hickory stick nearby, and followed a trail of blood and footprints in the snow that led to the Stone Arch Bridge over Callicoon creek. There had clearly been a violent struggle between two or three men, and the marks in the snow suggested that a body had been thrown over the bridge. The two men went to notify Philip Hembdt and others, including the local constable Charles Heidt—a nephew of Markert's and the cousin of Joseph Heidt. Several boats were launched into the creek and the water dredged with hooks. Markert's body was found, dragged on to land, placed on a sledge, and taken to Hembdt's hotel. The men present had all heard of Adam Heidt's accusations, and now reached the conclusion that he must be responsible for Markert's death.

At the Half-way House an examination of Markert's body showed that he had been shot in the head several times. Two letters were found on him, one in English and the other in German. The latter read as follows:

> Kenoza Lake
> March 19, 1891
>
> George Markert –
>
> You seeming friend and sly enemy. Nothing done so fine but what it will appear in the daytime. God has opened my eyes. You should take your witchcraft back. You know I have a judgement against you. You came to me on a Sunday and got receipt. If you do not take the torture back I will sell the judgement and pay the doctor bill which you have caused. You came to my house and stroked your beard. I was sick all the time. I forbid you my house and my barn, my flesh and blood. In the name of God.
>
> A. Heidt.

The letter in English was roughly the same. Adam clearly suspected that Markert aimed to bewitch him to death to avoid honouring his debt.

On the Friday a party of local men went to arrest Adam and his son Joseph. Armed with a search warrant they found a revolver hidden in a pile of hay and a bloody handkerchief. The two Heidt men were taken to Sullivan County Jail, while the coroner John Dycker launched an investigation. At the inquest, both Adam and Joseph denied any knowledge of the murder, but the jury decided there was sufficient evidence for the Heidts to be indicted for murder. Their case was to be considered by the county grand jury in the spring, but both the prosecution and defence requested more time to gather evidence. Meanwhile, in the spirit of impartiality, the press reported the widely held view that they were guilty.[10]

The trials of Joseph and Adam began on the 17 August 1892 at the courthouse in Monticello. Joseph's trial came first, and was relatively straightforward as he had already confessed to the crime while in jail. He told his version of events on the night of the 19 January to the court:

> I made up my mind to ask my uncle to remove this spell from him [Adam]; remember the fatal evening; was at Kenoza Lake to see the blacksmith concerning the shoeing of our horses the next day; saw him at Curtis Alley's hotel; after leaving there I went to Markert's; had a pistol in my possession at the time, which I found in the barn; did not see uncle when I went down to his home that night; then went over to the bridge and waited awhile and I met him at the bridge and he replied, good evening, and asked what I wanted. I asked him to if he would be so kind as to take the torture back from my father; his reply was that he would take nothing back; again repeated the request, to which he again refused; told him that I would have him arrested in the morning if he did not; he said that if I said another word he would knock the life out of me, calling me a damned lummix; he then attempted to strike me; he was angry and did strike me; I grabbed the club and wrestled it away from him; we had by this time crossed the bridge to the scene of the affray; he clinched me, took out his knife and told me that I would have to die on the spot. In trying to escape I slipped and fell; grabbed hold of him and pulled him down; drew the revolver and fired for his head; cannot say how many times; when I regained my footing I again grabbed him and threw him over the bridge; then went home; did not know what I was doing at the time, have had a headache since then; was afraid to tell of the deed for fear of being lynched.

Joseph's defence attorney pleaded that he was a simple, misled boy with a formerly irreproachable reputation. At 7.50 p.m., the jury processed back into the court room. The acting County Clerk then addressed them: 'Gentlemen of the jury, look upon the prisoner; prisoner, look upon the jury. How find you this man, guilty or not guilty?' Jury foreman Maverick Ingraham arose and pronounced that they had agreed on a verdict of murder in the second degree. Joseph's life had been saved. He was sentenced to thirty-years' imprisonment in Dannemora state prison, which is known today as Clinton Correctional Facility.

The next day, a Thursday, it was Adam's turn in the dock. The presiding judge was Edgar L. Fursman. The first business of the court was to convene a panel of sixty jurors who were then questioned as to their suitability. Then as now, it was not a responsibility that many citizens enjoyed. Isaac Quinlan said his bones ached, but the judge refused to dismiss him. M. D. Pierce said he had diarrhoea, but the judge told him to get a prescription and return to the courthouse. Several hours later the jury panel had been whittled down to the required twelve men. Their task was to decide if Adam had aided and abetted Joseph that tragic night. Had Joseph been economical with the truth? The judge addressed them: 'This man is on trial for his life. He is either guilty of murder in the first degree or nothing. It won't do to convict a man on suspicion. Human justice rests on a foundation of law.'

Friends and neighbours, such as Philip Hembdt, Adam Bernhart, and Conrad Metzger, testified regarding their conversations with Adam on the subject of his bewitchment. Oliver Hofer, Callicoon Justice of the Peace, reported on the letters found on Markert's corpse. Joseph Heidt was also called back to give evidence. The trial concluded the next morning. By 9 a.m. the jury was seated, ready to hear the address of Judge Fursman. He advised them to give a verdict of not guilty as there was insufficient evidence to convict, not least of which was the fact that the tracks of only two people were evident on the bridge that snowy night. Without leaving their seats the jury expressed agreement. Fursman turned to Adam and said, 'Heidt you are discharged.' Adam's eyes filled with tears and he nodded an expression of thanks before being led away.[11]

Despite Markert's death, Adam's health did not recover. His mind deteriorated. In September 1892 a local newspaper editorial stated that Adam Heidt was 'not a safe man to be at large'. No sane man, it stated, could believe George Markert possessed the power of witchcraft. It recommended that he be taken to the asylum. This is exactly what happened the following June. Adam's wife Barbara requested the Overseer of the Poor to institute proceedings to have him declared insane and that he was not fit to be at large. Due process was duly gone through with two doctors certifying his insanity, and Adam was taken to the State Lunatic Asylum at Middletown. It was thought he would resist, but the officers told him he would be cured if he consented to go. 'Neighbours feel easier now that he is under duress', reported one paper.[12] There he stayed until his death in July 1897. The cause was melancholia and inflammation of the spinal marrow or chronic myelitis, which would explain the nervous symptoms and fatigue of which he complained.[13]

Barbara died in September 1901 after becoming bedridden with stomach cancer. She was buried in St George's Catholic cemetery, Jeffersonville. As a reporter noted, 'she was a mild-mannered woman, respected, and seemingly undeserving of so troublous a life as was hers'.[14] The same year a local sheriff, while taking a prisoner to Dannemora, had a chat with Joseph Heidt. He was described as a model inmate by the prison authorities. In 1913 he was paroled, having served twenty-one years of his thirty-year sentence. The following year he was pardoned. He settled in Malone, Franklin County, and was described in 1914 as an 'honest, hard-working man, much respected by the people who know him'.[15] He worked in a broom factory for a bit, and in 1930 we find him, at the age of sixty, employed as a labourer, married with a young daughter and stepdaughter. And there we shall leave this tragic family story.

Big trouble at Booger Hole

In 1900 Booger or Bogle Hole was a remote log cabin settlement in the wooded hills of Big Otter, Clay County, plumb in the middle of West Virginia. It was an isolated spot and its very name denoted its uncanny reputation, a booger being a menacing supernatural being, a frightening ghost or goblin usually seen at night in wild places. 'I can tell a million tales about that place', said the well-known fiddler Wilson Douglas, who used to live near Booger Hole. He recalled seeing ghostly figures that disappeared in front of his eyes, including one time a woman all in white, her hair as black as a crow, who cried and wailed, her face hidden from his view.[16]

The white population had deep Irish and Scottish roots, and the area had a reputation as a rough, lawless backwater. One journalist described it harshly at the time as 'one of the poorest and most ignorant counties in all the mountain regions . . . generation after generation they have intermarried, until the type has become incapable of mental or moral effort'. Several large extended families such as the Boggs, Moores, Cottrells, Lyons, and Mccumbers scratched a living from farming, hunting, timber, and nature's bounty. These were not first- or second-generation immigrants scrabbling for a living in an unfamiliar environment. They were well-established families that formed the backbone of their communities. Some had improved themselves to 'respectable' status, others remained dirt poor. Schooling was unwanted and the level of illiteracy high. The life of these hill folk was described well in 1899:

> The West Virginia mountaineer lives very close to Nature . . . juicy berries refresh him along the road; nuts drop to his path; 'sang' (ginseng), which makes one of his sources of revenue, reveals itself to his eye as he follows the cows to pasture; a cool brook springs up to quench his thirst when weary of following the plough; pine knots are always within reach to make light as well as warmth; mud and stones easily combine in his hand to shape a daub chimney; and a trough dug out of an old tree furnishes a receptacle that is as good for dough at one end as for a baby at the other. Often, however, this close relation to Nature assumes a war attitude, fierce and uncompromising. . . . When satisfied that he is not expected to pose as a 'freak,' but is met on the equal plane of human intercourse,

the mountain story-teller seems to enjoy recounting the traditions and beliefs of his people and their forefathers. Leaving himself a loophole of escape, he is very likely to finish his yarn with – 'tain't that I believe them things myself. I know they ain't nawthin' but superstition; but I kin qualify that right round here, not many miles away, there's people that believe in witches.'[17]

It was in 1899 that an elderly widow named Annie Boggs (*b.* 1827) came to settle in Booger Hole. Shortly after she was joined by her two granddaughters, Prudie, aged eighteen, and Mabel aged two. Annie requested a place to stay from a relative, Squire Boggs, who was described as one of the few intelligent, well-to-do men in the area. Years back he had built a log schoolhouse on his property to educate the local children, but few parents took advantage of the opportunity. By the late 1890s it had been abandoned, and so Annie and her granddaughters were allowed to occupy it. They placed thick blankets over the broken windows, and they set about creating a little garden to grow a bit of corn, tobacco, and vegetables. With the help of the squire they made it through the first winter and they settled into the community. Unfortunately Annie possessed some tell-tale attributes: she was elderly, widowed, independent, sharp tongued, and living on the margins.[18]

In the spring, rumours began to circulate that 'Mother Boggs' was a witch. They seem to have originated from the Cottrell family who had received word from relatives in neighbouring Roane County, where members of the Bogg family had also long settled, that Annie had been ejected from there because of her witchery.[19] Local misfortunes soon began to be blamed on the suspected witch. One of the most vocal of the accusers was 'Old Man Cottrell'—probably Marshal Cottrell who was the same age as Annie. He accused her of riding him mercilessly at night. The schoolhouse was avoided, though one of the Cottrell boys was rumoured to be seeing Prudie. There was apparently talk of lynching Annie. On a cold winter's night in 1900 someone drew aside one of the blankets that served as a curtain at the schoolhouse, poked a rifle through, and shot her in the back.

A murder investigation was launched by Deputy United States Marshal Daniel Cunningham (1850–1942), one of the most renowned lawmen in the state, who happened to be staying nearby at the time. He had plenty of business in the area, noting in his old age that 'near this Bogey Hole many murders and other crimes have been committed'. Around 1897 a watchmaker named Joseph Clark stopped at the old schoolhouse one night, and was never seen again. Officers found a bloody trail leading to a nearby creek. In the summer of 1899 a dirt-poor farmer named Louis Cohen was murdered in nearby Big Otter Creek.[20] Around the same time, Cunningham had been tracking down James Wayne who was responsible for a series of post office robberies in the area. Cunningham was a well-known figure in the region due to his involvement in a long-running, bitter, land feud on the border of West Virginia and Kentucky during which his brother Nathan, also a deputy marshal, had been murdered. Dan was also arrested and put on trial for his role in a revenge killing. In 1902, Cunningham would again attract notoriety through his bloody enforcement of injunctions against striking miners at the New River coalfields.[21]

Back to Booger Hole, though, and Cunningham's analysis of the bullets that killed Annie suggested that they had been fired from a rifle especially bored out for the purpose. Tracks outside indicated that two people had approached the window. Further inquiries revealed that Old Man Cottrell had borrowed such a rifle from a neighbour a few days before. This was enough for Cottrell and his nephew—the young man courting Prudie—to be arrested on suspicion of murder. They were taken to Clay County Courthouse for examination by Squire Norval Shannon.[22] The court room was packed with Cottrell supporters from Booger Hole. They were ordered to leave the guns and rifles they had brought with them outside under guard for fear of disturbance.

Cottrell and his nephew pleaded not guilty to the murder but were adamant that Annie Boggs was a witch, and others in the courtroom were vociferous in support of this claim. The old man explained how she had ridden him one stormy night when there was a surge of water down the Big Otter river:

> She called me, I tol' you, Squire. She called me with a witch-call'. 'Then you got up out of bed and went out into the night?' 'No, it ain't just that way. You don't go. You just lies abed shiverin' an' sweatin' an' asleep all the time. It wasn't exactly me that went that night or any other night. It war my seconds, another of me. So I flew out through the window. That boy there, Linn, he was standin' shiverin' outside, all hitched up with a rope of poison oak. She hitched me to him an' we went up in the air nigh to the moon. When we went too slow a buzz of snake-doctors [dragon flies] stung us up.

A voice from the crowd shouted: 'Them wa'nt no real snake-doctors. Them was witch flies. Snake-doctors that's real don't fly nights.'[23] Old Man Cottrell continued, 'Whatsoever they was they stung right hard. She drove us up to Blue Knob [one of the highest hills in Clay County] an' hitched us to a pawpaw bush an' left us there.'[24] 'What did she go to Blue Knob for?' Asked the squire. 'Maybe for a ride, just. Maybe to meet some other witch. Then I expect she did a little pelverin' [pilfering] thereabouts—eggs an' milk, or maybe a strip of meat.'

'What happened next?' he was asked. 'We was left there fast to the pawpaw bush, moanin' an' cryin' with the wind an' rain an' cold, an not knowin' what minute the lightnin' would hit us.' At this point a woman in the crowd interjected,

'You can't get stricken by lightin' when you're bein' witch-ridden. Lightnin' don't hit witch horses.' After another brief exchange, another woman complained: 'I wouldn't tell anything about it. It's mighty onpearten [unwholesome] to be talkin' so much abouten witch folk even if she is dead.'

Old Man Cottrell continued nevertheless: 'She'll never witch naryun [anyone] no more. I ain't afraid of her now. She's done her worst on me. I'll tell all I know. When the storm begun to die down she come back for us an' rode us home again. Next mornin' our hands an' feet were full of burrs an' briers. They always are after she's ridden of us.' Another member of the Cottrell clan now spoke up: 'Squire, I can swear to havin' sat by Old Man while he was in bed sweatin' and groanin' and him asleep all the time, an' I knowed she was a-ridin' of him, an' seen him next mornin' with his hands an' feet like as if he'd been trompin' around a brier bush.'

Cottrell explained that he had been ridden about twenty to thirty times, and to other landmarks in or near Clay County, such as Yankee Dam and Strange Creek. His nephew also testified to having been ridden in a similar manner. Under questioning, Cottrell said he had not tried to kill Annie Boggs, 'Don't you know she'd a killed me if I had?' He told the squire that witches were in the Bible. 'Preacher read it out in meetin' last church day, not a month back.' Another woman then piped up and complained of all this talk of witches, 'I wouldn't wonder that we was all ridden after this.' To which a man in the room replied, 'Not by Mother Boggs. That was a right good killin'.'

Despite his claims of innocence, the hostility Cottrell expressed towards Boggs and the obvious motive for murder, Squire Shannon felt he had no alternative but to indict Cottrell and have him brought to trial. It never happened though. Dan Cunningham recalled many years later in his unpublished memoir on the criminal history of the area that Cottrell's sworn statement about his witch torments could be found in the old dockets belonging to the squire. But Cunningham noted that the '*corpus delicti*' was never proven, and to the best of his knowledge the murderers of Annie Boggs were never brought to justice.[25] They were—and they were not, as we shall now find out.

In February 1905 the case of Annie Boggs was resurrected with the arrest of her former neighbours, Frederic Moore, his twenty-eight-year-old sister Rosa Lyons, and another female acquaintance. Moore apparently confessed to shooting Boggs with the help of his two female accomplices. He was fifteen at the time and lodging with his sister and John Lyons. What their interrogation revealed was that the murder of Annie Boggs was not connected with her witchery but the threats she made regarding her knowledge of another murder in the neighbourhood. Booger Hole was clearly buzzing with mystery, gossip, and rumour. It transpired that Annie Boggs had quarrelled with Rosa Lyons, née Moore, wife of John Lyons.

In anger, Boggs threatened Rosa that 'she could light her pipe and before it burned out could go to the place where the ashes of Henry Hargus were'. A few days later she was dead. Fred Moore was never convicted of the killing.

Who was Henry Hargus?[26] He was the son or nephew of Margaret Moore, a women with an adventurous and shady past, hence the undetermined nature of Henry's relationship to her. Margaret's first husband had been a volunteer in the Union Army. After his death she formed a relationship with a man named Minner. In the 1870 census we find her keeping house in Union, Clay County, with her four-year-old son James, two daughters, and a twenty-four-year-old farm labourer George Minner—possibly her stepson. James was apparently the offspring of her lover after the death of Minner, a man named James Fletcher from Calhoun County. Margaret secured an officer's widow's pension by fraudulent pretences to the sum of several thousand dollars. Several hundred dollars of this she gave to Henry Hargus before she was arrested and imprisoned for fraud, while James Fletcher was imprisoned for a murder near Charleston. She gave nothing to her son James, though.

Around 1883 Hargus disappeared from his home in Booger Hole. He was rumoured to have been murdered but no one was caught and the body never found. But while under arrest, James Wayne had told Dan Cunningham that John Lyons and James Moore had murdered Hargus, and they had told him where the body had been hidden. Cunningham apparently dismissed the claim at the time, believing Wayne was trying to mitigate his own crimes. Still, many years later, Cunningham would recall that on passing through Booger Hole on several occasions he would stop and chat with James Moore: 'while in conversation . . . he would leave me and go out to a rock, stump, or log or tree and gaze as though something was coming up out of the ground. Moore would do this at least three times in 30 minutes. He would spend about five minutes at a time in this harrowing manner.'

After his mother's incarceration, the teenage James had lodged with a farmer named James Lanemn in Union, working as a farm labourer. By 1900 he was thirty-four and had worked as a labourer in Booger Hole for several years. It was here that his past caught up with him. Following the arrest of Fred Moore and Rosa Lyons a detective named A.W. Sell, of Clay, got to work and found that Caroline Moore, elder sister of James and Rosa, had also been talking about how John Lyons and James Moore disposed of Hargus's body. Sell conducted a search under the Moore's cabin and found clear evidence of a grave. The body had been burned, but bits of bone, hair, and clothing remained. One cuff button bore the initials of Hargus and there was a whetstone inscribed with his name. This was enough to arrest Lyons and Moore. During the Grand Jury hearing, Caroline Moore broke down and recalled how on the night of the murder, Lyons and her brother had wrapped her up in a sheet so that she could not witness them burying Hargus's corpse. She managed to gnaw a hole in the sheet, however, and saw the two men bring a body swathed in a sheet into the house. The body was later exhumed, burned, and reinterred. Aaron Runion, who had married into the Moore family, testified that he had overheard Lyons and James Moore saying ominously that Caroline 'knew too much about something'. This time the Grand Jury considered there was enough evidence to indict the two men. But, again, no one was found guilty.

In 1917 the murder of Annie Boggs once again made headlines when residents of Booger Hole formed a lynch mob to rid the community of several individuals who were suspected of having been involved in a series of murders that stretched back to the Hargus affair. As well as the killings already mentioned, a peddler named John Newman had also disappeared while passing through Booger Hole, and Thurman Duffield of Calhoun County had been fatally shot by Laura Sampson, wife of farm labourer Harvey Sampson. Thurman's brother Scott launched a posse to arrest her, and, during a shoot out, her hand was shot off. At the subsequent trial Sampson claimed self-defence and was acquitted. Things came to a head in 1917 because of the recent murder of a respected Booger Hole resident named Preston Tanner who had burned to death. It was widely believed that neighbour Howard Sampson and his father Andrew were responsible for setting fire to his home. An old resident recalled many years later that Howard had taken a fancy to Preston's wife and wanted him out of the way. The more prosaic motive was the sum of $30. The Sampsons were arrested along with Fred Moore, although Fred was later released while the Sampsons stood trial for murder with Howard sentenced to life imprisonment. While Andrew and Howard lay in jail awaiting trial in Clay, a mob of sixty men from Booger Hole attempted to storm the jail and exact lynch law. If there was any doubt about their intentions, the following poster was pasted around Booger Hole

> We the citizens of Clay county seeing that we cannot get justice by law, have organized the Clay county mob. We have pledged our lives to drive these people from our county or kill them. If we cannot catch and hang you, we shall sneak upon you and kill you as you killed Henry Hargis, Lucy Ana Boggs, the old peddler and Preston Tanner.
>
> If before you leave there is any stealing, killing or burning, we will get bloodhounds and detectives and run you to the ends of the earth. Bill Sampson, Kooch Sampson, Fred Moore, and Aaron Runyon are hereby notified to leave the state in ten days. Rose Lyons, Bill Moore and Elizabeth Sampson are notified to leave in thirty days.
>
> Clay County Mob

An old citizen of Booger Hole recalled in 1971 how the Clay County Mob got their way in the end. He was awoken one night in his youth by dynamite explosions ripping through the valley. He looked out of his bedroom window and saw the glow of burning buildings. Five families were forced out of the area by daybreak.[27] One can guess their names. Booger Hole no longer exists on the map. The spot now consists of Rush Fork and the nearby settlement of Dink, and has become an area visited for its supposed high level of paranormal activity.[28]

Apart from their brief space in the limelight as witch believers, the Cottrells of Booger Hole were not mixed up in any of these foul deeds. Indeed, in the mid-twentieth century the Cottrell family members played a significant role in restoring the reputation of the place, preserving the fine craft skills of the much-maligned hill folk. Jenes Cottrell became well known in folk-music circles as 'The Banjo Man from Dead Fall Run'. A brief newspaper feature on him in 1965 described how the sixty-three-year-old lived in the old farm the family had built around 1904 between Booger Hole and Ivydale, living pretty much as they had done in his parents' day.[29] There were no mains water or electricity, and Jenes made all his own furniture and grew his own food. He regularly demonstrated traditional wood-turning techniques at local fairs in the 1960s, and the banjos he made ingeniously from pressure cookers and other used parts are sought after today. His sister Sylvia (O'Brien), another fine banjo player, likewise continued the same hill-folk life on the family farm after Jenes's death. An interview with her in the 1980s takes us back to the life and beliefs of the area of the beginning of the century.

Sylvia (b. 1909) and Jenes (b. 1902) grew up next to members of the Boggs family and she no doubt heard of the murder of Annie and the many other goings on at Booger Hole. It may explain her cagey response when asked by an interviewer if she knew any witch stories, 'Ah, I don't know. I've heard some talk about witches taking milk from cows. And I think they did do that.' She went on to describe how a 50-cent piece would be put in the bewitched churns. When the interviewer asked if it was the silver that was efficacious or the motto on the coin 'In God We Trust', she said it was the motto. Still, years later, shortly before she died, Sylvia felt the urge to write down numerous stories of witches and supernatural happenings for the West Virginia ethnographer Gerald Milnes.[30]

So this case is something of a red herring. I could easily have been fooled into assuming that Annie Boggs had been shot as a witch if I had stopped my research at the conclusion of the trial of Old Man Cottrell. This would have been an understandable moment to terminate interest in the case, leaving the reader with the suspicion, fuelled by prejudice against the perceived backwardness of hillbilly folk, that the Cottrells had got away with murder. After all, I have provided accounts of numerous such shootings, and Cottrell and his nephew seem good candidates despite their protestations of innocence. It was only by following these peoples' histories in the years after the event that an entirely different story emerged, and the identity of the murderer and the reason for the crime were revealed. Assumptions about the relationship between witchcraft belief, rural isolation, and lack of education are pernicious. As we shall now see as we move westwards.

Solomon Hotema: Choctaw witch killer

The Choctaws were an ancient culture of the Mississippi river valley who came to be defined as one of the 'Five Civilized Nations' due to their adoption of European and generally pacific ways. This did not protect them from being ejected from their ancestral lands when they signed away their Mississippi territory under the 1830 Treaty of Dancing Rabbit Creek. The Nation was split asunder. Those that remained, the Mississippi Band, knuckled under and submitted to federal and state law, but between 1831 and 1833, some 15,000 Choctaws made their way westwards to the Indian Territory that would later form part of the state of Oklahoma. It was an arduous trek remembered as the 'Trail of Tears': over 2,000 never made it.

The newly settled Nation initially maintained its legal authority in the territory and all those who applied for citizenship came under its jurisdiction, although through successive treaties accommodations were made with federal authorities. In 1866, for instance, it was agreed that the Choctaws would hand over criminals whose apprehension was demanded by state and federal authorities. As the Choctaw economy prospered from mining and timber, it sought to restrict citizenship to preserve social, cultural, and economic harmony. In 1875 the previous custom of admitting white men married to Choctaws to the Nation was restricted although not stopped. Those Choctaws who had remained in Mississippi were, however, encouraged to join the Nation with funds being made available in the 1890s to help poor families to remove to Oklahoma. In 1891 two commissioners, one of them named Solomon Hotema, were appointed to travel to Mississippi to facilitate the relocation of eighty new citizens.[31] But external political pressure was increasingly being placed on the Nation to open up land to white interests and end Choctaw legal self-determination.

Solomon Hotema was a full-blood Choctaw born in Grant, Oklahoma, in May 1854. He was educated locally at Old Spencer Academy for Indians before, in 1878, becoming one of thirty-five young Choctaws given a bursary to attend Roanoke College, Salem, Virginia, which had been founded by Lutheran pastors in 1842. The college had an ethos of education for all and in the 1870s, was proactive in recruiting students from the Choctaw Nation. On his return to Oklahoma in 1881, Solomon, now trained in law, immersed himself in serving his people. He was a county judge between 1884 and 1886 and became a minister of the Cumberland Presbyterian church. He was active in Choctaw politics, considered a progressive and a follower of Green McCurtain, principal chief of the Nation during most of the 1890s and early 1900s. Hotema entered the Nation's senate in 1890 where he made a name for himself as a fine orator, and he also sat on the Choctaw National Education Commission, gaining funds for the creation of a mission school near his home. He had become a prosperous as well as an influential man, with mercantile interests and a farm sustaining a hundred head of cattle and two hundred hogs in the neighbourhood of Cold Spring Church, of which he was the founder and pastor, some six miles from Grant. But in the spring of 1899 this widely respected citizen and fine public servant, described in 1891 as 'a kind, good neighbour', went on a killing spree.

Married in April 1883 to Nancy Coleman, the couple produced three children over the next few years, only one of which, Cornelia, born in 1887, survived. A few years after Cornelia, they had a young son, Solomon's pride and joy. But in 1898 an outbreak of disease spread through the community and in the spring of the following year Solomon's son became one of its victims. Rumours rumbled around the neighbourhood that the epidemic was caused by witches, although it was later diagnosed as meningitis. Meetings were held at the church about what to do, and it was agreed to send for a reputed forty-nine-year-old medicine man named Sam Tarnatubby, who lived some twenty miles to the east. Tarnatubby confirmed that witches were, indeed, responsible and divined that the only way to end the plague was to kill them. During this time the grief-stricken Solomon spent much of his time praying. He beseeched God that the witches might be overcome, and dwelled on Bible stories of sorcery as proof of their existence. He preached on the subject at church, telling his congregation that he feared his people were going back to the witchery and evil of the past. He told them that during prayer he had seen witches coming through the air in the shape of fire balls.

On the 14 April not long after preaching this sermon, Hotema, as headman in the community, felt it was his duty to act. After a few drinks for Dutch courage he summoned two neighbours, Sam Fry (aged thirty) and Tobias Williams to his home. They armed themselves with a Winchester rifle and a shotgun, got into Hotema's buggy, and set off to the home of his sister-in-law Vina Coleman. Many years later, in her old age, Vina's daughter Louisa recalled what happened next:

> Mr Hotema, he keeping coming nearer to our house and then he pointed
> his gun our way as he raise it to his shoulder. I run into the house and my
> mama push baby toward floor. He missed them once, I think, and Mama

grabbed baby and tried to run from him. I don't know just what happened next, but when shooting stopped I looked outside the house. Mr Hotema, he was gone, but Mama was lying on ground near gate. She did not make no noise but little baby was crying. Mama was laying on it, one shoulder holding baby to ground. I told my brother, who was in house, 'Mr Hotema, he killed Mama... we must run...' and we run away. I don't think I ever saw Mama again... I don't never hate Mr Hotema. He was good man. He was our pastor. But I don't think my mama was a witch. I think he was wrong about that but he thought she was.[32]

Hotema and his two accomplices moved on to the home of Hull Greeenwood. They asked where his wife Lucy was, and when she appeared and pleaded for her life, she too was shot dead. Next on their list was Amos Morris. Their final destination was the home of Eastman Missippi, but fortunately for him, he was out. Panic surged through the community as news of the killing spree spread. Some hid out in the brush fearful that they might be the next to be accused of witchcraft. Deputy Marshals Ennis and Everidge got up a posse and set out from Grant to find the killers. They tracked down Hotema the next day as he was about to take a train to Paris, Texas. He was going to give himself up he said. He was escorted to the jail at Antlers while the posse went after Fry, Williams, and Tarnatubby, who were all subsequently arrested.[33]

At the ensuing examination before Commissioner Benjamin F. Hackett, Hotema seemed tranquil, talkative, and clear minded. There were no words of remorse. When asked why he had murdered three people, he replied 'I have the authority to do so.' 'Where did you get this authority?' he was asked. 'In the book of all books, the Bible, in the passage wherein it says: "Thou shalt not suffer a witch to live"', he answered. While in jail at Antlers he asked the jailer to forward a letter to the press. It began, 'I have on yesterday killed one man and two women. A man certainly does not know what his destiny shall be.' He then provided a brief biography and an account of his good works, before moving on to matters at hand:

> Since 1898 an opposition to the work has been manifested, threatened to wipe us out of existence with mal practice, and threats have been repeated on Thursday night April 13 1899. The people are afraid of them and have been dodging for about a week and saw them in their fires. Appeared and took it upon myself to sacrifice my life for the Lord's cause and for the love of the people. Now I am numbered with the law breakers, only awaiting for trial, not only for trial, but humbly submit my neck to the gallows.
>
> I ask all the Christian people of the land to remember me and my dear wife, Nance Hotema, and my loving little daughter, Cornelia, and my

darling little son, Frank Hotema, for their consolation and denying themselves for Christ, so that we may meet each other in heaven, where there is not parting. Yours in Christ, S. E. Hotema.[34]

The three defendants were taken to the holding jail at Atoka where Tobias Williams suddenly died of unknown causes. Hotema, and the two other defendants were then removed to Paris, Texas, to await trial before a federal judge. There we find them in the 1900 census, languishing in Lamar county jail.

A year earlier, with the passing of the Curtis Act, written by the 'mixed-blood' Congressman of Kansas, Charles Curtis, Choctaw customary law had pretty much been junked after years of smaller-scale erosion. Thereafter all peoples in the Indian Territories of the 'Five Civilized Nations' were subject to federal law.[35] The Major Crimes Act of 1885 had already imposed federal jurisdiction over murders committed in Indian territories. Under federal law the three men applied for bail, Fry and Hotema were denied, but Tarnatubby was admitted to bail for $2,000 because he was not present during the killings, but was nevertheless an accessory before the fact. As he sat in jail Hotema began writing a book on the 'Passing of the Indian' and biographical notes that he hoped would be published. He believed that within a few years the Native American would become extinct, absorbed into the larger American culture. Here was a man not only struck with terrible personal grief but also grappling with the complex balance he and his fellow leaders of the Choctaw Nation had pursued with both the white population and the judiciary and legislature of the United States. While eschewing the 'old ways', perhaps he thought he and his fellow Choctaws had gone too far.

Despite his apparent intention to provide a written record of his life and times, when the days of his trial finally came in 1901, he proved remarkably reticent about events. Further drama was to occur in the meantime. In February 1901 the bailed Tarnatubby was standing around a fire near Goodwater, near Grant, when he was struck with paralysis and fell in the fire, suffering serious burns. Shortly before the trial of Hotema and Fry, Deputy Marshall John B. Walter went to pick up Hotema's nephew, Stuart Pierce, to give testimony. Pierce was found shot dead on some rocks not far from Cold Spring Church, his Winchester rifle at his feet. It was not known whether he killed himself or was murdered.[36]

When the trial of Hotema and Fry began some fifteen local physicians were examined as to Hotema's sanity, with a majority of the opinion that he was insane. So on 13 April 1901, two years nearly to the day since the killing spree, Hotema was acquitted of the murder of Lucy Greenwood and Amos Morris on account of temporary insanity. Sam Fry was acquitted for his role as accomplice. Tarnatubby was acquitted separately as an accessory due to insufficient evidence.[37] Now Hotema faced trial before Judge Bryant for the murder of Vina Coleman. He pleaded not guilty, but was reticent as to his motives, although his defence introduced evidence that he believed in witches based on his reading of the Bible, and was convinced his people were being afflicted by witchcraft. This resulted in a hung jury, and a second trial was set for 26 November. Some forty witnesses were called to attend. This time he was found guilty of first-degree murder and on 5 December he was sentenced to be hanged on 14 February 1902. When a journalist interviewed him in jail, Hotema blankly refused to discuss the subject of witchcraft. Why he killed was a mystery to him and to others he said, but made it clear it had nothing to do with whisky.[38] An appeal was made to the United States Supreme Court, and his execution was stayed until his appeal was considered on the 28 April.

The appeal rested in part on double jeopardy, in other words the ruling under the Fifth Amendment that persons cannot be convicted of a crime for which they have been acquitted. The defence based this plea on the fact that Hotema had been acquitted of the other two murders. This was described as 'wholly without merit' by the Supreme Court. The remaining defence rested principally on his belief in witchcraft. The court's decision rested on whether:

> The evidence shows that the defendant Hotema believed in witches, and that it was the result of his investigation and belief as to what the Scriptures taught, and that he acted upon that belief, thinking he had the right to kill the party he is charged with killing, because he thought she was a witch, but at the time he knew it was a violation of human law and that he would be punished therefore, in that event it would not be an insane delusion upon the part of Hotema, but would be an erroneous conclusion, and, being so, would not excuse him from the consequences of his act.[39]

The Supreme Court agreed, and although Hotema's letter to the press in April 1899 was not considered, it confirmed that he knew he was violating human laws as set down by the United States legislature

A campaign now began to seek a presidential pardon to commute the death sentence. The eminent psychiatrist Dr Alonzo Blair Richardson, superintendent of the Government Hospital for the Insane at Washington DC (now St Elizabeth's Hospital), a published authority on melancholia and delusions, and recently elected president of the American Medico-Psychological Association, was requested to investigate Hotema's mental state. He concluded that Hotema earnestly believed in witches and that there was no evidence of insanity 'outside of the belief in witches'. The motive for the killing and the act itself were attributed to defective reasoning stemming from 'racial characteristics, the degeneration of brain due to habits of intoxication, or more probably the increase in the strength of his racial characteristics'. Richardson, who died shortly after writing this, recommended that the sentence of death be commuted to life imprison-ment.[40] One of the key petitioners on Hotema's behalf was Republican Judge Thomas Chauncey Humphry (1846–1937), an active member of the Paris First Methodist Church. President Theodore Roosevelt obliged. Connected or not, in 1904 Humphry was appointed by Roosevelt as United States District Judge for the Central District of the Indian Territory. Roosevelt faced some criticism for the decision, but as the *Dallas Morning News* commented:

> If the convict really believed the persons to be witches, and that they were using the power of Satan to destroy his family, as he claimed, then he should not be hanged for the crime. It has not been so long a time since some of our ancestors were doing the same thing, and, however revolting the chase after witches may now appear to be, we should not forget to be merciful to the benighted Indian who has not yet caught up with the procession.[41]

While criminals convicted by the Paris court usually ended up at Fort Leaven-worth, Kansas, because of his age and having lived in a southern climate all his life, the Department of Justice agreed that Hotema be incarcerated in the Atlanta Penitentiary. One of the Texas marshals who escorted him to Atlanta remarked,

> I have guarded the prisoner all through his incarceration and I never saw a man with a better disposition. His meetings with his family and friends have been particularly affecting. He is a proud man and has never com-plained. We have never placed a handcuff on him. As you saw us bring him in, so we have always treated him. During his term in jail he has always read his Bible and prayed daily.[42]

Hotema now claimed that he was temporarily insane when he committed the murders, and expressed confidence that he would be pardoned and so be allowed to spend the rest of his days at home with his family. In December 1906 a meeting of evangelical ministers in Atlanta, amongst them E. C. Cronk, and J. F. Purse, passed a resolution to campaign for Hotema's pardon. He was by now in failing health, and it was thought he did not have long to live. They were unsuccessful, for Solomon died in prison on 23 April 1907 from phthisis pulmonalis, tubercu-losis, in other words; the white plague. He was buried in an unmarked grave in the prison cemetery.[43] No one knows what happened to his prison manuscripts. An attempt to trace the trial records in 1999 proved unsuccessful.[44]

Hotema's case proceeded in a relatively straightforward manner. It was not always the case when Native-American witch slayers were prosecuted. The Major Crimes Act of 1885 should have clarified the law, but well into the twentieth century, witch killings continued to expose unresolved tensions regarding the boundaries between Native American, state, and federal law. When, in 1886, a Zuni man was put on trial for witch murder in the district court at Albuquerque, New Mexico, for instance, the presiding judge ruled that the offence was not against the United States and referred the case to the territorial Grand Jury.[45] The following year Dick Wyneco shot dead a medicine man in the Yakima Agency, Washington, believing he had bewitched his son. He was arrested by the agency authorities and a council of Yakima asked what would happen to him. They were informed of the Major Crimes Act of 1885. In response they complained they knew nothing about this law, and that while they were satisfied with its application in the future, they felt it was unfair that Wyneco be tried under this federal law when he and they were unaware of it.[46] In 1902 two headmen of the Umatilla tribe in Oregon named Toy Toy and Columbia George murdered a medicine woman named Anna Edna believing her to have witched Toy Toy's father to death. George killed her by dosing her with strychnine. A county court found the two men guilty—they did not deny it—and sentenced them to hang. After an appeal, the Oregon Supreme Court ruled surprisingly that state courts did not have jurisdiction over killings between Indians. They were tried again at a federal district court in Portland before an all-white jury, where it was reported that 'an odder plea and a more picturesque trial have never been known here'. The defence played the witchcraft card 'for all it was worth', making reference to the Salem trials. The two men were found guilty but the jury recommended life imprisonment rather than hanging. Toy Toy continued to launch appeals over the next few years, and US President William Howard Taft eventually pardoned both men in 1911 and 1912.[47]

Even when the supremacy of US law was clearly established, prosecutions were difficult to pursue because sometimes Native Americans were reluctant to give evidence or gave false information, unwilling to submit their own people to the scales of 'white man's' justice. An Indian agent supervising the Mescaleros of New Mexico reported in 1885 that an attempt had been made to execute an old woman after a medicine man had identified her as a witch. She was shot through the hip, and survived after treatment by an agency doctor. 'The punishment of the perpetrators of this dastardly outrage is next to impossible, as the Indians will give no information', he complained.[48]

Then there were the cultural issues about imposing the full weight of American jurisprudence where it clearly conflicted with native moral and judicial conceptions of justice. Considering the pervasive racism towards Native Americans at the time, white juries and judges sometimes demonstrated surprising sensitivity to cultural defence arguments. Salem nagged the white conscience of course. When a Mescalero Apache agent reported in 1883 that an old woman had been burned to death for witchcraft, he remarked that while people might be shocked, the Indians were only a century behind the Puritan fathers, and in this light it was not 'such a strange thing after all'.[49] In 1874 an all-white jury at Olympia, Washington territory, returned a verdict of not guilty on a mixed-race Indian named Harry Fisk who shot dead a Squaxin medicine man who he believed was responsible for his wife's long illness and death, accusing him of throwing an evil spirit into her. Fisk pleaded self-defence and his case was successfully argued by Judge Dennison. Fisk and his wife sincerely believed that she would die if the medicine man was not killed. Still, the court's decision smacked of double standards to some in the Squaxin community. When, in 1879, an old man of another Washington tribe, the Puyallup, was tried for killing a medicine man he accused of bewitching his children, the grand jury refused to indict him. 'This was unfortunate as it leads them to believe our laws do not punish for such matters', reported the local Indian agent. 'I will now have to turn the old man over to the council of the reservation to be punished as they may direct.'[50] Thirty-three years later, two Navajos killed a medicine man with an axe because they said he had done much harm in the community and had to be killed. They had been appointed to do it by the community, and if they had not done it then others would have: the witch had to die. Again their defence team did a good job. There was a hung jury, and after long delays for a retrial it was decided that they be paroled to the superintendent of the Fort Defiance agency.[51]

Why could the cultural defence not also be applied to some European-American witch killers as well? Joseph Heidt could have argued that the custom and belief of his Bavarian ancestors considered witches real and deserving of death. In his father's grandfather's time witches were still being executed by the state. Was another double standard at work? The fundamental legal difference of course, was that some Native American tribal laws had 'from time immemorial' ruled that witchcraft was a capital offence, and, as with the Navajo, they had not been changed or expunged. In America and Europe, the law, at least by the nineteenth century, was clear that witchcraft was no longer recognized as a crime. The belief in witches might mitigate a murder but only if it could be proven that witchcraft belief was symptomatic of insanity. The argument that the killer did not know that witchcraft was no longer a crime, while plausible, as evident from examples in a previous chapter, was never mentioned as mitigation. After all, execution was murder if not sanctioned and performed by the state.

So Hotema's lawyers had few options. A cultural defence stood no chance, partly because he was so thoroughly westernized and educated in US law, but principally because his offence also contravened the Choctaw laws against witch-craft drawn up in 1834, though this was not raised in reports of the trial. What made Hotema's case more unusual was that rather than appealing to indigenous custom, his defence argued on the basis of his profound belief in the supremacy of

Mosaic law. While the courts may have decided Hotema's biblical conviction was 'an erroneous conclusion', the decision raises intractable issues about cultural moral equivalency before the law. In essence, the Bible on which American society was often claimed to be founded, was deemed a less convincing justification for witch killing than the customary law of peoples often decried as pagans.

TIMES A-CHANGING

Americans had a lot on their minds in the early 1950s. The Cold War was intensifying, American troops were dying in Korea, and Senator Joseph McCarthy was pursuing his corrosive 'witch hunt' against real and illusory communists. In 1952 Arthur Miller's *The Crucible* dramatized the Salem witch trials as a trenchant allegory of McCarthyism. Racial segregation was still deeply entrenched, and the Civil Rights movement was moving into a new phase, with the growing influence of the Nation of Islam. Yet witches were still very much on the minds of some across the country. 1950 was the year that the trial of Helen Evans caused the Delaware authorities so much national embarrassment. It was also the year that Carl Walters, a forty-year-old resident of Carters Valley, Rogersville, Tennessee, walked into the local store where Alberta Gibbons and her mother Alta Woods were drinking pop and shouted at them, 'This has gone far enough.' He drew a pistol and shot Alberta dead as she held her baby in her arms. Alta pleaded, 'Please don't kill me', but Walters put three bullets in her anyway. He then got into his car, drove to Kingsport some twenty miles away, went to the police station and reported matter-of-factly, 'I have just shot two women down in Hawkins County. I was tired of being bewitched.' It was the 15 August.

Walters' wife Ruby, sister of Alta Woods (née Blair), had recently fallen down stairs, breaking her hip. One of their children had died not long before, and Walter was suffering from a strange complaint. In April and May 1949 he had been to see Dr Herbert Pope at Knoxville. Walter confided in Pope that ever since he was thirteen people had been 'against him', and related a story of an eleven-year-old boy he knew who hanged himself while under a witch's spell. On one occasion

Walters brought his eleven-year-old daughter Sylvia and said she was bewitched too. Pope gave Walters some shock treatment and recommended he go to a clinic. Walters agreed and spent two weeks at St Albans psychiatric hospital, in Radford, Virginia. It evidently did not help. When he returned home he told numerous neighbours that he and his family were bewitched.

As Walters lay in Rogersville jail a few days after the shooting, the residents of Carters Valley organized a lynch mob some seventy-five strong, which assembled at midnight and marched on the jail. There followed one of the more remarkable shoot-outs of the era. At least twenty shots were exchanged during an hour-long siege, with one of the mob managing to fire through the jail door. Leading the defence was Sheriff Bradley Blair, a cousin of Ruby and Alta. He and his officers shot two of the crowd before it finally dispersed. Blair subsequently got wind of plans to cause a riot when Walters was due to appear at the county courthouse. Blair knew who the ring leaders were and managed to prevent any such occurrence. Walters was tried in December. Nineteen of his neighbours and acquaintances gave evidence that they had heard him complain of his troubles with witchcraft. Most testified that they believed Walters sane. A separate insanity jury also found him sane despite the evidence of three psychiatrists that he suffered from *dementia praecox*—the same condition diagnosed in Albert Shinsky. Walters calmly chewed gum as he heard the Hawkins county court jury return a guilty verdict. He was sentenced to die in the electric chair on 3 February 1951. The defence immediately launched an appeal, and in May, Walters was taken to Nashville hospital to undergo further psychiatric tests.[1] These proved more convincing and he avoided the chair. So another witch murderer sat out his days in the asylum.

Meanwhile in Knoxville, Tennessee, the latest round in the long drawn-out trial of an African-American woman, Alberta Jefferson, for shooting dead a young conjure doctor, Obie Lee Roddie, had recently come to an end. Alberta, aged thirty-one, claimed Roddie had put a 'death hex' on her and her husband. Police searched his premises and found herbs, powders, and a little black book containing spells and recipes written in green ink. It included one for 'laying a burden on your enemy's heart'. His paperwork showed he had treated 174 patients in 1947, and had been paid more than $2,000. Finally, in 1952, the Tennessee Supreme Court ruled that Jefferson's belief in 'voodoo' did not mitigate her crime, but nevertheless affirmed a lenient three-year sentence.[2]

1952 was another notable year in the annals of witch shooting. In Mission, Texas, Alfredo Medrano shot waitress Maria Acevedo in the chest with 0.22-calibre pistol. She was not serious hurt fortunately. Medrano and Acevedo had been friends but when he began to suffer headaches and his family fell ill he came to the conclusion that she had paid a witch doctor to put a hex on him.[3] The same year, Joe S. Chavez, a forty-two-year-old Arizona rancher shot dead Mrs Maria Estrella Miranda.[4] Chavez ran a cattle ranch and alfalfa farm in the aptly named Superstition Mountains, some thirty-five miles east of Phoenix. Around 1942, Chavez's wife Josie, who he had married in 1929, started going blind and experienced constant spinal pain. He spent many days and much money travelling America and Mexico seeking out doctors and healers who might cure her eyesight. Chavez heard gossip, though, that one of his female relatives had paid a healer named Miranda to put a spell upon Josie.

The forty-one-year-old Maria Estrella Miranda, wife of Antonio Miranda, lived near the village of Guadalupe, south-east of Phoenix. At the time it was a settlement of some 850 people, mostly Hispanics and Yaqui Indians who had fled to the area from their Mexican homeland during the late nineteenth and early twentieth century as a result of political persecution. Miranda had a reputation for witchery or *brujería*. The local sheriff, L. C. Boies, observed, 'Everyone in Guadalupe who suffered any kind of a disease blamed Mrs Miranda. Lots of people thought they had a reason to kill her.' Then again, he said, she had her friends who considered her a devout religious woman. A neighbour told Chavez that she had seen pictures of him and his wife in Miranda's cabin and that she used them to work her spells. Chavez said he pleaded with Miranda to make Josie well again, even offering her $9,000. She replied dismissively that he should try and take her to court.

On 12 September 1952 Chavez decided to pay Miranda a visit to demand the return of the pictures. He brought a pistol with him. According to Chavez's version of events, Miranda refused and ordered him to leave. He took a step forward towards a box of photos, and Miranda reached for a shotgun. Chavez took out his pistol and shot her four times. He was arrested five days later. When police searched Miranda's home they found a small Catholic shrine on which were some 100 photos, amongst them, curiously, three depicting Democratic politicians defeated in that year's elections, Ernest McFarland who was running for the Senate, Joe C. Haldiman for governor, and Ralph Watkins for the House of Representatives. It would seem that Miranda was praying either for their good or ill fortune. Chavez's trial was originally scheduled for 15 December but it was postponed as most of the witnesses only spoke Spanish and it took time to hire an interpreter. It finally began in April 1953. The defence team put together a case based on temporary insanity and self-defence. Six neighbours testified that Miranda was a witch. Chavez was convicted of a second degree murder, a verdict that judge Ralph Barry described as 'more than merciful'. Barry was unwilling to countenance that the belief in witchcraft was instrumental in such a crime, and told Chavez 'you do not believe in hex'. He suspected that Chavez had murdered Miranda to 'shut her mouth' because she knew about his extra-marital affairs.

Chavez was sentenced to twenty-five to forty years in prison. Miranda's family filed a suit for damages against him with the Maricopa County Superior Court. $34,500 was demanded but only $2,000 was awarded.

After this last rash of witch shootings, witchcraft disputes were covered less and less in the press. The age-old neighbourly suspicions and accusations still occasionally played out between individuals. In 1960, for instance, eighty-three-year-old Minnie Gilland of Detroit suspected an elderly neighbour, Mary Donaldson, aged seventy-five, of witching her much younger husband away from her, so she painted a 'hex sign'—a ring of tar and chicken feathers—on Donaldson's house. Donaldson, who bought her coal from Mr Gilland, sued for damages, saying it would cost $75 to remove the tar sign. 'I had to do something', said Gilland. 'After I had done it I felt better'—that old refrain of the bewitched who went on the offensive.[5] But by 1960 the assault and abuse of suspected witches had largely become a thing of the past. That does not mean that belief in witchcraft had likewise disappeared. Folklorists continued to collect stories about witches, but few people complained of being victims.

The witch doctors continued to ply their trade. In 1950 a New Jersey Bureau of Employment report on disability relief noted that they had received one claim certified by a Pennsylvania 'hex doctor'.[6] State disability claims had to be signed by a medical practitioner but there was no sanction against non-licensed physicians doing so. Moving south, in 1958 a police investigation was launched regarding a series of arson attacks against the home of an African-American labourer named Calven Tuck, of Talladega, Alabama. It transpired that Tuck had visited a hoodoo doctor to hex the person responsible. The doctor instructed him to bury a bottle containing a half pint of vinegar, nails, pins, and a biscuit upside down at a forty-five degree angle. The arson attacks ceased afterwards, leaving the police puzzled. A year later, John Jernigan, Chief Deputy Prosecutor of Little Rock, Arkansas, issued a raft of summonses against African-American conjure doctors after he had been visited on several occasions by a man who claimed a local conjure doctor named Dr Snake had put a spell upon him. Snake, John Richmonds, and another practitioner nicknamed 'The Bishop', were charged with practising medicine without a licence.[7]

No doubt witchcraft constituted less and less of the business of the doctors. Although they had always offered more than just counter-witchcraft services for their respective communities, they were becoming increasingly irrelevant due to the diminution of this part of their trade. The profession was undoubtedly losing its identity, becoming culturally marginalized, just as we saw with the Native-American medicine men in the early twentieth century. German-American pow-wow doctors in comparison had never been reliant on witchcraft belief for their custom; their practice depended on a broader conception of illness and medicine, and was attuned to a strong Christian brand of faith healing and self-help. As a consequence, the pow-wows retained a distinct identity and a significant role in folk healing as witch belief waned. In 1969 the journalist and best-selling author Arthur H. Lewis interviewed several Pennsylvania practitioners. 'One needn't be a detective to locate powwowers', he revealed. 'None of them are inclined to conceal their talents or seem the least bit reluctant to discuss their *modus operandi*.'[8]

One could try and argue that the rise of the Cold War and the fear of communist infiltration into every nook and cranny of American society (note I do not use the psychiatric term 'paranoia'), somehow displaced the concern regarding witches: reds under the bed replacing witches riding you in bed. There are certainly parallels, as Arthur Miller and others observed. Propaganda such as the US Army pamphlet issued in 1954 explaining how one could identify closet communists by the way they talked, the terms they used, and the people they associated with, certainly fed into the deep-seated suspicion of the enemy within.[9] But parallel lines do not intersect. The communist booger was an abstract global threat to national American security, and not relevant to domestic personal well-being on a day-to-day level. The analogy works well regarding the old theological concerns of a satanic conspiracy heralding the apocalypse, but in everyday life communists did not replace witches as the killers of pigs, the nocturnal riders of horses, and evil-eyed baby kissers. No, witchcraft accusations declined because they became less relevant as personal well-being became more secure thanks to the state: at the same time, Americans' sense of insecurity regarding a global threat grew to epic proportions.

Witchcraft belief became more private. Those who considered themselves bewitched no longer felt confident in discussing their suspicions with friends and neighbours. Communities no longer generated outsider witches through gossip and collective memory. Twentieth-century sanitary and medical advances, such as the introduction of penicillin and painkillers, no doubt played their role in attenuating witch belief born of medical conditions, but the institution of a comprehensive welfare state also had an impact, albeit less obvious. Compared with Western and Northern Europe, the United States was relatively late in introducing such safety nets for the poor as unemployment benefit and pension insurance. But the New Deal of the 1930s introduced a raft of radical legislation, so that for a time the US was in advance of the welfare state provision of Europe. Most witchcraft accusations were born of necessity, the inability to understand or cope with misfortune. The creation of a welfare state created a comfort zone for the masses, so that the need *to explain* misfortune became less of an impulse, less necessary. The child fell ill and the cows ailed but witchcraft was no longer required as a diagnosis leading to a solution, and consequently witches did not need to be identified. Take away this basic comfort blanket and maybe witchcraft will become an explanation once again. After all, a majority of Americans, like many Europeans, believe in divine and satanic intervention in earthly affairs.

In 1986, a survey of University of Texas students revealed that 22 per cent believed in witchcraft. A rather more representative national Harris Poll in 2007 showed that 31 per cent believed in witches, rising from 28 per cent in 2005, though the figure dropped to 23 per cent in 2009.[10] The population of the United States was over 308 million in 2010, so that makes some 70 million witchcraft believers. A recent American opinion poll on book censorship revealed that 41 per cent of respondents thought that books including witchcraft and sorcery should not be available in school libraries.[11] The concern over witchcraft has clearly not gone away. But what did the people answering these polls understand by the terms 'witch' and 'witchcraft'?

Reinventing witchcraft

In 1940s England a new era of witchcraft was brewing as a former colonial civil servant named Gerald Gardner (1884–1964) set about creating a modern pagan religion called Wicca.[12] Building on his knowledge of folklore, occultism, spiritualism, and freemasonry, and inspired by Charles Leland's book *Aradia*, which claimed to reveal the existence of an ancient Italian pagan cult, and the works of Margaret Murray, who proposed that those persecuted as witches in the early modern era were members of a pre-Christian fertility cult, Gardner invented a founding myth for his new movement. He claimed that one night in 1939 he was initiated into a coven of witches in the New Forest, Hampshire. This group, headed by a priest and priestess, had kept alive the 'Old Religion' of the witches, worshipping a fertility goddess and a horned male deity. He revealed all in *Witchcraft Today*, published in 1954, and Wicca was born. If Gardner and his followers were correct then the history of witchcraft had to be completely rewritten.

Back across the Atlantic, 1964 was a watershed in the history of witchcraft in America. The year that Gardner died was also the year that the American comedy hit *Bewitched* first screened, and when a flamboyant English woman named Sybil Leek brought Wicca to the consciousness of the American public. While the writings of Gardner and his followers were not completely unknown in the US, the idea of witchcraft as a *religion* was a new concept for 99.9 per cent of the population at a time when the old traditional concerns regarding witches, as recounted in this book, were waning but far from forgotten. Now here were witches who formed covens and met for sabbats as in the legends of old, but who were claiming to be followers of an ancient pagan fertility religion, motivated by good intentions, celebrating the power of nature; not outsider, conflict, or accidental witches destroying humans and livestock out of malicious pleasure. It was a tough sell only a decade or so after people were being shot dead as witches.

Still, the United States was far from being virgin territory for esoteric groups espousing a mix of magic and ancient wisdom.[13] The country hummed with prophets, cults, masonic orders, and occultists. The terms 'Hermeticism' and 'Rosicrucianism' were frequently bandied about in some quarters of this mystic milieu. The former was based on a series of Greek philosophical and religious texts originating in late antiquity that were thought to be the profound musings of Hermes Trismegistus, a man–god combination of the Greek deity Hermes and the Egyptian Thoth. A version of this *Corpus hermeticum* was translated into Latin in the late fifteenth century and became a key source for Renaissance magic. Rosicrucianism referred to the tenets of a legendary fifteenth-century German knight who led a Brotherhood of the Rosy Cross. Their mission was to institute a spiritual reformation through the embrace of Hermetic and Kabbalistic magic. Rumours of the Brotherhood first emerged in the early seventeenth century, and despite their being no proof of its existence, it caught the imagination of eighteenth- and nineteenth-century freemasons and occultists.

The earliest American groups were born out of the era of spiritualism and mesmerism, such as the Rosicrucian Fraternity founded by African-American spiritualist Beverley Randolph (1825–1875), who espoused the use of magic mirrors and ritual sex. Then there was the Hermetic Brotherhood of Luxor founded in 1888 by a Scottish violin maker, Peter Davidson, who scratched a living in Georgia selling occult paraphernalia and herb doctoring. Back in Britain, in the same year, the Hermetic Order of the Golden Dawn was founded on the basis of a series of rites and rituals culled from ancient Egyptian and Greek texts, freemasonry, Kabbalah, and Renaissance Christian mysticism. The tensions between those members subscribing to Christian esotericism and those to pre-Christian religion and magic contributed to its demise in the early years of the twentieth century. One of the troublesome former members of the Golden Dawn, the notorious magician Aleister Crowley, went on to set up a British franchise of a German ritual magical order known as the Ordo Templi Orientis (OTO).

Crowley made a couple of visits to America during the early twentieth century. A lodge of the OTO was set up in California in 1914, and a short-lived offshoot was founded in Chicago in 1931. By the end of the 1930s, America was the last surviving home of the OTO, with the British Order disbanding in the 1920s and the Nazis suppressing the German branches. Lodges of the Rosicrucian Order of the Alpha and Omega, an outgrowth of the disbanded Golden Dawn, were created in Chicago and New York by 1914, and new lodges sprung up in New

York, Philadelphia, Los Angeles, and San Francisco between 1919 and 1921, but they did not flourish for long. One of those who joined the New York lodge in 1920 was a former Vaudeville musician, Paul Foster Case, whose occult interests stemmed back to his childhood. Case was expelled from the lodge two years later and embarked on creating a new 'school of wisdom' in Boston called the Builders of the Adytum or B. O. T. A., which he subsequently relocated to Los Angeles in the early 1930s. The school offered correspondence instruction on a range of occult subjects such as astrology, tarot, and Kabbalah, as well as borrowing heavily from Golden Dawn material and ritual.

During the early twentieth century various other home-grown Rosicrucian groups sprung up, such as the Order of the Rosicrucian Fellowship founded by Max Heindel in Oceanside, San Diego, which claimed to have 7,000 members in 1913.[14] The most successful and most publicized was the Ancient Mystical Order Rosae Crucis (AMORC), which was founded in 1915 by New Jersey commercial artist, Harvey Spencer Lewis. It claimed to be based on the mystery schools of pharaonic Egypt. Its headquarters moved from New York to Tampa before settling in San Jose, California. Lewis had grand visions. In Tampa he tried to build a fifteen-storey temple, and briefly set up the Order's own radio station. Then in 1928 he announced he was taking some members on a trip to Egypt where they would hold an ancient rite in full costume at the Karnak temple complex.[15]

None of these American occult groups of the nineteenth and first half of the twentieth century linked themselves with witches or witchcraft though. So as in Britain, Wiccans had the task of establishing their ancient inheritance by earnestly but dubiously rebranding the persecuted witches of the past as their benign pagan ancestors, thereby having to overcome centuries of ingrained prejudice and tradition about witchcraft. The process was not helped by a penchant amongst some early Wiccans, following in Gardner's footsteps, for myth-making about their own pasts. Leek was no exception. She claimed her family had been witches since 1134, and that she was descended from a legendary early eighteenth-century witch of Burslem, Staffordshire, named Molly Leigh. According to her autobiography she was brought up on an English estate and the French Riviera, where she was first initiated into a witch coven in the hills above Nice. Aleister Crowley was a highly improbable family guest during the 1920s. At sixteen she said she married a famous but unnamed pianist who died two years later. Back in England, she spent time living with the gypsies learning their secret lore and was initiated into an ancient coven in the New Forest. What civil records reveal is that she was born on 22 September 1917, near the smoky potteries town of Stoke-on-Trent, Staffordshire. Her father was Christopher E. Fawcett (d. 1955), and her mother's maiden name was Booth. In 1944 Sybil Fawcett married John

B. Delves, a butcher's son, at a ceremony near Cheadle, not far from Stoke. Then, in 1952, she married again to antique dealer Reginald B. Leek in Bournemouth, Hampshire.

In the early 1960s we find her in the village of Burley, in the New Forest, running an antiques shop, and beginning her campaign to educate the public about the witch religion. A feature spread in the *News of the World* in October 1963 called her 'Britain's No. 1 Witch' and reported Sybil's intention to set up a school for witches. It was one of numerous photo opportunities in which she posed with a pet jackdaw nicknamed Hotfoot Jackson on her shoulder.[16] In early 1964, she was involved in the creation of the Witchcraft Research Association and the founding of its magazine *Pentagram*. In its first edition one of its other founders, Doreen Valiente, expressed the hope that the WRA would act 'as a kind of United Nations of the Craft'.[17] Sybil was briefly its first president but clearly put the backs up of her fellow founders.

Leek began to attract coverage in the America press in late 1963. Early the following year reports appeared with titles such as 'Black Rumors Oust White Witch', in which it was revealed that Sybil was being evicted from her home and her antiques shop due to accusations that she was involved in orgies and black magic. Over the previous months churches and churchyards across the country had been vandalized and desecrated in a manner that suggested ritual activity. The press went into overdrive, and the police did not help by suggesting that in some cases Black Masses had been held by satanists. At Clophill in Bedfordshire, for instance, a vault was smashed, and the skull of its eighteenth-century occupant, Jenny Humberstone, taken and impaled on an iron spike, with the rest of her bones scattered around. There is no evidence that such acts of desecration were the work of satanists or 'black witches'. The culprits were most likely delinquents influenced by Dennis Wheatley's black-magic novels, and the hit film version of one of them, *The Devil Rides Out*, and who enacted copy-cat desecrations inspired by the lurid press reports.[18] Leek's public expressions of interest in the cases harmed her reputation though, despite her explicit condemnation of such dark doings. The New Forest locals turned against her she complained, 'It is heartless. They are taking away my livelihood.' 'I'm a white witch', she insisted, 'my witchcraft does nothing but good.'[19]

She first visited America in the spring of 1964 to promote a book on her experiences of the antiques trade, *A Shop in the High Street*. Within weeks she was appearing on the long-running syndicated talk show, the Mike Douglas Show, one of many television appearances over the next decade. In May she told reporters that she had sold the idea of a television comedy series called 'Dear Witch' to an American company, and intended to use the proceeds to set up her long-planned school of witchcraft back in Britain.[20] Seeing an opportunity for further reinvention, she swiftly adopted the title of Dame, something she could not get away with back in England. When asked once as to why the honour was bestowed upon her, she replied evasively that it was 'for bravery for something but it was so long ago, I can't remember', before then recalling as an afterthought that she had saved some lives as nurse while tending to wounded soldiers in the Hebrides during the Second World War.[21]

Leek returned to Britain in June, announcing to the press that she intended to emigrate to the US to escape continued persecution.[22] She resigned as president of the Witchcraft Research Association, claiming she was forced out because her colleagues frowned upon her interest in black magic.[23] Whether this was true or not, Leek, in turn, had issues with her fellow witches. For one, she disliked the use of ritual nudity as employed by Gardnerians and others. 'I can get enough power for occult healing with six fur coats on. All I need is my mind to generate power', she argued.[24] As to her coven meetings, she described them to one journalist as consisting of 'lots of singing and dancing and drinking. Rather like one of your debutante parties, I should imagine'.[25]

She moved around America drumming up interest in herself and her numerous publications. Ever patient with the habitual enquiry as to whether she had arrived on a broomstick, she was always ready with a newsworthy soundbite or extraordinary claim. No Halloween passed without Sybil being interviewed somewhere. In 1966 she claimed that America's 400 witches had more power than the Mafia. The same year she told *Sports Illustrated* that she was turning her psychic power to the Kentucky Derby, having picked six winners out of six at Ascot a few years before.[26] It was claimed that she foresaw the assassinations of John F. Kennedy and his brother. *Playboy* stated that an impressed military at Cape Kennedy consulted her. Yet Leek's powers failed to prevent the burglary of her St Louis motel room in July 1966. A purse, which she said was a gift from Ian Fleming of Bond fame, containing $450, was taken along with three magic rings, one of which she warned could 'have a disastrous effect on anyone else who wears it'. Leek was so angry that she declared she was weaving a hex on the thief: 'it's been 20 years since I've felt this vicious and the hex I conjured then was so terrible I won't even tell you about it'. She was also sorely tempted to hex a female journalist who called her 'a jolly little pudding of a woman'.[27] By 1968 Britain's former 'No. 1 Witch' was being described as 'America's most famous resident witch'. But she increasingly preferred to be known for a much wider portfolio. As described by the *Los Angeles Times* in 1972, she was an astrologer, entrepreneur, lecturer, publisher, radio and television producer and personality, mother, and manufacturer of sailboats and jewellery. Oh, and she had previous claimed to be a scriptwriter for the BBC.[28]

The earliest investigations into the modern witch religion in America were conducted from unusual quarters. In the summer of 1964, Don Shepherd of

Channel 6 Philadelphia did some research on witchcraft in connection with the station showing the first series of *Bewitched*. This led him to former actress Mary Manners Hammerstein, one-time wife of Reginald Hammerstein, brother of the famed lyricist and theatre impresario Oscar. Mary, who seems to have described herself as a white witch, made 'witch brooms' for distribution to children, invented cooking utensils, and marketed a pie-making kit. In early May 1964 it was reported that Mary's hilltop home Sky Island, in Upper Black Eddy, Pennsylvania, was haunted by a noisy ghost, causing Mary to lose her beauty sleep. Flying saucers had also been spotted in the area. She invited the Polish parapsychologist Alexander Imich and his wife, who had emigrated to the US in 1952, to investigate. A member of Mary's coterie, artist Tavis Teichman, painted a portrait of Sybil during a visit to a psychic party at Sky Island that also included a spiritualist and the Philadelphia television presenter Bill Hart, who hoped to record the spirit activity for his afternoon show on WCAU.[29]

Don Shepherd told Bob Feldman of television station WHYN about Hammerstein, and Bob then had a chat with Massachusetts newspaper columnist Brian F. King, who related their conversation in his column in September. 'What I'm looking for is a real live witch that I can book for an interview on one of our television shows', said Bob. He was having problems finding one, though. King suggested he try Sybil Leek. 'Don't think I haven't thought about her', he replied, 'but what I'd really like to find is a real live witch who lives right here in Western Massachusetts.' Three weeks later King reported in his column how Bob had faired. 'I'd say the results were good', said Bob, 'even though I didn't hear from a witch or a warlock who was willing to publicly identify her or himself as such.' He received a few telephone calls from people who claimed to be witches, 'but they were sort of vague, and what they had to say didn't seem to ring true'. A few letters trickled in, one from a person who explained, 'I never knew I had some qualification for becoming a witch', but after reading Bob's description of witches having extra-sensory perception and clairvoyance, felt that her own experiences in these fields now made sense. Another more knowing correspondent, signed 'A Warlock', wrote:

> Dear Mr Feldman:
> You are quite right in assuming that there are those of us who practise the 'Old Religion' in this area. I myself am a warlock and have been for years. I am a descendant of Alice and Mary Parker, who were hanged as witches at Salem on Sept. 22 1692.
>
> Your interview in Mr. King's column was honest, and I trust it will help lift the heavy censure placed on us by those who would persecute us, especially here in Massachusetts.

> I would like to mention, however, that not all of us belong to covens, especially here in Massachusetts. Fear of detection and reprisals force us to practice in deepest secrecy, with perhaps the assistance of an apprentice witch or warlock.

The mystery warlock was unwilling to be interviewed, though, suggesting that Sybil Leek might be of assistance. Bob was left still looking for an American witch to interview. They would begin turning up within a few years.[30]

Sam Tate of Edison, New Jersey, a buyer of baby clothes for a major department store, was another contemporary witch-finder, who attracted press attention in 1965 when he placed this advertisement in the *New York Times*: 'Author wishes to interview witches for completion of serious book on Witchcraft Religion. Legitimate replies only'. Tate was not overwhelmed with correspondents. 'A lot of newspapermen have called', he revealed, 'and a couple of researchers, two sweet little old ladies, three drunks and a man looking for an apartment.' Described as a big, blonde fellow, Tate began to research American witches after he was approached by a New York radio producer to talk on the subject. He had seen some magazine articles Tate had written on psychic phenomena. Tate confessed he was no expert on witchcraft though. 'How long would it take you to become an expert on witches?' asked the producer. 'When was the show on?' Tate replied. 'Tomorrow night', came the answer.[31] Tate was inspired and began his researches. He said his family did not mind his interest in witchery but preferred him not to join a coven.

Tate had learned about the movement from three main sources: *Pentagram* magazine; Patricia Crowther, a leading Gardnerian who had set up a coven in the northern English town of Sheffield, and who with her husband had written a book that year called *The Witches Speak* (1965); and Fanny Carby, an actress he described as a 'lonely' or solitary witch. Carby had appeared on Broadway in the hit show 'Oh, What a Lovely War', and in 1970 appeared in a British television adaptation of James Herlihy's play 'The Season of the Witch' about a teenage girl's immersion in the hippie subculture. She had roles in many other British television programmes and films between the 1950s and 1990s, including *The Elephant Man* (1980). Tate declared that the Old Religion was 'as genuine as Druidism but it's gotten a bad press ever since that messy business up in Salem in the 17th century'.[32] He estimated that there were no more than fifty or so witches in the US at that time. The book he intended to write, 'The Working Witch', seems never to have made it into print.

In 1969 Leek estimated that there were 300 covens in the USA. It does not sound improbable if the meaning of coven is interpreted broadly, as there must have been a fair few groups that had only a fleeting existence.[33] The witch religion was growing. Some covens were founded by other British arrivals during the 1960s, most notable amongst them Raymond and Rosemary Buckland, followers of Gerald Gardner, who settled in Long Island in 1962 where they set up the first Gardnerian Wiccan group in America, and created the Buckland Museum of Witchcraft and Magick in New York. Their profile grew after the publication in 1971 of Raymond's book *Witchcraft from the Inside*, and a few years later he created a breakaway group following what he called 'Seax-Wicca' or Saxon Witchcraft. This new tradition accepted self-initiation, thereby opening up a new path for the involvement of curious individuals. Another early Wiccan coven was founded in Chicago by Donna Cole after she had gone to England to be initiated into Gardnerian Wicca in 1969.

'If I were 18', said Sybil Leek in 1969, 'you would see the hippiest, yippiest, yappiest hippie you've ever seen!'[34] But, as she recognized, a new generation was taking over the scene, and she stepped back into the shadows as far as witchcraft was concerned. Most of her numerous publications were on astrology, psychic phenomena, reincarnation, and prediction. She repeatedly told journalists that she did not want to be styled an evangelist for the witch religion. 'I'm not the Billy Graham of Witchcraft', she said with her typical flair for a neat phrase. By the mid-1970s Leek had pretty given up talking about witchcraft to the media.[35] She died of cancer at her home in Melbourne, Florida, in October 1982.

The new generation of American witches was more strident—as much concerned with the social challenges of the present as fantasies about the ancient past. As a religion, witchcraft developed in distinctive ways through its embrace by the counterculture and civil rights movements of the era. American witches were pioneers in espousing environmentalism and feminism, for instance.[36] Indeed, interest in feminism and ecology were pathways into Wicca. As one historian of the movement has noted, while England may have given Wicca to America, the United States exported eco-feminist witchcraft back across the Atlantic.[37] The feminist movement adopted witchcraft as an example of the crushing and terrible misogyny of a patriarchal past that had yet to be eradicated from western society. One women's rights group called itself WITCH—the Women's International Terrorist Conspiracy from Hell, though other sources of the acronym were also formulated. They picketed the 1968 Miss America contest, and on Halloween that year, one cell dressed up as witches to picket and humorously hex Chase Manhattan Bank in an action called 'Up against the Wall Street'. The movement also funded practical services such as judo classes and an abortion referral service in New York.[38]

The one big negative in the coming together of feminism and the witch movement was the promulgation of the 'Burning Times'. This was a term coined by Gerald Gardner to describe the historic persecution of the witches he had adopted as pagan ancestors. As the majority of those executed as witches in the early modern period were women, the notion was propagated in feminist circles, particularly by the American radical Mary Daly, that the Burning Times represented 'gendercide', a female holocaust instigated by a male patriarchal society that used the fear of witchcraft to exterminate millions of women across Europe. This was a monumental distortion of the historical record, based on a completely unsubstantiated calculation for the number of people executed as witches. Probably no more than 50,000 people were executed in the European witch trials, a tragic figure but nevertheless far from a female holocaust. It took a couple of decades to drain this misinformation from the Wiccans' narrative of their own past and the pseudo-sense of grievance and victimhood, and yet the myth of millions of victims continues to be repeated in books like Dan Brown's *Da Vinci Code*.[39]

In the late 1960s Morgan McFarland, the daughter of a Protestant missionary, set up a Dianic witchcraft group that had a strong ecological and feminist underpinning.[40] She was inspired in childhood by reading Roman and Greek myths, and in adulthood was active in the Women's Liberation Movement. Her home in Dallas was notable for having a coffin in the front yard, and one interviewer described her as a woman 'with Mary Poppins sincerity and mystic persuasion'. Her ecological message was simple, 'if you destroy nature you are destroying Mother and you are destroying me'.[41] Morgan and her fellow founder of the Dallas Dianic group, Mark Roberts, published a witchcraft journal *New Broom*, and created a short-lived business named Witch Way Tours inc. In 1972 they announced a fifteen-day tour of Britain. The itinerary began with a visit to the Buckland Museum of Witchcraft followed by a Pan Am flight to London. Once in Britain ticket holders would be given membership of the Spiritualist Association of Great Britain, hear talks by Druids, Wiccan priests and priestesses, attend séances by England's leading mediums, and spend several nights in haunted inns and ghost-ridden manor houses.[42] The eco-feminist message of witchcraft was further defined by Miriam Simos, better known as Starhawk, who promoted witchcraft as a Goddess nature religion with a strain of transcendentalism that can be traced through America's past. Her book *The Spiral Dance* (1979), which expressed the rebirth of an ancient religion, apparently sold around 50,000 copies in the first six years, and is still in print today. In it she explained that witchcraft was 'a religion, perhaps the oldest religion extant in the West. Its origins go back before Christianity, Judaism, Islam—before Buddhism and Hinduism . . . [it] is closer in spirit to Native American traditions or to the shamanism of the Arctic.'[43]

In an era of protest and activism, it would be surprising if Wicca did not develop a militant wing. Leading it from New York was Leo Martello, a graphologist, hypnotist, and gay rights activist. On Halloween 1970 he organized a 'witch-in' event in Central Park, New York, that the authorities tried to ban, mimicking the 'sit-in' protests of the previous decade and the 'bed-in' by John Lennon and Yoko Ono in protest at the Vietnam War. He then founded the Witches' Liberation Movement and later the Witches Anti-Defamation League, and demanded reparations from the Catholic Church for their role in the Burning Times. 'Today witches are treated like refugees from a psychotic ward', Martello complained to a journalist in 1974, as they sat in his red and black ritual chamber.[44] Thanks to his energies and media savvy, though, 'for the first time in history, modern witches are fighting for their constitutionally guaranteed civil rights'.[45] That said, there was nothing actually illegal about practising witchcraft as a religion. The old state laws against obtaining money by fortune-telling, palmistry, mediumship, and other 'crafty science', were still in place, tinkered with and updated here and there. The District of Columbia innovated, for instance, by licensing this occult trade. But the laws were rarely stringently enforced and did not impinge on the new witch religion.[46]

Two clear indicators that modern witchcraft had lodged itself firmly in American culture were when it was linked with *Playboy* and when it was recognized by the Internal Revenue Service. In 1970, Playboy Bunny Starr Maddox, a member of a Miami Wiccan coven, was photographed in glamorous witch pose alongside one of her in a Bunny costume. Maddox told journalists, 'It bothers my parents'— Wicca that was, not posing as a Bunny. 'They're strict fundamentalists and they don't believe in witches.' Her parents sent a minister round to talk to her, but he soon made his excuses once she began questioning him. A couple of years later she was in Chicago promoting a Playboy production of *Macbeth*, confiding that in a previous life she had been burned at the stake for witchcraft.[47] The same year, 1972, the IRS certified that the Church and School of Wicca was a religious association and therefore tax exempt. The Church had been founded by British engineer Gavin Frost and his American wife Yvonne in Missouri in 1968. They created the first and longest-lasting correspondence course in pagan witchcraft.[48]

Who were these modern witches? They were nearly all white, urban, mostly middle class, and over half, female. Morgan McFarland's seventy-five members seem representative. They included dentists, solicitors, secretaries, students, professionals with postgraduate degrees, nurses, and truck drivers. Most were in their mid-twenties and mid-thirties.[49] The media coverage pioneered by Leek helped normalize interest in the movement, but outside the main cities, those wanting to join a coven faced challenges. Desiring to be a witch was not something to discuss with the parents over Sunday lunch or to pin on the local town noticeboard. So advertisements began to appear in the personal columns of the regional press, such as this one from an Ohio newspaper in 1973, 'I am interested in Wicca. Persons with information please call...'; this from a Louisiana paper, 'WICCA study group forming. For information, write . . . '; and from Alabama, 'Couple interested in Wicca Traditions wish to contact other persons with similar interests'.[50]

By no means was all media coverage neutral, relaxed, or humorous. Wicca took off at a time when fears of satanic cults had been fuelled by other darker strains in the late sixties counterculture.[51] Roman Polanski's superbly atmospheric film *Rosemary's Baby* caused a sensation in 1968 with its creeping paranoia that a New York occult group was engineering the sacrifice of an infant. It transpires that they are Satanists heralding the birth of the child as a satanic messiah. Then, the following year, the Charles Manson murders shocked America, further fuelling concerns over the growing influence of satanic cults. Scare stories multiplied shortly after. 'Hippie commune witchcraft blood rites told', screamed a headline from the *Los Angeles Herald Examiner*. It reported that police in Santa Cruz were concerned about the growth of 'witchcraft cults that sacrifice animals and turn humans into "slaves of Satan"'.[52] In 1972, a Christian evangelist named Mike Warnke published a best-selling book entitled *The Satan-Seller* in which he shocked and fascinated readers with his purported former life as the leader of a satanic cult in the late 60s, practising magic, invoking demons, taking drugs, indulging in orgies, and committing rape. It was denounced by some as a tissue of lies, but the template was repeated in other spurious 'I was a Satanist' books over the next couple of decades. No wonder that Morgan McFarland complained to a journalist in 1972, 'too many people in the United States confuse it with Satanism, and how could it be? Witchcraft, real witchcraft, doesn't recognize the existence of Satan or the Devil. That's a Christian concept'.[53] Unfortunately an increasingly powerful evangelical media stoked the fires of misinformation and suspicion.

In 1972 the Rev Hershel R. Smith travelled across America in his funky 'witchmobile', a van containing an anti-occult display of paraphernalia that had been constructed by Warnke and the controversial Pentecostal evangelist Morris Cerullo, head of the World Evangelism, Inc. ministry. Cerullo was a vocal campaigner against the modestly burgeoning witchcraft movement, preaching that 10 million Americans were dabbling in the occult, and that there were 100,000 practising Satanists. At the age of twenty, Smith claimed he was a member of a coven in San Francisco; that would have been in the early 1960s if true, but it was not. He said he was a morphine addict and alcoholic, supporting himself by drug dealing, emanating demonic pressures, and hexing people. He made a pact with the Devil to take his life at the age of twenty-five, but found God before sacrificing himself. Ordained a minister, he ran Teen-Power, a centre for rehabilitating witchcraft believers in San Bernardino, California, and took to the road in the witchmobile.[54] While attracting the interest of the press, his local visits were not necessarily a smashing success. An encounter arranged in St Louis between Smith and the Frosts, who were well prepared with an audio-visual presentation of their craft, ended as a damp squib. Smith failed to turn up and the eight Wiccans present outnumbered an audience of five.[55]

Still, the drip of satanism scare stories made an impression on the American public. When, in 1972, the decomposed body of a girl was found in a quarry in Union County, New Jersey, police reported that they found bits of what they described as wooden crosses over her head, and pieces of wood around the body 'like a coffin'. The authorities said the murder might be linked to a witchcraft coven that was rumoured to exist in the area. The girl's parents agreed that she might be the victim of black witchcraft or satanism. The following year the murder of a seventeen-year-old amusement park worker on Daytona Beach was described as a 'witchcraft slaying' committed by a gang of transient teenage beach-bums. A local resident reported that a satanic witchcraft coven operated at a house nearby, and he had heard that they signed their names in blood in a register.[56] As with some of the so-called hex slayings of the 1920s and 1930s the introduction of witchcraft and satanism was sensational spin generated by press reportage and an overly loquacious police, with the murders usually turning out to have more mundane origins.

Finding an American heritage

'The Mormons and Christian Scientists began right here in the United States', Leo Martello explained to a journalist in 1974. 'They own millions of dollars of property and have full rights.' Martello intimated that the witchcraft religion should aspire to the same.[57] But what would a truly American witchcraft religion look like?

In the early years most American pagan witches were of British, northern or central European ancestry, and considering that Wicca originated in Britain, it is no surprise that the Wiccan conception of witchcraft and magic was firmly rooted in English, Welsh, Irish, and Scottish folklore and myth. The notion of a Celtic tradition was and is very strong. In 1967, for instance, American *Y Tylwyth Teg* covens were founded whose members reclaimed what they described as the 'Faerie Faith' of Wales. Scandinavian and Baltic neopagan groups emerged in America later but this takes us away from the conception of a witch religion.[58] Considering the strength of American-German identity, it is somewhat surprising that it was only in the 1990s that the idea of German Wicca joined the pagan mainstream thanks to a raft of publications by Pennsylvania neopagan author Jenine Trayer, a.k.a. Silver RavenWolf. She has adapted/appropriated (delete as you feel inclined) Pennsylvania Dutch 'pow-wow magick' into her pagan world view and practices. The addition of a 'k' is a giveaway as to the pagan spin on what is a Christian healing tradition.

Italian pagan witchcraft was an early significant departure from the Anglo-Celtic mainstream. The seeds of an Italian tradition had been sown seventy years before, when American journalist and folklorist Charles Godfrey Leland published *Aradia, or The Gospel of the Witches* (1899), which claimed to contain the rituals and lore of a Tuscan pagan witch sect purportedly based on the revelations of a female adherent of this 'Old Religion'. The followers worshipped a goddess named Aradia, and they possessed an ancient Italian explanatory text called the *Vangelo* that she allowed Leland to translate. While hardly making a splash at the time, this highly dubious book was an important influence on the foundation of Gardnerian Wicca. The founders of neopagan Italian witchcraft in the 1960s, Leo Martello, the son of a Sicilian immigrant farmer, and fellow Italian-American Wiccan, Lori Bruno, whose mother's family came from around Naples, were inspired by but did not fully embrace Leland's Tuscan flavour of paganism. They emphasized their own family hereditary traditions regarding who their fellow *streghe* worshipped and what they practised. From the 1990s the conception of Italian pagan magic was given a boost, and developed in new ways, by the writings of an Italian-American *strega* named Raven Grimassi who claims to have been initiated into the tradition by an aunt on his Italian mother's side.[59]

The American Wiccan adoption of European ancestral religions, imaginary and otherwise, is part of a broader pattern of how second-, third-, or fourth-generation emigrants sought to reconnect with their ancestral homeland cultures through religion, language or custom. There is often a degree of fabrication, adaptation, or change in this process of simulation. Norwegian-Americans, for instance, have adopted the Norwegian expression *uffda* to enunciate mild discomfort or displeasure as a badge of ethnic identity, and in doing so they use it in contexts that have no resonance back in Norway, and they are even more enthusiastic about *lutefisk* (dried fish preserved in lye—an acquired taste) than contemporary Norwegians.[60] The adoption of religions and practices from completely separate cultures is far more problematic however. This is evident from the relationship between the newly self-identified pagans and Native Americans—people denounced and harried as pagans by *others* ever since Europeans embarked on North American shores.

Native-American medicine men, who by the mid-twentieth century were regularly being termed 'shamans', were thought to possess a pure tradition of spiritual wisdom and nature worship untainted by 2,000 years of Christianity. Theirs was a convincing unbroken history of religion. Neopagans could learn from the Native Americans; they were brothers and sisters in pagan spirit, persecuted for practising their ancient religion. They could point to studies by European historians arguing that elements of shamanism could be identified in the records of the sixteenth- and seventeenth-century witch trials. Still, implicit in this embrace was a sense that the continuity of ancient lines of European paganism were somehow less authentic—a fact that some Wiccans were beginning to acknowledge by the 1980s.

The British Gardnerian Frederic Lamond recalled how in 1958 his coven experimented with Native American ritual: 'Someone mentioned that the Lakota Sioux dance for hours on end until they drop from exhaustion to raise power for their spells: we never managed more than 5 minutes at most, but the spells still worked.'[61] A decade later, counterculture America became entranced by the publications of anthropologist and cult leader Carlos Castaneda, in which he recounted his supposed initiation by a Yaqui shaman through the use of psycho-active plants such as peyote. The inner circle of Castaneda's followers was known as 'The *Brujas*'. The neopagan fascination with Native-American religion was not just about the ritual use of drugs; the concept of the Great Spirit, and the dances, chants, dream catchers, and sweat lodges used in communal and individual rituals were all adopted. But some Native-American groups have seen this practical interest as the culturally insensitive appropriation of their sacred beliefs and traditions, a continuation of the earlier European appropriation of medicine bundles and other sacred artefacts as curios and museum pieces.[62] Their rituals were rendered meaningless, void of power, denigrated, once inserted into another culturally alien religion.

American witches have been less interested in borrowing from African-American religious and magical traditions, perhaps because of the obvious Christian influences in Voodoo, hoodoo, and conjure; likewise the Hispanic tradition of *Santería*.[63] But then again, the witch religion is a broad church these days, and there are those who style themselves Christian witches, with Voodoo and *Santería* providing templates as to how Catholicism and non-Christian faiths and practices can be blended to create new traditions that have legitimacy in the eyes of others.[64] Most of those neopagans who do embrace African-American and Hispanic faiths have an ethnic connection, and seek to explore their cultural roots. There are few African-American or Hispanic Wiccans, though.

Witches, *streghe*, *brujas*—the notion of a pagan witch heritage is obviously historically problematic. Up until this chapter I have spent most of the book discussing witches in different American cultures, yet the only time I have referred to paganism has been with regard to European denunciations of Native-American religion and African-American 'superstition'. While some American Wiccans have argued that those executed and persecuted in colonial America were members of European pagan cults who had secretly re-established their faith in the new land, there has been a general silence about the many Americans from many different cultures who were accused of witchcraft after the 'Burning Times', simply because they do not fit the narrative of persecution, secrecy, ancestry, and cultural antiquity. Cunning-folk and witch doctors tend to be used to fill the gap between the witch trials and the emergence of Wicca, but these were not witches as understood at the time, though they were sometimes accused of witchcraft. The witch, as understood by Europeans, African Americans, and Native Americans was a malicious, destructive, and repugnant individual bent on destroying individuals and communities. He or she was never the benign and sympathetic witch of Wicca. Native Americans executed witches into the twentieth century not because they were pagans. Their medicine men were killed if they were suspected of turning to witchcraft to harm their communities. Alberta Gibbons, Alta Woods, and Maria Miranda were not shot dead as witches in the 1950s because they were part of a pagan underground.

That said, as this book has also shown, America is a land of transplanted hereditary magical traditions. Africans and Europeans brought their fears of witches, and their means of identifying and punishing them. They continued to practise the folk medicine of their ancestors, and adapted to what the American environment and other Americans offered in the way of knowledge. Magical practitioners travelled from Europe and Africa to the new land offering their services to all and sundry. But once paganism is injected into this narrative it instantly becomes historically problematic. Martello claimed, for instance, that there was still a large underground network of pagan *streghe* operating in Italy. That would be news to anyone living in rural Sicily and elsewhere in the country. Much of the basic folk magic and healing lore that he and other Italian-American pagans practised is shared with the old country but not the conception of a witch religion.

In a sense, American Wicca does not need witches. For centuries an exchange of magical knowledge has taken place between different ethnic and cultural groups, blending traditions from non-Christian and Christian faiths alike. Modern American pagans can claim all these traditions as being part of a true and continuous American heritage stretching back several centuries without referring to witchcraft as an ancient religion brought to America. Many Wiccans already acknowledge this, and are sensitive about referring to themselves as witches. Who knows how it will develop in the future, and what role it will play in society—after all, who in 1850 would have believed that Mormons would number in the millions. Maybe in this respect Martello was on to something profound in his vision of a pagan future.

And so back to Salem

Guilt over Salem was an itch that some could not resist scratching. In 1946 the Georgia industrialist H. Vance Greenslit, who would later become President of Southeastern Greyhound Bus Lines, petitioned the Massachusetts legislature to pardon one of his Salem descendants Ann Pudeator, and six others who were executed for witchcraft. It was rejected, as were further requests in 1946 and 1953, although a resolution was finally passed in 1957.[65] Greenslit then ceased pursuing any further public interest in the matter, leaving a Salem resident, John Beresford Hatch, to carry on a one-man crusade to have the British parliament exonerate all those executed at Salem. Hatch, who was not related to any of the Salem accused, sent numerous letters to Buckingham Palace and to the Prime Minister's office. In 1960 he petitioned Congress, the State Department, and the Massachusetts legislature to pressure the British government. A letter to the British Consul General in Boston received the curt reply that Her Majesty's government no longer had jurisdiction over the witch trials. Another missive to Prime Minister Harold Macmillan, suggested he and Hatch meet at Salem's Gallows Hill 'to settle one and for all time' the exoneration of the Salem accused. He did not receive a reply.[66] Then, in 1992, the tercentenary of the Salem trials was marked by the installation of a new monument commissioned after a competitive process. It was unveiled by playwright Arthur Miller, and the human-rights campaigner and Holocaust survivor Elie Wiesel gave a memorial speech. The event provided a sober moment of reflection about Salem's status, underlining its role in reminding the nation of the dangers of persecution, prejudice, and scapegoating.[67]

Meanwhile the popular image of the witch was changing, and not just because of the rise of Wicca. There was a flipside to the satanic image being peddled by evangelists. Writing in November 1964, Joy Miller, Women's Editor at the Associated Press, complained, 'This may go down as the year of the kook—the year the weirdo achieved status, the year Halloween lasted around the calendar.' She was referring to the success of *The Adams Family* and *Bewitched* which had both begun airing on ABC that year. The old films of vampires and werewolves used to send shivers down the spine, but now television was sanitizing such figures of supernatural fear, 'the ghoul next door is pure Pollyanna, and the witch is a homebody who conjures up dinner. By a twitch of her pretty nose'.[68] By the 1960s witches had become sexy, overshadowing the venerable stereotypical old crone so strikingly represented in the *Wizard of Oz* and the Disney animation *Snow White*. Young beautiful witches had been depicted in nineteenth-century literature, but it was the advertising industry, commerce, film, and television that provided the real makeover in popular culture.[69]

In the romantic comedy *I Married a Witch* (1942), based on the novel *The Passionate Witch* by Thorne Smith, Veronica Lake plays Jennifer, an attractive young seventeenth-century Salem witch burned at the stake along with her father Daniel—perpetuating the mistaken belief that witches were burned in America. Their spirits are imprisoned in a tree until one day in 1942, it is split asunder by lightning and they are freed to exact revenge on the descendant of their

Puritan persecutor, played by Frederic March. True love overcomes hate, of course, and the film ends happily with the spiteful, sozzled Daniel trapped in a bottle, and Jennifer marrying March. *Bell, Book and Candle* (1958), based on a successful 1950 Broadway play, presented a modern-day witch Gillian Holroyd, played by Kim Novak, who lives alone in Greenwich Village with her cat familiar Pyewacket—which was the name of an imp mentioned in an English witch investigation conducted by Mathew Hopkins the Witchfinder General in 1644. Gillian finds herself attracted to her neighbour played by James Stewart, and faces the dilemma that she will lose her witch powers if she truly falls in love. A strong message in both was that a good witch had to be not only nubile but domesticated, as came across loud and clear in the most influential sexy witch of the era, Samantha Stephens, in the television comedy *Bewitched*. ABC made 254 episodes between 1964 and 1972. Elizabeth Montgomery, she of the pretty nose, was Samantha, married to her mortal husband Darren, played by Dick York for most of the series.[70] In June 1970, the cast of *Bewitched* made a rare venture out of the studio to record scenes at Salem for two Halloween-based episodes, 'Samantha's Bad Day in Salem' and 'Samantha's Old Salem Trip'. For the occasion, the show's producer explained to the press, 'the directional traffic signals which carry the face of an old hag on a broom will be changed to carry the much prettier profile of Samantha'.[71] The town was about to undergo a witch revolution.

The commercial exploitation of 1692 had begun back in the early 1890s when a local jeweller began making 'Salem Witch Souvenir Spoons' on which were depicted witches, hanging ropes, cats, brooms, and the moon. A few years later a number of the town's businesses were using a 'made in Witch City' brand. In 1940 the makers of a line of female toiletries called 'Early American Old Spice', launched a marketing campaign depicting a beautiful woman hanging by a noose from a gnarled tree, a rose clasped in one hand, with a verse underneath that began:

> *Hung! As a witch –*
> *Much too much for the Puritans of Salem –*
> *Her charming witchery quite overcame them*

Readers were enticed with the prospect that they too could possess 'the radiant charm that baffled our Founding Fathers'.[72] Salem witchcraft could be fun as well as seductive! In 1889 Parker Brothers produced a Salem game called *Ye Witchcraft Game*, but sensitivities were such that the company decided to pull it from production a few years later. No such problem eighty years on. At the 67th annual America Toy Fair in 1970, a Salem company presented *Witch Pitch* in which players tossed discs into a revolving cupola on top of a witch's house. The packaging announced, 'Made in Witch City, U.S.A.'[73]

Small-scale tourism in Salem had been going on for much of the century but there had long been a struggle between those in the town who wished to promote its rich heritage *sans* witches, and those that wanted to exploit further a brand with huge potential.[74] The scales tipped decidedly during the 1970s. The Halloween episodes of *Bewitched* played their part. Then the town's chamber of Commerce finally fully embraced the Witch City brand, and the Wiccans came to town. Leading the way was Californian Wiccan Laurie Cabot who opened a store called 'A Witch Shop' in 1971 selling Wiccan paraphernalia and witch-related curios. She was an entrepreneurial witch in the Sybil Leek mould, courting the media, writing popular books, and even managing to brand herself successfully as the 'Official Witch of Salem' with a little unwitting help from Massachusetts Governor Michael Dukakis. Some on the city council were not best pleased, with the mayor explaining in 1977 that they thought 'the historical recognition of the city would be internationally demeaned by allowing a commercial capitalization by one individual'.[75] There was undoubtedly also a Christian cringe at the promotion of witchcraft however defined.

Similar uneasiness emerged during attempts to turn the 1928 'hex murder' house of Nelson Rehmeyer in North Hopewell Township, Pennsylvania, into an educational heritage experience. Rehmeyer's house still stands, repeatedly broken into by thrill seekers, and so in 2007 one of his great-grandsons spear-headed a venture to have it listed on the National Register of Historic Places, restore it, and turn it into a museum exploring the beliefs behind the murder and the tradition of pow-wowing. It was soon clear, however, that the local planners and the North Hopewell Township authorities were resistant to the idea. 'Thank goodness Elvis' Graceland isn't located in North Hopewell Township', one local journalist wryly observed.[76]

The embrace of the witch was also due in part to the commercialization of Halloween. A Dallas journalist recalled in 1964 that in the 1930s, the Halloween tradition of mischief night, which was primarily an Irish introduction, was a pretty violent affair. The youths of Dallas would grease the railway tracks, puncture tyres, smash windows, and turn over outdoor toilets. But during the early 1960s the more innocent version of costumed trick-and-treating we know today was in the ascendancy and ripe for commercialization. The journalist reported that 'for weeks supermarkets, drug stores and variety stores have been structured for the coming festival, featuring hundreds of special Halloween items for parties'.[77] It took a while, but Salem businesses finally saw it as an opportunity not to be missed. In 1982 a group of business people led by the owner of the Salem Witch Museum devised a 'Haunted Happenings' event for the autumn holiday, advertising the town as the 'Halloween Capital of the World'. The initiative grew and grew until it attracted the hundreds of thousands who flock there today. Danvers, née Salem

Village, where the accusations began, has been left relatively untouched by the tourist boom, its remembrance of the trials rendered more discreet.

A new generation of young attractive witches hit American screens in the 1990s. Following on from the modest impact of the fantasy comedy *Teen Witch* (1989), series such as *Sabrina the Teenage Witch* (1996–2003), *Buffy the Vampire Slayer* (1997–2003), and *Charmed* (1998–2006) were hugely successful, and culturally significant—at least for a time. Matching the generational changes taking place in society, these witches were more independent and less domesticated than their mid-century screen counterparts. The creators of the shows injected elements of the Wiccan tradition, introducing a pre-teen and young teen audience to the movement, albeit largely shorn of its paganism. This exposure coupled with the advent of the publishing sensation that was *Harry Potter*, the first volume of which appeared in 1997, helped generate the 'teen witch' phenomenon of the late 1990s and early 2000s. Hundreds of thousands of teenagers, girls in particular, were inspired to dabble in making their own spells to enhance their social and emotional situation, and some moved on to exploring the notion of witchcraft as the Old Religion. Authors, some pagan like Silver RavenWolf, pumped out heaps of 'how to' empowerment books for an eager youthful audience. The response was predictable, with evangelical groups up in arms over this new outbreak of diabolic heathenism perverting America's youth. That old persecutorial tendency was roused once again with high-profile book burnings of *Harry Potter* novels.

So here we are in twenty-first century America with witchcraft as much a matter of the present as the past, the idea of the witch refracted by twentieth-century culture. Yet ever since 1692 the narrative regarding witchcraft has been distorted by the constant manipulation of history and slanted by racial prejudice. Much of the story of witchcraft in modernizing America has been conveniently forgotten or obscured by myth-making and seductive assumptions about progress. The pre-occupation with Salem has served as a smokescreen for some uncomfortable truths regarding the people who built the United States. Thousands of Americans, Native, European, and African, were persecuted, abused, and murdered as witches after 1692. Where are the monuments to them? They are as much a part of America's heritage as the witches of colonial New England. It is time this history was taught as a lesson in how the past is not a foreign country.

ENDNOTES

Chapter 1 Notes

1. The most recent calculation of the number of executed witches is in Marion Gibson, *Witchcraft Myths in American Culture* (New York and London, 2007), p. 12. The literature on Salem is vast, and need not be sifted through here.

2. Gibson, *Witchcraft Myths*, pp. 44–9.

3. Cited in Gibson, *Witchcraft Myths*, p. 49; Gretchen A. Adams, *The Specter of Salem: Remembering the Witch Trials in Nineteenth-Century America* (Chicago, 2008), p. 102. On the rhetorical use of Salem see also Philip Gould, 'New England Witch-Hunting and the Politics of Reason in the Early Republic', *New England Quarterly* 68 (1995) 58–82.

4. *State*, 1 March 1919.

5. *Albany Evening Journal*, 26 March 1852; *Boston Daily Globe*, 31 July 1885. See also, Gibson, *Witchcraft Myths*, pp. 57–61.

6. Thomas P. Slaughter, 'Crowds in Eighteenth-Century America: Reflections and New Directions', *Pennsylvania Magazine of History and Biography* 115 (1991) 3–35; Edmund S. Morgan, 'The Witch & We, The People', *American Heritage* 34 (1983) 6–11; Cooper, *The Statues at Large of South Carolina*, p. 743.

7. *Rising Sun*, 13 December 1796; *Biddeford-Saco Journal*, 25 February 1961.

8. To date, the most thorough account of eighteenth-century witchcraft is still Herbert Leventhal's, *In the Shadow of the Enlightenment: Occultism and Renaissance Science in Eighteenth-Century America* (New York, 1976), ch. 3. Other important works on magic in the period, couched within religious cultures, are: David D. Hall, *Worlds of Wonder, Days of Judgement: Popular Religions Belief in Early New England* (New York,

1989); Jon Butler, *Awash in a Sea of Faith: Christianizing the American People* (Cambridge, Mass., 1990); D. Michael Quinn, *Early Mormonism and the Magic World View*, 2nd edition (Salt Lake City, 1998); Alison Games, *Witchcraft in Early North America* (Lanham, 2010).

9. Brian Levack, *The Witch-Hunt in Early Modern Europe*, 3rd edition (Harlow, 2006), pp. 279–81; Wolfgang Behringer, *Witchcraft Persecutions in Bavaria: Popular Magic, Religious Zealotry and Reason of State in Early Modern Europe* (Cambridge, 1997), pp. 347–55.

10. On early perceptions of Native Americans as devil worshippers and witches see Elaine G. Breslaw, *Tituba, Reluctant Witch of Salem: Devilish Indians and Puritan Fantasies* (New York, 1996); Games, *Witchcraft in Early North America*, pp. 21–36; Richard Godbeer, *The Devil's Dominion: Magic and Religion in Early New England* (Cambridge, 1992), pp. 192–3.

11. Daniel R. Mandell, 'The Indian's Pedigree (1794): Indians, Folklore, and Race in Southern New England', *William and Mary Quarterly* 3rd S., 61, 3 (2004) 524; Elsie Worthington Clews Parsons, *Pueblo Indian Religion* (Chicago, 1939), Vol. 2, p. 1065.

12. Marc Simmons, *Witchcraft in the Southwest: Spanish & Indian Supernaturalism on the Rio Grande* (Lincoln, 1974), p. 26.

13. Parsons, *Pueblo Indian Religion*, Vol. 2, p. 1065. Transcripts of the case are also printed in Games, *Witchcraft*, pp. 143–52.

14. Tibo J. Chavez, 'Early Witchcraft in New Mexico', *El Palacio* 77 (1970) 7–9.

15. Malcolm Ebright and Rick Hendricks, *The Witches of Abiquiu: The Governor, the Priest, the Genízaro Indians* (Albuquerque, 2006).

16. Tracy Brown, 'Tradition and Change in Eighteenth-Century Pueblo Indian Communities', *Journal of the Southwest* 46, 3 (2004) 463–500.

17. *David Zeisberger's History of the Northern American Indians*, Archer Butler Hulbert (ed.) (Columbus, 1910), p. 125.

18. Earl P. Olmstead, *David Zeisberger: A Life Among the Indians* (Kent, 1997), p. 195.

19. See Michael C. Coleman, *Presbyterian Missionary Attitudes Toward American Indians, 1837–1893* (Jackson, 1985), pp. 82–5.

20. *Albany Argus*, reprinted in the *Lancaster Journal*, 10 August 1821.

21. Matthew Dennis, 'American Indians, Witchcraft, and Witch-Hunting', *Magazine of History* 17, 4 (2003) 22.

22. Charles E. Hunter, 'The Delaware Nativist Revival of the Mid-Eighteenth Century', *Ethnohistory* 18, 1 (1971) 47.

23. Adam Jortner, *The Gods of Prophetstown: The Battle of Tippecanoe and the Holy War for the American Frontier* (New York, 2012); Matthew Dennis, *Seneca Possessed: Indians, Witchcraft, and Power in the Early American Republic* (Philadelphia, 2010); R. David Edmunds, *The Shawnee Prophet* (Lincoln, 1983); Alfred A. Caves, 'The Failure of the Shawnee Prophet's Witch-Hunt', *Ethnohistory* 42, 3 (1995) 445–75; Alfred A Caves, *Prophets of the Great Spirit: Native American Revitalization Movements in Eastern North*

America (2006); Jay Miller, 'The 1806 Purge among the Indiana Delaware: Sorcery, Gender, Boundaries, and Legitimacy', *Ethnohistory* 41, 2 (1994) 245–66.

24. See Jortner, *The Gods of Prophetstown*, ch. 9.

25. Jean Van Delinder, '"Wayward" Indians: The Social Construction of Native American Witchcraft', *Quarterly Journal of Ideology* 26 (2004); Amanda Porterfield, 'Witchcraft and the Colonization of Algonquian and Iroquois Cultures', *Religion and American Culture: A Journal of Interpretation* 2, 1 (1992) 103–24.

26. Joseph R. Washington, *Anti-Blackness in English Religion, 1500–1800* (New York, 1984); Laura A. Lewis, *Hall of Mirrors: Power, Witchcraft, and Caste in Colonial Mexico* (Durham, NC, 2003), p. 149; John Jea, *The Life, History, and Unparalleled Sufferings of John Jea, the African Preacher* (Portsea, c.1811), p. 9.

27. Thaddeus Norris, 'Negro Superstitions', *Lippincott's Monthly Magazine* 6 (1870) 91; Yvonne P. Chireau, *Black Magic: Religion and the African American Conjuring Tradition* (Berkeley, 2003), pp. 18–19.

28. *Indianapolis Sentinel*, 18 June 1879.

29. *Philadelphia Times*; reprinted in *Aberdeen Daily News*, 30 May 1890; *Brooklyn Eagle*, 21 July 1880.

30. *St Louis Republic*, cited in *Inter Ocean* 19 November 1896.

31. Demos, *Entertaining Satan*, pp. 387–400; Godbeer, *The Devil's Dominion*, pp. 229–30. See also Leventhal, *Shadow*, 100–6.

32. Julian P. Boyd, 'State and Local Historical Societies in the United States', *American Historical Review* 40, 1 (1934) 10–37.

33. Terry A. Barnhart, '"Elegant and Useful Learning": The Antiquarian and Historical Society of Illinois, 1827–1829', *Journal of the Illinois State Historical Society* 95, 1 (2002) 7–32.

34. George Faber Clark, *A History of the Town of Norton* (Boston, 1859), p. 582; Jeptha R. Simms, *History of Scholarie County, and Border Wars of New York* (Albany, 1845), p. 164; A. P. Marvin, *History of the Town of Winchendon* (Winchendon, 1868) pp. 408, 409; John Langdon Sibley, *A History of the Town of Union* (Boston, 1851), p. 228.

35. James Monroe Buckley, 'Witchcraft', *The Century: A Popular Quarterly* 43, 3 (1892) 409. I could have produced graphs and concentration maps showing where each case I have found took place, looking for regional and density patterns, but considering the selectivity and patchiness of newspaper reporting in many parts of America, such analysis could easily distort or mislead, reinforcing ethnic perceptions, as has certainly happened with regard to the Pennsylvania Dutch. Besides, those cases that came to court are merely the tip of the iceberg of witchcraft disputes. We know as much thanks to the work of folklorists.

36. Frank Luther Mott et al., *American Journalism: A History of Newspapers in the United States* (London, [1941] 2000), Vol. 5, p. 216.

37. *New-Bedford Mercury*, 24 December 1847.

38. *New-Bedford Mercury*, 24 December 1847.

39. *Winona Daily Republican*, 27 February 1899; 3 March 1899.

40. *New York Times*, 14 January 1881.

41. *Los Angeles Times*, 9 March 1903.

42. *Philadelphia Inquirer*, 18 October 1895.

43. *The Norwood News*, 31 October 1899; *Fort Wayne Sentinel*, 17 November 1899; *Hutchinson News*, 20 November 1899; *Fort Wayne News*, 25 November 1899. This is almost certainly the same John Dalke of Center, Outagamie, mentioned in the 1900 census who became a prominent enough member of the community to merit a mention as an admirable farmer in Thomas Henry Ryan's *History of Outagamie County* (Chicago, 1911), p. 1226, and attracted a newspaper obituary in 1940.

44. *The Times* [Hammond, Indiana], 5 July 1907; *Atlanta Constitution*, 15 February 1903.

45. For a useful summary of these issues, see Beverly J. Robinson, 'Africanisms and the Study of Folklore', in Joseph E. Holloway (ed.), *Africanisms in American Culture*, 2nd edition (Bloomington, 2005), pp. 356–72.

46. Rosan Augusta Jordan and Frank De Caro, '"In This Folk-Lore Land": Race, Class, Identity, and Folklore Studies in Louisiana', *Journal of American Folklore* 109 (1996) 31–59.

47. Jeffrey E. Anderson, *Conjure in African American Society* (Baton Rouge, 2005), pp. 6–7.

48. J. Hampden Porter, 'Notes on the Folk-Lore of the Mountain Whites of the Alleghanies', *Journal of American Folklore* 7 (1894) 105–17.

49. *Cincinnati Daily Gazette*, 17 May 1873; See also <http://www.legendsofamerica. com/ks-benders.html>.

50. *New York Times*, 10 September 1911.

51. See Owen Davies, 'Urbanization and the Decline of Witchcraft: An Examination of London', *Journal of Social History* 30 (1997), 597–617.

52. Frances M. Malpezzi and William M. Clements, *Italian-American Folklore* (Little Rock, 1992), p. 146.

53. *The Universalist and Ladies' Repository* 7 (1839) 393.

54. *New York Spectator*, reprinted in the *Providence Patriot* 18 March 1829. on the Five Points and Water Street, see, Emelise Aleandri, *Little Italy*, pp. 7–8.

Chapter 2 Notes

1. *The Daily Gazette* [Fort Wayne], 10 November 1885; *Newark Advocate*, 22 November 1901.

2. Samuel Kercheval, *A History of the Valley of Virginia*, 2nd edition (Woodstock, 1850), p. 240; *The Mirror*, 16 July 1825, 58; *Winona Daily Republican*, 12 October 1867; *London Nonconformist*, 27 November 1867.

3. Theda Kenyon, 'Witches Still Live', *North American Review* 228, 5 (1929) 623.

4. On the American German pow-wow tradition see, for instance, David Kriebel, *Powwowing Among the Pennsylvania Dutch: A Traditional Medical Practice in the Modern World* (University Park, 2007); Don Yoder, 'Hohman and Romanus: Origins and Diffusion of the Pennsylvania Dutch Powwow Manual', in Wayland D. Hand (ed.), *American Folk Medicine: A Symposium* (Berkeley, 1976), pp. 235–48; Gerald C. Milnes, *Signs, Cures & Witchery: German Appalachian Folklore* (Knoxville, 2007).

5. Vance Randolph, *Ozark Superstitions* (New York, 1947), ch. 7.

6. George Struble, 'The English of the Pennsylvania Germans', *American Speech* 10, 3 (1935) 170.

7. Leonard W. Roberts, *Up Cutshin and Down Greasy: Folkways of a Kentucky Mountain Family* (Lexington, 1959), p. 93; Jason Semmens, 'On the Origin of Peller', *Old Cornwall* 14, 1 (2009) 43–50.

8. William E. Van Vugt, *Britain to America: Mid-Nineteenth-Century Immigrants to the United States* (Urbana, 1999), pp. 92–3.

9. Richard M. Dorson, *Bloodstoppers & Bearwalkers: Folk Traditions of the Upper Peninsula* (Cambridge, Mass., 1952), pp. 113–14. See also, Wayland D. Hand, 'The Folklore, Customs, and Traditions of the Butte Miner', *California Folklore Quarterly* 5,1 (1946) 1–25.

10. On cunning-folk see Owen Davies, *Cunning-Folk: Popular Magic in English History* (London, 2003).

11. On African American terms for magical practices and practitioners see, Chireau, *Black Magic*, esp. pp. 21, 55; Anderson, *Conjure*, pp. 27–8; Wonda L. Fontenot, *Secret Doctors: Ethnomedicine of African Americans* (Westport, 1994), pp. 39–44; Jason R. Young, *Rituals of Resistance: African Atlantic Religion in Kong and the lowcountry South in the Era of Slavery* (Baton Rouge, 2007), ch. 3.

12. The term has survived in twentieth-century language to refer to an awkward clumsy person; John Algeo and Adele Algeo, 'Among the New Words', *American Speech* 64, 2 (1989) 152–6.

13. *Berks and Schuylkill Journal*, 21 September 1822. See also M. P. Handy, 'Witchcraft among the Negroes', *Appleton's Journal: A Magazine of General Literature* 8 (1872) 666–7.

14. For a discussion on *wanga* in West Africa see, John Middleton and E. H. Winter (eds), *Witchcraft and Sorcery in East Africa* (London, 1963), 143–75.

15. See, for example, Portia Smiley, 'Folk-Lore from Virginia, South Carolina, Georgia, Alabama, and Florida', *Journal of American Folklore* 32, 125 (1919) 380.

16. For an overview of European folk medicine see Owen Davies, 'European Folk Medicine', in Stephen B. Kayne (ed.), *Traditional Medicine: A Global Perspective* (London, 2009), pp. 25–44.

17. Thomas Short, *Medicina Britannica* (Philadelphia, 1751), pp. 141, 282.

18. Chireau, *Black Magic*, pp. 72, 181; Milnes, *Signs, Cures & Witchery*, p. 98.

19. Charlotte Erichsen-Brown, *Use of Plants for the Past 500 years* (Aurora, 1979), pp. 88–9.

20. Randolph, *Ozark Magic*, p. 284.

21. William Wous Weaver, *Sauer's Herbal Cures: America's First Book of Botanic Healing, 1762–1778* (New York, 2001), p. 41.

22. Newbell Niles Puckett, *Folk Beliefs of the Southern Negro*, p. 15.

23. Anderson, *Conjure*, p. 72. See also the Online Archive of American Folk Medicine; <http://www.folkmed.ucla.edu/>.

24. Mary L. Galvin, 'The Creation of a Creole Medicine Chest in Colonial South Carolina', in David Buisseret and Steven G. Reinhardt (eds), *Creolization in the Americas* (Arlington, 2000), pp. 79–80.

25. *Daily Journal*, 14 November 1729.

26. Leventhal, *Shadow of the Enlightenment*, ch. 5; Boria Sax, 'The Basilisk and Rattlesnake, or a European Monster Comes to America', *Society and Animals* 2, 1 (1994) 3–15.

27. Laurence Monroe Klauber, *Rattlesnakes: Their Habits, Life Histories, and Influence on Mankind*, 2nd edition (Berkeley, 1997), Vol. 2, p. 1192.

28. William Meyrick, *The New Family Herbal: Or, Domestic Physician* (Birmingham, 1790), p. 392.

29. Galvin, 'Creole Medicine Chest', p. 81.

30. Reprinted in *The William and Mary Quarterly*, 2nd S., Vol. 5, 2 (1925) 110–12.

31. Charlotte Erichsen-Brown, *Medicinal and Other Uses of North American Plants: A Historical Survey with Special Reference to the Eastern Indian Tribes* (New York, [1979] 1989), pp. 359–62; Laurence Monroe Klauber, *Rattlesnakes: Their Habits, Life Histories, and Influence on Mankind* (Los Angeles, 1956), Vol. 1, pp. 1160–8.

32. Tennant, *The Vegetable Materia Medica*, p. 369.

33. Galvin, 'Creole Medicine Chest', pp. 74–6.

34. Elizabeth Brandon, 'Folk Medicine in French Louisiana', in Hand (ed.), *American Folk Medicine*, p. 219.

35. Weaver, *Sauer's Herbal Cures*, p. 23; John Langdon Sibley, *A History of the Town of Union* (Boston, 1851), p. 323.

36. Abel Tennant, *The Vegetable Materia Medica and Practice of Medicine* (Batavia, 1837), p. 410. See also, Kay K. Moss, *Southern Folk Medicine 1750–1820* (Columbia, SC, 1999), pp. 126–7.

37. *Atlanta Constitution*, 20 September 1901.

38. Kay K. Moss, *Southern Folk Medicine 1750–1820* (Columbia, SC, 1999), ch. 10; Richard Swiderski, *Poison Eaters: Snakes, Opium, Arsenic, and the Lethal Show* (Boca Raton, 2010), ch. 8; Galvin, 'The Creation of a Creole Medicine Chest in Colonial South Carolina', pp. 82–4; Kevin J. Hayes, *A Colonial Woman's Bookshelf* (Knoxville, 1996), p. 91.

39. Peter H. Wood, '"It was a Negro Taught Them": A New Look at African Labor in Early South Carolina', in Roger D. Abrahams and John F. Szwed (eds), *Discovering Afro-America* (Leiden, 1975), p. 41.

40. See Walter Rucker, 'Conjure, Magic, and Power: The Influence of Afro-Atlantic Religious Practices on Slave Resistance and Rebellion', *Journal of Black Studies* 32, 1 (2001) 84–103; Bernard Moitt, *Women and Slavery in the French Antilles, 1635–1848* (Bloomington, 2001), pp. 40–2.

41. Chireau, *Black Magic*, p. 71; Fett, *Working Cures*, pp. 162–3; Joseph Cephas Carroll, *Slave Insurrections in the United States, 1800–1865*, p. 63.

42. R. B. Medbery (ed.), *Memoir of William G. Crocker, Late Missionary in West Africa* (Boston, 1848), p. 116.

43. Thomas Winterbottom, *An Account of the Native Africans in the Neighbourhood of Sierra Leone* (London, 1803), Vol. 1, p. 269.

44. Hyatt, *Hoodoo, Conjuration*, Vol. 1, p. 376; Zora Neale Hurston, *Mules and Men* (New York, [1935] 1990), p. 284.

45. On Norwegian American folk-medical borrowings see Kathleen Stokker, *Remedies and Rituals: Folk Medicine in Norway and the New Land* (St Paul, 2007), pp. 16–17.

46. For example, 'Folk-Lore from Buffalo Valley, Central Pennsylvania', *Journal of American Folklore* 4, 13 (1891) 127.

47. For example, Joseph Doddridge, *Notes on the Settlement and Indian Wars: Of the Western Parts of Virginia and Pennsylvania from 1763 to 1783, inclusive, together with a Review of the State of Society and Manners of the First Settlers of the Western Country* (Pittsburgh, [1824] 1912), p. 125.

48. Heyrman, *Southern Cross*, p. 90.

49. *Iowa State Reporter*, 5 May 1875; *Cincinnati Daily Gazette*, 13 March 1875. This is probably the same Nancy Lewis recorded in the census of 1880 (Council bluffs, Iowa) as being 48 years of age, married to George Lewis, with four young daughters.

50. Vance Randolph, 'Ozark Superstitions', *Journal of American Folklore* 46, 179 (1933) 20; Richard L. Brown, *A History of the Michael Brown Family of Rowan County, North Carolina* (Granite Quarry, 1921), p. 29.

51. 'Concerning Negro Sorcery in the United States', *Journal of American Folklore* 3, 11 (1890) 286; *The Ohio Cultivator* 14 (1858) 280; *Western Farmer & Gardener* 1 January (1846) 3; 2 February (1846) 38; 1 April (1846) 105.

52. G. H. Dadd, *Dadd On the Nature and Treatment of The Diseases of Cattle* (Boston, 1859), p. 375.

53. John T. Plummer, 'Proximative Analysis of a Concretion of Hairs found in the Esophagus of a Slaughtered Ox', *American Journal of Pharmacy* 25 (1853) 102.

54. '*Western Farmer & Gardener*, 1 January 1846; 1 April 1846; Conjuring and Conjure-Doctor in the Southern United States' *Journal of American Folklore* 9, 33 (1896) 144; 'Concerning Negro Sorcery in the United States', *Journal of American Folklore* 3, 11 (1890) 286.

55. W. Soltau Fenwick, 'Hair-Balls and other Concretions in the Stomach', *British Medical Journal* 2, 2187 (1902) 1696–98. See also John E. Cannaday, 'Foreign Bodies in the Stomach and Intestines', *Annals of Surgery* 94, 2 (1931) 218–32.

56. Vance Randolph, 'Ozark Superstitions', *Journal of American Folklore* 46, 179 (1933) 20; Josiah Henry Combs, 'Sympathetic Magic in the Kentucky Mountains: Some Curious Folk Survivals', *Journal of American Folklore* 27, 105 (1914) 328.

57. Grace Partridge Smith, 'Folklore from "Egypt"', *Hoosier Folklore* 5, 2 (1946) 45–70; 'Concerning Negro Sorcery in the United States', *Journal of American Folklore* 3, 11 (1890) 286.

58. See Daniel G. Hoffman, 'Jim's Magic: Black or White?', *American Literature* 32, 1 (1960) 47–54; Ray W. Frantz Jr, 'The Role of Folklore in Huckleberry Finn', *American Literature* 28, 3 (1956) 314–27.

59. William Henry Perrin, *History of Effingham County, Illinois* (Chicago, 1883), pp. 13–14.

60. <http://en.wikibooks.org/wiki/Muggles%27_Guide_to_Harry_Potter/Magic/Bezoar>. On recent interest see Suzanne M. Shultz, 'Bezoars: A Not-So-Magical Therapy from the Past', *Journal of Consumer Health on the Internet* 14, 3 (2010) 303–7.

61. Eliza Brightwen, 'Bezoars', *Science* 21, 521 (1893) 50–1; H. C. Erik Midelfort, *Mad Princess of Renaissance Germany* (1994), p. 90.

62. John Mason Good et al., *Pantologia: A New Cyclopædia* (London, 1813), Vol. 2. The porcupine bezoar is also mentioned in Samuel Stearns, *The American Herbal; Or, Materia Medica* (Walpole, 1801), p. 267.

63. John Lawson, *A New Voyage to Carolina* (London, 1709), p. 49.

64. William H. Harding, 'On the Chinese Snake-Stone, and its Operation as an Antidote to Poison', The *Medical Repository* 4 (1807) 248–50.

65. *Star and Republican Banner*, 5 May 1840.

66. *The Republican Compiler*, 20 April 1830.

67. Loman D. Cansler, 'Madstones and Hydrophobia', *Western Folklore* 23, 2 (1964) 95–105; Thomas R. Forbes, 'The Madstone', in Hand (ed.), *American Folk Medicine*, pp. 11–21.

68. 'Mad-Stones', *Journal of American Folklore*, 15, 59 (1902) 292; Cansler, 'Madstones', 101; Walter James Hoffman, 'Popular Superstitions', *Appletons' Popular Science Monthly* 50 (1896–7), p. 98.

69. Sidney L. Spahr and George E. Opperman, *The Dairy Cow Today: U.S. Trends, Breeding and Progress since 1980* (Fort Atkinson, 1995), p. 47; Everett E. Edwards, 'Europe's Contribution to the American Dairy Industry', *Journal of Economic History* 9 (1949) 72–84; Edith H. Whetham, 'The Trade in Pedigree Livestock 1850–1910', *Agricultural History Review* 27 (1979) 47–50.

70. *Edwardsville Intelligencer*, 28 August 1896.

71. G. R. Smith, 'History of Crimson Clover in the USA', <http://www.ihsg.org/subsites/conference2010/documents/IHSC2010OralProceedings(24).pdf>.

72. Cited in C. Grant Loomis, 'Sylvester Judd's New England Lore', *Journal of American Folklore* 60 (1947) 154.

73. Wayland D. Hand, 'European Fairy Lore in the New World', *Folklore* 92, 2 (1981) 141–8.

74. Peter Narváez, 'Newfoundland Berry Pickers "In the Fairies": Maintaining Spatial, Temporal, and Moral Boundaries Through Legendry', Peter Narváez (ed.), *The Good People: New Fairylore Essays* (New York, 1991), pp. 338–41.

75. The point is well made in Richard M Dorson, *America in Legend: Folklore from the Colonial Period to the Present* (New York, 1973), pp. 14–15.

76. See, for example, J. A. Teit, 'Water-Beings in Shetlandic Folklore, as Remembered by Shetlanders in British Columbia', *Journal of American Folklore* 31 (1918) 180–201; W. J. Wintemberg, 'Folk-Lore Collected in Toronto and Vicinity', *Journal of American Folklore* 31 (1918) 129; Margaret Sweeney, 'Tales and Legends Collected by Jeffersonville Students', *Hoosier Folklore Bulletin* 3, 3 (1944) 43.

77. 'Lutins in the Province of Quebec', *Journal of American Folklore* 5, 19 (1892) 327–8; Barbara Rieti, *Strange Terrain: The Fairy World in Newfoundland* (St John's, 1991); Gary R. Butler, 'The *Lutin* Tradition in French-Newfoundland Culture: Discourse and Belief', in Peter Narváez (ed.), *The Good People: New Fairylore Essays* (New York, 1991), pp. 5–22;

78. Richard M. Dorson, *Bloodstoppers & Bearwalkers: Folk Traditions of the Upper Peninsula* (Cambridge, Mass., 1952), p. 78.

79. Narváez, 'Newfoundland Berry Pickers', p. 340.

80. Barbara Rieti, *Making Witches: Newfoundland Traditions of Spells and Counterspells* (Montreal, 2008), p. xii.

81. See Alaric Hall, *Elves in Anglo-Saxon England* (Woodbridge, 2007).

82. Samuel Deane, *The New-England Farmer; Or Georgical Dictionary*, 2nd edition (Worcester, 1797), pp. 97–8.

83. *A Statistical Account, Or Parochial Survey of Ireland* (Dublin, 1819), Vol. 3, p. 27; John Henderson, *General View of the Agriculture of the County of Sutherland* (London, 1812), p. 100.

84. Walter W. Skeat, '"Snakestones" and Stone Thunderbolts as Subjects for Systematic Investigation', *Folklore* 23, 1 (1912) 45–80; Charles Rau, *Early Man in Europe*, p. 144; Thomas Wilson, *Arrowpoints, Spearheads, and Knives of Prehistoric Times*, pp. 22–6.

85. Lizanne Henderson and Edward J. Cowan, *Scottish Fairy Belief* (East Linton, 2001), pp. 77–9.

86. Joseph Meehan, 'The Cure of Elf-Shooting in the North-West of Ireland', *Folklore* 17, 2 (1906) 200–10.

87. William Jack Hranicky, *Prehistoric Projectile Points Found Along the Atlantic Coastal Plain* (Boca Raton, 2003).

88. James Britten, 'Amulets in Scotland', *Folk-Lore Record* 4 (1881) 168–9.

89. See Charles Cobb (ed.), *Stone Tool Traditions in the Contact Era* (Tuscaloosa, 2003).

90. Ishi's story has been told in a number of publications. Regarding his arrowhead-making skills see, Steven Shackley, 'The Stone Tool Technology of Ishi and the Yana of North Central California: Inferences for Hunter-Gatherer Cultural Identity in Historic California', *American Anthropologist* 102, 4 (2001) 693–712.

91. Parsons, 'Witchcraft Among the Pueblos', 109; John G. Bourke, 'Vesper Hours of the Stone Age', *American Anthropologist* 3, 1 (1890) 62; John O'Kane Murray, *A Popular History of the Catholic Church in the Unites States* (New York, 1876), p. 56; H. Henrietta Stockel, *The Lightning Stick: Arrows, Wounds, and Indian Legends* (Reno, 1995), p. 106.

92. Katherine Briggs, *A Dictionary of Fairies* (London, 1976), p. 7; Grace Partridge Smith, 'Flint Charms in Southern Illinois', *Folklore* 67, 3 (1956) 174–5.

93. Puckett, *Folk Beliefs*, p. 315; Laurie Wilkie, *Creating Freedom: Material Culture and African American Identity at Oakley Plantation, Louisiana, 1840–1950* (2000), pp. 188–9; Anderson, *Conjure*, p. 61.

94. Lauri Honko, *Krankheitsprojektile: Untersuchung über eine urtümliche Krankheitserklärung* (Helsinki, 1959); Jesse W. Harris, 'German Language Influences in St. Clair County, Illinois', *American Speech* 23, 2 (1948) 108.

95. *David Zeisberger's History of the Northern American Indians*, p. 126.

96. Horatio Cushman, *History of the Choctaw, Chickasaw and Natchez Indians* (Greenville, 1899), p. 138.

97. *Winona Republican-Herald*, 19 July 1923. Amongst the Kiowa there was a belief that the buffalo had their own medicine men who gained their power from having a hair ball in their stomachs; Weston La Barre, 'Kiowa Folk Sciences', *Journal of American Folklore* 60, 236 (1947) 108.

98. Stephen Wilson, *Feuding, Conflict and Banditry in Nineteenth-Century Corsica* (Cambridge, 1988), pp. 92–3; Joyce Malcolm, *Guns and Violence: The English Experience* (Cambridge, Mass., 2002).

99. Michael A. Bellesiles, *Arming America: The Origins of a National Gun Culture* (New York, 2000); Bellesiles, 'Exploring America's Gun Culture', *William and Mary Quarterly* 3rd S, 59 (2001) 241–68; Robert H. Churchill, 'Gun Ownership in Early America: A Survey of Manuscript Militia Returns', *William and Mary Quarterly* 3rd S, 60 (2003) 615–42.

100. *Iowa State Reporter*, 9 April 1901.

101. Doddridge, *Notes on the Settlement and Indian Wars*, p. 125.

102. *The Gospel Advocate, and Impartial Investigator* 6 (1828) 191; *The Quincy Daily Whig*, 19 August 1891; Tom Painter and Roger Kammerer, *Forgotten Tales of North Carolina*, p. 13; Elisabeth Cloud Seip, 'Witch-Finding in Western Maryland', *Journal of American Folklore* 14, 52 (1901) 42.

103. Milnes, *Signs, Cures & Witchery*, p. 173; *Brown Collection*, pp. 489–90.

104. Owen Davies, 'Witchcraft accusations in France 1850–1990', in Willem de Blécourt and Owen Davies (eds), *Popular Magic in Modern Europe* (Manchester, 2004), pp. 107–33.

105. L. Winstanley and H. J. Rose, 'Scraps of Welsh Folklore. I. Cardiganshire; Pembrokeshire', *Folklore* 37, 2 (1926) 166; Mary M. Banks, 'Witch Lore from the Borders of Sussex and Surrey (1895–1898)', *Folklore* 52 (1941) 74; Ruth Tongue, *Somerset Folklore* (London, 1965), p. 71; John Symonds Udal, *Dorsetshire Folk-Lore* (1922), p. 208; Ethel Rudkin, 'Lincolnshire Folklore, Witches and Devils', *Folklore* 45, 3 (1934) 263; L. F. Newman, 'Some Notes on the History and Practice of Witchcraft in the Eastern Counties', *Folklore* 57, 1 (1946) 32; Bodil Nildin-Wall and Jan Wall, 'The Witch as Hare or the Witch's Hare: Popular Legends and Beliefs in Nordic Tradition', *Folklore* 104 (1993) 69, 72.

106. *Kansas City Times*, 22 February 1891.

107. *Sun*, 22 September 1838; *Hagerstown Mail* 26 October 1838.

Chapter 3 Notes

1. Leventhal, *Shadow of the Enlightenment*, pp. 80–1; *Acts and Laws, of His Majesty's Colony of Rhode-Island* (Newport, 1745), p. 116.

2. L. Lynn Hogue, 'Nicholas Trott: Man of Law and Letters', *South Carolina Historical Magazine* 76, 1 (1975), p. 27.

3. See Owen Davies, 'Decriminalising the witch: The origin of and response to the 1736 Witchcraft Act', in John Newton and Jo Bath (eds), *Witchcraft and the Act of 1604* (Leiden, 2008), pp. 207–32.

4. See Davies, *Witchcraft, magic and culture*, pp. 61–76; Malcolm Gaskill, *Hellish Nell: Last of Britain's Witches* (London, 2001).

5. Daniel D. Blinka, 'Jefferson and Juries: The Problem of Law, Reason, and Politics in the New Republic', *American Journal of Legal History* 47, 1 (2005) 92; *Laws of the State of New-Jersey* (1821), p. 248.

6. *Laws of the Commonwealth of Pennsylvania* (Philadelphia, 1810), Vol. 1, pp. 114–15; *Votes and Proceedings of the House of Representatives of the Province of Pennsylvania. Beginning the Fifteenth Day of October 1744* (Philadelphia, 1774), p. 283.

7. Davies, *Witchcraft, magic and culture*, p. 48.

8. James C. Humes, 'The Nation's First Civil Disobedient', *American Bar Association Journal* 58 (1972) 259–63.

9. Thomas Cooper, *The Statutes at large of South Caroline* (Columbia, 1837), Vol. 2, p. 742. On his library see, Dumas Malone, *The Public Life of Thomas Cooper, 1783–1839* (Columbia, 1961), p. 391.

10. Robert A. Gross, 'Squire Dickinson and Squire Hoar', *Proceedings of the Massachusetts Historical Society*, 3rd S, Vol. 101 (1989) 1–23; Cynthia A. Kierner, *Scandal at Bizarre: Rumor and Reputation in Jefferson's America* (New York, 2004), esp. pp. 43–5.

11. William Cobbett, *Porcupine's Works; Containing Various Writings and Selections, Exhibiting a Faithful Picture of the United States of America* (London, 1801), Vol. 9, p. 353.

12. 'Squire Jock', *The American Monthly Magazine* 6 (1835) 380.

13. John A. Conley, 'Doing it by the Book: Justice of the Peace Manuals and English Law in Eighteenth Century America', *Journal of Legal History* 6, 3 (1985) 257–98.

14. William Nelson, *The Office and Authority of a Justice of Peace* (London, 1729), p. 732.

15. See, for example, Joseph Shaw, *The Practical Justice of Peace* (London, 1751); Theodore Barlow, *The Justice of Peace: A Treatise Containing the Power and Duty of that Magistrate* (London, 1745), p. 137; Leventhal, *Shadow of the Enlightenment*, pp. 83–4.

16. *Baltimore Federal Republican*, 4 March 1820.

17. A. B. Wright, *Autobiography of Rev. A. B. Wright* (Cincinnati, 1896), p. 262.

18. Albert Virgil Goodpasture, *Life of Jefferson Dillard Goodpasture* (Nashville, 1897), pp. 66–8; Nashville Herald, reprinted in *Brattleboro Messenger*, 27 August 1831.

19. The identity of the French family is confirmed by genealogical research. For details see <http://www.frenchfamilyassoc.com/FFA/CHARTS/Chart110/>.

20. <http://www.rootsweb.ancestry.com/~tnfentre/fent.htm>.

21. <http://www.newsarch.rootsweb.com/th/read/TNOVERTO/2003-11/1069692709>.

22. *The Revised Statutes of the State of Maine, passed October 22, 1840* (Augusta, 1841), p. 740; Davies, *Grimoires*, pp. 201–2. See also *The Public Statute Laws of the State of Connecticut* (Hartford, 1808), Vol. 1, p. 689. Blewett Lee's various articles on spiritualism, fortune telling, and the law are useful, e.g. 'Psychic Phenomena and the Law', *Harvard Law Review* 34, 6 (1921) 625–38.

23. *Statutes of the State of New Jersey* (Trenton, 1847), p. 262.

24. *Quincy Daily Whig*, 14 December 1892; *St Albans Daily Messenger*, 14 December 1892.

25. *Cedar Rapids Gazette*, 23 March 1950; *Tucson Daily Citizen*, 14 March 1950; *Evening Journal*, 22 March 1950.

26. <http://courts.delaware.gov/CommonPleas/municipal.stm>.

27. *Laws of the State of Delaware* (New-Castle, 1797), Vol.1, p. 68.

28. Claudia L. Bushman, Harold B. Hancock, and Elizabeth Moyne Homsey (eds), *Proceedings of the Assembly of the Lower Counties on the Delaware, 1770–1776* (Cranbury, 1986), p. 267.

29. *Laws of the State of Delaware* (1829), p. 139.

30. *Revised Statutes: The State of Delaware* (Dover, 1852), p. 487.

31. Yoshinobu Hakutani (ed.), *Theodore Dreiser's Uncollected Magazine Articles, 1897–1902* (Cranbury, 2003), p. 258.

32. See Graham Caldwell, *Red Hannah, Delaware's Whipping Post* (Philadelphia, 1947).

33. Hakutani, *Theodore Dreiser's Uncollected Magazine Articles*, p. 257.

34. *State of Delaware: Journal of the House of Representatives*, Vol. 1939 (s.n., 1905), p. 70.

35. *Chester Times*, 16 March 1927. On legal discrimination against gypsy fortune-tellers in this period, see also, Mary Walker, '"A Fool, Idiotic, and Insane Kind of Business": Fortune Tellers in the Long Beach Amusement Zone in the 1920s', unpublished paper.

36. *The Dothan Eagle*, 21 March 1950; *Bakersfield Californian*, 4 May 1950.

37. *State of Delaware: Journal of the House of Representatives* (1951) p. 130.

38. *Tucson Daily Citizen*, 13 February 1953.

39. *Charleston Daily Mail*, 10 April 1953; *Laws of the State of Delaware* (1955), Vol. 1, p. 380.

40. Eric Homberger, *New York City: A Cultural and Literary Companion* (New York, 2003), p. 87.

41. *New York Herald*, 17 February 1889.

42. *Macon Weekly Telegraph*, 21 April 1893.

43. *Philadelphia Inquirer*, 19 July 1914.

44. Forrest Morgan et al., *Connecticut as a Colony and as a State* (Hartford, 1904), Vol.1, p. 228; John M. Taylor, *The Witchcraft Delusion in Colonial Connecticut* (New York, 1908), p. 155.

45. Cornelia Hughes Dayton, *Women Before the Bar: Gender, Law and Society in Connecticut, 1639–1789* (Chapel Hill, 1995), pp. 295, 302, 316, 325.

46. Peter Charles Hoffer, *Law and People in Colonial America* (Baltimore, 1992), pp. 79–81; Kierner, *Scandal at Bizarre*, p. 45; Cornelia Hughes Dayton, *Women Before the Bar*, p. 304; Joan R. Gundersen, *To Be Useful to the World: Women, Revolutionary America, 1740–1790* (New York, 1996), p. 138.

47. Thomas Starkie, *A Treatise of the Law of Slander, Libel, Scandalum Magnatum, and False Rumours* (London, 1813), p. 87.

48. Charles Viner, *A General Abridgment of Law and Equity*, 2nd edition (London, 1791), Vol. 1, pp. 420–5. See also Thomas Coventry and Samuel Hughes, *An Analytical Digested Index to the Common Law Reports* (Philadelphia, 1832), Vol. 2, p. 1286.

49. William Halsted, *Reports of Cases Argued and Determined in the Supreme Court of Judicature of the State of New Jersey* (Trenton, 1824), Vol.2, p. 298.

50. Cited in Andrew J. King, 'The Law of Slander in Early Antebellum America', *American Journal of Legal History* 35, 1 (1991) 15.

51. S. M. Waddams, *Sexual Slander in Nineteenth-Century England: Defamation in the Ecclesiastical Courts, 1815–1855* (Toronto, 2000).

52. See Andrew J. King, 'Constructing Gender: Sexual Slander in Nineteenth-Century America', *Law and History Review* 13, 1 (1995) 63–110.

53. A transcript of the records was printed in James D. Hopkins, *Address to the Members of the Cumberland Bar* (Portland, 1833), pp. 30–2.

54. *The New England Historical and Genealogical Register* 28 (1874) 70, 71.

55. John Hayward, *The New England Gazetteer*, 7th edition (Boston, 1839); George Augustus Wheeler, *History of Brunswick, Topsham, and Harpswell* (Boston, 1878), p. 220.

56. Hopkins, *Address*, p. 32. Hopkins was possibly referring to court documents pertaining to the Arundel, York County, case.

57. Quoted in Conley, 'Law of Slander', 14.

58. See Ann Goldberg, *Honor, Politics and the Law in Imperial Germany, 1871–1914* (Cambridge, 2010), esp. pp. 33–74.

59. Quoted in Goldberg, *Honor*, p. 37.

60. *Wilkes-Barnes Times*, 12 August 1915.

61. *Lake County Times*, 3 June 1918; *Quincy Daily Journal*, 17 September 1917. Both the Dissingers and Sigfried had been born in Pennsylvania.

62. *Cincinnati Commercial Tribune*, 13 June 1877.

63. *New York Herald*, 14 February 1885; *New York Times*, 14 February 1885. It would seem a similar argument was mounted in the slander case brought by Elizabeth Dissinger of Auburn, Pennsylvania; *Philadelphia Inquirer*, 19 September 1918.

64. *New York Times*, 2 September 1883; *A Compilation of the Laws Applicable to the City of Scranton* (Scranton, 1877), p. 206.

65. *Washington Post*, 6 March 1917.

66. Samuel June Barrows, *New Legislation Concerning Crimes, Misdemeanors, and Penalties* (Washington, 1900) p. 191.

67. *Winona Daily Republican*, 27 February 1899; 3 March 1899. Details of both families have been researched by family members on <http://www.ancestry.com>.

68. Hohman, *Long Lost Friend* (1850), p. 10.

69. *The World*, 5 July 1891.

70. *St Louis Republic*, 10 July 1898.

71. James G. Kiernan, 'Race and Insanity', *Journal of Nervous and Mental Disease* 13, 2 (1886) 74–6.

72. *Trenton State Gazette*, 31 June 1850; *Public Ledger*, 5 July 1850. Other instances include: John Gardner of Reading attempting to bring a suit against a Mrs Staub for witchcraft (*Newark Daily Advocate*, 12 September 1883); another Pennsylvania case was reported in the *Daily Nevada State Journal*, 11 March 1894.

73. *Newark Advocate*, 22 November 1901; *Chicago Tribune*, reprinted in *Des Moines Daily News*, 25 November 1901; *Locomotive Engineers Journal*, 30 (1896) 516.

74. *Suburbanite Economist*, 16 August 1907; *Evening Herald* [Montpelier, Indiana], 3 July 1907; *The Times* [Hammond, Indiana], 5 July 1907. John Paris was almost certainly

the 41-year-old of Vincennes mentioned in the 1910 census. He was married to Lydia Paris, with three young children.

75. *The Times* [Hammond, Indiana], 3 July 1907.

76. See Peter D. Edgerton, 'Banishment and the Right to Live Where You Want', *University of Chicago Law Review* 74, 3 (2007) 1023–55.

77. *Morning Oregonian*, 4 February 1924; *Tyrone Daily Herald*, 26 April 1924.

78. On American editions see Paul C. Gutjahr, *An American Bible: A History of the Good Book in the Unites States, 1777–1880* (Stanford, 1999).

79. *Columbus Messenger*, reprinted in the *Inter Ocean*, 2 July 1875.

80. *The Evening Post* [Frederick], 1 June 1912.

81. *New Albany Ledger*, reprinted in *Cincinnati Daily Gazette*, 19 July 1871.

82. *Pittsburgh Gazette*, 26 July 1875.

Chapter 4 Notes

1. On the value of global comparisons see Ronald Hutton, 'Anthropological and Historical Approaches to Witchcraft: Potential for a New Collaboration?', *Historical Journal* 47, 2 (2004) 413–34; Wolfgang Behringer, *Witches and Witch-Hunts: A Global History* (Cambridge, 2004). The idea of regional and local cultures in America is explored in David Hackett Fischer, *Albion's Seed: Four British Folkways in America* (New York, 1989).

2. Frances M. Malpezzi and William M. Clements, *Italian-American Folklore* (Little Rock, 1992), p. 61; Randolph, *Ozark*, p. 265.

3. Combs, 'Sympathetic Magic in the Kentucky Mountains', 329; Barden, *Virginia Folk Legends*, p. 96; *Brown Collection*, p. 110; Ricardo Arguijo Martínez, *Hispanic Culture and Health Care: Fact, Fiction, Folklore* (Saint Louis, 1978), p. 106.

4. The figure for England and Wales in the same period is 91 per cent; Davies, *Witchcraft, Magic and Culture*, p. 193.

5. *David Zeisberger's History of the Northern American Indians*, p. 124.

6. Dennis, *Seneca Possessed*, p. 105; Games, *Witchcraft*, p. 80.

7. On the gendered nature of magic in African-American culture see Yvonne Chireau, 'The Uses of the Supernatural: Toward a History of Black Women's Magical Practices', in Susan Juster and Lisa MacFarlane (eds), *A Mighty Baptism: Race, Gender, and the Creation of American Protestantism* (Ithaca, 1996), pp. 171–89.

8. Joseph Doddridge, *Notes on the Settlement and Indian Wars: Of the Western Parts of Virginia and Pennsylvania from 1763 to 1783, inclusive, together with a Review of the State of Society and Manners of the First Settlers of the Western Country* (Pittsburgh, [1824] 1912), p. 126.

9. Marion Gibson, *Reading Witchcraft: Stories of Early English Witches* (London, 1999), ch. 3.

10. See Linda Dégh and Andrew Vázsonyi, 'Does the Word "Dog" Bite? Ostensive Action: A Means of Legend-Telling', *Journal of Folklore Research* 20 (1983) 5–34; Bill Ellis, 'Death by Folklore: Ostension, Contemporary Legend, and Murder', *Western Folklore* 48, 1 (1989) 201–20; Bill Ellis, *Lucifer Ascending: The Occult in Folklore and Popular Culture* (Lexington, 2004); Stephen Mitchell, 'A Case of Witchcraft Assault in Early Nineteenth-Century England as Ostensive Action', in Willem de Blécourt and Owen Davies (eds), *Witchcraft Continued: Popular Magic in Modern Europe* (Manchester, 2004), pp. 14–29.

11. Richard Day and William Hopper, *Images of America: Vincennes* (Charleston, 1998), p. 86.

12. *The Times* [Hammond, Indiana], 5 July 1907.

13. *Cincinnati Commercial Tribune*, 12 June 1878.

14. Rebecca Kugel, 'Of Missionaries and Their Cattle: Ojibwa Perceptions of a Missionary as Evil Shaman', *Ethnohistory* 41, 2 (1994) 227–44.

15. *Wilkes-Barre Times*, 15 September 1911; *New York Times*, 10 September 1911.

16. John Powell, *Encyclopedia of North American Immigration*, p. 115.

17. Ronald B. David, *Clinical Pediatric Neurology*, 3rd edition (New York, 2009), pp. 192–3.

18. *New Orleans Delta* and *The Crescent*, reprinted in the *Trenton State Gazette*, 31 July 1855.

19. *Rochester Sentinel*, 9 March 1937.

20. *Omaha World Herald*, 12 May and 13 May 1938; *Logansport Press*, 13 May 1938; *Plain Dealer*, 19 June 1938.

21. Louis C. Jones, 'The Evil Eye among European-Americans', *Western Folklore* 10, 1 (1951) 11–25; Hand, *Magical Medicine*, ch. 16 'The Evil Eye in Its Folk Medical Aspects: A Survey of North America'; Alixa Naff, 'Belief in the Evil Eye among the Christian Syrian-Lebanese in America', *Journal of American Folklore* 78 (1965) 46–51; Robert T. Trotter II, 'A Survey of Four Illnesses and Their Relationship to Intracultural Variation in a Mexican American Community', *American Anthropologist*, N.S. 93, 1 (1991) 115–25; Malpezzi and Clements, *Italian-American Folklore*, pp. 117–28. See also, Howard F. Stein, 'Envy and the Evil Eye among Slovak-Americans: An Essay in the Psychological Ontogeny of Belief and Ritual', *Ethos* 2, 1 (1974) 15–46.

22. *Joplin Globe*, 28 June 1929; *Ogden Standard-Examiner*, 4 August 1929.

23. *Naugatuck Daily News*, 11 October 1901.

24. *Trenton Evening Times*, 12 January 1907.

25. Charles Bradbury, *History of Kennebunkport* (Kennebunk, 1837).

26. *Rising Sun* (N. H.), 13 December 1796; *Biddeford-Saco Journal*, 25 February 1961.

27. See, for example, Lyndal Roper, *Witch Craze: Terror and Fantasy in Baroque Germany* (New Haven, 2004), ch. 7.

28. *St Louis Republic*, 10 July 1898.

29. *St Louis Republic*, reprinted in *Ticonderoga Sentinel*, 20 July 1899.

30. *Newark Advocate*, 20 November 1901.

31. *Logansport Journal*, 20 August 1903; *Atlanta Constitution*, 16 August 1903.

32. *Newark Daily Advocate*, 12 September 1883.

33. *Salt Lake Tribune*, 25 January 1903.

34. Andre Jackson Davis, *The Magic Staff: An Autobiography of Andrew Jackson Davis* (New York, 1857), pp. 143–52.

35. Parsons, 'Witchcraft Among the Pueblos', 107; William S. Simmons, 'Indian Peoples of California', *California History* 76, 2/3 (1997) 61; John G. Bourke, 'Notes Upon the Religion of the Apache Indians', *Folklore* 2, 4 (1891) 431; David Blanchard, 'Who or What's a Witch? Iroquois Persons of Power', *American Indian Quarterly* 6 (1982) 231.

36. Quoted in Blanchard, 'Who or What's a Witch?', 231. See also, *Missionary Herald* 15 (1819) 223.

37. Kate Masur, *An Example for the Land: Emancipation and the Struggle over Equality in Washington, D.C.* (Chapel Hill, 2010), pp. 114–15.

38. *Washington Star*, reprinted in the *Albany Evening Journal*, 3 September 1867.

39. *Galveston Daily News*, 8 January 1895.

40. *New York Sun*, reprinted in the *State* [South Carolina], 31 March 1895.

41. Roland Steiner, 'Observations on the Practice of Conjuring in Georgia', *Journal of American Folklore* 14, 54 (1901) 180.

42. Frances Cattermole-Tally, 'The Intrusion of Animals into the Human Body: Fantasy and Reality', *Folklore* 106 (1995) 89–92; Puckett, *Folk Beliefs*, p. 255.

43. *Kansas City Times*, 24 May 1888.

44. *Syracuse Standard*, 11 September 1885; *Kansas City Star*, 2 November 1885.

45. Bill Cecil-Fronsman, *Common Whites: Class and Culture in Antebellum North Carolina* (Lexington, 1992), p. 118.

46. *Ogden Standard Examiner*, 17 June 1934.

47. Wyatt MacGaffey, *Kongo Political Culture: The Conceptual Challenge of the Particular* (Bloomington, 2000), pp. 78–115; Laura L. Porteous, 'The Gri-Gri Case: A Criminal Trial in Louisiana During the Spanish Regime, 1773', *Louisiana Historical Quarterly* 17 (1934) 48–63.

48. 'Concerning Negro Sorcery in the United States', *Journal of American Folklore* 3, 11 (1890) 281–2.

49. See, for example, Reg Crowshoe and Sybille Manneschmidt, *Akak'stiman: A Blackfoot Framework for Decision-Making and Mediation Processes*, 2nd edition (Calgary, 2002), ch. 4; William Wildschut, *Crow Indian Medicine Bundles* (New York, 1975); Charlotte Johnson Frisbie, *Navajo Medicine Bundles or Jish* (Albuquerque, 1987).

50. Ellis, 'Southwest: Pueblo', p. 205.

51. Bernard Coleman, 'The Religion of the Ojibwa of Northern Minnesota', *Primitive Man* 10 (1937) 50.

52. Louise Spindler, 'Great Lakes: Menomini', in Deward E. Walker Jr and David Carrasco (eds), *Witchcraft and Sorcery of the American Native Peoples* (Moscow [Idaho], 1989), pp. 49, 56, 64.

53. Anderson, *Conjure*, pp. 38–9.

54. Franz Boas, 'Current Beliefs of the Kwakiutl Indians', *Journal of American Folklore* 45, 176 (1932) 248.

55. Roland Steiner, 'Observations on the Practice of Conjuring in Georgia', *Journal of American Folklore* 14, 54 (1901) 179.

56. Alanson Skinner, *Material Culture of the Menomini* (New York, 1921), pp. 333–4.

57. Wells, 'Southwest: Pueblo', pp. 207–9; Ebright and Hendricks, *Witches of Abiquiu*, pp. 133, 143.

58. I agree with Anderson on this; Anderson, *Conjure*, p. 179, n. 50.

59. *Galveston Daily News*, 8 December 1906.

60. <http://chesterfield-sc.com/History%2008.htm>; William Gilmore Simms, *The Geography of South Carolina*, p. 60.

61. Cooper, *The Statutes at large of South Caroline*, Vol. 2, pp. 742–3; Viola C. Floyd, *Lancaster County Tours* (Lancaster, SC, 1956), pp. 14–16.

62. *Portsmouth Journal of Literature and Politics*, 2 October 1824.

63. For example, Hand, *Magical Medicine*, ch. 15; Patricia Rickels, 'Some Accounts of Witch Riding', *Louisiana Folklore Miscellany* 1, 2 (1961) 1–17; Josiah Henry Combs, 'Sympathetic Magic in the Kentucky Mountains: Some Curious Folk Survivals', *Journal of American Folklore* 27, 105 (1914) 328.

64. Kristina Tegler Jerselius, *Den stora häxdansen: Vidskepelse, väckelse och vetande i Gagnef 1858* (Uppsala, 2003).

65. Hyatt, *Hoodoo, Conjuration, Witchcraft, Rootwork*, Vol. 1, p. 136.

66. Hand, *Magical Medicine*, p. 229.

67. Robert Farris Thompson, *African Art in Motion: Icon and Art* (Berkeley, 1974), ch. 3.

68. See, for example, Robert F. Gray, 'Some Structural Aspects of Mbugwe Witchcraft', in Middleton and Winter (eds), *Witchcraft and Sorcery in East Africa*, p. 166; J. R. Crawford, *Witchcraft and Sorcery in Rhodesia* (Oxford, 1967), pp. 115–16.

69. Owen Davies, 'The nightmare experience, sleep paralysis and witchcraft accusations', *Folklore* 114, 2 (2003), 181–203; Owen Davies, 'Hag-riding in Nineteenth-Century West Country England and Modern Newfoundland: An Examination of an Experience-Centred Witchcraft Tradition', *Folk Life* 35 (1996–7), 36–53; David Hufford, *The Terror that Comes in the Night: An Experience-Centred Study of Supernatural Assault Traditions* (Philadelphia, 1982); Shelley R. Adler, *Sleep Paralysis: Night-Mares, Nocebos, and the Mind-Body Connection* (New Brunswick, 2011).

70. *Life of William Grimes, the Runaway Slave, Brought Down to the Present Time* (New Haven, 1825), pp. 24–5.

71. *New Orleans Bee*, 7 June 1844, reprinted in *Age*, 5 July 1844; *Times Picayune*, 7 June 1844.

72. Joe Ross, 'Hags Out of Their Skins', *Journal of American Folklore* 93, 368 (1980) 183–6; 'Beliefs of Southern Negroes Concerning Hags', *Journal of American Folklore* 7, 24 (1894) 66–7; Chireau, *Black Magic*, pp. 86–7.

73. Giselle Anatol, 'Transforming the Skin-Shedding Soucouyant: Using Folklore to Reclaim Female Agency in Caribbean Literature', *Small Axe* 7 (2000) 44–59; Jeffrey W. Mantz, 'Enchanting Panics and Obeah Anxieties: Concealing and Disclosing Eastern Caribbean Witchcraft', *Anthropology and Humanism* 32, 1 (2007) 18–29.

74. Fred B. Kniffen, Hiram F. Gregory, and George A. Stokes, *The Historic Indian Tribes of Louisiana: From 1542 to the Present* (Baton Rouge, 1987), p. 261.

75. Akers, *Living in the Land of Death*, pp. 27, 28.

76. *Trenton State Gazette*, 31 July 1855.

77. Tom Peete Cross, 'Folk-Lore from the Southern States', *Journal of American Folklore* 22, 84 (1909) 254.

78. Spindler, 'Great Lakes: Menomini', pp. 48, 49.

79. Porter, 'Notes on the Folk-Lore of the Mountain Whites', 114.

80. *Dallas Morning News*, 3 October 1936; *Chicago Daily Tribune*, 4 October 1936.

81. *Philadelphia Inquirer*, 28 July 1902.

82. *Lock Haven Express*, 20 August 1904.

83. *Memphis Daily Avalanche*, 17 March 1866.

84. For a detailed study of this see Catherine L. Albanese, *A Republic of Mind & Spirit: A Cultural History of American Metaphysical Religion* (New Haven, 2007).

85. Lawrence Foster, *Women, Family, and Utopia: Communal Experiments of the Shakers, the Oneida Community, and the Mormons* (Syracuse, 1991), ch. 3; Clarke Garrett, *Spirit Possession and Popular Religion: From the Camisards to the Shakers* (Baltimore, 1987); Albanese, *Republic of Mind & Spirit*, pp. 182–90.

86. Allen Putnam, *Mesmerism, Spiritualism, Witchcraft, and Miracle: A Brief Treatise* (Boston, 1858), pp. 28, 33.

87. W. G. Le Duc, 'Introduction', James Stanley Grimes, *Etherology, and the Phreno-philosophy of Mesmerism and Magic Eloquence*, 2nd edition (Boston, 1850), p. 12.

88. On mesmerism in America see, David Schmit, 'Re-visioning Antebellum American Psychology: The Dissemination of Mesmerism, 1836–1854', *History of Psychology* 8 (2005), 403–34; Betsy van Schlun, *Science and the Imagination: Mesmerism, Media, and the Mind in Nineteenth-Century English and American Literature* (Berlin, 2007); Robert C. Fuller, *Mesmerism and the American Cure of Souls* (Philadelphia, 1982).

89. David Christy, *A Lecture on African Civilization* (Cincinnati, 1850), pp. 13–14; David Christy, *Pulpit Politics; Or, Ecclesiastical Legislation on Slavery* (Cincinnati, 1862), p. 41.

90. William Denton, *Nature's Secrets: Or, Psychometric Researches* (London, 1863), p. 293.

91. Buchanan, 'Sympathetic Impressibility', *Buchanan's Journal of Man* 1, 8 (1849) 358.

92. *The Ohio Medical and Surgical Journal*, 4, 5 (1852) 437; *The Western Lancet*, 13, 1 (1852) 42–52.

93. W. H. Hunter, 'The Pathfinders of Jefferson County', *Ohio Archaeological and Historical Publications* 8 (1900) 155.

94. Andrew Jackson Davis, *The Great Harmonia* (Boston, 1867), Vol. 3, p. 243.

95. Emerson W. Baker, *The Devil of Great Island: Witchcraft and Conflict in Early New England* (New York, 2007). On the development of spiritualism in America see, for example, Owen Davies, *Ghosts: A Social History*, 5 Vols (London, 2010), Vols 3–5.

96. *Baltimore Gazette*, 10 November 1832.

97. *Easton Gazette*, 20 August 1831; *Albany Daily Advertiser*, reprinted in *Rhode Island Republican*, 13 September 1831; *New Hampshire Sentinel*, 7 October 1831.

98. William McDonald, *Spiritualism Identified with Ancient Sorcery, New Testament Demonology, and Modern Witchcraft* (New York, 1866), pp. 5, 112. On McDonald, see Benjamin L. Hartley, *Evangelicals at a Crossroads: Revivalism and Social Reform in Boston, 1860–1910* (Lebanon, 2011), p. 11.

99. *Church Review* 18 (1866) 113. On the sceptical equation of spiritualism with Salem, see Adams, *Specter of Salem*, pp. 66–8.

100. Heather D. Curtis, *Faith in the Great Physician: Suffering and Divine Healing in American Culture, 1860–1900* (Baltimore, 2007), pp. 125–6.

101. See Stephen Gottschalk, *The Emergence of Christian Science in American Religious Life* (Berkeley, 1973), esp. pp. 144–5, 227. See also Rennie B. Schoepflin, *Christian Science on Trial: Religious Healing in America* (Baltimore, 2003).

102. Joseph Jastrow, The *Psychology of Conviction: A Study of Beliefs and Attitudes* (Boston, 1918), pp. 192, 193.

103. *Boston Daily Globe* 13 May and 15 May 1878; Gillian Gill, *Mary Baker Eddy* (Reading, Mass., 1998), chs 13–14; Willa Cather and Georgine Milmine, *The Life of Mary Baker G. Eddy & the History of Christian Science* (New York, 1909), esp ch. 12.

104. Frank Podmore, *Mesmerism and Christian Science: A Short History of Mental Healing* (London, 1909), p. 271.

105. Roy M. Anker, *Self-Help and Popular Religion in Modern American Culture* (Westport, 1999), p. 83; Gottschalk, *The Emergence of Christian Science*, p. 149.

106. *New York Times*, 21 May 1907.

107. *Ogdensburg Advance*, 18 November 1909; *New York Times*, 27 April 1910; Augusta Stetson, *Vital Issues in Christian Science: A Record of Unsettled Questions which Arose in the Year 1909* (New York, 1914).

108. James G. Kiernan, 'Race and Insanity', *Journal of Nervous and Mental Disease* 13, 2 (1886) 74–6.

109. *Ogdensburg Advance*, 8 August 1907; *Anaconda Standard*, 8 August 1907; *Logansport Reporter*, 8 August 1907; *Oakland Tribune*, 7 August 1907; *Washington Post*, 8 August 1907.

110. *Fort Worth Morning Register*, 24 December 1901; *Des Moines Daily News*, 21 December 1901; *Dubuque Telegraph-Herald*, 21 December 1901.

Chapter 5 Notes

1. Davies, *Witchcraft, Magic and Culture*, pp. 86–100; Nils Freytag, 'Witchcraft, witch doctors and the fight against "superstition" in nineteenth-century Germany', in Willem de Blécourt and Owen Davies (eds), *Witchcraft Continued: Popular Magic in Modern Europe* (Manchester, 2004), pp. 29–46; Peter Dinzelbacher, 'Swimming Test', in Richard Golden (ed.), *Encyclopedia of Witchcraft: The Western Tradition* (Santa Barbara, 2006), Vol. 4, pp. 1097–9; Russell Zguta, 'The Ordeal by Water (Swimming of Witches) in the East Slavic World', *Slavic Review* 36 (1977) 220–30; Heikki Pihlajamäki, '"Swimming the Witch, Pricking for the Devil's Mark": Ordeals in Early Modern Witchcraft Trials', *Journal of Legal History* 21 (2000) 35–59; Bartosz Marcińczak, 'Krytyka pławienia czarownic w *Objaśnieniu błędami zabobonów zarażonych* Józefa Andrzeja Załuskiego', *Literatura Ludowa* 3 (2006) (my thanks to Bartosz Marcińczak for providing me with an English version of his article); Péter Tóth, 'River Ordeal—Trial by Water—Swimming of Witches: Procedures of Ordeal in Witch Trials', in Gábor Klaniczay and Éva Pócs (eds), *Witchcraft, Mythologies and Persecutions* (Budapest, 2008), pp. 129–64.

2. Richard Weisman, *Witchcraft, Magic, and Religion in 17th-Century Massachusetts* (Amherst, 1984), pp. 104, 236; Godbeer, *Devil's Dominion*, p. 167; Demos, *Entertaining Satan*, p. 287, 363; Games, *Witchcraft*, p. 141.

3. *Thomas's Massachusetts, Connecticut, Rhode-Island, Newhampshire and Vermont Almanack* (Worcester, 1797); *Beers's Almanac . . . for 1798*; Robert K. Dodge, *Early American Almanac Humor* (Bowling Green, 1987), pp. 121–2; John Smith Futhey and Gilbert Cope, *History of Chester County, Pennsylvania* (Philadelphia, 1881), Vol. 1, p. 414.

4. Randolph, *Ozark*, p. 282. On early modern prickers see Peter Maxwell-Stuart, *Witch-Hunters: Professional Prickers, Unwitchers and Witch-Finders of the Renaissance* (Stroud, 2003).

5. See, for example, Nasario García, *Brujerías: Stories of Witchcraft and the Supernatural in the American Southwest and Beyond* (Texas, 2007), pp. 266–80; Arthur J. Rubel, 'Concepts of Disease in Mexican-American Culture', *American Anthropologist* N.S., 62, 5 (1960) 801; Aurelio M. Espinosa, *The Folklore of Spain in the American Southwest*, J. Manuel Espinosa (ed.) (Norman, 1985), pp. 75–6.

6. Weisman, *Witchcraft, Magic, and Religion*, p. 40.

7. *The Herald* [Syracuse], 27 October 1889; Wayland Hand (ed.), *Popular Beliefs and Superstitions: A Compendium of American Folklore* (Boston, 1981), p. 1093; George

Benson Kuykendall, *History of the Kuykendall Family since its Settlement in Dutch New York in 1646* (Portland, 1919), p. 508.

8. de Blécourt, 'Boiling Chickens and Burning Cats', p. 99. See also, Hans de Waardt, *Toverij en samenleving* (The Hague, 1991), p. 216.

9. *Boston Daily Globe*, 20 August 1883.

10. Willem de Blécourt, '"Evil People": A Late Eighteenth-Century Dutch Witch Doctor and his Clients', in Davies and de Blécourt (ed.), *Beyond the Witch Trials*, pp. 147, 149. An earlier eighteenth-century Dutch example is also reported in *The Athenian Oracle*, 2nd edition (London, 1704), p. 73. See also, de Blécourt, 'Boiling Chickens and Burning Cats', p. 99.

11. Marijke Gijswijt-Hofstra, 'Witchcraft after the Witch-Trials', p. 170; Douglas R. Holmes, *Cultural Disenchantments: Worker Peasants in Northeast Italy* (Princeton, 1989), p. 157.

12. Harry Hyatt, *Folk-Lore from Adams County* (New York, 1935), pp. 488–98.

13. *Syracuse Daily Standard*, 2 April 1896.

14. *Waterloo Daily Courier*, 13 May 1893. This is likely to be the Peter Sandford mentioned as a foundry worker in Paterson in the 1880 census. He was born in the Netherlands, was aged 26 (in 1880), and was married with young children.

15. *The Herald* [Syracuse], 27 October 1889.

16. *Quincy Daily Journal*, 12 August 1896. For other cases from Ohio and Kentucky, see *Cincinnati Daily Enquirer*, 12 September 1875; *Daily Journal* [Tennessee], 26 August 1895; *Logansport Journal*, 16 August 1913.

17. E. B. Knebb Atchison, 'Concretions', *Transactions of the Annual Meetings of the Kansas Academy of Science* 16 (1897–8) 45–6.

18. *Wilkes-Barre Times*, 6 September 1877.

19. Gustav Henningsen, 'Witchcraft in Denmark', *Folklore* 93, 2 (1982) 132.

20. *Wilkes-Barre Times*, 19 November 1914; *Wilkes-Barre Times*, 15 December 1914.

21. *Atlanta Constitution*, 15 June 1893.

22. See, for example Fanny D. Bergen, 'Some Saliva Charms', *Journal of American Folklore* 3, 8 (1890) 51–9.

23. *Morning Telegraph* [New York], 10 September 1876.

24. *Portland Courier*, reprinted in the *Portsmouth Journal* 31 September 1830.

25. Leland L. Duncan, 'Further Notes from County Leitrim', *Folklore* 5, 3 (1894) 199. See also E. Estyn Evans, *Irish Folk Ways* (London, 1957), p. 304; Arthur Moore, *Folklore of the Isle of Man* (London, 1891), p. 156.

26. *Logansport Journal*, 20 August 1903; *Atlanta Constitution*, 16 August 1903; *Quincy Daily Journal*, 2 December 1915.

27. *St Paul Daily Pioneer*, 28 September 1872.

28. *Daily Confederation*, 30 March 1860; *Waterloo Daily Reporter*, 20 June 1901; *Logansport Pharos*, 14 June 1901.

29. *Norfolk Herald*, 3 June 1822; *Berks and Schuylkill Journal*, 21 September 1822; *Huntingdon Gazette*, 31 October 1822. A petition launched in 1826 by Absolom Scarborough, Hyde County, North Carolina, on his conviction for the murder of May Midyeht, detailed that while he denied he committed the act, he believed May was a witch responsible for the losses of several boats, and admitted he had expressed the opinion that 'if he believed her a witch, he would as willingly kill her as a snake'; Cecil-Fronsman, *Common Whites*, p. 119.

30. The *San Francisco Call*, 25 November 1905; *San Francisco Call*, 18 January 1906.

31. Rennard Strickland, *Fire and the Spirits: Cherokee Law from Clan to Court* (Norman, 1975), pp. 28–9; *The Panoplist, and Missionary Herald*, 15 (1819) 462.

32. *New-Bedford Mercury*, 20 November 1829. See also, Donna Akers, *Living in the Land of Death: The Choctaw Nation, 1830–1860* (East Lansing, 2004), pp. 27–8.

33. *Constitution and Laws of the Choctaw Nation* (*c.*1846), p. 18.

34. *Public Documents Printed by the Order of the Senate of the United States* (Washington, 1836), Vol. I, p. 275.

35. Grant Foreman, *The Five Civilized Tribes* (Norman, 1934), p. 33.

36. Simmons, *Witchcraft in the Southwest*, pp. 98–9; *Annual Report of the Commissioner of Indian Affairs, for the Year 1854* (Washington, 1854), p. 173.

37. Simmons, *Witchcraft in the Southwest*, p. 102.

38. *Mariposa Gazette*, reprinted in *Daily National Democrat*, 16 October 1858.

39. See Martha Blue, *The Witch Purge of 1878: Oral and Documentary History in the Early Navajo Reservation Years* (Tsaile, 1988); Clyde Kluckhohn, *Navajo Witchcraft* (Boston, [1944] 1962).

40. *Times Picayune*, 23 November 1873; *New Haven Register*, 17 September 1888.

41. Hand, *Magical Medicine*, pp. 218, 222.

42. *New York Times*, 2 September 1883.

43. See, for example, *Brown Collection*, p. 440; Doughty, 'Folklore of the Alleghanies', 395.

44. *Monroe Commercial*, reprinted in the *San Francisco Bulletin*, 12 September 1879. For early modern examples see Demos, *Entertaining Satan*, p. 183; Godbeer, *Devil's Dominion*, pp. 42, 63.

45. Demos, *Entertaining Satan*, p. 183; Godbeer, *Devil's Dominion*, pp. 44–6; Joseph Doddridge, *Notes on the Settlement and Indian Wars: Of the Western Parts of Virginia and Pennsylvania from 1763 to 1783, inclusive, together with a Review of the State of Society and Manners of the First Settlers of the Western Country* (Pittsburgh, [1824] 1912), p. 126.

46. Pers. comm. Daniel B. Davis, Archaeologist Coordinator, Kentucky Transportation Cabinet; Rebecca Morehouse, 'Witch Bottle', *Curator's Choice* (August 2009) <http://www.jefpat.org/CuratorsChoiceArchive/2009CuratorsChoice/Aug2009-

WitchBottle.html>; Chris Manning, 'Buried Bottles: The Archaeology of Witch-craft and Sympathetic Magic'; Marshall J. Becker, 'An Update on Colonial Witch Bottles', *Pennsylvania Archaeologist* 75, 2 (2005) 12–23.

47. Hand, *Magical Medicine*, ch. 6.

48. Cited in Moss, *Southern Folk Medicine*, p. 161.

49. Reprinted in the *Winona Daily Republican*, 28 July 1886.

50. *Pennsylvania Agriculture and Country Life: 1840–1940* (1971) p. 546. For examples of witches supposedly using the same method, see Milnes, *Signs, Cures, & Witchery*, pp. 80, 81.

51. James Frazer, *Golden Bough* (London, 1920), pp. 56–9, J. G. Owens, 'Folk-Lore from Buffalo Valley, Central Pennsylvania', *Journal of American Folklore* 4, 13 (1891) 126; Kriebel, *Powwowing among the Pennsylvania Dutch*, pp. 39–40; Hand, *Magical Medicine*, p. 221; Puckett, *Folk Beliefs*, pp. 255, 370.

52. *Wilkes-Barre Times*, 12 August 1915; *Quincy Daily Journal*, 29 May 1897.

53. George Henry Loskiel, *History of the Mission of the United Brethren among the Indians in North America* (London, 1794), p. 119; *David Zeisberger's History of the Northern American Indians*, p. 126; Sarah Tuttle, *Conversations on the Choctaw Mission* (Boston, 1830), Vol. 1, p. 28; Ellis, 'Southwest: Pueblo', p. 204.

54. *The Torch Light and Public Advertiser*, 2 October 1828; *Farmer's Cabinet*, 4 October 1828.

55. Colin Palmer, 'Afro-Latinos and the Bible: The Formative Years in Mexico, Brazil, and Peru', in Vincent L. Wimbush (ed.), *African Americans and the Bible: Sacred Texts and Social Textures* (New York, 2000), pp. 184–5; Rosanne Marion Adderley, *'New Negroes from Africa': Slave Trade Abolition and free African Settlement in the Nineteenth-Century Caribbean* (Bloomington, 2006), pp. 220–2; Angelita Dianne Reyes, *Mothering across Cultures: Postcolonial Representations* (Minneapolis, 2002), pp. 44–6; Carole Boyce Davies (ed.), *Encyclopedia of the African Diaspora* (Santa Barbra, 2008), Vol. 1, p. 815.

56. *Brown Collection*, pt 2, pp. 106–7; William Henry Perrin, *History of Effingham County, Illinois* (Chicago, 1883), p. 14; *Iowa State Reporter*, 5 May 1875.

57. *Grand Forks Herald*, 14 July 1885.

58. Roud, *Superstitions*, pp. 314, 411; M. C. Balfour, *County Folklore: Northumberland* (London, 1904), pp. 53, 54; Mary Julia MacCulloch, 'Folk-Lore of the Isle of Skye. IV', *Folklore* 34, 1 (1923) 91. See also, W. A. Craigie, 'Some Highland Folklore', *Folklore* 9, 4 (1898) 378.

59. Caesar Otway, *Sketches in Erris and Tyrawly* (Dublin, 1841), p. 381. See also Joseph Meehan, 'The Cure of Elf-Shooting in the North-West of Ireland', *Folklore* 17, 2 (1906) 200–10.

60. For example, William Henry Jones and Lewis L. Kropf, 'Székely Folk-Medicine', *Folk-lore Journal* 2, 4 (1884) 105; M. Edith Durham, 'High Albania and its Customs

in 1908', *Journal of the Royal Anthropological Institute of Great Britain and Ireland* 40 (1910) 463.

61. Also confirmed in 'Letters to the Editor', *Folklore* 72, 2 (1961) 414–16; Ewen, *Witchcraft and Demonianism*, p. 161; Kittredge, *Witchcraft*, p. 167; *Folk-Lore Record* 3, 1 (1880) 134; Roud, *Superstitions*, pp. 264–5.

62. *Drums and Shadows: Survival Studies Among the Georgia Coastal Negroes* (Athens, 1940), p. 13.

63. *Atlanta Constitution*, reprinted in *Biddeford Daily Journal*, 5 May 1884.

64. *Huntingdon Globe*, 16 June 1887; *Daily Hawk-Eye*, 21 February 1885; *Kokomo Tribune*, 18 April 1894.

65. See Bill Ellis, 'Why is a Lucky Rabbit's Foot Lucky? Body Parts as Fetishes', *Journal of Folklore Research* 39, 1 (2002) 51–84.

66. *Muskogee Phoenix*, 5 May 1892; *San Antonio Daily Light*, 15 March 1894; *Kokomo Tribune*, 18 April 1894; *Weekly Herald-Dispatch*, 21 April 1894.

67. W. L. Hildburgh, 'Images of the Human Hand as Amulets in Spain', *Journal of the Warburg and Courtauld Institutes* 18 (1955) 67–89; W. L. Hildburgh, 'Notes on some Contemporary Portuguese Amulets', *Folklore* 19, 2 (1908) 213–24; Malpezzi and Clements, *Italian-American Folklore*, p. 121; Leo Pap, *The Portuguese-Americans* (Boston, 1981), p. 122; Fennell, *Crossroads and Cosmologies*, pp. 72–4; Kathleen A. Deagan, *Artifacts of the Spanish Colonies of Florida and the Caribbean, 1500–1800* (Washington DC, 2002), Vol. 2, pp. 95–9; Hand, *Magical Medicine*, p. 245.

68. *Semi-Weekly News* [Lebanon, PA], 5 June 1922.

69. See Robert Blair St. George, *Conversing by Signs: Poetics of Implication in Colonial New England Culture* (Chapel Hill, 1998), pp. 181–95.

70. Louis P. Nelson, *The Beauty of Holiness: Anglicanism and Architecture in Colonial South Carolina* (Chapel Hill, 2008), pp. 159–60.

71. Robert Means Lawrence, *The Magic of the Horse Shoe With Other Folk-Lore Notes* (London, 1898), pp. 101–2.

72. *Cleveland Plain Dealer Pictorial Magazine*, 16 July 1950.

73. Don Yoder and Tom Graves, *Hex Signs: Pennsylvania Dutch Barn Symbols and their Meaning* (Mechanicsburg, 2000), esp. p. 69. See also, Milnes, *Signs, Cures & Witchery*, pp. 49–51.

74. *Memphis Daily Avalanche*, 17 March 1866; *Newark Daily Advocate*, 12 September 1883; Vance Randolph, 'Ozark Superstitions', *Journal of American Folklore* 46, 179 (1933) 20.

75. Robert Means Lawrence, *The Magic of the Horse Shoe With Other Folk-Lore Notes* (London, 1898), pp. 103–16. For its use in seventeenth-century America, see Demos, *Entertaining Satan*, p. 182; Godbeer, p. 82.

76. *The Gospel Advocate, and Impartial Investigator* 6 (1828) 191; Buckley, 'Witchcraft', *The Century* 43, 3 (1892) 409. See also, See also *Brown Collection*, pp. 121–2; Mary Willis

Minor, 'How to Keep off Witches', *Journal of American Folklore*, 11, 40 (1898) 76; Puckett, pp. 158, 477–8.

77. Hyatt, *Hoodoo, Conjuration, Witchcraft, Rootwork*, Vol. 1, p. 154.

78. Malpezzi and Clements, *Italian-American Folklore*, p. 145; Puckett, *Folk Beliefs*, pp. 156–7; Alan Dundes, '"Jumping the Broom": On the Origin and Meaning of an African American Wedding Custom', *Journal of American Folklore* 109 (1996) 324–9.

79. *Monroe Commercial*, reprinted in the *San Francisco Bulletin*, 12 September 1879.

80. Blair St. George, *Conversing by Signs*, pp. 190–2.

81. Dina Eastop, 'Outside In: Making Sense of the Deliberate Concealment of Garments within Buildings', *Textile* 4,3 (2006) 238–55; Brian Hoggard, 'The Archaeology of Counter-witchcraft and Popular Magic', in Owen Davies and Willem de Blécourt *Beyond the Witch Trials: Witchcraft and Magic in Enlightenment Europe* (Manchester, 2004), pp. 167–86; Ian Evans, 'Deliberately Concealed Objects in Old Australian Houses and Buildings', PhD thesis, University of Newcastle, New South Wales, 2010. On recent American research see Megan E. Springate, 'The Sexton's House has a Ritual Concealment: Late Nineteenth-Century Negotiations of Double Consciousness at a Black Family Home in Sussex County, New Jersey', *African Diaspora Archaeology Network Newsletter* (June 2010); C. Riley Augé's website, <http://www.crossingthethreshold.org/>; M. Chris Manning, 'Hidden Footsteps: Analysis of a Folk Practice', <http://ballstate.academia.edu/ChrisManningPratt/Papers/907688/Hidden_Footsteps_Analysis_of_a_Folk_Practice>.

82. Mark P. Leone and Gladys-Marie Fry, 'Conjuring in the Big House Kitchen: An Interpretation of African American Belief Systems Based on the Uses of Archaeology and Folklore Sources', *Journal of American Folklore* 112 (1999) 372–403; Lynn Jones, 'Crystals and Conjuring at the Charles Carroll House, Annapolis, Maryland', *Newsletter of the African-American Archaeology Network* 27 (2000).

83. *Record Herald*, 20 November 1918.

84. *Plattsburgh Sentinel*, 8 April 1892.

85. See Davies, *Grimoires*, chs. 6 and 7.

86. W. W. Newell, 'Tales of the Blue Mountains in Pennsylvania', *Journal of American Folklore* 11, 40 (1898) 78.

87. *New York Times*, 2 September 1883. For an *in situ* example see Milnes, *Signs, Cures & Witchery*, pp. 177–8.

88. August C. Mahr, 'A Pennsylvania Dutch "Hexzettel"', *Monatshefte für deutschen Unterricht* 27, 6 (1935) 215–25.

89. See Adolf Spamer, *Romanus-Büchlein* (Berlin, 1958), pp. 95–108.

90. See Davies, *Grimoires*.

91. Roger Finke and Rodney Starke, *The Churching of America, 1776–2005: Winners and Losers in our Religious Economy*, 2nd edition (New Brunswick, 2005), ch. 4.

92. Thomas Meade Harwell, *Studies in Texan Folklore—Rio Grande valley* (New York, 1997), p. 6.

93. Ann Taves, *The Household of Faith: Roman Catholic Devotions in Mid-Nineteenth-Century America* (Note Dame, 1986), p. 58.

94. *New York Times*, 29 November 1872; Simmons, *Witchcraft in the Southwest*, p. 46.

95. *Sixtieth Anniversary of the Dedication of Most Holy Name Church Troy Hill* (Pittsburgh, 1928); Keith Sniadach, *Relics of God: A Supernatural Guide to Religious Artifacts, Sacred Locations and Holy Souls* (Charleston, 2011), pp. 131–2.

96. Chaim M. Rosenberg, *Goods for Sale: Products and Advertising in the Massachusetts Industrial Age* (2007), pp. 97–8.

97. *The Olean Democrat*, 18 June 1891.

98. *Bay City Times*, 2 August 1904.

99. *Plain Dealer*, 4 November 1901.

100. W. Scott Robison, *History of the City of Cleveland* (1887), p. 382.

101. *Cleveland Leader*, reprinted in *Boston Daily Globe*, 31 July 1886.

102. See Robert Anthony Orsi, *The Madonna of 115th Street: Faith and Community in Italian Harlem, 1880–1950* (New Haven, 1985).

103. Joseph Doddridge, *Notes on the Settlement and Indian Wars: Of the Western Parts of Virginia and Pennsylvania from 1763 to 1783, inclusive, together with a Review of the State of Society and Manners of the First Settlers of the Western Country* (Pittsburgh, [1824] 1912), p. 126.

104. *Wilkes-Barre Times*, 16 March 1916.

105. Peter Benes, 'Fortunetellers, Wise Men, and Magical Healers in New England, 1644–1850', in Peter Benes (ed.), *Wonders of the Invisible World: 1600–1900* (Boston, 1992), pp. 127–49.

106. Benes, 'Fortunetellers, Wise Men', pp. 132–3.

107. *The Southern Medical and Surgical Journal* 16 (1860) 308; *Drums and Shadows*, pp. 15, 197; Snow, *Walkin' Over Medicine*, pp. 58–60.

108. Richard M. Dorson, *Bloodstoppers & Bearwalkers: Folk Traditions of the Upper Peninsula* (Cambridge, Mass., 1952), pp. 81–2. On French printed magic books, see Davies, *Grimoires*, passim.

109. *Nashua Gazette*, reprinted in the *Sun* [Maryland], 6 October 1843. For an example of Nevens' press advertisements see *Morning News* [Connecticut], 20 July 1846.

110. *Jackson Sentinel*, 9 September 1886; *Portsmouth Journal of Literature and Politics*, 2 October 1824.

111. *New York Sun*, cited in *Hopewell Herald*, 3 October 1883; *San Francisco Bulletin*, 3 October 1883.

112. *Philadelphia Inquirer*, 27 August 1901.

113. *New Albany Ledger*, reprinted in *Cincinnati Daily Gazette*, 19 July 1871.

114. *New York Times*, 2 September 1883.

115. *Newark Daily Advocate*, 12 September 1883.

116. *Sun* 18 March 1861.

117. Q. K. Philander Doesticks, *The Witches of New York* (New York, 1859), p. 18. On Thomson's work see Joe Lockard, *Watching Slavery: Witness Texts and Travel Reports* (New York, 2008), pp. xiv–xvii; Justine S. Murison, *The Politics of Anxiety in Nineteenth-Century American Literature* (Cambridge, 2011), pp. 95–6. On press advertising and magic in the period see Davies, *Grimoires*, ch. 6; Owen Davies, 'Newspapers and the Popular Belief in Witchcraft and Magic in the Modern Period', *Journal of British Studies* 37 (1998), 139–66; Davies, *Witchcraft, Magic, and Culture*, pp. 160–4.

118. *The World* [New York], 9 July 1893.

119. Account based on reports in *The Quincy Daily Journal*, 11 July 1888; *Quincy Daily Whig*, 8 January 1901, 4 May 1901; *Quincy Daily Journal*, 3 May 1901; *Quincy Daily Whig*, 19 April 1902; *Quincy Daily Journal*, 21 April 1902; *Quincy Daily Whig*, 28 September 1904, 29 September 1904, 13 October 1904, 17 October 1905; *Illinois Medical Journal*, 8 (1906) 430; *Quincy Daily Journal*, 26 August 1913.

Chapter 6 Notes

1. William Henry Perrin, *History of Effingham County, Illinois* (Chicago, 1883), p. 14.

2. Fischer, *Albion's Seed*, pp. 715–24.

3. *Baltimore Patriot*, 17 March 1831.

4. *American Journal of Dental Science* 1 (1839) 192.

5. *Maryland and Virginia Medical Journal* 12 (1859) 132.

6. *Baltimore Sun*, 19 December 1848; Charles Grafton Page, *Psychomancy: Spirit-Rappings and Table-Tippings Exposed* (New York, 1853), p. 22.

7. *Daily Inter Ocean*, 20 June 1889.

8. *Duluth News-Tribune*, 13 January 1921; *Philadelphia Inquirer*, 23 December 1920; *Fort Wayne Journal-Gazette*, 20 January 1921.

9. *Cincinnati Commercial Tribune*, 27 March 1883. Details of the Schefflers from the census and *Williams' Cincinnati Directory* for 1883, and 1885.

10. Peter Charles Hoffer, *Law and People in Colonial America*, p. 77; Susan Juster, 'Sinners and Saints: Women and Religion in Colonial America', in Nancy A. Hewitt (ed.), *A Companion to American Women's History* (Oxford, 2002), pp. 71–2.

11. Futhey and Cope, *History of Chester County*, Vol. 1, p. 413.

12. Adelaide L. Fries (ed.), *Records of the Moravians in North Carolina* (Raleigh, 1941), Vol. 5, pp. 2131, 2231; Moss, *Southern Folk Medicine*, p. 162; Jon F. Sensbach, *A Separate Canaan: The Making of an Afro-Moravian World in North Carolina* (Chapel Hill, 1998), p. 292.

13. *Cincinnati Daily Gazette*, 8 November 1877.

14. *Chicago Daily Tribune*, 4 October 1936. On Lenyi, see Virginia B. Troeger, *Woodbridge: New Jersey's Oldest Township* (Charleston, 2002), p. 101.

15. *The Gospel Advocate, and Impartial Investigator* 6 (1828) 191.

16. *Winona Daily Republican*, 29 September 1885; 17 October 1885; *The World* [New York], 16 October 1885.

17. *Philadelphia Record*, 13 January 1929; reprinted in J. Ross McGinnis, *Trials of Hex* (Davis/Trinity Publishing Co. 2000), p. 433.

18. *Salem Daily News*, 23 May 1893; 24 May 1893; *The World* [New York], 9 July 1893.

19. *Salem Daily News*, 13 June 1893.

20. *Salem Daily News*, 27 November 1893; 25 January 1894; *The Sumner Gazette*, 1 March 1894.

21. 'The Great Salem Witchcraft Trial of 1894', *Echoes* 16–17 (1977) 96.

22. John J. Honigmann, 'Witch-Fear in Post-Contact Kaska Society', *American Anthropologist* N.S. 49, 2 (1947) 222–43.

23. *Dictionary of American Naval Fighting Ships*, <http://www.history.navy.mil/danfs/j2/jamestown-i.htm>.

24. Sergei Kan, *Memory Eternal: Tlingit Culture and Russian Orthodox Christianity through Two Centuries* (Seattle, 1999), pp.144–5.

25. *New York Herald*, 14 June 1879; *Philadelphia Inquirer*, 14 June 1881; George Thornton Emmons, edited with additions by Frederica de Laguna, *The Tlingit Indians* (Seattle, 1991), pp. 410–11.

26. *Report on Education in Alaska*, p. 1447.

27. *Quincy Daily Whig*, 13 October 1882.

28. *Brooklyn Eagle*, 19 February 1882.

29. Ted C. Hinckley, *The Americanization of Alaska, 1867–1897* (Palo Alto, 1972).

30. Printed in Sheldon Jackson, *Alaska and Missions on the North Pacific Coast* (New York, 1880), p. 84.

31. S. Hall Young, *Hall Young of Alaska: The Mushing Parson* (New York, 1927), p. 116.

32. Young, *Hall Young of Alaska*, pp. 131, 141.

33. *Dearborn Independent Magazine*, 28 May (1927), 20.

34. Robert E Coontz, *From the Mississippi to the Sea* (1930), p. 164.

35. Emmons and de Laguna, *Tlingit Indians*, pp. 371–2, 411–12; Eliza Ruhumah Scidmore, *Alaska: Its Southern Coast and the Sitkan Archipelago* (1885), p. 111; Young, *Hall Young of Alaska*, p. 213.

36. Thomas A. Morehouse, Gerald A. McBeath, and Linda E. Leask, *Alaska's Urban and Rural Governments* (Lanham, 1984), pp. 16–17.

37. Ted C. Hinckley, '"We Are More Truly Heathen Than the Natives": John G. Brady and the Assimilation of Alaska's Tlingit Indians', *Western Historical Quarterly* 11, 1 (1980) 51.

38. Sidney L. Herring, *Crow Dog's Case: American Indian Sovereignty, Tribal Law, and United States Law in the Nineteenth Century* (Cambridge, 2004), pp. 232–3; Claus-M. Naske and Herman E. Slotnick, *Alaska: A History of the 49th State*, 2nd edition (1987), pp. 73–4.

39. John G. Brady, 'Witchcraft in Alaska', *The Independent*, 29 December 1898.

40. *Quincy Daily Journal*, 1 April 1898.

41. *Quincy Daily Journal*, 4 November 1895.

42. *The Alaska Searchlight*, 17 December 1894; *Quincy Daily Journal*, 19 January 1895; *Tacoma Daily News*, 14 December 1898; *Daily Alaska Dispatch*, 11 February 1902. Jackson was possibly the nephew of Chief Aanyalahaash, who petitioned the governor in 1915 to have his chieftainship transferred to him; Anne Chandonnet, 'Southeast Sagas: Chief Aanyalahaash', <http://juneauempire.com/stories/082903/nei_sesagas.shtml>.

43. Victoria Wyatt, 'Interpreting the Balance of Power: A Case Study of Photographer and Subject in Images of Native Americans', *Exposure* 28, 3 (1992) 26; Sharon Gmelch, *The Tlingit Encounter with Photography* (Philadelphia, 2008), p. 77.

44. *Daily Alaska Dispatch*, 10 May 1910.

45. *Cedar Rapids Evening Gazette*, 18 May 1896.

46. *Morning Olympian*, 13 December 1898.

47. *Daily Alaska Dispatch*, 14 February 1900.

48. *Atlanta Constitution*, 10 November 1902; *Cranbury Press*, 5 December 1902; *Daily Alaska Dispatch*, 23 December 1902;

49. *Report on the Work of the Bureau of Education for the Natives of Alaska* (Washington, 1917), pp. 84–5.

50. *Charlotte Observer*, 5 December 1915.

51. *Daily Alaska Dispatch*, 17 August 1919.

52. *Daily Alaska Dispatch*, 7 December 1917, 31 October 1917; *Wyoming State Tribune*, 30 July 1919. One of the last reported cases of witch torture amongst the Tlingits occurred in 1919 when chiefs of the Bear Lake community were arrested after a sixteen-year-old girl was found tied to a tree by her hair, her hands tied behind her back.

53. See Sergei Kan, 'Shamanism and Christianity: Modern Day Tlingit Elders Look at the Past', *Ethnohistory* 38, 4 (1991) 363–87.

54. Kan, *Memory Eternal: Tlingit Culture*, p. 277.

55. Young, *Hall Young of Alaska*, p. 118.

56. *Baltimore Republican*, 10 October 1911.

57. *Daily Inter Ocean*, 20 June 1889.

58. *Newark Daily Advocate*, 12 September 1883.

59. *Quincy Daily Whig*, 20 February 1889; *Bismarck Tribune*, 26 March 1889.

60. *Philadelphia Inquirer*, 1 November 1891.

61. *Philadelphia Inquirer*, 28 July 1902.

62. *Grand Forks Herald*, 14 July 1892.

63. *North American*, 22 May 1900; 11–14 March 1903; *Lebanon Daily News*, 14 March 1903. See also Lewis, *Hex*, pp. 35–6; Carleton F. Brown, 'The Long Hidden Friend', *Journal of American Folklore* 17 (1904) 90, 149.

64. *American Medicine* 7 (1904) 804.

65. *Philadelphia Inquirer*, 22 September 1900.

66. *Pawtucket Times*, 14 February 1910.

67. *Lebanon Daily News*, 30 January 1913.

68. *Wilkes-Barre Times*, 11 August 1909; *Philadelphia Inquirer*, 10 July 1910.

69. Karen Buhler-Wilkerson, *No Place Like Home: A History of Nursing and Home Care in the United States* (Baltimore, 2001); Harriet Fulmer, 'History of Visiting Nurse Work in America', *American Journal of Nursing* 2, 6 (1902) 411–25.

70. *Pawtucket Times*, 13 September 1912.

71. Aurand, *Pow Wow Book*, p. 12.

72. *New York Times*, 10 September 1911.

73. *Patriot* [Harrisburg], 15 July 1915.

74. Davies, *Murder, Magic, Madness*, pp. 184–92.

75. *Oregonian*, 25 August 1918; *Record Herald*, 19 November 1918, 20 November 1918, 26 November 1918, 11 January 1919; *Gettysburg Times*, 13 November 1919; *Star and Sentinel*, 30 April 1921.

76. The best account is J. Ross McGinnis, *Trials of Hex* (privately printed, 2000). See also, Joseph David Cress, *Murder and Mayhem in York County* (Charleston, 2011), pp. 80–6.

77. Lewis, *Hex*, pp. 94–5.

78. John Lineaweaver, 'Hexa Buch', *North American Review* 232, 1 (1931) 13–25.

79. *The Daily Mail* [Hagerstown], 6 December 1932; *Dallas Morning News*, 21 July 1933; Gerald Martin Bordman, *American Theatre: A Chronicle of Comedy and Drama, 1930–1969* (New York, 1996), p. 94; Armond Fields and L. Marc Fields, *From the Bowery to Broadway: Lew Fields and the Roots of American Popular Theatre* (New York, 1993), p. 509; Earl F. Robacker, *Pennsylvania German Literature* (Philadelphia, 1943).

80. *Sunday World Herald*, 18 February 1934.

81. Clara Louise Leslie, 'Science Studies Pow-Wowing', *Every Week Magazine*; reprinted in *The Springfield Sunday Union and Republican*, 11 January 1931.

82. See A. M. Aurand, W. J. Klose, and J. P. Keller, *History of Beaver Springs, Penn'a, and Centennial Souvenir Book* (Beaver Springs, 1906).

83. Donald B. Kraybill and Marc Alan Olshan, *The Amish Struggle with Modernity* (Hanover, 1994), pp. 115–16.

84. David Weaver-Zercher, *The Amish in the American Imagination* (Baltimore, 2001), pp. 53–4, 115, 129.

85. *Indiana Evening Gazette*, 19 September 1933.

86. See George Cooper, *Poison Widows: A True Story of Witchcraft, Arsenic, and Murder* (New York, 1999).

87. *Indiana Evening Gazette*, 9 January 1930; *Huntingdon Daily News*, 9 January 1930.

88. *News Comet*, 23 January 1931; *Gettysburg Times*, 24 January 1931.

89. *Tyrone Daily Herald*, 18 September 1933.

90. *New Castle News*, 6 April 1934.

91. *Indiana Evening Gazette*, 23 February 1935.

92. *Lebanon Daily News*, 12 March 1940, 14 March 1940.

93. John Andrew Hostetler, *Amish Roots: A Treasury of History, Wisdom, and Lore* (Baltimore, 1992), pp. 106, 107.

94. See, for example, C. Virginia Palmer, 'The Health Beliefs and Practices of an Old Order Amish Family', *Journal of the American Academy of Nurse Practitioners* 4, 3 (1992) 117–22; Judith Offner, 'Pow-Wowing: The Pennsylvania Dutch Way to Heal', *Journal of Holistic Nursing* 16 (1998) 479–86; Paul L. Reiter et al., 'Complementary and Alternative Medicine Use Among Amish and Non-Amish Residents of Ohio Appalachia', *Journal of Rural Nursing and Health Care* 9, 2 (2009) 33–44.

95. John A. Hostetler, 'Folk Medicine and Sympathy Healing among the Amish', Hand (ed.), *American Folk Medicine*, pp. 249–59.

Chapter 7 Notes

1. *Hampshire Gazette*, 19 October 1825; *Sentinel and Witness* (N. H.) 19 October 1825.

2. Frederick Coombs, *Coomb's Popular Phrenology* (Boston, 1841), p. 58. See also Davies, *Murder, Magic, Madness*, p. 31.

3. George Combe, *A System of Phrenology* (New York, 1842), p. 149.

4. 'Exemption of the Cherokee Indians and Africans from Insanity', *American Journal of Insanity* 1 (1845) 287.

5. E. Y. Williams, 'The Incidence of Mental Disease in the Negro', *The Journal of Negro Education* 6, 3 (1937) 377–92; Peter McCandless, *Moonlight, Magnolias & Madness: Insanity in South Carolina from the Colonial Period to the Progressive Era* (Chapel Hill, 1996), p. 155; J. S. Haller Jr, 'The Negro and the Southern Physician: A Study of Medical and Racial Attitudes 1800–1860', *Medical History* 16, 3 (1972) 238–53.

6. Martin Summers, '"Suitable Care of the African when Afflicted with Insanity": Race, Madness, and Social Order in Comparative Perspective', *Bulletin of the History of Medicine* 84, 1 (2010) 58–91. Ana Maria G. Raimundo Oda, Claudio Eduardo M. Banzato and Paulo Dalgarrondo, 'Some Origins of Cross-Cultural Psychiatry', *History of Psychiatry* 16, 2 (2005) 155–69.

7. James G. Kiernan, 'Race and Insanity', *Journal of Nervous and Mental Disease* 13, 2 (1886) 74.

8. See, for example, M. M. Drymon, *Disguised as the Devil: How Lyme Disease Created Witches and Changed History* (South Portland, 2008); Laurie Winn Carlson, *A Fever in Salem: A New Interpretation of the New England Witch Trials* (Chicago, 1999); Thurman Sawyer and George Bundren, 'Witchcraft, Religious Fanaticism and Schizophrenia—Salem Revisited', *The Early American Review* 3, 2 (2000). See also, Robin DeRosa, *The Making of Salem: The Witch Trials in History, Fiction and Tourism* (Jefferson, 2009), pp. 93–6.

9. See Jonathan Metzl, *The Protest Psychosis: How Schizophrenia Became a Black Disease* (Boston, 2009), p. 26.

10. *Pittsburgh Gazette*, 26 July 1875.

11. *Davenport Gazette*, reprinted in the *Logansport Journal*, 11 January 1878.

12. See, for example, John Reid, 'Understanding the New Hampshire Doctrine of Criminal Insanity', *The Yale Law Review* 69, 3 (1960) 367–420.

13. Susanna L. Blumenthal, 'The Deviance of the Will: Policing the Bounds of Testamentary Freedom in Nineteenth-Century America', *Harvard Law Review* 119, 4 (2006) 959–1034; Harry Hibschman, 'Witches and Wills', *North American Review* 230, 5 (1930) 622–7.

14. For a similar link between strange farming ideas and supernatural belief, see Davies, *Murder, Magic, Madness*.

15. David James M'Cord, *Reports of Cases Determined in the Constitutional Court of Appeals of South Carolina* (Columbia, 1830), Vol. 4, pp. 183–97; *Niles' Register*, 1 December 1827, 220–1.

16. Albert G. Porter, *Reports of Cases Argued and Determined in the Supreme Court of Judicature of the State of Indiana* (Indianapolis, 1855), Vol. 5, pp. 137–40.

17. Horace Gray, *Reports of Cases Argued and Determined in the Supreme Judicial Court of Massachusetts* (Boston, 1859), Vol. 7, 467–73; *Brooklyn Eagle*, 19 May 1856.

18. Stewart Chaplin, *Principles of the Law of Wills: With Selected Cases* (New York, 1892) pp. 76–8; *Boston Daily Globe*, 28 February 1888.

19. *Quincy Daily Journal*, 8 October 1903.

20. Glenn D. Walters, *Foundations of Criminal Science: The Use of Knowledge* (Santa Barbara, 1992), pp. 71–3.

21. *Montana Butte Standard*, 2 March 1937, 6 March 1937, 7 March 1937, 30 March 1937, 31 March 1937, 17 June 1937, 18 June 1937, 19 June 1937, 20 June 1937, 26 June

1937, 13 February 1938; *Helena Daily Independent*, 15 February 1938; *Independent Record*, 28 April 1944.

22. *The Trenton Times*, 23 September 1884; *St Paul Daily Globe*, 24 September 1884. On the diabolic plea see Owen Davies, 'Talk of the Devil: Crime and Satanic Inspiration in Eighteenth-Century England', available at <http://herts.academia. edu/OwenDavies/Papers/157535/Talk_of_the_Devil_Crime_and_Satanic_Inspiration_in_Eighteenth-Century_England>.

23. *Evening Independent* [Ohio], 7 April 1910; *Van Wert Daily Bulletin*, 20 August 1910; *Belleville News Democrat*, 8 April 1910; *Marion Daily Star*, 2 September 1910.

24. *Gastonia Daily Gazette*, 25 August 1938 and 27 August 1938; *The Daily Times-News* [North Carolina], 4 July and 9 December 1938; *Sheboygan Press*, 27 August 1938.

25. *Statesville Landmark*, 31 December 1928.

26. Trina N. Seitz, 'Electrocution and the Tar Heel State: The Advent and Demise of a Southern Sanction', *American Journal of Criminal Justice* 31, 1 (2006) 103–24; Scott Christianson, *The Last Gasp: The Rise and Fall of the American Gas Chamber* (Berkeley, 2010).

27. *The Daily Times-News* [Burlington, NC], 9 December 1938.

28. *Baltimore Medical Journal* 1 (1870) 495.

29. Mary de Young, *Madness: An American History of Mental Illness and its Treatment* (Jefferson, 2010), ch. 6; Benjamin Reiss, *Theaters of Madness: Insane Asylums and Nineteenth-Century American Culture* (Chicago, 2008).

30. Principal reports of the case in, *Ames Daily Tribune-Times* 3 August 1935; *Hamilton Daily News Journal* [Ohio] 3 August 1935; *Lima News* 4 August 1935; *Circleville Herald* 10 August 1935; *Mansfield News-Journal* 13 November 1935; *The Lima News* 20 December 1938; *The Chronicle-Telegram* [Ohio] 6 January 1939; *Lima News* 26 February 1939; *The Advocate* [Ohio] 13 March 1939.

31. The only close match in the census records are a Samuel and Tillie (a contraction of Matilda) Waldman who lived with their two children in New York in the 1920s and early 1930s. This Samuel is listed as a Hungarian-born salesman.

32. H. M. Turk, 'A Psychiatrist Evaluates the Hospital Library', *Hospitals: The Journal of the American Hospital Association* 15 (1941) 45–6.

33. *The Advocate* [Ohio] 13 March 1939.

34. *Pottsville Republican*, 19 March 1934; *New Castle News*, 23 March 1934; *Indiana Evening Gazette*, 24 March 1934, 26 March 1934; *Springfield Republican*, 25 March 1934; *Tyrone Daily Herald*, 27 March 1934; *Reading Eagle*, 29 March 1934.

35. Walter G. Bowers, 'Hydrotherapy: Methods of Application with Results: As Used in the Philadelphia Hospital for the Insane', *Journal of the American Medical Association* 51 (1908) 1420–1; *Schuylkill County, Pennsylvania: Genealogy-Family History-Biography* (Chicago, 1916), Vol. 2, pp. 639–40.

36. Richard Noll, *American Madness: The Rise and Fall of Dementia Praecox* (Cambridge, Mass., 2011); Adityanjee, Y. A. Aderibigbe, D. Theodoridis, and V. R. Vieweg, 'Dementia Praecox to Schizophrenia: The First 100 Years', *Psychiatry and Clinical Neurosciences* 53, 4 (1999) 437–48; See also the useful overview at <http://en. wikipedia.org/wiki/Dementia_praecox>.

37. *Indiana Evening Gazette*, 6 February 1937; *Gettysburg Times*, 21 July 1947; Lewis, *Hex*, p. 197.

38. *Schuylkill Legal Record* 70–1 (1976) 160–6; *Lebanon Daily News*, 10 January 1976.

39. See John R. Sutton, 'The Political Economy of Madness: The Expansion of the Asylum in Progressive America', *American Sociological Review* 56 (1991) 665–78; Historical Statistics of the United States, Millennial Edition Online, <http://hsus. cambridge.org/HSUSWeb/HSUSEntryServlet>; Edward Shorter, *A History of Psychiatry: From the Era of the Asylum to the Age of Prozac* (New York, 1997), p. 46; Edwin Fuller Torrey and Judy Miller, *The Invisible Plague: The Rise of Mental Illness from 1750 to the Present* (New Brunswick, 2001), pp. 277–9. More generally see, for example, Carla Yannim *The Architecture of Madness: Insane Asylums in the United States* (Minneapolis, 2007); David Rothman, *The Discovery of the Asylum*, revised edition (Boston, 1990).

40. James Vance May, *Mental Diseases: A Public Health Problem* (Boston, 1922), pp. 58–60; John Koren, Samuel Warren Hamilton, and Roy Haber, *Summaries of State Laws Relating to the Insane* (New York, 1917).

41. *Davenport Gazette*, reprinted in the *Logansport Journal*, 11 January 1878.

42. *Los Angeles Times*, 27 March 1903.

43. Paul E. Carpenter, 'Some of the Legal Phases of Insanity', *American Lawyer* 102 (1903) 102. For a good case study of these changes, see C. Peter Erlinder, 'Of Rights Lost and Rights Found: The Coming Restoration of the Right to a Jury Trial in Minnesota Civil Commitment Proceedings', *William Mitchell Law Review* 29, 4 (2003) 1269–83; 'The "Crime" of Mental Illness: Extension of "Criminal" Procedural Safeguards to Involuntary Civil Commitments', *Journal of Criminal Law and Criminology* 66, 3 (1975) 255–70.

44. *Simpson's Leader-Times*, 9 January 1929; Cress, *Murder and Mayhem in York County*, p. 85.

45. James G. Kiernan, 'Race and Insanity', *Journal of Nervous and Mental Disease* 13, 2 (1886) 74.

46. *Omaha World Herald*, 27 January 1907; *Duluth News-Tribune*, 18 February 1907; *Winona Republican Herald*, 18 June 1907.

47. *Portsmouth Daily Herald*, 1 June 1907; *Grand Forks Herald*, 9 November 1909.

48. *Winona Republican-Herald*, 4 April 1907.

49. Margaret B. Hay, 'Law and Social Work in a Rural Community', *Annals of the American Academy of Political and Social Science* 145, 1 (1929) 139–40.

Chapter 8 Notes

1. Harring, *Crow Dog's Case*, p. 268.

2. *Boston Daily Globe*, 29 January 1892.

3. Raymond L. Cohn, *Mass Migration Under Sail: European Immigration to the Antebellum United States* (Cambridge, 2009), p. 122; L. Edward Purcell, *Immigration* (Phoenix, 1995), pp. 29–31.

4. Quoted in Edith Abbott, *Historical Aspects of the Immigration Problem: Select Documents* (Chicago, 1926), p. 96.

5. James Eldridge Quinlan, *History of Sullivan County* (New York, 1873), pp. 164–8.

6. *Republican Watchman*, 16 January 1891.

7. *Republican Watchman*, 27 April 1888.

8. *Republican Watchman*, 1 June 1888.

9. *The Athens Messenger*, 26 July 1888.

10. *The Sun* [New York], 28 January 1892; *Middletown Daily Times*, 26 May 1892.

11. *Middletown Daily Times*, 17 August 1892; *Middletown Daily Press*, 17, 18, and 19 August 1892; *Republican Watchman*, 19 August 1892.

12. *Republican Watchman*, 2 September 1892, 9 June 1893; *Middletown Daily Press*, 7 June 1893.

13. *The Argus*, 23 July 1897.

14. *Republican Watchman*, 13 September 1901.

15. *Middletown Daily Times-Press*, 29 August 1914.

16. Briggs, *A Dictionary of Fairies*, pp. 30–3; Jesse Harris and Julia Neely, 'Southern Illinois Phantoms and Bogies', *Midwest Folklore* 1, 3 (1951) 171–8; Gerald Milnes, *Play of a Fiddle: Traditional Music, Dance, and Folklore in West Virginia* (Lexington, 1999), p. 29.

17. Frances Albert Doughty, 'Folklore of the Alleghenies', *Popular Science* (July 1899) 390, 391.

18. The story is pieced together from the censuses, memoir of Dan Cunningham, and newspapers: *Sun*, 3 November 1900; *Daily Herald*, 16 December 1900; *Los Angeles Times*, 5 October 1902; *Morning Herald* [Kentucky], 18 February 1905; *Bluefield Daily Telegraph*, 29 April 1905; *Logansport Pharos-Reporter*, 29 January 1917; *Bluefield Daily Telegraph*, 1 February 1917; *Messenger* [Beckley], 23 January 1917.

19. See William Henry Bishop, *History of Roane County, West Virginia* (Spencer, 1927), pp. 454–5.

20. *Portsmouth Herald*, 8 July 1899.

21. Kenneth R. Bailey, 'Dan Cunningham', *West Virginia Encyclopedia*, <http://www. wvencyclopedia.org/articles/1697>.

22. <http://www.polsci.wvu.edu/wv/Clay/clahistory.html>.

23. Snake-doctor was a term for a type of dragonfly; Puckett, *Folk Beliefs*, p. 438.

24. The pawpaw was associated with witchcraft and the Devil; Randolph, *Ozark*, p. 261.

25. 'Memoirs of Daniel W. Cunningham: The Criminal History of Roane and Jackson Counties', manuscript dated 1929. <http://www.newrivernotes.com/misc/cunningh.htm>.

26. He was referred to variously as Hargess, Hargust, Hargus, and Hargis. I have stuck with Hargus due to the mention of numerous Harguses in the 1880 census of neighbouring Roane County.

27. *Charleston Daily Mail*, 2 November 1971.

28. Mary Lucinda Curry, *Booger Hole: Mysteries, Ghost Tales, and Strange Occurrences* (Maysel, 1990).

29. *Beckley Post-Herald*, 13 August 1965.

30. John Lilly (ed.), *Mountain of Music: West Virginia Traditional Music from* Goldenseal (Urbana, 1999), p. 95; Milnes, *Signs, Cures & Witchery*, pp. 138–41, p. 172.

31. For brief biographical details on Hotema see H. F. O'Beirne, *Leaders and Leading Men of the Indian Territory* (Chicago, 1891), Vol.1, pp. 135–6; Angie Debo, *The Rise and Fall of the Choctaw Republic* (Norman, 1961), p. 181.

32. Frances Imon, *Smoke Signals from Indian Territory* (Wolfe City, 1976), pp. 75–6.

33. *Fort Gibson Post*, 27 April 1899; *Bismark Daily Tribune*, 21 April 1899.

34. *Dallas Morning News*, 20 April 1899.

35. Arrell Morgan Gibson, *Oklahoma, a History of Five Centuries* (Norman, 1965), p. 193.

36. *Dallas Morning News*, 2 March 1901; 18 April 1901.

37. *Dallas Morning News*, 23 April 1901.

38. *Dallas Morning News*, 1 December 1901.

39. Solomon Hotema v. United States, April 28, 1902; <http://www.law.cornell.edu/supremecourt/text/186/413>.

40. *Annual Report of the Attorney General for the United States for the Year 1903* (Washington, 1903), p. 49.

41. *Dallas Morning News*, 6 November 1902.

42. *Dallas Morning News*, 22 January 1903; *Atlanta Constitution*, 15 February 1903.

43. *Augusta Chronicle*, 4 December 1906; *Annual Report of the Attorney General of the United States for the Year 1907* (Washington, 1907), Vol. 1, pp. 90, 92; *Atlanta Georgian*, 24 April 1907.

44. *Paris News*, 14 April 1999.

45. *Quincy Daily Journal*, 25 May 1886.

46. Harring, *Crow Dog's Case*, p. 269.

47. *Pittsburgh Press*, 21 January 1902; Harring, *Crow Dog's Case*, pp. 271–2; *Anaconda Standard*, 26 January 1912.

48. *Annual Report of the Commissioner of Indian Affairs, for the Year 1885* (Washington, 1885), p. 151.

49. *Annual Report of the Commissioner of Indian Affairs, for the Year 1883* (Washington, 1883), p. 118.

50. Brad Asher, 'A Haman-Killing Case on Puget Sound, 1873–1874: American Law and Salish Law', *Pacific Northwest Quarterly* 86, 1 (1994) 17–24; *Annual Report of the Commissions of Indian Affairs, for the Year 1879* (Washington, 1879), p. 152.

51. Franc J. Newcomb, *Navaho Neighbours* (Norman, 1966), 189–92. On the cultural defence issue see Andrew M. Kanter, 'The Yenaldlooshi in Court and the Killing of a Witch: The Case for an Indian Cultural Defense', *Southern California Interdisciplinary Journal* (1995) 411–54; Alison Dundes Renteln, *The Cultural Defense* (New York, 2004), pp. 39–40. Culture defences have been made more recently in cases of apparent witch murder. In 1993 a 24-year-old Mexican immigrant, Celerino Galicia, stabbed his girlfriend forty-three times after the couple had separated. In his defence Galicia claimed she was a *bruja*, and having failed to find a *curanderos* felt he had no alternative but to kill her to break the spell or *embujada* he believed was upon him. A professor of intercultural psychology was called to give evidence. In 1988 an Ethiopian refugee, Hagos Gebreamlak shot dead his girlfriend in Oakland, California, claiming that she was a *bouda* or witch.

Chapter 9 Notes

1. *Anniston Star*, 16 August 1950; *Star-News*, 23 August 1950; *Chicago Daily Tribune*, 24 August 1950; *Kingsport Times*, 29 October 1950, 12 December 1950, 14 December 1950, 15 December 1950, 1 February 1951, 11 March 1951, 11 May 1951.

2. *Delta Democrat-Times*, 30 September 1949; *Arkansas State Press*, 14 October 1949; *Kingsport News*, 10 June 1950; *Delta Democrat-Times*, 28 February 1952.

3. *Morning Advocate* [Baton Rouge], 22 July 1952.

4. *Tucson Daily Citizen*, 18 September 1952; *Tucson Daily Citizen*, 10 December 1952; *Time*, 11 May 1953; *El Paso Herald-Post*, 15 May 1953; *Lima News*, 24 May 1953; *Prescott Evening Courier*, 3 June 1955.

5. *Free Lance-Star*, 11 February 1960.

6. Monroe Newman, 'Joint Administration of Social Insurance Programmes', *Journal of Insurance* 25, 4 (1959) 49.

7. *Pittsburgh Post-Gazette*, 5 September 1958; *Calgary Herald*, 19 December 1959.

8. Lewis, *Hex*, p. 198.

9. Eric Alterman, *Who Speaks for America? Why Democracy Matters in Foreign Policy* (Ithaca, 1998), p. 96.

10. *Oregonian*, 31 October 1986; <http://www.harrisinteractive.com/Insights/Harris-Vault.aspx>.

11. <http://www.harrisinteractive.com/vault/HI-Harris-Poll-Book-Censorship-2011-04-12.pdf>.

12. The seminal history of Wicca is Ronald Hutton, *Triumph of the Moon: A History of Modern Pagan Witchcraft* (Oxford, 1999). See also Leo Ruickbie, *Witchcraft out of the Shadows: A Complete History* (London, 2004); Aidan Kelly, *Crafting the Art of Magic* (St Paul, 1991).

13. See Mitch Horowitz, *Occult America* (New York, 2009); J. Gordon Melton, *Encyclopedia of American Religions* (Detroit, 2003).

14. *San Diego Union*, 15 March 1913.

15. *Tampa Tribune*, 16 December 1928.

16. *News of the World*, 20 October 1963; <http://www.thewica.co.uk/SL%20schoola.htm>.

17. Copies of the *Pentagram* can be seen at <http://www.thewica.co.uk/Pentagram.htm>.

18. Bill Ellis, *Raising the Devil: Satanism, New Religions, and the Media* (Lexington, 2000), pp. 211–15. Ronal Hutton provides a useful personal insight into such teenage activities in this period; Hutton, *Triumph of the Moon*, p. 268.

19. *Omaha World Herald*, 2 January 1964.

20. *Albuquerque Journal*, 26 May 1964.

21. *Tuscaloosa News*, 29 October 1972.

22. *Omaha World Herald*, 10 June 1964.

23. *Omaha World Herald*, 2 July 1964.

24. *Morning Advocate*, 4 November 1964.

25. *Philadelphia Inquirer*, 28 October 1982.

26. *Sports Illustrated*, 12 December 1966.

27. *Toledo Blade*, 4 July 1966; *Rockford Morning Star*, 27 October 1968.

28. *Los Angeles Times*, reprinted in *Tuscaloosa News*, 29 October 1972.

29. *Springfield Sunday Republican*, 27 September 1964; *Trenton Evening Times*, 7 May 1964; 14 May 1964; 1 June 1964; *Philadelphia Inquirer*, 28 October, 1982.

30. *Springfield Sunday Republic*, 18 October 1964.

31. *Newport Daily News*, 1 June 1965.

32. *Morning Advocate*, 1 January 1966.

33. Marcello Truzzi, 'The Occult Revival as Popular Culture: Some Observations on the Old and the Nouveau Witch', *The Sociological Quarterly* 13 (1972) 25.

34. *The Plain Dealer*, 6 November 1969.

35. *Toledo Blade*, 4 July 1966; *Tuscaloosa News*, 29 October 1972.

36. See Chas S. Clifton, *Her Hidden Children: The Rise of Wicca and Paganism in America* (Lanham, 2006), ch.2, esp, p. 43.

37. Clifton, *Her Hidden Children*, p. 122.

38. Wendy Griffin, 'Webs of Women: Feminist Spiritualities', in Helen Berger (ed.), *Witchcraft and Magic: Contemporary North America* (Philadelphia, 2005), pp. 57–8.

39. See Diane Purkiss, *The Witch in History: Early Modern and Twentieth-Century Representations* (London, 1996), ch. 1.

40. Adler, *Drawing Down the Moon*, pp. 127, 224.

41. *Dallas Morning News*, 9 May 1976.

42. *Dallas Morning News*, 1 April 1973.

43. See Catherine L. Albanese, *Native Religion in America: From the Algonkian Indians to the New Age* (Chicago, 1990), pp. 180–4; Vivianne Crowley, 'Wicca as Nature Religion', in Joanne Pearson, Richard H. Roberts, Geoffrey Samuel (eds), *Nature Religion Today: Paganism in the Modern World* (Edinburgh, 1998), pp. 176–7; Gibson, *Witchcraft*, pp.154–9.

44. *Omaha World Herald*, 24 February 1974.

45. Leo Martello, Witchcraft: *The Old Religion* (Secaucus, 1973), p. 23. For biographical details see Leo Martello, *Weird Ways of Witchcraft*, foreword by Reverend Lori Bruno (San Francisco, 2011).

46. See Jack Fritscher, *Popular Witchcraft: Straight from the Witch's Mouth*, 2nd edition (Madison, 2004), pp. 45–50.

47. *Mobile Register*, 8 September 1970; Curtis D. MacDougall, *Superstition and the Press* (New York, 1983), p. 360.

48. See the Frosts' blog <http://gavinandyvonne.blogspot.com/2010/12/true-history-of-wicca.html>.

49. See also Danny L. Jorgensen and Scott E. Russell, 'American Neopaganism: The Participants' Social Identities', *Journal for the Scientific Study of Religion* 38, 3 (1999) 325–38.

50. *Plain Dealer*, 10 July 1973; *Morning Advocate*, 21 June 1972; *Mobile Register*, 29 September 1974.

51. Bill Ellis, *Raising the Devil: Satanism, New Religions, and the Media* (Lexington, 2000), pp. 167–202.

52. Ellis, *Raising the Devil*, p. 178.

53. *Reading Eagle*, 7 December 1972.

54. *Morning Advocate*, 7 February 1973. On Hershel, see Mike Hertenstein and Jon Trott, *Selling Satan: The Evangelical Media and the Mike Warnke Scandal* (Chicago, 1993), pp. 144, 160–5. For Hershel's own account see Hershel Smith and Dave Hunt, *The Devil and Mr Smith* (Old Tappan, 1974).

55. *Dallas Morning News*, 4 December 1972.

56. *Trenton Evening Times*, 3 October 1972; *Omaha World News*, 3 May 1973.

57. *Chicago Sun-Times Midwest Magazine*, 24 March 1974; cited in MacDougall, *Superstition and the Press*, p. 356.

58. Ethnicity in American neopaganism is explored in *Witching Culture: Folklore and Neo-Paganism in America* (Philadelphia, 2004), esp. pp. 212–15. On the variety of traditions see, for example, James R. Lewis, *Witchcraft Today: An Encyclopedia of Wiccan and Neopagan Traditions* (Santa Barbara, 1999).

59. Sabina Magliocco, 'Imagining the Strega: Folklore Reclamation and the Construction of Italian-American Witchcraft', in Joseph Sciorra (ed.), *Italian Folk: Vernacular Culture in Italian-American Lives* (New York, 2011), pp. 197–215.

60. Odd S. Lovoll, *The Promise Fulfilled: A Portrait of Norwegian Americans Today* (Minneapolis, 1998), p. 54.

61. Frederic Lamond, *Fifty Years of Wicca* (Sutton Mallet, 2004), p. 21.

62. Philip J. Deloria, *Playing Indian* (New Haven, 1998), ch. 6; Sarah M. Pike, *Earthly Bodies, Magical Selves: Contemporary Pagans and the Search for Community* (Berkeley, 2001); Magliocco, 'Reclamation, Appropriation and the Ecstatic Imagination in Modern Pagan Ritual', in Murphy Pizza and James R. Lewis (eds), *Handbook of Contemporary Paganisms* (Leiden, 2008), pp. 223–41.

63. Helen A. Berger, Evan A. Leach, and Leigh S. Shaffer, *Voices from the Pagan Census: A National Survey of Witches and Neo-Pagans in the United States* (Columbia, 2003), p. 29.

64. See, for example, Stephanie Urquhart, 'Onward Pagan Soldiers: Paganism in the U.S. Military', in Michael Strmiska (ed.), *Modern Paganism in World Cultures: Comparative Perspectives* (Santa Barbara, 2005), p. 329.

65. *The New Yorker*, 11 September 1954.

66. *Oregonian*, 21 August 1960.

67. Judith Wasserman, 'Retail or Re-tell?: The Case of the Salem Tercentenary Memorial', *Landscape Journal* 22 (2003) 1–11.

68. *Advocate*, 4 November 1964.

69. Bernard Rosenthal, *Salem Story: Reading the Witch Trials of 1692* (Cambridge, 1993), p. 172.

70. See Gibson, *Witchcraft*, pp. 194–216; Walter Metz, *Bewitched* (Detroit, 2007).

71. Peter Alachi, 'The Salem Saga 1970', <http://www.harpiesbizarre.com/salemsaga.htm>.

72. See Susanne Saville, *Hidden History of Salem* (Charleston, 2010), pp. 9–18.

73. Frederick J. Augustyn Jr, 'The American Switzerland: New England as a Toy-Making Center', *Journal of Popular Culture* 36, 1 (2002) 7; *Omaha World Herald*, 28 February 1970.

74. Stephen Olbrys Gencarella, 'Touring History: Guidebooks and the Commodification of the Salem Witch Trials', *Journal of American Culture* 30, 3 (2007) 271–84; Francis Hill, 'Salem as Witch City', in Dane Anthony Morrison and Nancy Lusignan

Schultz (eds), *Salem: Place, Myth, and Memory* (Lebanon, 2004), pp. 283–99; DeRosa, *The Making of Salem*, ch. 5.

75. See Russ Ely, *Bewitched in Salem: Witch City or City of Peace?* (New York, 2004), ch. 8. As a Salem pastor, Ely has his own agendas as well.

76. *York Dispatch*, 19 June 2007; *York Daily Record*, 16 April 2009; www.yorkdispatch. com/ci_6730841 (27 August 2007).

77. *Dallas Morning News*, 31 October 1964.

FURTHER READING

On witchcraft and witch trials in seventeenth and early eighteenth-century North America:

Baker, Emerson W. *The Devil of Great Island: Witchcraft and Conflict in Early New England* (New York, 2007).

Breslaw, Elaine G., *Tituba, Reluctant Witch of Salem: Devilish Indians and Puritan Fantasies* (New York, 1996).

Demos, John, *Entertaining Satan: Witchcraft and the Culture of Early New England* (Oxford, 1982).

Games, Alison, *Witchcraft in Early North America* (Lanham, 2010).

Godbeer, Richard, *The Devil's Dominion: Magic and Religion in Early New England* (Cambridge, 1992).

——, *Escaping Salem: The Other Witch Hunt of 1692* (New York, 2005).

Hall, David D. *Worlds of Wonder, Days of Judgment: Popular Religious Belief in Early New England* (New York, 1989).

Karlsen, Carol, *The Devil in the Shape of a Woman: Witchcraft in Colonial New England* (New York, 1987).

Reis, Elizabeth *Damned Women: Sinners and Witches in Puritan New England* (Ithaca, 1997).

Wiseman, Richard, *Witchcraft, Magic, and Religion in 17th-Century Massachusetts* (Amherst, 1984).

Much has been written about the Salem trials. Notable contributions include:

Boyer, Paul and Nissenbaum, Stephen, *Salem Possessed: The Social Origins of Witchcraft* (Cambridge, MA, 1974).

Hoffer, Peter, *The Devil's Disciples: Makers of the Salem Witchcraft Trials of 1692* (Baltimore).

Norton, Mary Beth, *In the Devil's Snare: The Salem Witchcraft Crisis of 1692* (New York, 2002).

Rosenthal, Bernard, *Salem Story: Reading the Witch Trials of 1692* (Cambridge, 1993).

Some of the more original recent work on Salem concerns its use as a metaphor and how it has been re-imagined and marketed:

Adams, Gretchen A., *The Specter of Salem: Remembering the Witch Trials in Nineteenth-Century America* (Chicago, 2008).
DeRosa, Robin, *The Making of Salem: The Witch Trials in History, Fiction and Tourism* (Jefferson, 2009).
Gibson, Marion, *Witchcraft Myths in American Culture* (New York and London, 2007).

There are few dedicated studies on the social history of witchcraft in European American societies in the eighteenth and nineteenth centuries, but valuable discussions are contained in books that explore the broader world of religion and culture in the period:

Benes, Peter (ed.), *Wonders of the Invisible World: 1600–1800* (Boston, 1995).
Brooke, John L., *The Refiner's Fire: The Making of Mormon Cosmology, 1644–1844* (Cambridge, 1994).
Butler, Jon, *Awash in a Sea of Faith: Christianizing the American People* (Cambridge, Mass., 1990).
Leventhal, Herbert, *In the Shadow of the Enlightenment: Occultism and Renaissance Science in Eighteenth-Century America* (New York, 1976).
Quinn, Michael, *Early Mormonism and the Magic World View* (Salt Lake City, 1987).
Seeman, Erik R., *Pious Persuasions: Laity and Clergy in Eighteenth-Century New England* (Baltimore, 1999).
Sobel, Mechal, *The World They Made Together: Black and White Values in Eighteenth-Century Virginia* (Princeton, 1987).

Attitudes towards Native Americans and their witchcraft beliefs in the period have attracted some significant recent studies:

Caves, Alfred A. *Prophets of the Great Spirit: Native American Revitalization Movements in Eastern North America* (2006).
Dennis, Matthew, *Seneca Possessed: Indians, Witchcraft, and Power in the Early American Republic* (Philadelphia, 2010).
Ebright, Malcolm and Rick Hendricks, *The Witches of Abiquiu: The Governor, the Priest, the Genízaro Indians* (Albuquerque, 2006).
Herring, Sidney L., *Crow Dog's Case: American Indian Sovereignty, Tribal Law, and United States Law in the Nineteenth Century* (Cambridge, 2004).
Jortner, Adam, *The Gods of Prophetstown: The Battle of Tippecanoe and the Holy War for the American Frontier* (New York, 2012).

The study of magical cultures amongst the African American population in the nineteenth- and early twentieth century, and their representation, has been advanced considerably by:
Anderson, Jeffrey E, *Conjure in African American Society* (Baton Rouge, 2005).

Chireau, Yvonne P., *Black Magic: Religion and the African American Conjuring Tradition* (Berkeley and Los Angeles, 2003).

Murray, David, *Matter, Magic, and Spirit: Representing Indian and African American Belief* (Philadelphia, 2007).

Moving into the twentieth century, the continuation of witchcraft beliefs and magical practices in German American communities are detailed in:

McGinnis, J. Ross, *Trials of Hex* (Davis, CA, 2000).

Milnes, Gerald C., *Signs, Cures & Witchery: German Appalachian Folklore* (Knoxville, 2007).

Kriebel, David, *Powwowing Among the Pennsylvania Dutch: A Traditional Medical Practice in the Modern World* (University Park, 2007).

Insights into witchcraft beliefs at the other end of the country are provided in García, Nasario, *Brujerías: Stories of Witchcraft and the Supernatural in the American Southwest and Beyond* (Texas, 2007).

As to modern manifestations of witchcraft and American Wicca see:

Berger, Helen, *A Community of Witches: Contemporary Neo-Paganism and Witchcraft in the United States* (Columbia, 1998).

——(ed.), *Witchcraft and Magic: Contemporary North America* (Philadelphia, 2005).

Clifton, Chas S., *Her Hidden Children: The Rise of Wicca and Paganism in America* (Lanham, 2006).

Ellis, Bill, *Raising the Devil: Satanism, New Religions, and the Media* (Lexington, 2000),

Magliocco, Sabina, *Witching Culture: Folklore and Neo-Paganism in America* (Philadelphia, 2004).

Picture Acknowledgements

Plate 10: Alaska State Library, Case & Draper Photograph Collection, P39-0448; Plate 2: Archives/The Spokesman-Review; Plates 17, 18 Associated Press; Plate 14: Daily Press 17 August 1892; Plate 20 Doug Winemiller; Plate 19: © Everett Collection, Inc.; Plate 3: Evening Telegram, 2 December 1911; Plate 7: From the collection of the York County Heritage Trust, York, PA.; Plate 5: Library of Congress, Chronicling America: Historic American Newspapers site. http://chroniclingamerica.loc.gov/lccn/sn85066387/1905-11-25/ed-1/seq-3/; Plate 16: Library of Congress, Chronicling America: Historic American Newspapers site. http://chroniclingamerica.loc.gov/lccn/sn86071197/1901-12-26/ed-1/seq-8/; Plate 4: Library of Congress, Prints & Photographs Division [reproduction number, LC-DIG-cph.3a02009]; Plate 1: Library of Congress, Prints & Photographs Division [reproduction number, LC-DIG-ppmsca-05086]; Plate 13: From, August C. Mahr, 'A Pennsylvania Dutch "Hexzettel"', Monatshfte fur deutschen Unterricht 27, 6 (1935) 215; Plate 6: National Museum of Health and Medicine; Plates 8, 11, 12: newspaperarchive.com; Plate 9: NY Times; Plate 15: West Virginia State Archives.

The publisher apologizes for any errors or omissions in the above list. If contacted they will be pleased to rectify these at the earliest opportunity.

INDEX